MW01143055

A Rebirth of Freedom

*The Calling of an
American Historian*

Thomas P. Govan
1907-1979

A Rebirth
of Freedom

The Calling of an
American Historian

Thomas P. Govan
1907-1979

John Crocker, Jr.

To order additional copies of this book, contact:
Xlibris Corporation
1-888-795-4274
www.Xlibris.com
Orders@Xlibris.com
21365

Contents

PART I

The Emergence and Transformation of a Young Historian

PART II

A New Birth of Freedom

PART III
The Last Best Hope

APPENDICES

A Selection of Govan's Essays

Historians are not only the custodians of the nation's memory, they are also the keepers of its conscience, and on them lies the complex and difficult burden of seeking to distinguish right from wrong.

It was the admission of wrongdoing, not its avoidance, according to the biblical writers, that freed men from the burden of sin, that enabled them to be obedient to God of whom it was said, "His service is perfect freedom."

Thomas Payne Govan

Acknowledgements

This book could not have been written without Thomas P. Govan's papers, which he and his wife, Jane, left to me. They are a fundamental source and are now safely stored in the archives of the Episcopal Church in Austin, Texas, with copies of much of the material in the archives of the University of Oregon, Eugene. Nor could it have been written without the help by mail and taped telephone interviews with members of the Govan family, Tom's former colleagues and friends.

Several members of the family were indispensable: Tom's wife, Jane Dickson Govan, Elizabeth T. Conn (a niece), Thomas J. Tucker (a nephew), James Bunnell (a nephew-in-law), and Sarah E. Bunnell (a grandniece). I thank them especially for their help. Other family members with whom I was occasionally in touch were James F. Govan (a nephew and distinguished university librarian), Katherine Monges (a niece), and Richard Conn (Elizabeth's former husband).

Old and dear friends of the Govans shared their memories and made valuable contributions: Cora Louise Belford, Laura W. Roper, Elizabeth Cooper, Harriet Price, and Suzanne Reid. Former colleagues in the university and in the Episcopal Church did the same: Scott Bates, David Underdown, Robert Berdahl, Robert and Katherine Brady, J.C. Michael Allen, Robert Strider, F. Fitzsimmons Allison. And former students: G.P. Mellick Belshaw, Robert Ellis, Stanley Feldstein, and Jack Maddex.

I also consulted with a number of others: Owen C. Thomas (theologian and Episcopal priest); Gardner H. Shattuck (American church historian and Episcopal priest who graciously read and criticized the full text); Richard Brown (historian at the University of Connecticut); Elizabeth Sifton (editor); Lucia S. Tasker (former editor); Richard K. Winslow (former editor); and Donald R. Cutler (editor and retired Episcopal priest).

Three gifted editor-typists have been loyal friends who transcribed my longhand into an electronic version of the manuscript on their computers: Kathleen Jenkins (1990-1996), Erika M. Hetzner (1997-2001), and Elizabeth MacLean (2001 to the present). Margaret Cleveland did a superb final edit to made the book cohere.

Over the years, my son, Matthew H. Crocker, who teaches American history at Keene State College, Keene, New Hampshire, has talked with me for hours about American history, historians, and Govan. He has been a useful informant, critic and morale booster. And my wife, Agatha S. Littlefield: her patience is "up there" with Job's. Special thanks to all these people.

The libraries of Brown University, the University of Rhode Island, and the Episcopal Divinity School in Cambridge, Massachusetts have blessedly been open to me and unfailingly helpful.

West Kingston, R.I.
June 2003

Thomas P. Govan at Brown University, 1960-1962

Preface

The Moment of Meeting

In the fall of 1955, I was thirty-two years old, one year out of seminary, the curate at Trinity Church, Boston, and just ordained a priest, with the job of ministering to students in the Back Bay area of the city. In late October a regional conference was held in Whitinsville, Massachusetts, for Episcopal college chaplains and university faculty. Thomas P. Govan, the new Executive Secretary for Faculty Work for the national Episcopal Church was to speak. He was an American historian who had taught at the University of the South, University of Virginia and Tulane University. I went to the conference out of duty but hoped I would learn something. I did. Govan was a warm southerner with a charming drawl, who was new in his job and wanted us to know him. He spoke about his life, his fears, his struggles and how, through his research and experience, his life had been changed.

Here was a man, I realized, who had a beautifully integrated understanding of life which was woven out of his experience and study, which included an understanding of economics, politics, philosophy, government, American history and its meaning, all held together and energized by his Christian faith. God was real for him and mysteriously active in it all.

This was new! I had read and studied in all these areas, but to have them cohere seamlessly was the thing for which I had always yearned. Govan wanted to give and I wanted to receive. The experience was what he later would call trinitarian education: the

17

dynamic relationship of teacher and student with the subject matter and with each other. It is electric and alive when it happens and it changes people, heart and mind.

For me, Govan's address was an intellectual discovery and an emotional revelation. What he talked about concerned the deepest things in my own life: the biblical faith which I had learned and caught from my father on the one hand and on the other, my political faith in the United States for which I had risked service during World War II as a naval pilot. For Govan, these two elements, religious faith and political faith, were deeply interrelated. For me, his view would make new sense of my life.

I also experienced the magic of a personal relationship, which is the spirit and power of true education. It was obvious to me that he was eager to teach and had a personal investment in the reality of his subject matter. He must have sensed how eager I was to learn and that I had an investment in it too. I also liked him as a person, and so we became friends—teacher to student and student to teacher. I continued to listen, to argue with, and learn from him for the next twenty-four years.

The Man

Thomas Payne Govan, with his wife Jane, rebelled against the southern tradition of racism, against the South's pride in the lost cause of the Civil War, and the myth of a pastoral and agrarian southern past superior to the rest of the country. As a young man in graduate school, he became a "liberal with socialist leanings." Later, as a budding professional American historian and economist during the 1930s and 1940s, he was forced by what he was learning to change radically. His research was focused on the early national period of United States history, and was carried out during Franklin Roosevelt's New Deal in the 1930s. Research and experience together revolutionized Govan's thinking. First, his research into Alexander Hamilton and his administration of the U.S. Treasury; and second, his living experience with Roosevelt's administration led him to discover that these men had the same motives and the same policies. Both men sought to restore the country's entire economy with the intention of benefiting everyone, rich and poor alike, not just the rich.

Prior to Govan, most American historians approached their subject objectively and with the illusion that facts alone could reveal historical truth. Objectivity was their one goal. Not Govan. He understood the limits of the objective approach and knew life and history have meaning because people have purposes and deeply-held moral commitments and faiths. For Govan, the historian's task was to comprehend and interpret history integrating these influences—a task reflected in his professional life.

He was invested in the history he taught. He had a message that he cared about and wanted us to care about. He once said that he "could not help it if he was a prophet!" The term for him did not (emphatically not) mean a soothsayer who foretells the future. He meant "prophet" in the biblical sense: a person who calls people back to their true roots; insisting that there is a moral order in the world and that there are consequences to what people believe and do. His philosophy was reminiscent of the prophet Micah's call: "What does the Lord require of you but to do justice, to love mercy, and to walk humbly with thy God."[1] Throughout Govan's life he invited his students to remember and meditate upon the Declaration of Independence, the Preamble to the Constitution, Lincoln's Gettysburg Address and Second Inaugural Address. For him, these documents were at the heart of American history. He felt passionately about that history and wanted those of us who were his students to feel the same way. For him, these documents expressed the principles to which the country was committed and by which its history was to be measured and judged: "a new nation, conceived in Liberty and dedicated to the proposition that all men are created equal."[2] Govan had no illusions about the realities of that history: the nation constantly failed to live up to its principles. But they were the principles upon which the nation had been founded, and when the nation failed to live up to them, reform was necessary. In an imperfect world that meant constant reform.

Govan was therefore the enemy of perfectionists, on the right and the left. Both sides were doctrinaire, he believed, and would lead to a loss of freedom and the disillusionment of the people. On the contrary, recognition of imperfection and the need for constant reform would create hope by giving the citizens of the country the freedom to seek justice for themselves and for their neighbors. They would be free to be pragmatic, to experiment, to make mistakes without fear of censure, and to seek reform.

This recognition and reformation of imperfection was to Govan the essential message of the Bible. In 1966 he would write, "The English and American constitutions and laws are demythologized versions of biblical thinking."

His approach in the end, therefore, was a blend of the historical and the theological. What makes him different from other historians was his deep biblical understanding and his unique interpretation of American history in the light of that understanding.

This Book

Govan was not well known as a historian. Although he wrote a number of historical and theological essays, as well as a host of book reviews, he published only one big book, a revisionist biography of Nicholas Biddle.[3] This book permanently changed historians' understanding and evaluation of Biddle's role as president of the Second National Bank of the United States. These publications, however, encompassed only a fraction of the knowledge Tom felt compelled to share.

Twice he applied for grants to write a full American history into which all his thought and conviction could be poured. Circumstances and a tendency toward discouragement prevented his doing so. The detailed outlines he wrote for this book, however, are important in understanding him and his view of American history: that the United States, however imperfect, is still humanity's best hope for a society in which freedom and order co-exist.

From 1971-1973, while at the University of Oregon, Tom also collaborated with Forrest McDonald and Leslie E. Decker[4] in writing a two-volume American history text, *The Last Best Hope, a History of the United States*.[5] This text provided a conservative alternative to Samuel

Eliot Morison and Henry Steele Commager's liberal *The Growth of the American Republic*.[6] It corrected the book's sectional interpretation of United States history (North and East versus South and West), and presented a more positive view of the federal government's role in establishing and maintaining freedom, justice, and the prosperity of the nation. Tom placed his mark heavily on this book, but it remained only partly his. It was not until 1976, during the nation's bicentennial, and three years before his death, that he finally put together all he had to say about American history in an Oregon television lecture series, *Radical America, the Continuing Revolution*.[7]

As Tom got older and approached retirement, it seemed clear that he had no particular interest in collecting and publishing what he had written. For this reason and with his approval, I set about gathering his papers, with the purpose of publishing them together one day.

In the end Tom and Jane gave me all of his papers with the understanding that I would in some manner get his work published. What finally resulted is this biography. It is offered now, thankfully, as a long-standing promise finally fulfilled.

Introduction

The Providence of God has been mysteriously present [in American history], the God 'whose service is perfect freedom.'

Thomas P. Govan

Thomas Payne Govan: Economist, Historian and Theologian

Thomas Payne Govan was an unusual and complex man. Unlike most American historians of his era, he was a highly sophisticated political economist and accountant who knew not only economic theory, but also the practice of banking, large and small, and the details of accounting. He knew the history of economics: money, banking, double-entry bookkeeping, and the mysteries of debt, credit, and interest. Along with Bray Hammond, an official of the Federal Reserve Bank,[8] he knew more than anyone about the history of the political economy in the United States between 1789 and 1845.

As a historian, Govan was preoccupied with the question of how—in both the church and the state—freedom and order could be achieved simultaneously. These two goals were in conflict with each other. Early in his career, however, he became a convert to the English Constitution politically and the Church of England religiously as the best answer to the question. Both were essentially pragmatic in their approach, rather than ideological or doctrinaire. In both, reform was guided by compromise and what

23

worked, not theory. Tom liked that, and gradually became a convinced pragmatist. He also learned to take seriously the evil and cruelty in human nature along with the good, and soon realized that Christianity had the most realistic understanding of that dichotomy. As a result, he became a Christian pragmatist.

Many of Tom's fellow historians were enlightened liberals who believed that traditional moral standards were used in the past by the ruling elites primarily to justify and maintain their own dominance. Govan thought otherwise. He assumed the universality of human "sin"—that which leads people to rebel against a God who is transcendent over them. He felt that humans choose rationalization and self-justification over being forgiven or forgiving.[9]

So Govan was not only an economist and a historian; he was also becoming a theologian. Whether discussing the colonies, the Revolution, the Constitution, the economy, the Jefferson-Hamilton debates and power struggles, or slavery and the Civil War, he interpreted that history from his new-found theological view. The struggle for people in the United States, he believed, has always been to discover a way of governance that combines a maximum of freedom with enough of the right restraints to create and maintain order. In that struggle, Govan believed that the Providence of God was somehow mysteriously present, the God "in whose service is perfect freedom."[10] Economist, historian, and theologian, Govan was all of these, each endeavor informing the other.

Govan Among American Historians

A brief review of American historiography clarifies Govan's place among American historians and reveals the context within which he worked, wrote, and thought. It also clarifies the nature of his unique place as a historian—and my reasons for writing his biography.

American historiography can best be described as a pendulum swinging between extremes of interpretation followed by swings back toward a balanced consensus in the middle, which then becomes overstated, inducing further swings.

Puritan, Deist and Patrician Historians

American history lay, first of all, in the hands of the seventeenth-century Puritans who saw their history as the working out of God's Providence among His chosen people. William Bradford's *Of Plymouth Plantation* is probably the best example of this view. Puritan lives and communities were to be beacons of light to the world.[11]

When Isaac Newton's physics revealed his theory of God's natural laws in the eighteenth century, historians (now drawn mostly from the business and professional classes) soon moved God's role from an active participant in history to the Great Creator who set the world going and left it to run on its own according to natural law. Thomas Jefferson's *Notes on the State of Virginia,* for example, argued that God may have been creator, but human reason and natural law, not divine Providence, governed historical processes.[12]

The nineteenth century, well after the Revolution, produced a long period of romantic nationalism. Patricians wrote American history as the story of the gradual advancement of freedom led by the United States. The most important of these writers was George Bancroft, a tax collector for the port of Boston during Martin Van Buren's presidency. He wrote twelve volumes between 1834 and 1882 praising the democratic tradition, and the democracy that followed it, as the fruition of God's will.[13]

Bancroft's aim as a historian was to educate the American people about the meaning of their history and to inspire them to keep the country moving in the direction of increased freedom, justice, and equality. He believed that the Anglo-Saxons were a superior people, especially gifted in the development of institutions, and that beyond English constitutional monarchy, the United States Constitution was the capstone of democratic progress.

Between 1832 and 1844, Richard Hildreth, another patrician, wrote a six-volume pro-Federalist nationalist history, which set the pattern for the rest of the century.[14] For Hildreth, Hamilton and Jefferson symbolized two opposed theories of government, interpretations of the Constitution, parties (Federalist and

Republican), ideas of human nature, of life, and of American destiny. "Hamilton represented conservatism, capitalism, nationalism, and the anti-slavery sentiment of the North and East; Jefferson represented democracy, agrarianism, states' rights, and the pro-slavery sentiment of the South and West."[15]

In 1888, one year before the centennial of the Constitution, the historian John Fiske wrote that the Revolution had been fought for self-government and liberty, and that the Constitution had been written by an extraordinary and statesmanlike group of patriots who had, thereby, saved the nation and set its course for the future.[16] Like Bancroft, Fiske believed in the racial superiority of white Anglo-Saxon Protestants who, in England and the United States, had built strong and democratic national governments. He even traced the roots of their democratic institutions back to the ancient Teutonic tribes of Germany. The Constitution was, for Bancroft and Fiske, the fulfillment of a long and glorious process. Fiske and a majority of nineteenth-century historians leaned strongly toward the Federalist-Whig-Republican view and away from a Jeffersonian-Jacksonian-Democratic view of American history.

Govan had great sympathy for the Federalist view of these three men and found their ideas tremendously suggestive. He noted these ideas but then recast them. He believed, for example, that the long-term progress toward freedom, justice and equality in England and the United States was the result, not of Anglo-Saxon racial superiority, as Bancroft and Fiske suggested, but of the steady long-term influence of biblical ideas on the law and government of the two nations. He also condemned the terrible history of United States slavery and racial discrimination, which, he felt, flew in the face of those ideas.

Govan liked Hildreth's "temperamental preference for experience over theory,"[17] but thought that he overstated the Hamilton-Jefferson dichotomy. There was more that united this country than Fiske's analysis suggested.

Professional Historians and History as Science

In the 1870s, for the first time, university-trained professional historians began to appear, and with them, the idea of history as a science. If there were laws of scientific development, there must be laws of historical development. A new level of accuracy and objectivity became their goal. Henry Adams was a brilliant example. He applied the scientific law of entropy (the theory that things inevitably get worse and end in disaster) to history, and in 1890, with a keen eye and some misgivings, described the administration of Jefferson and Madison as "the triumph of democracy over aristocracy and, inseparable from that, the triumph of politics over statesmanship," the latter a circumstance he deplored.[18]

Also in the 1870s, Frederick Jackson Turner took Darwin's idea of evolution and applied it to the American social scene. He wrote about successive frontiers in the West, each one further away from Europe and therefore less aristocratic and more democratic. He believed that the Jacksonian "democracy of the people" was created by the American people's frontier experience. Turner focused his history on sectional differences and sectional conflict: agrarian versus urban; North and East versus South and West.[19]

Govan was willing to grant the influence of different sections of the country upon the people who lived there. He rejected Turner's argument that sectional differences were the most important driving force of American history. Govan argued there was much more that united the people of the different regions than divided them. Americans of all sections, for example, came from Europe, the majority from England. English was the dominant language and culture. All sections of the country were agricultural in the colonial period. The Industrial Revolution had not yet arrived, and when it did, it affected the entire country, not only the North and East. All sections were commercial, more or less, and were parts of the British Empire, so for Govan, Turner's sectional argument was a failure. The only true sectional conflict had been between the North and the South over slavery. On balance, however, the study and research of the professional historians favored the Federalist view of the nation and added significantly to the known facts about what had actually happened.

The Progressive Historians

Early in the twentieth century, the first radical swing of the historical pendulum occurred, led by Charles A. Beard, Carl Becker, Vernon L. Parrington, and others. These were the "new" or "progressive" historians and they turned American history on its head. Although they accepted much of the basic pattern of events in American history as laid out by earlier historians, including the Hamilton-Jefferson split, they insisted on a new set of materialistic and economic factors that had determined that history. They believed it was the materialistic circumstances under which people lived—the work they did, whether in a rural or urban setting, whether poor or well-off—that determined people's economic self-interest, and that economic self-interest, in turn, determined their behavior. Those who were well-off necessarily would be conservative, fighting to maintain the status quo and keep their advantage, while the poor would necessarily be radical, seeking change, reform, and a better life for themselves.

Carl Becker, writing shortly after World War I, claimed that the American Revolution, supported by the lower class majority of Americans, was fought for "home rule" and democracy. Tom Paine was its prophet. In the end, however, the lower classes achieved home rule but not democracy because, according to Becker, the Constitutional Convention of 1789, held under the rule of silence by the upper class intellectual aristocracy, was, in effect, a counterrevolution. It assured the aristocracy of their place in and their control of the country for a long time to come.

Beard essentially agreed, showing how the interaction of economic group interest explained the emergence of the new nation and the two political parties, Federalist and Republican, which vied for power and control. He pitted the merchants, manufacturers, shippers, creditors, and speculators against the farmers, laborers, those in debt, and the less well-off. He agreed with Becker that the Revolution was a move toward democracy and the Constitution a move away from it, a counterrevolution of the wealthy to protect their interests. Alexander Hamilton's financial program, he claimed, was intended to help the upper classes and hurt the poor.

The same thing happened, Beard believed, when Andrew Jackson was elected president and fought Nicholas Biddle and the Bank of the United States. Jackson was convinced that the Bank had monopolistic and unconstitutional control over the nation's economy, and that it stimulated corruption and helped the rich at the expense of the poor.

Parrington approached the American past in terms of intellectual history. His major theme was the Hamilton-Jefferson dichotomy. As a liberal, he was on the side of Jefferson, who stood for decentralized agrarian democracy and was supported, he said, by the mass of small farmers and urban laborers. Hamilton represented the upper-class aristocratic minority bent on maintaining its advantage. Parrington's influence was huge. Until the 1960s, almost every American literature student had to know his *Main Currents of American Thought*.[20]

In 1940, Govan's response to the Progressive historians, Becker, Beard, and Parrington, was three-fold. First, he accepted the fact that material circumstances and economic self-interest influenced people's behavior. Second, however, he rejected completely the Progressives' insistence that these were determinative factors and that class conflict was the driving force in history. Third, Govan rejected the implicit (sometimes explicit) insistence of the Progressives that people's ideas, thoughts, opinions, purposes, moral convictions, and faiths were meaningless and did not matter because these so-called "masks and rationalizations" were actually economic self-interest in disguise. This idea was nonsense to Govan. He knew that what people thought mattered to them and was their real motivation. People's convictions governed their behavior.

Govan made his point absolutely clear in 1940 in an essay entitled, "Slavery and the Civil War."[21]

There has been a growing tendency among historians to explain political and social actions in economic terms and to seek the origin of all conflicts in the material circumstances of the life of the people of the nation . . . . The economic interpretation has, on the whole, led to a better and more complete understanding of American history, but it has also, through overemphasis, caused some distortion . . . . It is the growing influence of this theory which gives particular importance to the publication this year of four books . . . [on the Civil War],[22] all denying by implication or explicitly its central thesis. None of these writers denies the validity of the economic interpretation of history. On the contrary, all find in the material and psychological environment the source of the ideas that move men to action. All, I think, would agree that it was the essential nature of capitalism, with its need for free markets and a free labor supply, that was responsible for the condemnation of slavery and unfree labor wherever it existed; but that once the condemnation had been accepted, it began to exert an independent influence, so that individuals who acted upon it were motivated not by economic interest, but by genuine moral fervor."[23]

Govan had made his point. But despite him and other historians, the Progressive historians dominated American historical interpretation right up through the 1940s, 1950s, and 1960s.

Post World War II History: The Consensus Historians

It was after World War II and to Govan's great relief that the pendulum began to swing back in a more conservative direction, led by historians like Louis Hartz, Daniel Boorstin, Robert E. Brown, Edward S. Morgan, and Ralph Gabriel. They came to be called "Consensus" or "neo-conservative" historians because they rejected the

Progressives' overemphasis on sectional and class conflict as the generators of history. They saw in American history the continuity and consensus of a stable society. Along with Govan, they rejected the Progressives' claim that ideas are merely rationalizations for the economic forces that motivate and govern behaviors. The implicit determinism in the Progressives' theory was an anathema to them. These men had great respect for tradition and found the Declaration of Independence and the Constitution to be the core of a widespread consensus on principles and beliefs that they traced back to John Locke and the English Constitution. They rejected progress as an article of faith; human nature was far too fickle and corrupt for that.

Each of these historians had his own focus. Louis Hartz denied the Progressives' claim that the American Revolution had been a radical movement that had fundamentally changed American society, arguing that America had been "born free," without a feudal past, titled aristocracy, or national church. It had been democratic from the start. He denied Locke's centrality to the consensus.[24]

Robert E. Brown discovered that the majority of colonists were people who had enough land or other property to qualify to vote and were more middle class than lower class. The society was open and prosperous enough to allow people to get ahead. So, in the Revolution, the majority of colonists were reluctant rebels who fought to preserve their democratic social order and to keep the traditional rights granted them by the English Constitution. The Revolution, therefore, was essentially conservative in its intent. Govan agreed, emphasizing the fact that at the beginning of the Revolution, it was the British, not the colonists, who were acting unconstitutionally.[25]

Daniel J. Boorstin postulated that in the new nation a consensus among Americans was born of the practical demands of their frontier environment. They were pragmatists who learned from their experience and distrusted theories. They were doers, not thinkers.[26]

Edward S. Morgan identified a continuity of ideals that most Americans shared and traced to British history and experience. He played down the conflict between Hamilton and Jefferson, insisting that they both shared a common faith within which they argued and fought.[27]

Richard Hofstadter in the mid-1940s argued that there was essential agreement between Jefferson and Hamilton. "However much at odds on specific issues, the major political traditions have shared a belief in the rights of property, the philosophy of economic individualism, the value of competition; they have accepted the economic virtues of capitalist culture as necessary qualities of men."[28] Govan was quick to reject this view. As we shall see, he saw the conflict between Hamilton and Jefferson as fundamental and still present in the country as we enter the twenty-first century. Hamilton represented the English constitution and Jefferson French Rationalism; they did not mix easily.

Govan was especially impressed, however, with Ralph Gabriel's *The Course of American Democratic Thought, an Intellectual History Since 1815*[29] in which he described the real genius of the United States as a realistic democracy that

> provides a middle-of-the-road solution for problems which arise . . . [in] an effort to harmonize the . . . doctrines of the free individual and nationalism . . . The American democratic faith is a system of checks and balances in the realm of ideas . . . a philosophy of the mean. It proclaims that, within broad limits of an ordered nature, man is master of his destiny.[30]

Govan liked the flexibility of this philosophy and its intention to provide standards by which democracy might be judged. Most important to him was Gabriel's insistence that it was a nonperfectionistic "democratic faith" (with emphasis on faith) that motivated the country. American democracy was a process of imperfect compromise, a balance that provided for humanity a freedom to become masters of their fates.

During the 1950s, the one historian with whom Govan shared almost complete agreement about American history was Bray Hammond, an economic historian who worked for the Federal Reserve Bank of the United States. Govan and Hammond never discussed religion, but otherwise, they were very much on the same wavelength: basically conservative, in the middle between the left and right swings of historical scholarship. They, with other Consensus historians, rejected class conflict analysis. Then, instead they suggested that the division in society was not between upper and lower classes, the rich and the poor, but between "two sets of capitalists—between newer entrepreneurs seeking to free themselves from the shackles imposed by the government regulation that was exercised through the Second Bank of the United States—and the older and more conservative entrepreneurs seeking to guide economic development through a . . . policy that gave the central government (through the national bank) an important role in regulating economic affairs."[31] Broadly speaking, they were part of the consensus group, but because of their economic expertise, were dubbed "entrepreneurial" historians.

Consensus Historians and the Problem of Thomas Jefferson

Although Govan agreed with the Consensus historians about the continuity between British and American history, he could not fully accept their consensus theories. One of the key problems was Thomas Jefferson and what he stood for. All of the Consensus historians played down the division between Hamilton and Jefferson, claiming that they both shared the same overarching liberal "Locke-ian" consensus and that their differences were minor squabbles within that consensus. Govan strongly disagreed.

Briefly put, Jefferson was a product of the eighteenth century Enlightenment. He assumed that the destructive forces associated with religion and nationalism could and should be overcome by a new liberal spirit of reason expressed politically in democracy: freedom from God and freedom from kings. Enlightened national policy could overcome the demons of the human spirit, Jefferson believed, by creating an agrarian society that left people free, kept them away from the corruptions of the city, urban commerce, and paper money, and protected them from both religious and government regulation. People would be virtuous enough to make democracy possible with a minimum of federal restraint.

Hamilton, following the Bible, believed to the contrary, that people were moved more by self-interest, avarice, and ambition than by reason and love, and would have to be restrained if they were to be free. Therefore, a strong federal government was necessary.

The division between Jefferson and the consensus, as Govan perceived it and as it was represented by Hamilton, was so deep and pervasive that he could not play it down as a minor squabble. Rather the division was profoundly theological as well as political. This fact made it more fundamental than any previous or subsequent analyses. In an article, "Hamilton and Jefferson, a Christian Evaluation," Govan argued his views on the two men.[32] He found Jefferson to be unrealistic and hence, a heretic, and Hamilton to be the realistic one and hence, the orthodox Christian—to the horror, of course, of Govan's fellow historians who thought that by mixing theology and history, he was mixing apples and oranges. Throughout United States history there have been these two theological, as well as political and economic, points of view: Federalists versus Republicans, Hamilton versus Jefferson, the federal authority versus states' rights, the Industrial Revolution versus agrarianism, hard money versus credit and paper money. These are two very different concepts of freedom: the freedom of radical individualism, which consists of the individual being left alone to do as he will, and the biblical conception of freedom, which comprises people in their community, aware of their need for those restraints that will protect them from one another and from their own worst selves.

In addition to their differences over human nature and politics, Hamilton and Jefferson held completely different views of God. Hamilton worshipped the biblical God, who had been essentially banished from history by the historians. Jefferson's God, at best, was the Divine Mechanic of Deism, the great impersonal Watchmaker, who started the world and then left it to run on its own. The biblical God was intensely personal, infinitely patient, forgiving, and history was the story of the conflict of wills between God and his willful and rebellious children.[33]

Govan insisted, therefore, that the differences between Jefferson and Hamilton were not only economic, political, and philosophical, but also theological.

Govan's Analysis: Deeper than the Consensus Analysis

Govan completed his Ph.D. thesis in 1937, taught for one year at the University of Chattanooga, and was teaching at the University of the South as this conservative historical swing was getting under way. The context for historians was primarily Progressive, so the Consensus group was very much a minority, swimming upstream against the prevailing current.

Tom had been a happy Progressive, only to find that his research into the economy of Georgia, the lives of Hamilton and Biddle, and his current experience with Roosevelt's New Deal were pointing him in a new direction. Govan discovered that he was really a conservative pragmatist like Hamilton and Biddle. He would soon discover that Anglican Christianity would provide him with a vastly informative and helpful theology to undergird his newfound pragmatism. In due time, Govan would realize that for several years while a pragmatist, he had also been a Christian without knowing it. His conversion was not an inner experience of the spiritual presence of God, although that came later through living the discipline of worship and prayer. It was a waking to the truth, an intellectual conversion: "Oh, so that is what is going on here! Oh, I get it." Getting it straight became his passion.

By the early 1940s, Govan had been forced by his study of American history[34] to become a neo-conservative. He was tremendously grateful for the company of the Consensus historians. He would have his differences with them, but in one respect he agreed completely: their emphasis on the continuity of American history with English history. Tom saw American history as part of English history, sharing in the constitutional understanding that came out of the English Reformation and the Glorious Revolution of 1689. That "revolution" produced a limited monarchy balanced by a partially democratic Parliament, a system of checks and balances, and a bill of rights that provided the English with a new level of freedom.[35]

At this point, Govan's analysis went deeper than any of his fellow neo-conservative historians. They were finding an American consensus in various theories, including the abstract theories of John Locke, which, for Govan, were no substitute for the organic historical reality of the English constitutional history. Tom accepted Locke's thought as part of the American consensus, but personally rejected his theories as "unhistorical."

The unique thing about English constitutional history, for Govan, was its fundamental grounding in theology. The *Book of Common Prayer* stated beautifully the attitude and principles of Anglican Church order and worship, and Govan found they were identical with the English constitutional monarchy and politics. These principles were both theological and political, operating in both realms because they were true not only to biblical faith and church life, but also universally true to human nature and experience in church and state. For example, from the 1549 *Book of Common Prayer*:

> There was never anything by the wit of man so well devised,
> or so sure established, which in the continuance of time
> hath not been corrupted.[36]

In other words, no matter how perfect a creation, humans will corrupt it. As a result, reform is always and continually necessary, in church and state. He also believed in the freedom of the human spirit. Both people and institutions can repent, reform, and change. Forgiveness is even more powerful than sin and corruption.

From the 1928 *Book of Common Prayer* of the American Episcopal Church:

> O God, who art the author of peace and lover of concord,
> in knowledge of whom standeth our eternal life, whose
> service is perfect freedom: Defend us, thy humble servants
> in all assaults of our enemies.[37]

Perfect freedom is never a human possibility. It is only possible as a gift from God, who loves and forgives.

In the Articles of Religion (originally drawn up during the reign of Queen Elizabeth I and included in the 1979 *Book of Common Prayer* mostly for historical reasons), there are several statements to which Govan often referred. For example, there is an affirmation that churches can and do "err, not only in their living . . . but also in matters of faith."[38] Infallibility is therefore an impossible claim.

The Preface to the 1789 *Book of Common Prayer* speaks of "keeping the happy mean between too much stiffness in refusing, and too much easiness in admitting variations in things once advisedly established."[39] Anglican (Episcopal) reform was carefully measured. In the United States, this reform came in the same year as the new Constitution and went no further than required by its new situation in a new republic. The Preface also clearly declares that the churches and their governments must be consistent "with the constitution and laws of their country."[40] Separation of church and state was implied from the start.

Above all, it was the opening statement of the Preface on liberty and worship that Govan cared about:

> It is a most invaluable part of that blessed 'liberty wherewith Christ hath set us free' that in his worship different forms and usages may without offense be allowed, provided the substance of the Faith be kept entire; and that in every Church what cannot be clearly determined to belong to Doctrine must be referred to Discipline; and therefore, by common consent and authority, may be altered, abridged, enlarged, amended, or otherwise disposed of, as may seem most convenient for the edification of the people, according to the various exigencies of times and occasions.[41]

As language, customs and forms change, so may the words, the usages and the forms of worship change so long as they edify the people and maintain the faith which they express. Nothing is absolute except faith and doctrine, a faith and doctrine that is resolutely undefined, thus leaving decisions about their meaning up to each generation of the Church. Pragmatism and freedom was the Episcopal Church's way of faith and way of life.

While at Sewanee in 1941, Tom discovered to his amazement that the attitude and spirit expressed in the preface to the American *Book of Common Prayer* was identical to the attitude and spirit of Benjamin Franklin's speech at the end of the Constitutional Convention, which won the day in 1789. This was the spirit of humility, the willingness to doubt one's own infallibility, to be pragmatic, and to learn from experience. There was no question in Govan's mind that the true consensus of the United States lay in this spirit and in these principles. They were simultaneously theological and political, and he would spell them out in his 1956 essay, "Free to Be Merely a Man,"[42] and in his 1962 Beloit lectures, "A New Birth of Freedom."[43]

To Govan's way of thinking, to be theologically realistic and sound was to be also politically realistic and sound, and vice versa. It meant accepting the evil, cruelty, destructiveness, and anomie in human nature that is latent in all human beings and all society. Slavery, the Civil War, World Wars I and II, and the Holocaust are such illustrations. At the same time there is also in human nature the capacity for self-sacrifice, compassion, creativity, love, forgiveness and realism. That realism, for Govan, denied both cynicism and Pollyanna-ism. It was the radical mean, and nowhere did Govan find it better represented than in the Bible.

Govan's theological perspective on American history made his life as a professional historian very difficult indeed because the fields of modern history and science were so separate from modern theology that they spoke exclusively different languages. God, after all, was not a character with whom most modern historians could cope. Even when they were "believers," they relegated God to the inner faith of individuals and, by definition, thought God irrelevant to the course of history. Whenever Govan tried to bring the two realms together so as to express his prophetic message, he inevitably had to use theological language that most historians would have to reject. This professional tension between history and theology was a constant drain on his energies. Yet, this was his vocation and he faithfully pursued it.

Fracturing of the Consensus

During the 1960s and 1970s, a new attitude toward history appeared. The old narrative, "from-the-top-down" history of national and political affairs was considered inadequate and elitist. Too many people in American society were forgotten; too many voices had not been heard; too many problems not considered in that history. External events had a lot to do with the change: the Civil Rights Movement, urban riots, the assassinations of John and Robert Kennedy, and Martin Luther King; a new awareness of minority groups, of injustice and poverty; the women's liberation movement, the Vietnam War, and Watergate. The New Left offered its critique from the radical view of complete "participatory democracy." "From the bottom up history," which took seriously the previously voiceless multitudes, began to challenge the history of the past. Sharecroppers, the urban poor, rural families, laborers, coal miners, factory workers, the lot of women: people in all these situations were being considered by historians for the first time.

Much of the impetus for change came from the universities. Research in many new fields surrounding history encroached on political history: the social sciences, psychology, sociology, anthropology, and political science, contributing much in content and methodology. Quantitative and comparative approaches began to appear.[44]

Govan's response to these changes, which began as early as 1948, was to welcome them, but conditionally. The new materials might be good and helpful in themselves, but very often confused the central political story or in many cases buried it entirely. This was disastrous when only the central political story could explain or interpret what was happening in the history under review. In his opinion, these additional approaches needed to be kept as helpful sub-texts, but when they took center stage, history became distorted. In a 1948 book review Govan wrote:

> The study of history in recent years has broadened its
> field of coverage to so many aspects of human life that it
> comes as a welcome relief to read a book definitely and
> frankly limited to past politics. The increased emphasis
> on economic, social, intellectual (and other) history has
> left unresolved many of the most important problems of
> United States political history . . . .

Contemporary commentators in the "Middle Period" (1825-1853), either in Georgia or other parts of the Union, when called upon to make a judgment or hazard a prediction concerning political affairs in the state, almost unanimously confessed their incapacity. Historians confronted with the same problems have confined their attention either to one particular phase of the political story or to a brief interval of time, leaving the general story virtually untouched or unexplained.[45]

Bernard Bailyn and Gordon S. Wood

Govan's life overlapped with two other important historians who more or less dominated American history throughout the 1960s and 1970s. The first, Bernard Bailyn, saw the American Revolution as a republican intellectual movement; and the second, Gordon S. Wood, who saw the Revolution as a social movement. Both rejected Beard's economic theory and took the motivating power of people's beliefs and convictions seriously. Govan was sympathetic to Bailyn for several reasons: first, Bailyn called for a return to narrative history. Most historians were writing analytical history. That is, they would propose a theory and then marshal all the evidence they could find to support it. Govan agreed that narrative had not only been neglected—it was out of style, looked down upon, and needed to be revived. Second, he supported Bailyn's conviction that ideas exerted real power in history. Third, Govan saw Bailyn's realistic understanding of the fallibility and self-interest of human nature as similar to his own. He could also accept Bailyn's insistence that the Revolution was a movement in the direction of republicanism so long as it was moderate republicanism, which allowed room for other legitimate political forces. Radical republicanism, he knew, would be a disaster.

Before the Revolution, Bailyn said, the colonies felt socially and politically inferior to the sophistication of England and Europe. After the Revolution, they felt superior. They were proud of their republican society and felt confident that they could create a republican government to match. Govan understood the emphasis of Bailyn's point perfectly because Bailyn was a Jeffersonian at heart. The colonist's post-Revolutionary sense of superiority to Britain came, according to Bailyn, from their confidence that they would create a government far superior to Britain's. Not only would they eliminate the monarchy, but would establish a true democracy without hierarchical divisions between aristocracy and the rest of the people. Govan disagreed. As a Hamiltonian, he saw the Revolution and the Constitution as an affirmative replication of the English constitution, but without the monarchy and with a modified republican government. Bailyn emphasized discontinuity with England; Govan emphasized continuity.[46]

Gordon Wood expanded Bailyn's republican theory.[47] The debate in the colonies over the Constitution, he said, was a social debate between aristocracy and democracy, federalism and anti-federalism. He explained that the Federalists were wealthy, educated elitists, who assumed that they were the "worthy, the natural social aristocracy of the country,"[48] who would staff the government that the Constitution had established, and run the country. The anti-Federalists, on the other hand, were majoritarian republicans who were convinced that aristocratic government would lead to tyranny. Wood was, in Govan's mind, as much a Jeffersonian at heart as Bailyn. And yet, despite his republican bias, Wood presented a fair picture of the Federalists. He described them as presenting

> an amazing display of confidence in constitutionalism, in
> the efficacy of institutional devices for solving social and
> political problems. Through the proper arrangement of
> new institutional structures the Federalists aimed to turn
> the political and social developments that were weakening

the place of "the better sort of people" in government back upon themselves and to make these developments the very source of the perpetuation of the natural aristocracy's dominance of politics. Thus the Federalists did not directly reject democratic politics as it had manifested itself in the 1780s, rather they attempted to adjust to this politics in order to control and mitigate its effects. In short they offered the country an elitist theory of democracy. They did not see themselves as repudiating either the Revolution or popular government, but saw themselves as saving both from their excesses. If the Constitution were not established, they told themselves and the country over and over, then republicanism was doomed, the grand experiment was over, and a division of the confederacy, monarchy, or worse would result . . . .

. . . The Federalists had by no means lost faith in the people, at least in the people's ability to discern their true leaders. In fact many of the social elite who comprised the Federalist leadership were confident of popular election if the constituency could be made broad enough . . . . Even if they had wanted to, the Federalists could not turn their backs on republicanism. For it was evident to even the most pessimistic "that no other form would be reconcilable with the genius of the people of America; with the fundamental principles of the Revolution . . . . Whatever government the Federalists established had to be "strictly republican" and 'deducible from the only source of just authority—the People.'[49]

Govan believed that the Federalists were right and that they were thinking of the common good. Wood seems to have believed they were wrong and that they were thinking primarily of their own interests.

Govan and Civil Religion

Govan understood and accepted the distinction between civil religion, which was understood to be the religious dimension of the secular public and political life of the nation, and the church religion of particular faiths, which were personal, voluntary, and denominationally specific (Episcopal, Methodist, Congregational, Roman Catholic, etc.). Essentially, he agreed with Robert Bellah, a sociologist at the University of California-Berkeley, who in 1967 published an article titled "Civil Religion in America,"[50] which spells out "the elaborate system of practices, beliefs and symbols born of America's unique historic experience." Among them are Lincoln's Gettysburg and Second Inaugural addresses; "The Star Spangled Banner" and "God Bless America;" the Pledge of Allegiance; "In God We Trust" and "E Pluribus Unum" on our coins; Memorial Day and Fourth of July celebrations.

Civil religion exists alongside of and liberally uses the symbolism of Protestant American church religion: ideas like "loyalty," "sacrifice," "die for," "faith" and "freedom." But, said Bellah, civil religion "is free of association with any single religious sect; it is the one religion in America that is broad enough for all citizens to accept."[51]

Govan simply identified in civil religion what he considered to be authentic biblical religion and then, because God is God of the Bible and America and of civil and church religion, considered the distinction irrelevant for his purposes. His God, the God of the Bible, could not be enclosed within the confines of religion of any kind. God was the Creator who stood above His creation and His people, their nations, and their history.

"The Last Best Hope": Freedom and How to Achieve It

The person who best expressed Govan's understanding of freedom was Abraham Lincoln in his Gettysburg and Second Inaugural addresses. Govan recognized in Lincoln a man influenced by the Bible in the same way he was—in a political as well as a religious sense. The principles of freedom, justice, and equality, of mercy and forgiveness, apply in national life as well as personal and religious life. Govan found these same principles in both economic and political forms within the laws and constitution of Great Britain, which the Federalists appropriated and adapted to the government of the United States in republican form. In this tradition, institutions were not understood to be hostile to personal freedom, nor were the restraints they imposed necessarily harmful. Liberty and authority were not opposing concepts; rather, one could not exist without the other. "There can be no freedom," Govan said, "unless there is an authority to establish and maintain it, but authority can exist only where it avoids perversion into authoritarianism through honoring and protecting the freedom of those who subject themselves to it. Some method of checks and balances such as those so beautifully exemplified in the Constitution of the United States are necessary to control unrestrained individualism and an unrestrained state."[52]

The Constitution abhorred perfectionism as much as absolutism. As Govan had said in his article "Free To Be Merely A Man": "It was not the intention of the American Revolution to provide a perfect society without corruption of misfortune,"[53] but rather to create a society with a maximum of freedom and order: freedom of citizens to "seek equal justice for themselves and for others;"[54] and order provided by lawful and generally accepted restraints.

This kind of government was what Lincoln called "the last best hope of earth."[55] The Civil War was a "fiery trial" that would prove whether the nation would "nobly save or meanly lose [this] last best hope."[56]

The United States survived the Civil War and has survived many other trials since from people left and right, "who have different purposes and views."[57] Those on the left, said Govan,

> . . . are distressed by the inequalities, injustices, and denials of freedom they continue to find in the nation. They believe these can only be remedied if the nation changes fundamentally. Each group has a different solution, but all agree that somehow there must be an easier, quicker, and more permanent way to establish freedom, justice, and equality for all. But those on the right reject freedom, and

they, too, like their predecessors in the seventeenth and eighteenth centuries, frequently have been in positions of power.[58]

Govan rejected both the left and the right because they sought to upset the truly revolutionary and balanced view set forth in the Declaration of Independence and the Constitution of the United States. And ironically, they often did so "in the name of the more profound and radical . . . hope set forth in these documents."[59] Both left and right, he believed led to authoritarianism. These documents were truly radical in their clarity about principles and their moderation, checks and balances in practice. They provided the best grounds for the pursuit of our imperfect freedom.

Govan believed, with Lincoln, that if the United States' freedom fails, freedom all over the world will also fail. He wrote

> If the United States does not work out, there is little hope that any can ever create and maintain a society in which they are free to seek equal justice for themselves and others . . . . This nation is still more nearly free, more nearly just, and more nearly equitable than almost any other that has existed on this earth.[60]

Govan saw the struggle of the right and the left and their questions involving the place and purpose of the Constitution as central issues confronting the nation in the present. These issues, he knew, were fundamentally theological. The struggle between good and evil is not over, and Govan felt bound in the tradition of Amos, Hosea, Isaiah, Jeremiah, and Ezekiel, to call his profession, his students and all who would hear, back to the true roots of our national life. Govan often found himself "crying in the wilderness" among his students, fellow historians, and colleagues in the church. However, he persisted because, he said, the historian has this duty, unwelcome though it be, for his is not solely the nation's memory, he is also its conscience, its teacher, and upon him lies the complex burden of seeking to distinguish right from wrong.[61]

PART I

The Emergence and
Transformation of a Young
Historian

1

The Govan Family

They were a group of unusual people who shared a respect and facility for discussion and debate . . . contentious, yes; difficult, yes . . . [but] serious people who thought about serious matters.

Thomas J. Tucker

Will and Kate

The origins of the Govan family[62] lie in Scotland, probably in the Glasgow area, where there are still many by that name. Because of overpopulation poverty, and economic changes early in the 19th century, thousands of Scots emigrated to the United States and Canada. They came in at the bottom of the social and economic ladder. In Glasgow, the name was pronounced Guv-un (as in "govern"), with the accent on the first syllable. In the United States, it became Go-van, with a long 'O' and the accent on the second syllable.

Thomas Payne Govan's parents represent an often-repeated pattern following the Civil War: a radical mix of North and South. Tom's father, William James Govan, was born in New Orleans in 1861. As a young man without a penny to his name, he worked for the railroad in Chattanooga, Tennessee, probably in a lower-level white collar or administrative job. There he met Katherine Clara Eaton, whose parents had moved to Chattanooga from her father's hometown in Haverhill, Massachusetts, when she was two. Albert Claude Eaton had been appointed manager of a large coal mine in South Pittsburgh, Tennessee, near Chattanooga. In the 1870s, the Civil War and Reconstruction were still so close that Eatons were tagged by the local people as northern "carpetbaggers."

The 10th Street House, approx. 1914. Front row: Roy, Carol, Tom, "Momma" Back row: Jack, "Uncle More," Gilbert, "Poppa." When asked why Uncle More lived there, Momma said, "I don't know. Poppa just brought him to dinner one evening and he stayed."

Will Govan and Kate were married in 1889, when he was twenty-eight and she was twenty-four. Soon after, they moved to Atlanta, Georgia, where Will opened and managed a successful cigar and tobacco store, which he financed with saved railroad money, help from Kate, and a bank loan. It comfortably supported the family for close to twenty years. At one point, he also owned a saloon. They moved initially into a boarding house owned by Senator Eugene Talmadge's mother when Talmadge was a newborn baby. Later, they bought a small house on Pine Street where, over the next eighteen years, all five of their children were born: Gilbert (1892), Jack (1895), Roy (1897), Carol (1901), and Tom (1907). The tobacco store must have been a success because in 1912, when Tom was five, Will was able to finance the building of a large new house for his family on Tenth Street in Atlanta. It was there that Tom grew up.[63]

Atlanta was a racist and violent city in the first decade of the twentieth century and the Govans did not entirely escape. One night, they heard a mob lynching and hanging a Jew named Frank, thought to be an "anarchist." It was close enough and terrible enough to be a subject for repeated discussion among the family for years after. They later likened the event to the Sacco-Vanzetti case in Boston during the 1920s.[64]

Kate, whom the children called "Momma," was a charming, attractive and very capable person, a good wife and mother. She was also the real power and center of the family: very strong, very steady, and endlessly patient. As chief manager and disciplinarian, she was unruffled and clearly in charge of a growing household enlivened not only by the children but also by innumerable comings and goings of other family and friends. She cared for a big family and a constantly full house—often without much help from her husband.

Will Govan was a complete contrast to his wife. Where she was steady and solid, he was variable and a dichotomy: on the one hand a warm and compelling person; on the other, erratic and obsessive. He was a kind man, instinctively full of feeling, who exuded a charm, even a charisma, which drew people to him. One example was "Uncle More" who lived with the Govans. When asked why "Uncle More" was there, Momma replied, "I don't know. Poppa brought him home to dinner and he just stayed."[65]

Will was also a loving father whom his children adored. Although he lacked formal education beyond high school, he loved to share books and ideas with them. He respected learning and cared about exposing his children to as much of it as he could. Reading out loud and discussing issues were a regular part of family life. "His beautiful reading voice was a pleasure"[66] for them all. Will's nephew, Thomas Tucker, described him as "a learned man . . . whose lack of formal education never deterred him from his love of learning . . . He had a profound effect upon many people," including his family. They were a group of "unusual people who shared a respect and facility for discussion and debate around the dinner table. They were contentious, yes; difficult, yes, but there was a strong drive for achievement. They were serious people and . . . thought about serious matters." Will Govan's influence had a lot to do with this. He was a genuine source of pride to his family. Gilbert, his oldest, and Tom, his youngest, especially caught his spirit and came to focus their lives on books and learning.[67] Will was also a realist about human nature. All of that was one side of the man.

William James Govan, "Poppa" in the 1930s

On the other side, Will was prone to enthusiasms, extreme behavior and addictions. He was a serious smoker and, as time went by, became a compulsive drinker, an alcoholic by today's standards. Apparently he came by his condition honestly: his father, James Fauntleroy Govan, died after being run over by trolley while he was drunk in New Orleans.

Will too enjoyed his share of benders. One day, Gilbert was "coming home from high school and came around the corner of Forsythe and Alabama Streets, where the cigar store was located. Gilbert saw people scrambling in the street for dollar bills that were floating down from the heavens. He looked up and saw that they were being thrown out the second floor window of the cigar store. He rushed in and, of course, it was 'Poppa drunk as a coot,' Gilbert said. He was furious with his father and immediately put an end to the dollar-throwing."[68] Poppa's drunkenness was becoming habitual, and he was embarrassing his family more often, yet no one accused him of being mean-spirited. The incident with the dollar bills was, after all, a sign of an exuberant generosity and goodwill. But Momma began looking for help and found it among the Christian Scientists.

Katherine Clara Eaton Govan, "Momma" in the 1950s

What the family's previous church affiliations had been is not clear. Kate's parents had her baptized in the Episcopal Church in Massachusetts, but there is no indication that she had any of her own children baptized. Nor is there evidence in Chattanooga of religious ties. As a child, Will had undoubtedly been exposed to and may have joined some form of evangelical Protestant church, possibly Southern Baptist. What is certain is that Kate, deeply upset by her husband's compulsive drinking, turned to the Christian Scientists because they were the only help at that time. They recognized alcoholism as an addiction and considered it an exclusively spiritual problem. They believed it could be cured by spiritual power, exerted by practitioners through counseling and prayer. No doubt Kate prevailed upon Will to accept the help of a practitioner, which, over a period of years, culminated in a conversion experience.

When Will was in his fifties, during a train trip to Chattanooga in 1915, "he had a bottle of clear southern moonshine liquor with him and had the bottle to his lips" when "suddenly he saw the light" and walked back to the station car at the end of the train and threw the bottle out onto the tracks and never drank again. He suffered with delirium tremens and, the family felt, was never the same.[69]

One grandson put it this way:

> He was a changed person, and his mind was slightly deranged. My memory of him was that he was the most wonderfully gentle, nice man I'd ever met. I loved him dearly . . . . [But] when you go from alcoholism to something that can save you, you hang onto it. And what he hung onto was the Christian Science faith.[70]

It turned out, he did not embrace Christian Science, but reverted to the old-fashioned southern Bible Christianity he had known as a young man. Momma, however, became the Christian Scientist.

Some family members attributed Will's drinking directly to having to share his house with his mother-in-law. She was apparently a controlling person who constantly interfered with his relationships with his children. Some family theorized the alcohol was the anesthesia he used to neutralize the pain she caused him. "The day she was no longer there, he stopped drinking."[71]

After his conversion, Will considered himself ordained by the Holy Spirit. He began preaching, teaching, distributing Bibles, forming new mission congregations around Atlanta, leading worship, baptizing, burying, and visiting people. Lists of his scheduled obligations were found by his son-in-law after Will's death.[72] Poppa was particularly concerned about alcoholics and the evils of drinking, and regularly visited people, black and white, in prison. He was filled with love and concern for the welfare of others, and the sweetness of his personality and warmth he exuded influenced people deeply. It also influenced Momma, who got interested in the prisoners and began working with him. When prisoners were released, they would visit the Govans' home and were always welcome.[73] But Poppa spent so much time and money on his religious work that both his family and his business suffered. Some family members felt he became more irresponsible sober than he had been drunk.[74] Their embarrassment over his alcoholism now became an embarrassment over his religion. He was becoming "peculiar" as they put it.

"After his conversion, he used to wear a Panama hat and an all-white seersucker suit, and a pair of webbed leather Oxford shoes with no socks, to keep his feet cool; this was his uniform year round. He did not like wearing an overcoat, jacket or tie. He carried a satchel made of stiff reeds on which was written in big black letters, 'OBEY THE LAW.' Inside were Bibles and Christian tracts on a variety of subjects, ready for distribution. His message was: "If you think you are bad because you drink, repent and just stop."[75]

He had a convertible sedan, which his sons thought was the hottest thing in town, except for the "Jesus Saves" sign on the driver's side door. Sometimes Roy would impress girls by taking them out for rides in his father's car with the top down and his fashionable raccoon coat carefully draped over the door covering the sign.

Sweet as Will was as a person, after his conversion he became a rigid moralist. For years, "he would not eat at Momma's table because she served meat, so she would set him up at a separate table, where he ate alone. He also refused to visit his daughter Carol's home because her husband, Thomas Tucker, served liquor."[76] Once, when serving on a jury, and after many days of deliberation, he came home in a dejected frame of mind. The jury had not been able to agree on a verdict. Poppa said the trouble was that on a jury of twelve, he had never seen a group of eleven men so "hard headed"—it was he who had hung the jury.

There were times when Will and Kate could hardly live under the same roof because they were so different. This was true during Will's drinking years and equally true during his religious years.

Momma once said of the Govans, "If you think they were bad when they drank, just wait until they stop."[77]

Sometimes when Will felt he had to leave the house, he went to Boggs Mountain outside Atlanta, where he had built a log cabin with a screened-in sleeping porch on one side. He would sometimes retreat for weeks at a time, and every morning, he would greet the sunrise by singing the Doxology, "Praise God from whom all blessings flow," over and over at the top of his lungs. His neighbors in the valley below would be woken by his songs of praise.[78]

Will had a horse named Jerry that he rode only going down the mountain to buy food. Coming back up, he lead the loaded-down horse on foot. In time, he became known by everyone around as the "Prophet of Boggs Mountain."

After 1925, when the children were gone and Will was in his late sixties, he and Kate had some very close and happy years, just the two of them in the Tenth Street home. But then Will began to get depressed and frightened, becoming more dependent on Momma and more possessive of her attention. Although she always responded with understanding, compassion, and humor, she found Will more and more of a burden. Momma would be ready to go out to play bridge with her friends when Will would say, "If you go and play bridge today, I'm going to commit suicide while you are gone." Momma was worried, felt she had to take him seriously and would call up her friends to decline playing that day. She described this to her granddaughter: "You can see my dilemma. I would have to call up Rosie Calder and say, 'I can't play bridge today because Will says he's going to kill himself.' I couldn't have drawn a comfortable breath the whole time I was gone."[79]

Will died in 1940, to the sorrow of the whole family. They had truly loved him as he had loved them. Will's manic enthusiasm and irresponsibility, however, juxtaposed with his tender sweetness and rigid moralism, made him a complicated husband and father to deal with. His inconsistent behavior inevitably affected his children, consciously and unconsciously.

Momma felt a huge sense of relief along with her sorrow, but above all she felt gratitude for a caring and well-intentioned husband. She remained the hub of the family until her death in 1967 at the age of 102.

Gilbert

The Govans' oldest son, Gilbert Eaton Govan, was born in Atlanta in 1891 when his parents lived on Pine Street after Will had his cigar store well established. Momma named him Gilbert after her maternal family from Auburn, New Hampshire, and Eaton after her paternal family from Massachusetts. Although he was bright and did well in school, it was not from school that he learned the passion of his life: good books.

> According to him, that passion came from a judge, Simpson B. Harris, who was adjutant general of Georgia just after the turn-of-the-century when Gilbert was in his early teens. He had been a colonel in the Sixth Georgian Infantry of the Confederate Army and now lived outside Atlanta on his estate named 'Carollton.' As it happened, the Govan family doctor was not a great believer in formal education—he was largely self-taught himself until he went to medical school—and knew the judge well. Whenever Gilbert got sick, the doctor would say, 'Oh, take him out of school and send him to Carollton!' Judge Simpson would talk and Gilbert would listen. The old man lent him books from his personal library and Gilbert would devour them. He loved every minute of it. And the treatment always worked.[80]

That experience got Gilbert started. His interest in the Civil War and local Chattanooga history never left him. He never finished high school or college because he had to work to support the family. Though nobody ever said so explicitly, this need for support was due in part to Will's irresponsibility. In 1916 at the age of twenty-four, Gilbert became a clerk in the book department of T.H. Payne Co., a department store in Chattanooga. When World War I intervened, he served in the army. He might not have returned to Chattanooga to live had he not met Christine Noble, a young schoolteacher, whom he married in 1918. Together they raised three children. In 1920 they returned to Chattanooga and Gilbert returned to work for T. H. Payne Co., and became head of the book department. "I was determined," he said, "to show that Southerners—who had few and far between bookstores to patronize—would buy books if they had a chance." Under his management, Payne's book department became "an oasis in what was a literary desert."[81]

In 1931, on the basis of his reputation, Gilbert was invited to become editor of the book page of the Chattanooga Times, a position he held with distinction for thirty-five years. His nephew, Thomas J. Tucker said he was "brilliant. His mind had an uncanny capacity to cut to the core of an issue. He also had an immense knowledge of literature, as well as local history of Chattanooga and the Civil War. His book on the Civil War General Joseph Johnston, *A Different Valor*, is still the definitive one."[82] With a friend, he also wrote the definitive history of the Chattanooga area up to the time of the Tennessee Valley Authority (TVA). Each week at the Times he wrote a "personal column on books, authors, and the publishing field in general" and solicited reviews of all sorts of books, just so long as they were "good" books.[83]

Gilbert Eaton Govan circa 1905

Gilbert Govan circa 1920

Gilbert was sixteen years older than Tom and realized early on that he and his younger brother were kindred spirits who shared a common interest in ideas and history. Gilbert filled in the gaps left by Will's inadequacies as a father and guided and encouraged Tom along his academic path.

In 1934, without giving up his book page in the Times, Gilbert joined the University of Chattanooga Library staff at the request of his friend and its president, Alexander Guerry, and very soon became its head. During his twenty-six years of leadership, the library tripled in size and tremendously increased its services to scholars and their research. He died in 1977 at the age of eighty-four.[84]

Jack, Roy and Carol

Jack and Roy, the two middle brothers in the family, were two and four years younger than Gilbert, respectively. Both had the charm and entrepreneurial spirit of their father and the drive of their mother. Both were married with children. Nothing in them had been academic, and they had little understanding or respect for Gilbert or Tom who made the academy their business. But because they understood that a college degree was an asset in any business, they completed bachelor degrees at Georgia Tech. Their hearts and aspirations though were in business and making money.

Carol, the only daughter, did not have an easy life as a child. She was a mystery to her father who understood and related better to the boys. Her mother was a powerhouse who did not always understand her feelings and fears. She was the younger sister of two boys who loved to tease and terrorize her. She grew up to be a very strong, very bright, very capable, but troubled person: controlling, impatient, and like everyone but Momma, with addictive tendencies.

Tom, the afterthought of the family, was born six years later and became a blessing to Carol. She doted on him and became a great help to Momma in caring for him. A sweet child, Tom was never a threat to the authority of his older sister. In later years he would become her chief defender and supporter.

Carol Govan 1903

Carol Govan Tucker circa 1946

2

The Young Historian

I cannot remember a time when I was not . . . awed and frightened by the mysteries of existence.

Thomas P. Govan

Tom's Early Interests

Born in Atlanta on January 9, 1907, Thomas Payne Govan was the youngest child in the family. His middle name came from the T. H. Payne department store where Momma shopped for years. She just liked the sound of that name. There was never any question about Tom's importance in the family. He was the youngest and favorite of his mother and his sister. Although they undoubtedly spoiled him, it was from them that he learned what unconditional love was. From his mother he also inherited an intellectual brilliance and combativeness which would be both a strength and a weakness later on. From his father came a special sweetness and charm which all his life drew people to him. From both parents he learned a love of books, the importance of ideas, and the pleasure of intellectual discussion. Tom was a sensitive and reflective little boy, definitely not an athlete, very bright and articulate, who learned to read early and in school was a pleasure to his teachers.[85] But from the start he was an anxious skeptic. As he would write later,

Thomas Payne Govan, the youngest child, circa 1909

I cannot remember a time when I was not . . . awed and frightened by the mysteries of existence, the world, other people, and myself, but dissatisfied with the apparently easy way in which these frightening mysteries were explained away by those around me. I wanted answers, but was given only comforting words; and did not realize that the purpose of these comforting words was to affirm the existence of the fundamental mystery of the human situation, not to dispel it. It seemed to me that the explanations offered were fairy stories, similar to and of the same quality as the story of the stork as an answer to where I came from and how my birth occurred, or of Santa Claus to explain the origins of the gifts and toys which appeared at Christmas.

I began to believe that I was almost alone in my fears and concern; that all others were indifferent; and that they were not afraid because they lacked the courage to compare their explanations with the mysteries they pretended to explain and find them wanting. The church and its ministers to me were the most guilty. They were the most certain, and their explanations the least believable.[86]

This indictment also applied to his father's religion which turned him off completely.

In his teens, faced with the confusion of puberty and awareness of the shadow of death and all its cohorts of sickness, conflict, injustice, violence, and the potential meaninglessness of life, Tom had deeper bouts of insecurity and fear. He began looking for the comfort of explanations and found them, not in religion, but in the certainties of mathematics and science, in logic and verifiable reality. They did not answer all of his questions or calm all of his anxieties, but they seemed to him tangible and solid—things that he could count on. It was not until much later than Tom would discover that even these certainties were only partial and were based upon unverifiable assumptions.[87]

From early on Gilbert recognized a kindred spirit in Tom and took a special interest in him. They were thinkers and became scholars. Poppa's death in 1940 was too early for Tom. He really missed him, maybe more than the other children, and into that gap Gilbert stepped. He became for a long time Tom's second father.

Tom was not all seriousness by any means. He was surrounded with a growing number of nieces and nephews for whom he played the role of the fun, available uncle. They would come by after school when he was doing his homework at the kitchen table, and would tease him until he quit to play with them.

After his Atlanta high school graduation in 1924, while still living at home, Tom attended Georgia Tech because he could do so as a day student. Fascinated by business and money, comforted by the precision of mathematics and science, he took all of the courses he could in business, bookkeeping, and economics. Unlike his brothers Jack and Roy, his was an intellectual interest in how the system worked, not simply in making money. He majored in communication, however, because there was no business major available. Tom knew even then that the world of finance would be a lifelong interest. He studied hard, enjoyed college, and became thoroughly versed in accounting and banking. In 1928, he graduated with a bachelor of science degree. Thanks to Gilbert's advice and influence, Tom immediately landed a job as a teller in the American Trust and Banking Company in Chattanooga. There he had an experience that transformed his life.

At the time, Tom accepted without question the racial attitudes of the nation, especially the South. Blacks did not vote in Atlanta; they were considered in every way inferior to whites, and so were destined to be lower class.

A reception was being held at the opening of a new branch office of the bank, and Tom, as the lowest person on the staff, was assigned to guard the front door and greet people as they came in. A large, elderly, and very impressive black man who had worked for the company for years came to the door. Tom realized that he was in the presence of a man vastly superior to himself, not just in size, but in presence. Even so, instinctively and abruptly, Tom told him he could not come in the front door but had to go around to the back door. Without hesitation or slightest sign of protest, the old man went around to the back door and entered the reception.

Tom knew even before the old man got to the back door what a horrible thing he had done. He felt sick inside and was ashamed of himself. He thrashed all that night about it, and from that moment on, his attitude and his behavior with regard to race, conscious and unconscious, changed. Tom recounted that story in his classes throughout his career. His point was: "how can we allow a society like that to develop in which a person like me could be allowed to speak to a man like him in those terms?" There was just something fundamentally wrong with a system that could allow that.[88] For the rest of his life he fought that system and the ideology that supported it.

After one year in the bank (1928-1929), Tom was convinced that he had learned all he could as a teller and was ready for graduate school. By that time, however, the Depression had struck. His family needed his financial support, and his mother wanted her youngest closer to home. Again, Gilbert intervened and helped Tom get a job in Atlanta as an insurance investigator with the Retail Credit Company, instead of pursuing his graduate studies.

Shortly thereafter, in 1931, Gilbert joined the Chattanooga Times as editor of the Sunday book page. He needed book reviewers, and there was his brother nearby, an avid student, marking time as an insurance investigator and needing stimulation. Gilbert began referring books to Tom for review. Tom would read six or seven books a month and review the one or two he thought worthy. With Gilbert's expert advice and coaching, Tom learned how to dig the heart out of a book and share it with his readers. He developed the skill of reading and reviewing, an avocation he continued for the rest of his life.

While working with the Retail Credit Company and writing reviews for Gilbert, Tom entered graduate school part-time at Emory in 1932. Although he was happy with his practical on-the-job education in banking, he wanted to place that experience in a theoretical and historical context, and so began his professional study in economic history. In his second year, he dropped the credit company job and moved full-time to Emory, financing himself with a teaching fellowship. Unimpressed with the value of economic theory, which sometimes seemed completely out of touch with reality, he followed Gilbert's advice and broadened his course of study to American history, earning his M.A. in that field in 1934. He immediately applied to Vanderbilt to pursue his Ph.D. The reaction of Tom's brothers, Roy and Jack, to his vocational decision was, "Does the damn fool want to go to school all his life?"[89] Will and Kate, on the other hand, were entirely supportive of the direction of Tom's career. Gilbert assured them of the soundness of Tom's decision. They were proud of Tom, and he appreciated their support.

At the time Tom began his professional study of history in the 1930s, historians were attempting to interpret the past with scientific precision. Initially Tom went along with the current trend, but he could not completely suppress his sense of the mystery that lay behind the facts. He was curious about what meanings were hidden in the patterns of history.

Later, Tom reflected on this period in his career:

> I had almost forgotten the mystery which surrounds us
> and intrudes into the center of our being. I no longer
> asked or concerned myself with fundamental questions,
> at least I tried to avoid them, and it was only infrequently
> that involuntarily they would intrude themselves into my
> mind. Each time the awe and fear reappeared and I was
> uncomfortable, so I strove to banish them to the realm
> of the undiscussed and unthought of, where, to my way
> of thinking, they properly belonged. As a beginning
> student of history . . . I was a scientist, a believer of facts,
> and I interpreted my task to be the use of scientific
> procedures to find out exactly what happened in the
> past and then to record it. I strove to free my mind from
> all preconceptions, all prejudice, all thought, and to
> become what would be, in effect, an investigating and
> recording machine.[90]

Tom found that he would have to live with tension between his
heart and his mind: his heart, sensitive, full of feeling, fearful,
wondering about the meaning of existence, always pressing to be
heard; and his mind, rational, committed to science, suppressing the
questions and feelings of the heart. It would take the next eight years
(in 1942 when he was confirmed in the Episcopal Church) to resolve
this conflict within himself.

The process would be a tortuous one. Trying to be a historical
"recording machine" was short lived because he soon realized that
trying to discover what really happened in history through the study
of empirical facts was futile. Whenever he settled on a set of facts,
there were always other facts that changed everything. The process of
writing down the facts seemed to distort them. No two historians,
even when they agreed on the facts, could agree on their meaning.
He was frustrated and challenged.

Tom would have to go at history in some other way, so he tried to
approach the facts from a previously chosen view, with a theory, a

guess at the underlying laws of history, and then see how the facts would cohere. The most powerful theories of the time were scientific laws, which he instinctively believed would create automatic historical progress. He assumed that "the modern, the contemporary, the new was better than the old."[91] He turned to the historians concerned with the interpretation and meaning of history. But here, instead of finding increased clarity and hope, he "came to complete despair."[92] He began reading Spengler, Henry Adams, Malthus, Ricardo, and James Mill, all of them heavily influenced by new empirical sciences, and found them all forecasting inevitable doom and claiming that humans could do nothing about it because scientific laws governed human life and that was that. Ethical behavior as a means to change things for the better, they said, was not only useless but wrong.

Thomas Jefferson, whom Govan had regarded as a spiritual forefather, turned out to be no better. Jefferson believed that American freedom and democracy depended upon a wealth of open land for a farming society that would be virtuous and produce good people. Crowded cities, commerce, industry and banks were corrupting society. This view was more than Govan could stomach. He was, after all, a city dweller, very much interested in economics, commerce and banks. He wanted to help create a better future for our cities, not give up on them. He became disillusioned with Jefferson.

As he later wrote,

> My search for comfortable words through science and natural law had thus ended in failure. There was no comfort in a philosophy and point of view which doomed all human struggle to defeat and assured me that the only outcome of life was death.

> I had for many years accepted this as my personal fate and prided myself on my willingness to accept it as a testimony to my personal courage, proving that I did not have to use the crutches that sustained other men, but I was unwilling to accept this conclusion as it effected mankind and the generations unborn. They, in spite of

all, I felt certain, would live, but to sustain this hope
[intellectually] I had to have a new philosophy, a new
science of man.

This new philosophy and its science of man was, of course,
there waiting for me in Marxism, which took the same
materials that had led Jefferson, Malthus, Ricardo, Mill,
Adams, and Spengler to enunciate a deterministic
philosophy of death, and from them wrought a new
synthesis promising life.[93]

Govan accepted Marx with welcome relief. As a historian, the
most important thing Tom learned from Marx was that "the facts
which [he] and other historians had tried to deal with were not
[real] facts at all. What [they] had been doing was to examine
consciously the conscious records of men who themselves were
unaware of the laws and forces which governed their actions."[94]
What historians needed to do according to Marx instead was to
look at the real facts: the physical and economic laws that governed
people's behavior. "There was a uniformity and regularity behind
the confused appearances of reality. Now that [he] had the clue,
the proper method, [he] could begin to ascertain what really
happened in the past."[95]

After receiving his M.A. in 1934, Tom stayed on at Emory for
another year as an instructor. As a neophyte Marxist, he also began
work on his Ph.D. at Vanderbilt.

I was in the south and my chief concern was with its
economic and political situation, relatively so much worse
off than the rest of the country, and I determined to examine
the circumstances in the early nineteenth century which
had produced this result. Marx himself in his articles on
the American Civil War . . . had provided the terms and
fundamental analysis. The war was not fought for political
or moral reasons. Slavery and states' rights were not the
issues.[96]

Rather, the war was the first stage of a revolution in which a rising bourgeois class in the North had successfully thrown off "the restraining shackles imposed upon its growth . . . by a feudal and agricultural South"[97] and thus set the conditions for the final stage of revolution in which the bourgeois class would overthrow capitalism in the North.

He later described his situation as a Ph.D. candidate:

> I was writing a thesis and time was short, so I selected as a proper unit for my study the subject of banking and the credit system in my native state of Georgia in the period between 1810 and 1860. I was involved in this task for two years between 1935 and 1937 and strange and, from my [Marxist] point of view, unpredictable things were happening in the world around me.[98]

Based on his own experience, Tom knew that

> the essentially pragmatic administration of Franklin D. Roosevelt, acting with courage, confidence, and intelligence, had begun to restore the American society and economy to a sound and healthy condition not by the destruction of individual liberty, but by a new birth of freedom. Internal peace and the rule of law was brought back into the country by a strengthened and invigorated government which protected the right of industrial labor to organize, provided useful work for the unemployed, increased the income of farmers, and restored profits and security to industrial, commercial, and financial enterprises.[99]

Then Tom discovered that Nicholas Biddle, faced with the panic of 1837, had done the same sort of thing as Roosevelt a hundred years before. Biddle and Roosevelt were "wealthy public leaders [who] believed in order and the rule of law, both valued freedom; and they found that individual liberty could be maintained only in a society in which government and its institutions were strong enough to restrain not only the weak and numerous but also the powerful and few."[100]

The outcome, according to Marx, should have been completely different. The crisis of 1837 and 1937 should have created a revolutionary sentiment in the minds of the exploited workers and farmers. This revolutionary sentiment in turn should have so frightened the well-to-do capitalist business interests (the bourgeoisie) "that they would throw off the liberal disguises which masked the fact of their rule and resort to naked and unlimited dictatorship. The United States, Great Britain, France, and other capitalist countries"[101] should have followed a path like that of Hitler and Nazi Germany. But they had not. Govan was faced with the inevitable conclusion that the resolution of these two crises a hundred years apart "could not be adequately explained in Marxian terms of class struggle"[102] and that he would have to give up Marx and look elsewhere for explanatory help.

Govan's research led him back to Alexander Hamilton, George Washington's secretary of the treasury, who, in 1789, had more to do with establishing the Bank of the United States and the credit system of the country than anyone else. Tom had believed Hamilton was a spokesman for the aristocracy, "a defender of monarchy and all its evils and one who had tried to fasten upon the United States all the inherited weaknesses of the British Constitution." With new eyes, Govan began to read what Hamilton had to say about human nature and society.

"Take all men," Hamilton once said, "and what are they governed by? Their passions and their interests."[103] Hamilton quoted David Hume, who said that in devising a government, we should consider all men to be knaves and governed by their interests; and later, Hamilton warned that, "If all power were given to the many, they would oppress the few." Similarly, "If all power were given to the few, they would oppress the many," so that " . . . in any proper form of government, each, the many and the few, must be possessed of power to protect itself from the other."[104]

This view of human nature, Govan discovered later, was reflected in the *Book of Common Prayer's* and the Bible's view of human sin, which he had long since rejected. The process of new understanding was underway, the first and major result of Tom's research into American history, and was almost entirely inadvertent.

This was not cynicism, Tom realized, but a realism about human nature which was reflected also in the Constitution of the United States. He would from that time on look at Hamilton and through Hamilton at United States history with new eyes. He was on his way to becoming a Hamiltonian conservative. This was the first and major result of his research.

The South's Economy Was Commercial

Tom began exploring the economics of slavery, cotton production, and cotton distribution. In November 1936, the annual meeting of the Southern Historical Association was held at Vanderbilt, and partly because he was at the university and partly because he had research to report, Govan was asked to lecture. He spoke on "The Georgia Planters and the Movement for Direct Trade with the Continent." This talk was an important moment for him. Lecturing to his peers was the best possible way of being introduced to the southern history profession. His address was an early version of a later article summarizing his thesis, called, "Banking and the Credit System in Georgia, 1820-1960."

He had found, he said, that most historians of the ante-bellum southern economy had focused almost exclusively on the economics of plantation slavery and considered it fundamentally unprofitable. To some extent this explained for them the reason that the South remained "backward" economically. The historians had failed, however, to understand and recognize the central importance of the commercial and credit system of the nation to the whole southern agricultural economy. Credit was its fundamental basis. Tom's research showed beyond any doubt that merchants and planters had used and depended upon this system ever since its founding after the Revolution. The planters regularly

> . . . went into debt to purchase land and Negroes, received
> advances from merchants for the necessary expenses of
> the growing season, and sold their crops (of cotton and

rice) to purchasers using funds supplied by banks on
security of the shipments of the same cotton and rice.[105]

In Govan's judgment, the system, though imperfect, worked well
and certainly to the satisfaction of most planters.

In the South, however, there were constant undercurrents of
hostility to the system. There were some politicians and planters who
distrusted credit, paper money, and banks entirely, and they wanted
hard-money currency and little use of credit. Others distrusted and
chafed against the power and control of credit exerted by the Bank of
the United States and wanted that power distributed down to the
state, city, and private banks. They wanted freedom from federal
regulation. Still others believed that they were being overcharged by
northern middlemen who managed the shipping, storing, and
marketing of southern crops overseas to England and Europe. These
undercurrents of dissatisfaction resulted in basically two initiatives:
first, the attempt of southern planters to gain financial control of the
cotton market and thus, free themselves from the "bonds" of the credit
system; and second, the attempt to establish direct trade with European
countries, thus bypassing the use of northern banks and the need for
the services of northern middlemen.[106]

Neither of these initiatives came to fruition but they suggested that
many planters felt caught in a system controlled by the North. They also
suggested that the planters needed to take hold of their own destiny.
Govan was able to show, on the contrary, that the vast majority of merchants
and planters in Georgia took "very little interest" in these schemes.

> Each was interested in his own particular operations and
> not the economic system as a whole. The average planter
> operated a comparatively small farm on which he raised
> relatively few bales of cotton. He needed supplies
> throughout the year that could be supplied by merchants
> in the nearest town. When his crop was harvested, he had
> neither the time nor the opportunity to send his cotton to
> a distant market. He desired to convert it into cash in the
> easiest and most convenient manner, consequently, he sold

73

it to the nearest buyer, and used the proceeds to pay the obligations that he had incurred during the year.

In the same way, the merchants were interested in the profits to be made from the sale of supplies and the purchase of cotton, and the bankers in discounting notes and furnishing exchange. They were little concerned whether the North was profiting at the expense of the South, or England at the expense of the United States.[107]

These close-to-home interests stood in the way of change in the financial and commercial system. Banks and middlemen were necessary to arrange the financial and delivery sides of the business transactions. Govan concluded that

. . . the existing system, while not perfect, did enable the southern planter to raise his cotton, transport it to the markets in the North and in England, and to receive in return the supplies he needed. The charges were moderate and the banks supplied the credit facilities which were necessary. It is hard to see how any system could have accomplished more.[108]

In fact, it worked so well that the farmers were never motivated to organize their potential power and take hold of the system as their own and use it for their own benefit. They made several efforts in this direction but they all failed, largely from lack of motivation.

The Role of the Bank of the United States

Govan's third finding was more a validation of what he already knew than a new discovery, involving the role of the Bank of the United States in the economy of the South. After receiving his Ph.D. from Vanderbilt in 1937, Govan went to England for a year on a grant to study the history of the English side of the cotton trade that had been central to the life of the South. While researching in Glasgow,

Liverpool, and London, he was struck by the crucial importance of the Bank of the United States in protecting not only the American cotton trade, but the economy of the U.S.

Govan was later asked to lecture on his findings at the Southern Historical Association meeting at the University of Kentucky in November 1939. The following year, he would write up his findings in an article entitled, "The Ante-Bellum Attempt to Regulate the Price and Supply of Cotton."[109] Cotton might be raised in the South, but its price was largely determined in the Liverpool market— controlled by financial and business conditions in England, not the needs and desires of the planters."[110] English spinners, for example, organized themselves to reduce the production of yarn in order to drive down the price of cotton, to the benefit of English buyers but loss to the American cotton farmers. The restrictive policies of the Bank of England were also calculated to drive down the price and for the same reason. The Bank of the United States, on the other hand, under the guidance of its president, Nicholas Biddle, was large and powerful enough to counteract English control by seeing to it that American cotton was bought and held in American hands until the price and profits for American planters were right and fair.

In all, the Bank served four crucial functions for the American economy. First, it provided a sound, flexible, and uniform currency; second, it protected farms and businesses of all kinds, large and small, from the boom-bust tendencies of the economy; and third, it regulated the state banks to prevent excessive speculation or competition. Fourth, it had an essential role in cushioning and countering the economic pressures from England and the Continent, and when necessary, stepping into the cotton trade in the interest of a fair price. The Bank was the southern planters' single most important support, although few of them could appreciate that fact, because most of them distrusted credit and bank manipulations, feared its monopoly, and desperately wanted their independence and control over their own produce. When the Bank finally went under in 1839, the commercial world, and especially the cotton planters of the South, lost their best friend. Without the Bank, the entire country suffered terribly, but the South most of all. Currency lost its uniformity and stability; the market was again vulnerable to its boom-bust tendencies, and the state banks were free to speculate as they chose. The cotton planters were again at the mercy of the English and European markets.

Worst of all, without the Bank's functioning power as a unifying force in the nation, the centrifugal forces of sectional rivalry and strong states' rights ideologies were free to run rampant.

Govan's research focused on the southern economy: its insecurity and its vulnerability. The economy was based on cotton, but the planters had never been able to "insure a regular and profitable return" on cotton.[111] That was a "constant grievance to the planters,"[112] and they were never able to resolve it. The loss of the Bank of the United States certified that they never would. Govan also believed that these two circumstances, the South's insecurity and the loss of the Bank as a unifying force contributed in a major way to the causes of the Civil War.

The war left the South economically devastated. Then, after Reconstruction, a general agreement among all white Americans, North as well as South, that blacks were inferior led to a series of Supreme Court decisions in 1876 and 1883 which essentially reversed the Fourteenth Amendment ("all persons are citizens") and the Fifteenth Amendment ("all citizens may vote"). These reversals gave back to the southern states the power to disenfranchise and re-enslave blacks in the tangled maze of tenant farming and sharecropping.

The Industrial Revolution, which was changing life in the North and in the urban areas of the South passed by the rural areas.[113] Cotton was still the cash crop of the region thanks to the cotton gin, and an oversupply of human labor, mostly black but including many whites who planted and harvested it by hand.[114] Tenant farming was a new kind of slavery that kept the cotton farmers in abject poverty.

Govan's final conclusion about the South was that it was far less well off than the North.

Upon his return from England to the United States in the summer of 1938, Tom received a year's appointment as a history instructor at the University of Chattanooga, through his older brother Gilbert, the university's librarian. Tom excelled as a teacher and was popular with students and faculty. He published his first historical article, previewed earlier in this chapter, summarizing his thesis, "Banking and the Credit System in Georgia, 1810-1860." It was published under the same title in *The Journal of Southern History.*[115] Over the years, his thesis has stood up to criticism very well, and was finally published by the Arno Press in 1979.

Gilbert was impressed with his brother's scholarship and teaching, and so decided to take Tom to the University of the South at Sewanee, Tennessee. The university had been founded before the Civil War by the Confederacy elite to be the "Harvard of the South." It was an Episcopal college and a majority of its board members were Episcopal bishops. In the early 1930s the university consisted of a college of two hundred to three hundred students and an Episcopal seminary of around sixty students.

The purpose of Gilbert's trip was to introduce Tom to the history faculty, but above all to meet his dear friend from University of Chattanooga, Alex Guerry, who became vice-chancellor at Sewanee. The unstated but implied purpose of the trip was to get Tom a new and better job. In due time he was appointed as an instructor in the history department, with the understanding that he could advance as openings appeared and on the condition that he prove himself. He began teaching in Sewanee in the fall of 1939, just before Germany's invasion of Poland. At the age of thirty-two, a new chapter in his life was opening.

3

Sewanee, 1939-1942

*Political and religious freedom came by the grace of God, not from
what we do in our presumptive virtue.*

Thomas P. Govan

Marriage

In 1940, Jane Davis Dickson arrived in Sewanee for the summer
with her mother, Mary Ellen (Nell) Dickson. At thirty-three, Jane was
a bright, attractive, mature, and savvy young woman quite free of vanity,
who loved beautiful things, though not attached to them. She also
had a quick and lively wit.[116] Her roots were deep in the Confederacy.
She had grown up as a child in Vicksburg, Mississippi, and had played
out back of the family house in the still-standing earthworks and
redoubts that had been built to defend the city against Grant's
siege in 1863. Years later, she had been deeply moved by Ken
Burn's television documentary, "The Civil War," which included a
number of shots of those very earthworks. Her great grandmother,
Jane Davis Farish, was a sister of Jefferson Davis, making Jane the
great-grandniece of the president of the Confederacy. The
Farishes continued to be a prominent and well-to-do southern
family, who later settled in Houston, Texas, where Jane and Nell
occasionally visited.

78

The men in Jane's family all died young: her grandfather, uncle, father, and only brother. Jane and her mother grew up essentially without men. Jane graduated from high school in Vicksburg, but following the southern tradition, did not go to college. She was, however, a voracious reader and her self-education was surprisingly thorough. Jane had been married in her early twenties, but had gone through a painful and disillusioning divorce in 1937. One day, Jane and Tom met while in line at the buffet table of the Tuckaway Inn in Sewanee, and were immediately drawn to each other. Soon, Tom invited Jane for a date. They had dinner together, were mutually charmed, and went for a walk in the warmth of a southern summer evening. They discovered they shared many interests and attitudes, and more important, despite their southern roots, agreed on the evils of racial segregation.

Jane reported that their first date lasted until dawn and that by summer's end, she and Tom had fallen in love. They knew they were going to get married.[117] For pre-marriage counseling, they went to the Reverend George J. Hall, chaplain of the University of the South. Tom was not baptized, as Jane was and as canon law required if they were to be married in the Episcopal Church. Jane was a more-or-less faithful Episcopalian whereas Tom was critical of the Episcopal Church. In a friendly way he made no secret of his feelings to Hall. Under the circumstances, however, he gladly (but without much conviction) agreed to baptism. In the chapel on December 10, 1940, just two weeks before the wedding and with two faculty friends as sponsors, the "deed" was done. George Hall later quoted Tom as saying to him, "I remember two things about your chaplaincy. First, you baptized me, and second, [during the war] you prayed for our enemies and people left the chapel."[118] Tom had approved of that prayer.

They were happily married "for love and companionship," as Jane put it, on December 22, 1940. Having failed to conceive a child during her previous marriage, she and Tom assumed they would have to do without children. Tom's family was there at the wedding, but his father, sadly, had died earlier that year, and Tom felt his absence.

Mary Ellen (Nell) Stout Dickson and her daughter
Jane Davis Dickson, aged five (?), circa 1912

A few months later in the spring of 1941, to their joy and amazement, Jane found that she was pregnant. Their joy was short-lived, however, because Jane soon lost the child.[119] The loss, close on the heels of the miracle and joy, was devastating. They never got over it. After that, Jane was unable to bear children, and they formed strong and poignant relationships with young people, many of whom they "adopted" and treated as their own children.[120]

Even with their sadness, Tom and Jane began their life together in harmony, delighted with each other. Tom was happy with his teaching and research, and Jane became a much-loved "house mother" for students.

Sewanee suited Tom as a young teacher. Though there were few students in the college (around two hundred fifty), they were good students and Tom enjoyed small classes of fifteen to twenty, which made it possible to teach seminar-style. Teaching in this way was especially important to Tom during these years because he learned and changed and shared his thinking with his students. The students engaged with Tom, both positively and negatively, and everyone learned. It was obvious to the students that Tom cared and spoke about his deepest feelings and commitments. In this period, his teaching was going well, he had a great deal of freedom in shaping his courses, faculty morale was generally high, and his scholarship was being recognized.

Birth of a Pragmatist

Tom had come a long way from his Marxist days. By the time he entered the classroom, he had become disillusioned by all of the historical theories that claimed to know the laws which determine human experience and history. Rather than provide hope for the world, these theories foretold disaster. Tom was learning that one had to be more humble before history; one could relate to history without being doctrinaire by not presuming to know its ways and means. He began making sense of history by focusing on living historical experience, and what that history had to teach. Roosevelt, for example, had no theory in 1937. Nicholas Biddle had no theory in 1837. Their very lack of theory left them free to experiment and do what they felt needed to be done to resolve the crises they faced in a more humble and pragmatic spirit.

Tom's teaching was changing in other ways. Increasingly he was drawn to Alexander Hamilton's views of man, society, and government. He came to believe that people are governed more by their passions and their interests than by anything else, and therefore needed to be restrained by law and given power by government to defend themselves from each other.[121] Tom felt that division and balance of power within the nation was essential because of the inherent passions of human nature.

This belief represented half of Hamilton's view. The other half was the conviction that the nation had to be strong and unified in order to survive pressures from without, and to maintain freedom and justice within. The way to achieve that strength and unity, Hamilton believed, was to appeal to the self-interest of the various parts (individuals, communities, cities, and above all, states) to join the country as a whole and remain loyal to its unity, rather than local interests. The nation would have a constitutional government and law with checks and balances, and the regular consent of the voters. It would have a national bank to create a stable currency and economy. The fundamental purpose of the founders, as Govan later expressed it, was "to create and maintain a society in which people are free to seek equal justice for themselves and for others."[122]

Govan's message to his students further insisted that the great tradition of freedom through national unity and strength had been seriously misunderstood from the beginning by leaders like Thomas Jefferson and Andrew Jackson, and was still misunderstood by many historians in the 1930s and 1940s, and by most of the American people. For the American people, Jefferson and Jackson had become the great heroes of American history. They affirmed individual freedom and states' rights against the federal government, especially the national treasury and the financial system. They saw national government as the enemy, the major threat to their freedom. They understood freedom to be measured in terms of the individual from central government's interference and control. Their faith was in local control and states' rights, which required the smallest and weakest federal government possible.

With this perspective, it was inevitable that Jefferson and Jackson would see Hamilton and Biddle as rich and corrupt aristocrats with too much power. Govan deemed these perceptions to be mistaken and set out in his teaching and writing to correct the wrong. His efforts were important because these issues and differences continue to be debated today.

As the specter of war came closer, Tom went through a transforming experience, which he described in his "Apologia Pro Sua Vita" (see Appendix 1). As a faculty member, he was expected to attend chapel daily with all of the faculty and students. One day he arrived early, and while waiting, picked up a *Book of Common Prayer* and read its Preface. He was surprised and startled by it: so different in attitude from his father's religion with its doctrinal certainties, its moral rigidity and perfectionism. The Preface assumed the imperfection of the Church and its members and affirmed the need for ongoing reform. It spoke of the freedom of the churches in America after the Revolution to become independent of their parent bodies in England. It spoke of the liberty of different Christian bodies to choose their own forms of worship. It spoke of their freedom to "alter, abridge, enlarge, amend or otherwise dispose of" these forms "by common consent and authority, as may seem most convenient for the edification of the people." It spoke of "seeking to keep the happy mean between too much stiffness in refusing and too much easiness in admitting variations in things once advisedly established." It spoke of these things with the intention of preserving the peace and unity of the Church. It expressed the hope that the *Book of Common Prayer* would "be received and examined by every sincere Christian, with a meek, candid, and charitable frame of mind, without prejudice or prepossessions; seriously considering what Christianity is and what the truths of the Gospel are."[123]

"There was," Govan said, "something familiar in these words, reminiscent of something I knew very well." After the service he went home and "took down the records of the Federal Convention [of 1789] and turned to a speech by Benjamin Franklin on the final day which requested everyone there to accept and sign the Constitution. Franklin's words echoed what Tom had read that morning,

> I confess that there are several parts of this constitution which I do not at present approve, but I am not sure I shall never approve them: For having lived long, I have experienced many instances of being obliged by better information or fuller consideration to change opinions . . . which I once thought right, but found to be otherwise. It is therefore that the older I grow, the more apt I am to doubt my own judgment, and to pay more respect to the judgment of others . . . In these sentiments . . . I agree to this Constitution with all its faults, if they are such; because I believe a general government necessary for us, and there is no form of government but what may be a blessing to the people if well administered, and believe further that this is likely to be well administered for a course of years, and can only end in despotism, as other forms have done before it, when the

people shall become so corrupted as to need despotic government, being incapable of any other. I doubt too whether any other convention we can obtain, may be able to make a better Constitution. For when you assemble a number of men to have the advantage of their joint wisdom, you inevitably assemble with those men, all their prejudices, their passions, their errors of opinion, their local interests, and their selfish views. From such an assembly can a perfect production be expected? It therefore astonishes me . . . to find this system approaching so near to perfection as it does . . . . Thus I consent . . . to this Constitution because I expect no better and . . . I cannot help expressing a wish that every member of the Convention who may still have objections to it, would with me, on this occasion, doubt a little of his own infallibility, and to make manifest our unanimity, put his name to this instrument.[124]

Govan was stunned. Franklin's statement seemed to be a "complete statement of [Govan's] own beliefs about history, politics, and life."[125] Franklin had a pragmatic message stated in political terms. The *Book of Common Prayer* had the same pragmatic message stated in religious terms. It was the same message. This recognition was the dawning of new light in Govan's life. As he sat in his study pondering Franklin and the *Book of Common Prayer*, he realized he was indeed a pragmatist and that Christianity and his political beliefs could co-exist. Christianity was now an option for him.

Alexander Hamilton, a Christian?

As Govan grew to know Hamilton better, he realized the important thing about Hamilton was not simply that he was a major architect of the new nation, but that he seemed to understand the theological principles that undergirded the nation. These were the principles that burst out of the Preface to the *Book of Common Prayer* that morning in the Sewanee chapel, the principles Franklin expressed in political form. Hamilton seemed to also have understood the connection.

84

Govan wondered how Hamilton had come by this understanding. Where had a Presbyterian from the Caribbean learned these things? Certainly he was brilliant and read voraciously; certainly he had grown up as a boy in an English colony; and yes, he had attended King's College in New York City (an Anglican college), but Tom's own experience suggested there might be more to it than that.

Tom's conjecture was that Hamilton had come by this spirit and these ideas under exactly the same circumstances and through exactly the same exposure that he himself had experienced in the Sewanee chapel. This is what Tom wrote about Hamilton:

> As a student in 1774 at King's College, Hamilton was required to attend Anglican services at least twice every day. Sermons and homilies were frequent and long, the book most available was that entitled the *Book of Common Prayer*, and it would be surprising if he, like other bright and easily bored young men, did not read more often than he listened. He most certainly was familiar with this magnificently written book, which, though religious and liturgical in content and language, was centrally political in its teaching. Its original purpose had been to justify a revolutionary break with the established order in religious affairs by appealing to the principles and to the principal (Almighty God) that the established order was charged with betraying.[126]

As Govan pointed out, these were the principles that supported the arguments made by the Church of England at the time of the Reformation and by the leaders of Parliament in resisting the royal absolutism of James I, Charles I, Charles II, the Protestant absolutism of Cromwell, and finally in 1688, James II, who was driven out and replaced by the limited monarchy of William and Mary. These were the principles upon which Hamilton would argue against the unconstitutional absolutism of King George III and his Parliament in 1775.

Alexander Hamilton by John Trumbull

Govan recognized Hamilton's prophetic role in politics and finance at a revolutionary moment in American history. He also believed his own life as a historian to be prophetic in a time when radical views, left and right, fought for position in church and state. There were right-wing ideologues wanting more authority for the institution, and left-wing ideologues wanting more authority for the people. There seemed to him to be very few speaking out for what he called the truly revolutionary and truly radical middle way of the United States Constitution and the federal system. The most radical and revolutionary conviction underlying both the nation and the church, in Tom's view, was that faith in the God "in whose service is perfect freedom" was the source and root of all true freedom, whether it be religious, intellectual, political, economic, or cultural freedom.[127] That faith meant freedom from the worship and subservience to anything else other than God, such as power or wealth or success. He saw that false idols enslave people; that God sets people free from such slavery. It also meant patient moderation in reform, the willingness to put up with imperfection because only God is perfect. It meant freedom from all simple, absolute answers and from all final and complete solutions. It meant freedom from trust in and claims for false idols of any kind, especially "good" idols like rigid morality or success in one's business.

Govan wrote:

> Political and religious freedom, to the extent that they exist in Great Britain and the United States, were not achieved through right actions by virtuous men acting on correct principles. Instead, they are almost accidental results of long years of conflict among selfish, self-centered individuals and groups; of 'sedition, privy conspiracy, and rebellion,' of 'false doctrine, heresy, and schism,' of 'hardness of heart,' and 'contempt of God's word and commandments.'[128] In other words, political and religious freedom come by the grace of God, not from what we do in our presumptive virtue. Once that is understood, then we can look at history and humbly discern who was more or less on the track of what God was doing, and who was not.[129]

Freedom came from the grace of God. That is what Govan believed. Although he did not always teach it directly, that faith was never far from the surface. It was the faith and spirit in which he tried to do his work in the field of history. At the deepest level, Govan was a historian whose vocation, like the Hebrew prophets before him, was to call the religious establishment and the nation back to their true roots.

Govan Essays, 1939-1942:

"Slavery and the Civil War"

Most historians in the 1920s and 1930s looked for what they considered new and better explanations for the events of history.

Many of them turned to economic and other materialistic and deterministic causes for these events. They were called Progressive historians. The most influential among them were Frederick Jackson Turner, Carl Becker, Charles A. Beard, and Vernon Parrington. Govan said of these men:

> Taking a simplified view of the economy of the United States before 1860, [these] historians have falsely pictured an industrial East in conflict with an agrarian South and West. The anti-slavery movement, in this interpretation was not a moral crusade, but a shrewd trick by 'Yankee' industrialists to separate two agricultural regions, and the resulting Civil War was a revolution ending in the triumph of the bourgeoisie over feudal landlords of the South and the independent farmers of the West.[130]

He deemed this view to be "naive economic determinism," which he "exposed" in his 1940 review article, "Slavery and the Civil War."[131] His message was simple: slavery alone was the cause of the war, and the issue between the North and South was primarily moral, not economic.

This essay reviewed four new books published in 1939 and 1940, which presented a very different view without denying the partial influence of economic reality as such.[132] Ralph Gabriel argued that the United States was sustained by the power of "a romantic national faith" in freedom, in a God-given "moral law, in the free individual, and the democratic mission of America in the world." Its central dynamic was a balance of power among different ideas and convictions.

The other three writers, Dumond, Phillips, and Eaton had a different focus. They agreed, contrary to the Progressive historians, that slavery was preserved not because of its profitability, but because southerners were terrified of "Negro insurrection, believed in Negro inferiority," and insisted that slavery was the only way whites and blacks could safely live together.

Govan's essay, "Slavery and the Civil War," is a manifesto for the motivating power of people's ideas, opinions, faith, and moral fervor. He asserted that power was universal. It was the moral perspectives of the two sides, North and South, not their economic interests that made compromise on the slavery issue impossible. After the war, reunion was possible only because northern and southern whites agreed that the blacks were inferior; both North and South had racial caste systems: the North de facto, the South de jure. The racism of the United States was universal.

The University of the South in Sewanee was no exception. Govan was already chafing over the issue, which would come to a head in 1952. When the Civil Rights Movement finally came in 1956-1957, Tom rejoiced and supported it wholeheartedly.

The essay "Slavery and the Civil War" caused a stir at the University of the South because desegregation was already an issue.

"Not Profit and Loss"

The "Not Profit and Loss" essay is a sharp, succinct, and surprising analysis of the causes of the Civil War.[133] Tom wrote it in the spring of 1942 as a review of a volume of northern newspaper editorials on secession edited by Howard Cecil Perkins and published by the American Historical Association.[134]

Tom's main point was that before Fort Sumpter was attacked in 1861, the North had no uniform opinion about slavery. Opinions in the North varied from abolitionists to business groups, manufacturers, merchants, and the wealthy, all of whom deplored conflict over "an abstract moral question" they felt would destroy economic prosperity for everyone. Many northern papers even "defended slavery and the validity of the southern position."[135]

Sufficient unity came only after Sumpter, when secession and war had become realities. The crucial issue between North and South was the moral question over extending slavery into the territories. For one side, it was an evil that must be stopped. For the other side, it was necessary for social order. So, the war came.

"Was Plantation Slavery Unprofitable?"

Govan's third article on slavery was published before World War II in 1942. It asked the question, "Was Plantation Slavery Unprofitable?" and was intended to call into question writer Ulrich B. Phillips's affirmative answer.[136] Phillips' view that slavery was unprofitable was widely accepted by historians who followed his lead in the early years of the twentieth century.

Ulrich B. Phillips was the best known student of William E. Dunning at Columbia University. Dunning was a southern racist who believed, like most Americans, in the inferiority of blacks. For him, Reconstruction after the Civil War was a dreadful disaster, which was rectified only when southern whites were able once again to take control of "inferior" blacks. That time came in 1883 when the Supreme Court found the 1875 Civil Rights legislation invalid. The 1883 decision had two devastating effects. First, it denied blacks equal rights in public accommodations and in jury service. Second, it effectively neutralized the Fourteenth Amendment to the Constitution, 1868 ("All persons born . . . in the United States are citizens") and the Fifteenth Amendment, 1870 ("the right of citizens to vote"). Thus, the states were given full legal authority to manage racial matters in their own ways. Since chattel slavery was now illegal, the States took control by a new but equally effective means: placing blacks on tenant farms and denying them the vote.

As Dunning's pupil, Phillips tried to explain the South in the most sympathetic way possible. He argued that slavery had proven to be unprofitable. Southern whites were nevertheless stuck with the blacks, and when colonization in Africa turned out to be impracticable, they institutionalized slavery "as the most responsible and humane system for controlling an inferior race that could be devised under the circumstances."[137] Slavery had failed economically, but was necessary as a means of social control.

Phillips also reasoned that if slavery was not profitable, then maybe it would have died out naturally, thus making the Civil War unnecessary. So the answer to the question of slavery's profitability was an important one. During the 1930s and 1940s, there were a few revisionist historians who argued that the war was avoidable: it was the moral extremism in the North, they said, that "blew up a relatively minor issue—human slavery—into a major one;" and had caused emotions to flare and a Civil War to be waged. The unprofitability of slavery was one piece of their argument that supported this view.[138]

To Govan, Phillips's views were an anathema, but Tom did not want to attack him outright. What he did do was write a careful, closely reasoned, impeccably researched, gentle, and tentative essay in which he redefined the meaning of profit by demonstrating that the cost of the planters' lifestyle had to be considered as income and therefore, as profit. He also used the 1850 and 1860 census reports of the thirteen southern states to show that over that ten-year period, the per capita "value of real and personal property" increased eighty percent and the aggregate value rose one hundred per cent.

Although these figures did not prove that slaves alone provided the increase—free labor and the fresh, productive land of Mississippi and Alabama may well have contributed to it—his conclusion was still sound: that historians "who have stated that slavery was profitable are more nearly correct than those who deny its profitableness."[139]

Govan's conclusion was so modest and so well supported by his research that it ended up being very effective. The essay marked the beginning of a nearly complete reversal of historical opinion on the subject; it undermined and the delegitimized the revisionist argument.

Subsequent scholarly research has found Govan's conclusion to be right. Twenty-four years later in 1966, his article was included in a book, *Pivotal Interpretations of American History, Volume I,* edited by Carl N. Deglar.[140] In 1971, it was reprinted three times: in *Slavery and Southern Economy* edited by Harold D. Woodman; in *Did Slavery Pay?,* edited by Hugh G. J. Aitkin; and in a reprint series in Black Studies published by Bobbs-Merrill.[141]

Deglar's evaluation of the essay is found in Chapter 21.

4

Christian Turning Point, 1941-1943

Man's capacity for justice makes democracy possible. Man's inclination to injustice makes democracy necessary.

Reinhold Niebuhr

On December 7, 1941, when Govan was 33, war exploded upon the United States in Pearl Harbor, and a united country joined the world conflict. Govan passionately supported the Allies in World War II, but could not bring himself to volunteer because, as he said, he was "too old to be a soldier." The real cause of his reluctance was his work on the life of Nicholas Biddle and his eagerness to continue his research. Govan also believed that pursuing his scholarship would be his most important contribution to his country.

Tom stayed at the University of the South, hoping he would not be drafted. As a compromise to military service, he accepted the role of "military service coordinator" at the university. This meant he was informed and up-to-date on the way the selective service system worked and able to assist and advise the students and faculty about their options for service: volunteering for particular specialties, applying for officers' training school, or pursuing the limited options granted within the draft.

But in October 1942, at thirty-five, Tom was drafted and began three and a half years in the army, entering as a private, and leaving in 1946 as a captain. Before induction, he and Jane traveled by railroad to say good-bye to his family in Chattanooga and Atlanta. Because he was ashamed of his status as a private, he did not want Jane to come to the bus station in Winchester, Tennessee to see him off to Chattanooga and basic training with "all those bums and riffraff." During basic training, a fellow private told Tom that he was the first person in the army he had seen reading a Bible. "What church are you?" he had asked. Tom replied, "I'm an unbeliever." Later he told Jane, "That shut him up."[142]

Reinhold Niebuhr's *The Nature and Destiny of Man*

During that year at Sewanee, and before he was drafted, Tom was influenced by a major event. In January 1941, Reinhold Niebuhr's *The Nature and Destiny of Man, Volume I* was published and became an immediate bestseller in theological and intellectual circles.[143] Not only did Niebuhr's "Christian realism" make sense to Govan, but he was bowled over by what he felt was Niebuhr's sheer brilliance and intellectual erudition. Niebuhr's work spoke to Tom not only in terms of his personal life and understanding, but in terms of his life as a professional historian. He devoured the book, and took it with him, along with the Bible and Plato's Republic, into the army.

No American theologian between 1935 and 1965 had more influence than Reinhold Niebuhr on people both inside and outside the churches in the United States, especially people searching for realistic moral and theological guidance in the areas of social ethics, politics, and public policy. The power of Niebuhr's influence stemmed from the realism that was his view of human nature, and that on which his social thought was based.

Niebuhr's thought came as a reaction to the idealism and utopianism of the Social Gospel, which had flourished in the United States more or less from the 1860s to the 1930s. Almost entirely a movement of the Protestant mainline churches, the Social Gospel emphasized the imminence and power of the Holy Spirit, and the unlimited potential of human goodness when those humans were properly educated and theologically informed. After the turn of the century, many Protestants came to believe that the kingdom of God could be literally established by "winning the world to Christ in this generation."[144] A major segment of the movement was convinced that the kingdom could be achieved by converting the rich and powerful leadership in every nation. This change of heart in the leadership would lead to changes in policies and institutions, they thought, and justice, peace, and harmony would gradually follow. An evolutionary progress in human affairs was inevitable if only the churches would fulfill their missionary responsibility. This extraordinary confidence was fueled in part by the new social sciences: psychological, sociological, and political. Walter Rauschenbusch, a major theologian of the time, enthusiastically claimed, "For the first time in religious history, we have the possibility of so directing religious energy by scientific knowledge that comprehensive and continuous reconstruction of social life in the name of God is within the bounds of possibility."[145]

Niebuhr began his ministry as an uneasy bedfellow of the Social Gospel, but soon became disillusioned by what he felt was its naiveté in failing to recognize the persistence of evil. He then began his search for what he believed was a more realistic form of Christianity. World War I had ended the nineteenth-century assumptions about steady and inevitable progress in the world. The values of the Industrial Revolution, particularly "social Darwinism" ("the survival of the fittest") were being called into question. No longer could the exploited classes of the poor be automatically considered inferior and deserving of their lot. No longer could it be assumed that the upper classes, the "captains of industry," were stronger, brighter and better than the lower classes and deserved their positions. The terrible inequalities, poverty, and suffering caused by the Revolution were having their moral impact upon society by raising the question of whether or not American society was inherently evil by its very nature. Was a good and just society possible? Many people began to question the goodness of human nature. Original sin was taking on new meaning. Niebuhr described himself in this transition period as moving from "being an optimist without falling into sentimentality" to being "a realist trying to save himself from cynicism."[146]

Niebuhr began his search with empirical reality. His approach was pragmatic. He wanted to explore the personal and social lives of people and discover what difference Christian faith was making in their lives. He also believed that no Christian doctrine that failed to foster concern for social justice was worthy of belief. In this respect, Govan discovered in Niebuhr a kindred pragmatic soul. Niebuhr's analysis confirmed Tom's own pragmatic experience, but added a theological, philosophical, and historical depth Tom had never known before. Niebuhr's clarity was what Tom needed to complete his faith. On the one hand, Niebuhr's biblical-Christian interpretation of human nature stood in contrast to other views such as the liberal Social Gospel and the idealistic and naturalistic views; on the other hand, it was a biblical-Christian interpretation of history, markedly different from either classical or modern alternatives and more realistic than both. As Niebuhr said in the preface to Volume II,

> ... the Christian faith assesses the spiritual stature of man[kind] more highly and has a lower estimate of man's virtue than alternate doctrines, both ancient or modern .... [And] the Biblical Christian faith has a more dynamic conception of history than classicism and a less optimistic view of historical dynamism than alternative modern views.[147]

Govan found Niebuhr's work compelling.[148] In 1943 when the second volume of *The Nature and Destiny of Man* was published, Tom asked Jane to send a copy to him in the army.

Reinhold Niebuhr's theology was important to Tom in three ways: in understanding myth; in his analysis of sin; and in his social ethics and politics. His analysis began by stating that the orthodox, mainline, ecclesiastical doctrines of Christian faith were no longer viable in western culture because if taken literally, the doctrines made no sense. Thinking people could no longer accept virgin birth or resurrection, or walking on the water literally. Furthermore, he said,

> Whenever orthodoxy insists on the literal truth of . . .
> [biblical] myths, it makes bad historical science out of
> true religious insights.[149]

Niebuhr knew that these fundamental doctrines were expressed in the Bible through symbolic language and in the form of mythical narrative. He believed that the "truth in myths" is more powerful than any rational or literal explanation. Only myth could cope with the mysteries and ambiguities of reality. "Myth alone," he said, "is capable of picturing the world as a realm of coherence and meaning without defying the facts of incoherence. Its world is coherent because all facts in it are related to [a] central source of meaning [God]; but [it] is not rationally coherent because myth is not under the abortive necessity of relating all [facts] to each other."[150] In other words, mythological truths remain true even though they do not fit with or conform to rational logic or empirical facts. Their truth is poetic or metaphysical and could be interpreted in a number of ways. Niebuhr never apologized for speaking in paradoxes. He felt reality is paradoxical. In the New Testament myth, for example, Jesus walked on the water, although in literal fact, he did not. The myth, however, is symbolically true. It says poetically that Jesus comes to us spiritually, especially when we are in trouble (in rough water!).

As important as Niebuhr's understanding of myth was to Govan, so was Niebuhr's understanding of sin as a fundamental condition of all people. To Govan's surprise, Niebuhr saw the precondition of sin as anxiety, not simply evil. He stated that because humans are physical beings and understand mortality, and can never be sure, they are chronically anxious. As self-conscious beings, people transcend nature in their freedom to choose their actions, and responsibility also creates anxiety. Because people often choose evil while believing it to be in their best self-interest, or miss the mark of the good they want to do, and so feel guilty. Anxiety and guilt, Niebuhr believed, are fundamental parts of the human condition, sources of insecurity that enslaves people and from which all try to escape. That universal attempt to escape Niebuhr called sin.

Govan knew this experience of anxiety very well and had done exactly as Niebuhr suggested: he had tried to escape into scientific certainty of one or another philosophical theory. These attempts had led, as he found out, to further slavery. Only the truth of Christian faith could finally set him free. Faith in the ultimate security of God's love can, Niebuhr believed, overcome the immediate insecurities of nature and history. This was a message Govan had never heard before, and he knew instinctively it was the truth.

Part of Niebuhr's understanding of sin was its persistence "even in the life of the redeemed."[151] Being a forgiven Christian, then, does not eliminate humans' sinful nature and its tendencies. Being a Christian may even heighten those tendencies. Being a Christian could numb rather than sensitize Christians to their duplicity. Later, Govan would say that he never understood the depth of sin until he became an insider in the Episcopal Church.

Niebuhr's social ethics and politics also rang true to Govan. Niebuhr suggested that self-interest is all-pervasive. Individuals may be capable of self-sacrificing love, but institutions never are. The best that can be expected of them is enlightened self-interest.[152] Or, put another way, in politics the highest goal is relative justice, not love. Jesus revealed God is love and that love is therefore the law of life. But in politics, love is never a simple possibility. One of Niebuhr's interpreters, Robert W. Lovin, put it this way:

> The ethics of Jesus do not deal at all with the immediate moral problem of every human life—the problem of arranging some kind of armistice between contending factions and forces. It has nothing to say about the relativities of politics and economics, or the necessary balances of power which exist and must exist in even the most intimate social relations.[153]

Niebuhr insisted that "realism denotes the disposition to take all of the factors in a social and political situation which offer resistance to established norms, into account, particularly the factors of self-interest and power."[154] All of these factors need to be weighed according to their effective influence upon events, he said, not simply "on a scale of Christian values."[155] We cannot, therefore, simply rely upon moral argument to guide political action.

This view was in radical contrast to the optimism of not only the Social Gospel, but the Enlightenment doctrines about the innate goodness of human nature and the inevitable progress of history. Yet Niebuhr's realism was protected from cynicism by the fundamental law of human nature: the capacity for love and justice. This duality of human nature prompted one of Niebuhr's most famous political aphorisms, a favorite of Govan's because it applies so beautifully to the United States, its Constitution, and Declaration of Independence:

> Man[kind]'s capacity for justice makes democracy possible; man[kind]'s inclination to injustice makes democracy necessary. Democracy is the form of social organization, in contrast to all others, which creates a system of human rights based upon consent, and in which 'freedom and order are made to support, not contradict each other.'[156]

In summary, Niebuhr's political realism rejected moral certainties on the one hand and moral relativism on the other. He opposed the Social Gospel's attempt to make Christian norms the only relevant criteria for action, pointing out that many other circumstances were crucial considerations. He also made the point that Christian norms could be distorted by self-interest, and he rejected political realism that treated moral norms as irrelevant to political choices. These norms, in spite of their relativity and possible falsehood, have tremendous political power simply because people believe them. Niebuhr's concern was to pay attention to political reality that included both established norms and the factors of self-interest and power. His method was dialectical, defining his position by rejecting the extremes. This approach resonated deeply within Govan and validated for him the approach followed by the reformers in the Church of England and the founders of the United States.

Stimulated by Niebuhr, Tom was at last ready to admit he was a Christian and wanted to make his commitment concrete. He had found a theological perspective that would set him free from his personal fears, his intellectual and moral confusions, and that would constantly nourish his professional work.

5

World War II, Army Historian 1942-1945

*Morale, engendered by thoughtful consideration for officers
and enlisted men by their commanders will produce a cheerful
and understanding subordination of the individual to the
good of the team.*

General George C. Marshall

Army Life

At thirty-five, Tom found army life difficult. His sergeant, sensing
Tom was well educated, asked each member of the platoon how many
years of schooling he had completed. When it became known that
Tom had a doctorate, he became a marked man. He was given the
worst work details and routinely heard comments such as, "You dumb
sons of bitches, watch this Ph.D. pick up cigarette butts and see if you
can learn anything." He constantly got demerits because he could
not make his bed properly. Finally, he befriended the sergeant by
teaching him fifth-grade arithmetic in exchange for lessons in
bedmaking and boot polishing. Still, daily life with the sergeant and
platoon was not the life Tom desired.[157]

During that first year of army duty in Memphis, however, Tom was
able to return to Sewanee often enough to attend confirmation classes

with Dr. Fleming James, Old Testament professor at the School of Theology at the University of the South. He had made up his mind officially to become an Episcopalian because he wanted to join Jane and because the Episcopal Church made sense to him. He was confirmed in Christ Church, Nashville, on April 24, 1943, by the Right Reverend Edmund P. Dandridge, Bishop of the Diocese of Tennessee. An important step in his spiritual journey was taken.

While Tom was in the army, Jane stayed in Sewanee. When the head of the university library went off to war, Jane was appointed acting librarian, a demanding position that she held from 1943 to 1945. Occasionally, she was able to get away to visit Tom in Memphis.

Tom wanted a commission because among other things, officers could have typewriters. He applied for Officers' Candidate School (OCS) requesting duty as an army historian. He was so pleased with his own résumé that he bet Jane ten dollars and a bottle of champagne that he would receive his acceptance before the end of basic training. The acceptance arrived late by one day; he paid Jane the money but never got around to the bottle of champagne.[158]

The army agreed that Tom could serve as a historian and sent him to OCS in Warm Springs, Georgia. Graduating as a second lieutenant in September 1943, thirty-six years old, he was assigned duty as historical officer at the Second Army Headquarters in Memphis, Tennessee. He replaced Lt. Bell I. Wiley, a history professor from the University of Mississippi. Tom's orders were to complete the history Bell had begun, a work he completed nine months later on July 1, 1944.[159]

The army's charge, first to Wiley and then to Govan, was to write "an administrative history" of the Second Army.[160] It was to tell the story of "what was done from the point of view of the command preparing the history, including a candid and factual account of difficulties, mistakes recognized as such, the means by which . . . they might have been avoided, the measures used to overcome them, and the effectiveness of such measures. The history was not intended to be laudatory,"[161] but true and useful for the future. This view reflected the thinking of two generals who led the Second Army during the War—Lt. General Ben Lear and then Lt. General Lloyd R. Fredendall, and theirs was the history Wiley and Govan provided.[162]

From its beginning in 1932, the Second Army had been a training army. In October 1940, it became a one-third part (later nearly half) of "the first large-scale peacetime training program in the history of the United States." The swift and decisive victories of the German armies in Norway, the Low Countries, and France, coupled with the expansion of Japanese power in the Far East, "represented a threat to which the United States had to respond."[163]

The history began with the difficult pre-Pearl Harbor period, before war was declared, when General Lear was in command. In the face of mass public blindness to the danger that lay ahead, of isolationist and antiwar sentiment throughout the country, and of low morale among the troops, Lear had the nearly impossible task of convincing the officers and men, as well as their families and the country at large that Germany, Italy, and Japan were in fact "real and present dangers" to the United States. An army "fit to fight" was essential; such fitness depended upon absolute discipline, scrupulous attention to detail, and a spirit of "self-control and pride, self-restraint and individual efficiency."[164] The creation of such an army depended upon training: superior, sophisticated training. Until Pearl Harbor, training had been a constant challenge. Then everything changed.

Between 1940 and 1943, the Second Army grew from 2,000 to 28,000 officers and from 63,500 to 500,000 men. Training had to be constantly upgraded to meet new conditions and deal with new war technology. The problem became not morale but continuity in the training army; three-quarters of the men were passing through and then leaving for active duty elsewhere. There was no opportunity to form these men into cohesive and interdependent units.

General Fredendall took over command soon after Pearl Harbor. By this time the nation was united in support of the army, shortages had been overcome, and the training program was well established. By 1944, Fredendall was convinced that the army was too casual and too soft and that the demands of war required a change of attitude and training. Govan outlined in the history what turned out to be the single most significant improvement of troop training in World War II. Fredendall ordered that

> All troops should undergo a course of training paralleling
> that of our Ranger Battalion. It should involve maximum
> physical hardening, training for personal physical combat,
> deception, surprise, night operation, thorough training in
> all weapons such as the knife, the pistol, the rifle, the
> machine gun, the mortar, and the rocket launcher . . . . [165]

Above all, the desire and willingness to "kill and destroy the enemy" had to be inculcated in the troops. Before long, ranger training became the order of the day for all ground forces.

It was also under Fredendall that large-scale army maneuvers became a continual, rather than occasional, process integral to the training. These maneuvers contributed in major ways to the army's ability to coordinate huge and complex operations such as the invasion of Europe and maneuvers involving the navy in the Pacific.

In spite of Tom's boredom with writing administrative history, what he called "the least interesting and rewarding of historical enterprises,"[166] he knew that "future historians would be in his debt and also that army officers . . . [might] find precedents and analogies for various possible solutions to their own problems in the future."[167]

Preparing the history also gave Tom a profound respect for the army and its leadership, above all for General George C. Marshall. Govan considered Marshall to be a brilliant organizer, coordinator, and planner—a visionary with an understanding of the precise details. Govan saw him as a wise and compassionate man who understood the interdependence of absolute discipline, personal decency, and valued cooperative care for one another within and between ranks in the armed forces. In the history, Govan cites a letter to General Lear in October 1940 in which Marshall sets the pattern of leadership for the entire war:

> First in importance will be the development of a high
> morale and the building of a sound discipline, based on
> wise leadership and a spirit of mutual cooperation
> throughout all ranks. Morale, engendered by thoughtful
> consideration for officers and enlisted men by their
> commanders, will produce a cheerful and understanding

> subordination of the individual to the good of the team.
> This is the essence of the American standard of discipline,
> and it is a primary responsibility of leaders to develop
> and maintain such a standard.[168]

In addition to researching and writing the history, Tom also lectured regularly to his superior officers about the training their soldiers received and the war's progress. He helped them to see the overall context in which they played a part and engaged them in conversations about where they had been, what they had done, and what their experience had meant.

The tediousness Tom felt with military history was somewhat relieved by civilian requests to write book reviews. *The Southern Historical Review* asked him to review *Monetary Banking Theories of Jacksonian Democracy* by Sister M. Grace Madeline.[169] Tom was critical of the author's objective approach of "confining herself rather strictly to the task of observer and recorder."[170] Andrew Jackson's financial policies between 1828 and 1848 decisively rejected central control of banking and monetary systems and laid open the way for "control by private persons and institutions for private ends."[171] The result was a series of violent up and down swings in the economy, a period during which the whole country—saving only the superrich and the speculators—suffered. "Many of the present-day economic policies and ideas," Govan said, "are but a continuation of this controversy of over a hundred years ago, and the arguments of the contending parties of the period need to be interpreted and evaluated,"[172] a job he was champing to get at.

One other review kept him in touch with his profession. It concerned a military biography of the extraordinary southern Civil War cavalry general, Nathan Bedford Forrest, whom Govan called "probably the greatest natural soldier in the history of warfare." He concentrated on "logistics, tactics, and strategy in that order" and was immensely successful.[173]

While at the Second Army headquarters, Govan sought reassignment in Europe, where he longed to go. But those orders never materialized; he was "too old for fighting," and the army needed his talents as a historian and teacher. Jane remembers that one day Tom looked in the mirror at his khaki tie and shirt, and exclaimed, "My God, am I ever going to get out of this?" He had respect for the army but he resented it as well. He felt it was a waste of his time and that his service was getting in the way of his career as a historian, but he found ways to cope. According to Jane, he was AWOL many weekends. He would hitch a ride, take the bus, and one way or another get to Sewanee to see her. Once he missed his return ride and was terrified that the army would discover his weekend getaways. They never did.

Writing at MacArthur's Headquarters

After nine months' duty in Memphis and the completion of the *History of the Second Army*, Tom was assigned to write a history of *Training in Mountain and Winter Warfare*.[174] When this task was completed in January 1945, Tom was sent immediately to the Pentagon. His transfer was rather mysterious, and he was not able to discuss its purpose with anyone. Late that spring, a diploma came through the mail to Jane in Sewanee stating that Tom had completed his studies in Far Eastern Intelligence and that he had been promoted to the rank of captain. He was cleared for work in G2 (Army Intelligence) in the Pacific theater.

By the time Tom received this promotion, the war with Japan was at its climax. The Japanese fleet had been largely destroyed the previous October 1944 at Leyte Gulf. Admiral Nimitz, at terrible cost to the navy, had absorbed 3,500 Japanese kamikaze attacks. Okinawa had been taken (April, 1945) and the bombing of Japan had begun. General MacArthur had just about finished his campaign in the Philippines and was planning the invasion of Japan.

In June 1945, Tom was dispatched to MacArthur's Manila headquarters and assigned to write *The Planning and Organization for the New Guinea Campaign*[175] and *The Preparation and Planning for the Invasion of Japan*.[176] Tom had become a respected and trusted historian.

Then came August 6, 1945, the day the atomic bomb was dropped on Hiroshima. On August 9, a second bomb was dropped on Nagasaki, and on September 2, Japan surrendered. Immediately, MacArthur was appointed Supreme Allied Commander of Japan and moved his headquarters to Tokyo.

Thomas P. Govan, Lieutenant in the United States
Army, Army Historian circa 1943

Tom went with him, continuing his writing work. He finished the two histories in early 1946, only to have them impounded by MacArthur's staff. They were never seen again. Tom (probably illegally) kept his own copies and brought both documents home. He later used them while teaching at the National War College at Haines Point in Washington, D.C. In the end, the War College somehow got hold of Govan's copies, which disappeared as well. In light of what is known about the extreme defensiveness of MacArthur and his staff, the disappearance was no real surprise.[177]

Govan's assignment in General MacArthur's headquarters was very different from his previous assignments. He was perceived as a newcomer and complete outsider who had no business digging into facts, making judgments, and presuming to write an authoritative history of things he knew nothing about. MacArthur's staff was uncooperative. Govan read the official files, interpreted messages, and pieced the history together from a thousand strands of information using as much as possible the language of his sources in an effort to be objective. There was information to which headquarters would not give Govan access, so he had to "steal" it. Some materials, it seems, were just too secret for him to see. According to Jane, Tom had found a colonel who was cleared for these sensitive materials and had asked that the colonel read the files and report to him. It is clear that Govan and MacArthur's staff differed about the facts and their interpretation.

There were also differences over policy. Govan tried to tell the truth, for example, about tensions between MacArthur and the Joint Chiefs, and between MacArthur and Admiral Nimitz.

In a review written by Govan in October 1953, he asserts:

> MacArthur . . . contended that the Allied offensive (in the Pacific) should be concentrated in his area while the Pacific fleet protected his right flank. . . . An advance through the Central Pacific (which Admiral Nimitz had already carried out by his speedy conquest of the Marshall Islands) 'would be time consuming and expensive' . . . and would accomplish no important strategic objectives. . . . The Joint Chiefs of Staff, in spite of MacArthur's repeated objections, ordered the offensive continued through both the Central Pacific (Nimitz) and Southwest Pacific areas (MacArthur) with the main effort to be made by Nimitz . . . while those of General MacArthur, as a secondary and diversionary effort, were to advance northwest along the coast of New Guinea, through the islands off Vogelkop Peninsula, and into the Philippines.[178]

Govan detailed the planning and history of that "diversionary" campaign, and no one knew more about it than he did. It seems clear, therefore, that Govan, intimately well informed and writing in the spirit of his earlier work for the army, may well have written much that

MacArthur could not tolerate. Is it plausible to imagine Govan writing "from the army's [that is, MacArthur's] point of view" as he had before for Lear and Fredendall? Could he have omitted reference to "difficulties" and "mistakes recognized as such?" The answer, of course, for Govan was no. This judgment is strengthened by Govan's scathing 1965 review of General MacArthur's *Reminiscences*:

> Make no mistake, these reminiscences are 'a folly,' a foolish act by a man who should have known better or been better advised, and will only damage him whom they [the reminiscences] are intended to praise. They are written entirely at the surface level, as if compiled by a public relations expert who was given the task of creating a 'favorable image,' for the hero of the narrative never makes a mistake, he is pure of heart and beyond reproach, and his only regret is that not all his superiors, civilian and military, were so fortunately endowed. A historian seeking to understand and evaluate MacArthur's truly distinguished military career will find almost nothing of value and use anywhere in the book, and even biographers will probably be misled, particularly if they accept MacArthur's unbelievable egotism as the true measure of the actual man. To list even the most obvious omissions, oversimplifications, and misinterpretations— to say nothing of misstatements of fact—would require more space than the original story.[179]

Govan's review highlights two critical points. First, MacArthur lets the reader believe that he operated independently in the Pacific, when actually he was "under the strategic command of the American Joint Chiefs of Staff, who gave him his orders and forced him to obey them, and that many of his operations, particularly the bypassing of enemy strength, were undertaken despite his persistent and continued objections."[180] The bypassing of Rabaul, on the island of New Britain, is an example. Originally, MacArthur had planned to take Rabaul before going on with his campaign. According to his story, it was his idea to change plans and bypass Rabaul, when in fact the Joint Chiefs of Staff made that decision independently of him, and actually in spite of MacArthur's resistance.

Second, Govan notes that MacArthur's role as general "was that of a coordinator of a large and complex planning staff and a settler of disputes the planners could not resolve," whereas MacArthur describes his Japanese campaigns "as if he were a Civil War commander, making instant decisions in the light of changing battle conditions."[181] The reality was quite different and MacArthur's accounts of the invasion of and repulsion from North Korea, as well as his view of the conflict with President Truman that led to his firing, are partial and one-sided. Both MacArthur the man, and MacArthur the general, Govan felt, were much better than *Reminiscences* suggests. MacArthur's own book was an unfair treatment of himself.

Thus, it is not likely that Govan and MacArthur would have agreed about what should and should not be said about MacArthur's role in either the New Guinea Campaign or in the planning for the invasion of Japan. It follows that MacArthur's headquarters most likely suppressed or destroyed Govan's work.

None of Tom's history writing, however, had been the waste of time that he expected it would be. It provided good training for his later biographical work, from which he learned the art of quoting from others to tell the story, and interspersing the quotations with his own commentary and interpretation. In writing *The Preparation and Planning for the Invasion of Japan,* for example, Govan used MacArthur's words as much as possible, not his own, in spelling out the plan, but he added lengthy commentary as the story unfolded.[182] Also, the chance to work with Lear, Fredendall, and MacArthur, to evaluate their strengths and weaknesses, their temperaments and moral characters, their judgment or lack thereof, their successes and their failures, provided Tom with invaluable experience.

By this time, he had applied to the Library of Congress for a grant to begin work on his Biddle biography, which was his priority and a project he had been passionate about since graduate school. When Govan had finished his work in Tokyo and the grant for the Biddle project had come through, he applied for discharge. The army excused him to fulfill what he called "his civic duty" because he had finished his military assignment and the war was over.

On Washington's Birthday, February 22, 1946, Captain Govan was discharged. Tom's three and a half years in the military ended, and he was ready to begin his major book project.

6

Biddle and the Bank, 1946

The issue was whether or not a great private monopoly should dominate the government, or whether the currency of the country should be paper or [coin]. It was whether the United States should have a controlled or uncontrolled financial and credit system.

Thomas P. Govan

Out of the army, supported by his grant from the Library of Congress where most of the Biddle papers were housed, and granted further leave from the University of the South, Tom began work in earnest on his Nicholas Biddle biography. In March 1946, he and Jane moved from Sewanee to Washington, D.C.

All might be well with Tom's work, but all was not well with their marriage. In fact, it was in serious jeopardy. What was wrong? What had happened? We do not know precisely, but we do know the circumstances. Tom had been away for three and half of the five years he and Jane had been married. The glow of young love may well have faded. One or both of them, being lonely, may have sought solace elsewhere. The fact that Jane could not have children drained some of the meaning from the marriage, and now that Tom was home, he seemed to be more married to his work than to Jane. Both of them felt let down at least, betrayed at worst. All of these tensions had caused bitter conflict between them. They agreed, however, to stick it out for now, to give themselves time to test out whether they could recover some the feelings they had known before the war.

Nicholas Biddle by George Freeman (1787-1868),
Anthony J. Drexel Biddle, owner. Courtesy of
Frick Art Reference Library

During the year in Washington, they made new friends who would become very important to them. In the Library of Congress Tom met two young women, Frances T. Schwab and Laura W. Roper,[183] who were doing research there. Franny was living with Laura and her husband, W. Crosby Roper. She and Laura had had an apartment together in Greenwich Village before her marriage to Crosby in 1940, and were close friends. They were a bright articulate group. Franny was the daughter of Dr. Sidney Schwab, a well-known neurologist at Massachusetts General Hospital in Boston. Laura "had written several biographies for teenagers and was later to write the definitive biography of Frederick Law Olmstead, the great landscape architect who, with his partner, Calvert Vaux, designed Central Park in New York."[184] Crosby was a Harvard-trained corporate lawyer and partner in the Washington law firm of Covington and Burling. Both couples were well-read, interested in ideas, literature, the arts, history, public policy, and business. They were immediately drawn to the Govans, and the Govans to them. Together they quickly found common ground and had lots to talk about.[185] As Laura put it, "We simply liked each other cordially, almost on sight, all four of us."[186] Those friendships would last for life and be a boon to the Govans. That winter and spring, they saw a lot of each other.

Conflict with Schlesinger

It had been ten years since Tom's interest in Biddle had first been aroused by William C. Brinkley and Fletcher M. Green, both historians at Vanderbilt University. Biddle was an articulate Brahmin from Philadelphia who had edited Lewis and Clark's expedition papers and the literary magazine Port Folio. He was a Federalist, a brilliant economist and banker who became president of the Second National Bank of the United States when James Monroe was U.S. President. At Vanderbilt, while working on his thesis, Tom had begun research on the Panic of 1837 and learned, to his surprise, of Biddle's remarkable and public-spirited response to it. He had been taught that Biddle was a wealthy and dishonest banker out to benefit from the interest of the well-to-do at the expense of the poor, especially the farmers. Yet here Biddle was in a depression doing just the opposite: trying to restore the profits of the cotton farmers and of agriculture in general. One hundred years later in 1937, the current Democratic administration of Franklin D. Roosevelt, deriving, as Govan believed from the tradition of Jefferson and Jackson, was doing exactly the same thing. In fact, Tom's observation of F.D.R. and his research into Biddle showed that both men were following policies first advocated by Alexander Hamilton in 1789. Needless to say, when he discovered this similarity between Biddle and Roosevelt, Govan's curiosity was stimulated.[187]

Govan began his research "with the intention of writing an objective, impartial biography that would do justice to Biddle and his opponents alike."[188] However, thirteen years later in 1959 when the book was finally published, he wrote "This ambition has not been fulfilled. I have written an apologia, a defense (one reader has called it 'a lawyer's brief'), but I could do nothing else and remain loyal to the evidence."[189]

That evidence consisted primarily of Biddle's own "personal and official correspondence" because "the Bank's records and general correspondence were sold for pulp after its failure and liquidation."[190] Govan read Biddle's correspondence more thoroughly than anyone had before and he became convinced of Biddle's financial soundness and moral honesty. It became clear to Tom that Biddle was not the corrupt and self-aggrandizing powermonger he had been depicted by the Jacksonian Democrats and by most American historians since that time. He was, rather, a brilliant financier committed to serving the common good of the young nation in the tradition of Hamilton. Through the Second Bank of the United States, Biddle recreated a stable and flexible currency and brought about unprecedented prosperity for the entire country.

During the spring of 1946, Govan worked at the Library of Congress on the Biddle correspondence and papers. In the summer, realizing he needed more income, he sought and accepted a visiting professorship at the University of Virginia nearby. There he continued to work on his biography as much as his teaching commitments would allow.

Tom's reputation as an expert on economic history brought him an invitation to address the American Historical Association's (AHA) annual meeting, December 27-30, 1946, to respond to the much-praised book by Arthur M. Schlesinger Jr., *The Age of Jackson*.[191] Govan called his address, "Jackson and the Credit System." Schlesinger had painted Jackson as the hero who had slain the corrupt and deadly monster, the Second Bank of the United States, which, under Biddle's powerful, manipulative control, had become a private and irresponsible monopoly. Schlesinger believed that Biddle had headed a financial oligarchy that strove to dominate the political and economic life of the nation, and to make the rich richer and the poor poorer. Schlesinger had been convinced by Jackson's interpretation of the Bank. He believed that American democracy and freedom were at stake.

The Bank of the United States, Philadelphia circa 1836,
courtesy Frick Art Reference Library

No one knew more about Biddle and the Bank than Govan. Unlike Schlesinger, Tom was an accomplished economist accountant, versed in economic theory and practice, and an expert on the details and mechanics of the American economy under Biddle's leadership. He was prepared to take Schlesinger's argument apart and replace it with his own. Schlesinger claimed that Jackson and his policies in the 1830s were parallel to those of Franklin D. Roosevelt in 1930s. But Govan disagreed. He knew that Roosevelt's policies to overcome the economic woes of the depression in 1936 were not like Jackson's at all, but were "essentially identical with those that had been advocated and followed almost a century before by Biddle, a banker and Hamiltonian nationalist, in a similar economic situation."[192] To Govan the issue was

> not whether a great private monopoly should dominate government, or whether the currency of the country should be paper or specie (coin). It was, stated in its simplest terms, whether the United States should have a controlled or uncontrolled financial and credit system.[193]

Jackson wanted an uncontrolled financial and credit system, because, as he claimed to his cabinet, the power to control the economy "belongs to the States and the people, and must be regulated by public opinion and the interests of trade."[194] Biddle knew that Jackson's theory was completely false. He was "certain that . . . the only practicable safeguard against the evils of irresponsible banking and depreciating paper money was a national bank to keep state banks in order." Only a national bank had the power necessary to control the national economy, keep it both stable and dynamic, and protect it from pressures of the British and European markets.[195]

Because Govan and another professor would be critically reviewing Schlesinger's book at the AHA meeting, and because of Schlesinger's scheduled appearance and controversy, tension among attendees was high. The meeting report read:

> On Saturday afternoon a capacity audience in the grand ballroom was treated to a display of intellectual pyrotechnics when . . . (a professor from Columbia and Thomas P. Govan of the University of Virginia) subjected certain of Schlesinger's concepts . . . to critical analysis . . . Govan . . . took up the cudgels for Nicholas Biddle and the Second Bank of the United States. He declared that the bank, if left alone, would have conducted its affairs in a conservative and impartial manner and provided a central banking system (along the lines of the Bank of England) so essential to the financial and commercial needs of the community. Favoring centralization of banking and joint private-public control, the speaker compared the Second Bank of the United States to the Federal Reserve System. . . . [Responding] to Professor Govan's thesis, Mr. Schlesinger denied that the Second Bank of the United States was impartially managed, refused to accept the view that centralized credit control in America would have avoided depressions in the 19th century, and asserted that any resemblance between the government's participation in the Federal Reserve System

and the Biddle Bank was strictly coincidental. He charged Mr. Govan with failing to appreciate the fact that concentration in private hands of control over the credit [system] is an anomaly in a democracy.[196]

Schlesinger Recants

The argument rested there for twelve years. Then in 1958, just a year before the publication of his Biddle biography, Govan restated in full the substance of what he had said in 1946—but without any reference to Schlesinger—in an article, "The Fundamental Issues of the Bank War," published in *The Pennsylvania Magazine of History and Biography*. The issue, he repeated, was whether the United States needed a controlled or uncontrolled financial and credit system.[197] As he said in 1946, the national economy had originally been controlled by the Bank of the United States and the country had flourished. After Andrew Jackson vetoed a bill to re-charter the Bank in 1836, the country suffered terribly until 1913 when, under the Federal Reserve Bank, control over the economy was once again established.

Later in 1958, Govan again addressed the American Historical Association, this time on "The Fall of the House of Biddle," which summarized the full biography, Nicholas Biddle, Nationalist and Public Banker, 1786-1844, about to be published the following year. American historians were forced to take another look at the issues. Govan's thesis has held up to this day. Schlesinger's understanding had changed, and he admitted that *The Age of Jackson*, in this respect, was "wrong."[198]

Schlesinger responded in writing, but not until 1989 when he wrote an article entitled, "The Ages of Jackson," in the *New York Review of Books* in which he finally admitted his errors. As he put it

> My critics have a point when they claim the Whigs, and not the Jacksonians, as the real forerunners of the Franklin D. Roosevelt's New Deal. The Tradition of affirmative government was the tradition of Hamilton, not Jefferson. Hamilton's faith in the dynamics of individual acquisition was always tempered by an

expectation of government control. Americans, he wrote had 'a certain fermentation of mind, a certain activity of speculation and enterprise which, if properly directed, may be made subservient to useful purposes but which, if left entirely to itself, may be attended with pernicious effect.' Subsequent statesmen in the tradition, especially John Quincy Adams and Henry Clay, elaborated the Hamiltonian vision into what Clay called the American System—a great dream of economic development under the leadership of the national state . . . .

Looking back, I think I did Hamilton, Adams, and Clay a good deal less than justice in *The Age of Jackson*. It is true that the American System, with its program of internal improvements, a protective tariff, Biddle's Bank of the United States was designed to benefit the business classes; but this was not the whole truth. The Whig program was also designed to benefit the nation and to accelerate the pace of economic growth. In retrospect, the Hamiltonians [and Govan would add, especially Biddle] had a sounder conception of the role of government and a more constructive policy of economic development than the anti-statist Jacksonians.

While I am confessing my error, I must say that . . . my bias was rather in favor of the [Jacksonian] hard-money policy— that is, the maintenance of a stable ratio between paper and specie [gold] . . . As I now reflect on the Jacksonian period, having been enlightened in the years between by kindly instruction from John Kenneth Galbraith . . . [I now see that] the hard-money policy, systematically pursued, would have held back development.[199]

Even in 1989 Schlesinger still failed to understand the full role of the Bank of the United States. He thought "the inflation and the subsequent depression of the 1830s were caused, not by Jackson's termination of the Bank of the United States and consequent overissue of notes by wildcat bankers, but by international monetary factors beyond Jackson's control."[200] Govan held that there was a depression not only because of irresponsible states' banks and depreciating paper money, but precisely because the Bank of the United States was not able to protect the American economy from international pressures.

From that time on, Tom was marked as controversial, but always respected. He and Jane continued at the University of Virginia through the spring and summer of 1947. In the fall, with the biography still incomplete though well on its way, they returned to Sewanee and Tom to a full schedule of teaching. Although he published a few articles on Biddle, all incidental to the biography,[201] Govan put his major project on hold again because of teaching commitments and personal troubles.

Govan's essay, "The Fundamental Issues of the Bank War," is in the Govan Archives. The same essay, slightly abbreviated, has been republished in several editions of *Taking Sides*, edited by Larry Modares and James M. SoRelle in 1995.[202]

Friends

Franny Schwab and her two brothers, Bob and Mack, owned a summer house in Cotuit on Cape Cod, Massachusetts. She invited the Govans to visit, which they did with pleasure several times during the summer of 1946. The Ropers also rented there so together their friendships deepened. During that summer, some of the Govans' unhappiness began to show. According to Laura Roper, "Jane told Franny, after [they had] all [Crosby and Laura, Jane and Tom, and Franny] had a lovely few days together at Franny's house in Cotuit, that she and Tom had been seriously thinking of divorce." That came as a terrible shock to both the Ropers and the Schwabs. What had happened? What could they do to help? Laura continued: "But when Tom and Jane realized how much all of us cared for them, they realized also that we cared for them not only separately but in conjunction, so they should try to maintain the combination." This was the unconditional love of close friends

"I think," said Laura, "they got along together more easily when on vacation: Tom not hag-ridden by . . . lack of time, lack of privacy. Then [on vacation] they really enjoyed each other."[203] There was no question about it: their vacation time with Franny Schwab and the Ropers was always a healing time for them. Jane and Tom did try and did succeed. The marriage held.

7

The Ups and Downs
of a Young Teacher

'History' is a demythologized word for the 'Providence of God.'

Thomas P. Govan

Govan's Work and State of Mind

After Govan's 1947 return to Sewanee and the University of the South, he rose from assistant professor to professor and finally to chair of the history department in 1950. While teaching, his views became deeper and more coherent. He worked it out in the classroom. He thought much about how the American revolution had as its primary purpose the increase of human freedom. Historians had offered a variety of opinions about how that freedom could best be achieved. After the Revolution, traditional conservatives, especially Alexander Hamilton and Nicholas Biddle, believed that society could be free "only where individual liberty, on the one hand, and government power, on the other hand, were restrained from becoming despotic."[204]

The traditional liberals, on the other hand, especially Thomas Jefferson and his followers, believed that "economic, social and political matters were controlled by natural laws with which men interfered at their peril, and that the government was best which governed least."[205]

Govan believed that the conservative view held the greatest hope for achieving reasonable security, freedom and prosperity. He felt that, "This anti-deterministic, non-dogmatic, essentially pragmatic . . . attitude advocated individual liberty and collective action but remained aware of the dangers inherent in both."

Thomas P. Govan, American Historian
after World War II

There was, however, one step more in Govan's analysis. By this time Tom's political philosophy was being influenced heavily by his Christian understanding. He became more aware of the fallibility of being human, the impossibility of moral perfection, and he yearned for comfort. Ironically he found it in the words of Thomas Cranmer's General Confession in the *Book of Common Prayer*.

> Most merciful father, we have erred and strayed from thy
> ways like lost sheep. We have offended against they holy
> laws. We have left undone those things which we ought to
> have done and we have done those things which we ought
> not to have done, and there is no health in us.

Tom realized that what he needed most was forgiveness, deep forgiveness; and he found it in Cranmer's words.

Tom was grappling with what he saw as the ambiguity of human progress toward a better society. He knew that human destiny cannot be controlled, but because he believed that human life and history have meaning, humans can—nay, they must—continually work at progress with hope.

But whose meaning? Who is in control? Govan asked. The answer echoed in his ears and heart: God's meaning, God's forgiveness, God's control. He suddenly knew it was all right to be merely an ordinary sinful human being. It was all right because God had forgiven him and set him free, not only from his sin but from the hapless task of avoiding sin. The freedom he felt as a result was exhilarating. Then it dawned on him: if this were true for him, it must be true for everyone. So, he concluded, all of history is shot through with the Providence of God. Tom realized that history is really a demythologized word for the Providence of God. Better still, history is the Providence of God.[206] He was home at last.

Tom's political philosophy rose out of his religious convictions, not the other way around. The understanding that history is God's Providence was so powerful and changed his life so radically that he taught with a new intensity. Not only did he teach objective history but passionately presented the view in which he deeply believed.

He focused more on the material and its meaning than he did on the students and their feelings. He desperately wanted to get through to them, to open their eyes and win their allegiance. When he felt students rejected his teaching or simply did not comprehend, he responded as though it was a personal rejection.

Students' reactions to his style were mixed. To some he was a terrifying figure, especially to those who were slow or disinterested. His intensity seemed like anger, confusing some students, and frightening others. Others rebelled against his ideas and teachings. But to some, Tom's energy and enthusiasm were exciting, and he engaged these students—the conversation was thrilling.

One of his students, G. P. Mellick Belshaw, later the bishop of New Jersey (1983-1994), who graduated in 1951, remembers a tutorial with Govan on the meaning of history. Each week his assignment was to write a paper, usually based on a book, to be read for discussion in the seminar. Belshaw describes a diagram Govan drew for him in class:

> One day in a compulsive way, he grabbed my paper, turned it over and with a pencil scribbled a few pictures and words to describe his view of history. As if to say, "Now do you get it?" Obviously, the compulsion on his part to tell me what his view of history was, and how he wanted me to understand it, made a strong impression on me, or I would not have saved it. The illustrations were done quickly and his comments were impatient. He liked me, but he wanted me to understand him. There was a kind of desperation about him—he seemed gruff and irritable to me, but he wanted to be liked and appreciated at the same time . . . .

> I really can't remember the details of what he was saying to me, but they had to do with the universe, infinity, and God; then with human achievement and failure, especially human pride; the [human] record of response [to God's self-revelation] and faith, that there is meaning in it all, which Scripture proclaims and which makes it [history] possible to interpret, so long as we don't get sucked into dogmatism.[207]

Personal Joys and Sorrows

Life for the Govans at the University of the South was intense, socially, politically, and emotionally. They were making new friends. Robert F. Gibson, the new dean of the School of Theology, was recruiting a group of young, bright faculty. Tom and Jane found them compatible, intellectually alive, and full of vitality. They came from the North and West, as well as from the South. They were obviously at home with theological thought and thus different from most of the university faculty. They shared Tom and Jane's convictions on race. With this new group of friends, the Govans' social life increased, the level of discussion rose, and they laughed a great deal more. Bob Gibson became one of Tom Govan's best friends, from whom he learned a lot about church history and with whom he loved to argue theology. When Gibson was elected Suffragon Bishop of Virginia, Tom was pleased because now he could say, "Goddammit Bob!" to a bishop.[208]

The Govans lived near the University in Sewanee in a small rented log house which they eventually bought. A small flower garden of Jane's and a small lawn Tom mowed graced its front yard. The house had a large living room and dining room, a kitchen, three bedrooms, a bath, and a study. Their daily routine during this period was relaxed and mutually supportive. Tom would be up early and come into the kitchen in his bathrobe and slippers, let their dachshund Judy out; "perk" a pot of coffee, the stronger the better, and drink most of it himself, always careful to save a full cup for Jane. He would have a bowl of cereal and then go into the living room with his coffee, smoke a series of cigarettes, and read the morning papers, *The New York Times* a day late, and the local paper, and then turn to a book or his lecture notes for that day.

Jane would get up early or late, as she chose, and come in dressed in an elegant bathrobe, with her hair carefully done. She would have her coffee and a cigarette, discuss the news with Tom, and then sit and read with him. When the time came, Tom would shave, dress and leave for his classes. Jane would clean up, dress, and often do some cooking, and then head off for her part-time volunteer job as librarian for the School of Theology.

She was a gregarious person, and loved to play the role of hostess. She was a good cook and occasionally had friends over for lunch, feeding them homemade bread, deli foods with Coke or coffee. For the students she had "open house" on occasion and they would gorge on better food than the commons provided.

The Govan house was always open to faculty at cocktail time. Jane was hostess and Tom presided. Good bourbon accompanied intense discussion, and his friends found Tom intellectually stimulating and fun. He held forth on a current or scholarly issue and sparked heated discussions. When he had a definite idea, he could be expansive and dogmatic, but he never resented an argument. It was part of the intellectual life he loved.

During the week, Tom attended daily chapel at the university which he found nourishing. On Sundays, Jane joined him at Otey Parish, the local Episcopal church in town. They found services uninspiring, though, and the congregation narrow and prejudiced. Even so, Tom, out of a sense of duty, served as a vestryman and tried unsuccessfully to break down the town-gown tensions and prejudices.

At Christmas, with the students gone, the Govans hosted an eggnog party. Jane made the fruitcake, heavily spiked, and Tom did an elaborate job on the eggnog: egg whites, cream, ice cream and Jack Daniels by the bottle. A Christmas tree graced the living room, and friends came to celebrate. The house would be bursting with holiday cheer.

Jane was more than a hostess though. She was very well-read, up on the latest literature and theater, and especially knowledgeable in the arts and architecture. She broadened and deepened Tom's understanding in these areas. She was a master of needlepoint. Several of their living room pillows were made by her.

Another factor in their lives were visits from the extended Govan family for whom Tom felt a responsibility. Nieces and nephews would visit Tom and Jane when there was a crisis at home, a need to escape, or board with them while attending the university. Without children themselves, they always welcomed family visitors. Jane, who had the time and her own ideas about bringing up children, would take them on and coach them as if they were her own. Jane loved this maternal role, but while Tom enjoyed these visits, he also suffered a lack of privacy and opportunities to concentrate on his own work.[209]

Conflict At Home

In addition to their active social life and visiting family, new academic responsibilities at the university interfered with Tom's scholarship. As history department chair, he was increasingly involved in committee work dealing with university administration and policy issues. In a small college, the faculty was expected to know and be available to students as advisors, counselors and friends, as well as teachers and mentors, day and night. Jane, of course, loved having students in and out of their house. She became an unpaid but valuable asset to the university staff. For Tom, these expectations made finding time for his research and book production difficult.

Jane's mother, Nell Dickson, had moved in to live with Jane while Tom was away in the army. When Tom and Jane moved back to Sewanee in the fall of 1947, Nell was waiting for them in their log cabin home. Tom's relationship with his mother-in-law was very cordial and warm initially; they had liked each other. But living in a small house together allowed too little privacy. Nell was a nonstop talker, mostly about trivia, and she inspired the same in Jane. Tom had no escape and they dragged on his energies and patience.

Jim Bunnell, the husband of Tom's niece, Kate Tucker, was finishing college at Sewanee on the GI Bill at the time and was one of Tom's students. Jim described the situation during that winter of 1947-1948:

> That was a very small house. The only place to sit and read in the evening was in the living room sitting around an open hearth. Here was Tom reading. He always had a couple of books on one side and a couple more on the other side. The walls of that room were lined with books. And there was his mother-in-law who never stopped talking. Tom would not be tuned into what she and Jane were saying. He was trying to read, study, and prepare his lectures, and so on. He would be interrupted by Nell to listen to some trite matter or other. And Tom put up with it . . . daily. But I could see that it got on his nerves. If Kate and I popped in for a visit some evening, or Tom asked us to come see him, there would be Nell and Jane. When Nell was talking, Jane was usually quite quiet and let her go on. I realized that Nell was doing all the talking. Tom and I could have a short conversation, and than Nell would butt in and introduce some utterly incongruous note. Tom would try to ignore it, but I could see that he

was gritting his teeth. I thought Tom did an awfully good job of tolerating her.[210]

Gradually Nell began to criticize Tom—first to Jane and then directly to Tom—he was not making enough money; he was married to his work and not to his wife; he was not caring for Jane properly; and, a sore point, he was not in control of his drinking. Tom knew these complaints were partially true, and he knew that Jane knew it. She had married him for love and companionship, and she was receiving precious little of either.

On the other hand, Jane was lonely and bored, and Nell was a big help to her. In return, Jane could minister to her mother who was partially crippled with arthritis. Tom understood this, yet he was struggling to teach, learn, and do research and write books, all of which required concentration, lots of quiet time, and support from his family. He was getting none of these things. He began to despise Nell. He and Jane wrangled over this and hurt one another. Both of them felt anger, guilt, and betrayal. Nell would say to others in the family, "I just hate to think about their living this way."

It was a difficult time, and Tom felt he had to make a decision for the sake of their future. He painfully told Jane that Nell had to go. Jane understood, but it hurt her deeply, and this in turn hurt him. Although they suffered, they learned out of all this agony they loved each other deeply and were still committed to their marriage.

During this painful time, Tom discovered two important realities about his marriage and himself. The first was that he and Jane would have to live with the inevitable tension between their personal life and his professional life as scholar. Tom hated hurting Jane; he hated being hurt by her and he found the inevitability of both occurring over and over profoundly depressing.

The second reality was Tom's realization that he might be more prone to depression than he felt was normal. He had spoken in his "Apologia" of "moments of doubt, despair, and torment,"[211] feelings that were very real to him. The knowledge that they were bound to return was in itself depressing to him. The fact that Jane did not seem to recognize these feelings only made them worse. Despite the confidence Tom had in his work, its quality and usefulness, he found these two realizations daunting. But that was not all. There was a third reality, one Tom probably would have denied: a tendency toward compulsiveness. He was a chain smoker and a regular, sometimes heavy, drinker. His students reported that very often in class he would have a cigarette going; it was allowed in those days. He began every morning with coffee and a series of cigarettes. The dangers of smoking, of course, were not known yet, so "everyone did it."

At best Tom's attitude toward drinking was ambivalent. He had grown up with an alcoholic father, but had also seen the negative consequences of his father's conversion to sobriety. He remembered Prohibition and despised how it trampled on individual freedom and, he felt, simply did not work. While recognizing alcoholism as a problem for some, it never occurred to him that it might be a problem for him. Rather, he believed, along with most of his contemporaries, that drinking was an integral part of sociability and social occasions. It loosened people up and was fun. He and Jane drank a good deal, a couple of bourbons before dinner, and maybe more after. When they were getting along, they thoroughly enjoyed it; when they were not, it exaggerated their conflicts. If alcohol contributed to Tom's depressions, as it must have, neither he nor Jane seemed to recognize it. It became clear as time went by that Jane had very little, if any, understanding of either Tom's tendency toward depression or his tendency toward alcoholism. She drank with him and criticized him as though neither existed.

Nevertheless, their relationship was supported by a shared Christian faith. Jane's faith had grown consistently since her divorce. Tom's faith was still in the flush of new discovery. Though they related to Christianity differently, they were together. That was a blessing to them.

"The Rich, the Well-Born, and Alexander Hamilton"

In spite of his troubles at the university and home, Tom's writing during this period was steady and of high quality. He was often asked to review and comment in his areas of expertise. For example, he reviewed a book on the tobacco industry,[212] and led a discussion on "Cotton, Sugar, and Hemp" at the Southern Historical Association (SHA) annual meeting in November 1948.[213] He also reviewed two books on the history of World War II,[214] and at the 1951 SHA annual meeting, he was asked to comment on an address by Robert Coakley about the American military supplies sent to the USSR during that war.[215] At that same meeting, he was appointed chair of the program committee for the 1952 meeting by one of his mentors, C. Vann Woodward, president of the association.

His review of *The Whig Party in Georgia, 1825-1853* by Paul Murray[216] noted that the study of history in recent years had broadened its field and increased its emphasis upon social, intellectual, and economic history, as distinct from political history. As a result, political analysis was left virtually untouched and unexplained to the detriment of historical understanding. He complimented Murray on tracing "the entire career of the Whig party in Georgia from its origins in . . . the States' Rights party to its dissolution in 1853 as a consequence of the failure of the national Whig party to achieve effective compromise on the question of slavery."[217]

Govan wrote one article of which he was particularly proud. "The Rich, the Well-Born, and Alexander Hamilton"[218] clarified Hamilton's political philosophy and the view of human nature upon which it was based. The prevailing criticism of Hamilton by many American historians was that Hamilton was antidemocratic and an elitist who believed that the rich and the well-born were virtuous, wise, and superior in every way to ordinary people and therefore could be trusted to "maintain good government." Govan demonstrated beyond any doubt that this claim was false. Hamilton distrusted all groups when they had too much power and wanted each to be a check on the others. It was true that he especially distrusted pure democracy as a dangerous form of government that could lead to chaos and then to tyranny. He firmly supported, however, the creation of a democratic republic in the United States.

It is worth noting that Govan's defense of Hamilton was, by implication, also a defense of Nicholas Biddle, very much one of the rich and well-born and Hamilton's heir on financial policy. Govan

130

surely remembered the attack by Arthur M. Schlesinger, Jr. on Biddle's Second National Bank and Schlesinger's belief that "the concentration in private hands of control over the credit system," which he had thought the Bank represented, "was an anomaly in a democracy."[219] Schlesinger's view at the time was not far from Andrew Jackson's: "the economy . . . must be regulated by public opinion and the interests of trade,"[220] that is, democratically. Hamilton, Biddle, and Govan would all reply, first, that the bank was a mixture of private and government control, each doing what it did best, with each acting as a check on the other; second, that the bank was sound and successful and served the interests of everyone in the nation; and third, that some form of more democratic control would be a formula for disaster. They were uniquely expert in the field of finance and knew what they were talking about. The critics were just plain wrong, Govan believed.

8

Mounting Crisis

*After as conscientious and prayerful a consideration of the subject
as I was able to make, I feel deeply convinced that the action taken
[not to desegregate] was in the best interest of both races.*

Edward McCrady, June 11, 1952

Desegregation Controversy at the University of the South

In 1951, events took a turn that changed the Govans' lives forever. Two years earlier, the Episcopal Church's only seminary for blacks, the Bishop Payne Divinity School in Petersburg, Virginia, closed as a result of difficulty with financial support and student recruitments, and a growing sentiment that opposed racially segregated Episcopal seminaries. Because the Theological Seminary in Alexandria, Virginia, and the School of Theology at the University of the South were segregated, after the Payne Divinity School closed, there was no place for the education of Episcopal black clergy in the South.

In June 1951, following the commencement at the University of the South, the School of Theology faculty met with the bishops present and urged them to join in an effort to have the School desegregated. They knew that the Virginia Theological Seminary faculty felt the same way. The bishops were divided. Several of them, led by Arthur C.

Lichtenberger, then Bishop of Missouri, were for immediate desegregation. Others were opposed or ambivalent. They approved of desegregation on Christian principles, but were not willing to act precipitously. They were "gradualists," who believed the time and circumstances were not right and considered the faculty's position too radical. Donald Armentraut, in his history of these events, nevertheless, reported that "many of the bishops agreed that Negroes should be admitted to the School of Theology."[221] The bishops left knowing exactly where the faculty stood.

During the summer, Virginia Theological Seminary opened its doors to its first black student, John T. Walker, who would later become Bishop of Washington, D.C. In October 1951, the Synod of the Fourth Province of the Episcopal Church, representing the twenty-two southeastern dioceses (all of its bishops and six clergy and six laity per diocese) met in Birmingham, Alabama to work out a common policy on desegregation for the province. This widely representative body debated what should be done and surprisingly resolved sixty-six to twenty-five that the Fourth Province thought

> It would not be desirable or advisable to establish a
> segregated seminary for theological education in our
> Province. But it thinks it desirable and advisable that we
> should open up our seminaries in the South to students
> of all races.[222]

This opinion was forwarded to the Board of Trustees at the University of the South and soon became public knowledge and the source of tremendous controversy. All winter the issue was debated in the seminary, the university, and the town. Govan agreed with the Synod. He did not support segregation.

The controversy spilled into all of the Govans' relationships, adding tension evident in their social life with friends in the town of Sewanee. Except for the School of Theology, it was present in their university relationships and painfully in Tom's undergraduate classes, where most of the students disagreed with him. But most painful of all was the division in the church. He was discouraged. On the one hand, the college chapel worship Tom and Jane attended embraced inclusion. But the nearby Otey Parish in town consisted of a small and almost entirely segregationist group, quite hostile to the university chaplain and the theological faculty. The tension grew worse as 1951 came to a close.

The Highlander School

Tom had known about Myles Horton and the Highlander School since 1940. Horton was a mountain Tennessean who had graduated from Cumberland College, studied at Union Theological Seminary, and explored progressive education methods as far away as Denmark. He had founded the school in 1932 in Monteagle, Tennessee, just "down the mountain" from Sewanee. The school was a polar opposite of the University of the South. Horton's purpose for founding Highlander was

> to bring about social change in the country and that there would be no discrimination, that we would deal equally with men and women, blacks and whites.[223]

In his role as facilitator, he encouraged people to work out their own answers to problems. He taught them to discover how to meet their needs and solve their problems. Education was a matter of cooperation, not competition, and through it, people learned confidence in themselves and were strengthened for action. He put this philosophy to work in the Highlander School first with the poor of the Appalachian Mountains, then with the industrial labor movement, in particular the CIO. In fact, Highlander became the quasi-official CIO educational training center for the entire South. It would soon serve the Civil Rights Movement in very much the same way.

Before World War II, Sewanee and Highlander developed a relationship. Fleming James, a distinguished biblical scholar and believer in the social gospel, was dean of the seminary and soon became a friend of Horton's. Gradually a few of Sewanee's liberal students and faculty took part in Highlander's life. It was the only place in the "old South" where whites and blacks could meet, eat and live together as equals.

It was not until after the war in 1947 when Tom returned to Sewanee that he met Horton. They recognized one another immediately as Niebuhrian progressives in conflict with the "old South." In the winter of 1952, just as the issue of desegregation at Sewanee was heating up, Tom and Jane became seriously involved with Highlander. A young CIO labor organizer, Richard L. Conn, who was courting and later married Tom's niece, arrived at Highlander and invited Tom down to share in the life of the school. He experienced Horton's methods first hand and was completely energized. Highlander changed peoples' hearts as well as their minds, and Tom was inspired—he wanted his own teaching to do the same.

At Highlander, Govan found his deepest commitments on race, class and education supported and he was strengthened by his contact there. He needed that strength because he realized that the desegregation issue, about which he had absolute clarity, might disrupt his career and change his life. The memory of sending the black man to the back door at the Atlanta bank some twenty years before still haunted him. Ending segregation was a deep and steady passion to him, but it was also a source of apprehension. With all its faults, Tom loved Sewanee but he knew he might have to leave.

During that winter Tom applied for a year-long grant from the Fund for the Advancement for Education to study in New York City. Whatever lay ahead, his scholarship had reached the point where he needed to test his ideas with the best minds in the country. For him, these were Reinhold Niebuhr and Paul Tillich at Union Theological Seminary and Jacques Barzun at Columbia. Jane was as eager as Tom for a chance to be in New York.

The Fire

On March 6, 1952, Tom and Jane arrived home from the movies to find their house in flames. Tom "dashed in and salvaged a few things, some silver" and other small objects of special meaning. "One or two efforts were all he could make because the heat and flames were too much."[224] It was a desperate and crushing blow: their beloved dachshund Judy died in the fire. Everything else they owned, and above all for Tom, his biography of Biddle, six years of work and all his research notes as well as the manuscript seemed lost.[225]

They were devastated. Jane described the half-finished manuscript and piles of notes and file cards lying unprotected on their living room floor when the flames broke out. The walls were floor-to-ceiling bookcases filled with books. Miraculously, the books burned off the walls and fell on top on the manuscript and notes on the floor, covering and largely saving them. Both the manuscript and notes were soaked but usable.[226] Tom Tucker, Govan's nephew, was a student at the university at that time and described the scene. Tom "had all his Biddle notes on three by five cards, which were watered down by the local fire department. And two friends of mine at the school took those three by five cards, separated them, and laid them out on the floor, one by one, so they would dry and could be used again. But Tom was unable to help. He had collapsed into shock; he was temporarily paralyzed, unable to do anything."[227] The total damage was later estimated at $13,176, only $5,000 of which was covered by insurance.[228]

The fire was a terrible shock both financially and psychologically. The catastrophe sent Govan from shock into depression. For more than a month he was barely able to cope with his day-to-day responsibilities, though he never missed a class. The tragedy added to the strain already present in their lives. There were rumors that the fire may have been set by a student, maybe a southerner who could not stand the version of history Tom was teaching. "Most Sewanee-ites, however, blamed the fire on the Govans' constant chain smoking."[229] Either way, the rumors made things worse for them.

The Govans began living in an available graduate student apartment and then housesitting for various faculty members. Along with the seminary crisis, their disillusionment with the university's leadership, and the near loss of the Biddle manuscript, they were now homeless. Tom and Jane felt uprooted and battered. With relief, they looked forward to their year in New York.

The Trustees' Decision and Its Consequences

At the June 6, 1952 meeting of the University board of trustees, a resolution was rejected that would have "closed the door tightly against the possibility of admitting Negroes."[230] As Christians, they could not deny the principle of church inclusiveness. Principle was one thing, the application of the principle, however, was another. They could claim that the time and the circumstances were not right without denying the principle, which was exactly what they did. After long debate, they considered the Fourth Province's resolution and voted it down 45-12. The majority present that morning at the meeting approved the following statement: "The furtherance of the church's work and happiness and mutual goodwill of both races will not now be served by the action requested by the Synod."[231] Those words had been the time-honored language of segregationists for the past century. Govan was distressed by the element of dishonesty in that language: Christian leaders claiming to believe in the Christian principle of inclusion, while hiding their racism behind the extenuating circumstances of time and occasion. Dishonest sanctimonious gradualism made him sick, and it was his church behaving that way. He asked Jane how she felt now about going to New York for a year. Her reply came from the heart: "I don't give a damn where we go. Just take me to an institution east of the mountains which doesn't claim to have any principles."[232]

Later that day, the Chattanooga Times and various radio stations reported the board's action not to desegregate. The message was clear. To change would be controversial and disruptive; education and morale at the university would suffer; standards would be called into question, and many students and faculty would be upset. The board had simply stonewalled the recommendation. Segregation would stand. Everywhere in the School of Theology and in many quarters of the university the reaction was swift and similar; the board of trustees had a revolution on their hands.

The next day, June 7, the theological faculty held its annual commencement meeting with the bishops present. In a heated discussion, the faculty presented their objections to the board's action. Again, they urged the bishops to join them in an effort to desegregate the School of Theology. Once again, the trustees' response was ambivalent. As one bishop put it, "I fail to see why a man may not accept an ethical principle and at the same time give careful consideration to the time and circumstances of its application." All too often the "gradualists" dishonestly used their position as a cover for intransigent racism and refused to act.

Two days later, the theological faculty met to discuss the situation, and decided to hold a secret meeting that night in one of their homes. Seven faculty members were present at the start of that evening meeting; two faculty were out of town. The new dean, Craighill Brown, whom they all liked and trusted, was not invited because they did not want to put him in a difficult position with the trustees. But Brown, equally committed to desegregation, walked the campus that night until he found them and was welcomed into the meeting.

Together, eight faculty members wrote and signed a petition to the trustees asking that the board reconsider its decision. One faculty member, then on leave in Japan, was called and immediately joined them, making nine signatures. Only one faculty member refused to join. Their protest was made in the name of Christian conscience and in response to a strong inclusive statement on race from the recent Lambeth Conference of Anglican Bishops from all over the world.[233] They could not in good conscience continue to teach in a Christian institution that denied entrance to blacks. They would act as a body for the sake of conscience if their request was ignored. "We are without exception prepared to resign our positions."[234] For each of them, especially those with tenure, this was a wrenchingly costly decision. That night they sang hymns and prayed together.

Govan called their petition the best document since the Declaration of Independence.[235] Like the Declaration, it specified their principles and grievances, backed up with the threat of action if their grievances were not acknowledged and rectified. Tom's name was not on the petition because he was not a member of the seminary faculty, but the signers welcomed his strong moral support as a fellow Christian. They knew that if he had been a member of the theological faculty, he would have joined them. At the time, they did not know that three years later he would give up his tenure and never return because of the desegregation issue.

The faculty's petition was formally delivered to the offices of Bishop Mitchell, the chancellor (who was not there, having driven home to Little Rock, Arkansas), and to Edward McCrady, the vice-chancellor. Simultaneously, the faculty sent the petition to both the Episcopal Church national press and the secular national press. McCrady had hardly read the document before phone calls from the press came pouring in. Bishop Mitchell had phone calls at home before he even knew there was a petition. They were furious. The faculty apologized for their timing, but reiterated their position.

From then on, everyone took sides, and as Jane said, "It was bitter war."[236] Accordingly, it did not take McCrady, Mitchell and the board long to strike back. One of the first things they did was to rescind the promotion to associate professor of Christian ethics they had just granted to Robert McNair. The executive committee of the Association of American University Professors (AAUP), which McNair asked to investigate the situation, reported that " . . . the sole ground for withholding the promotion was McNair's participation in the action of June 9." The committee also noted that "this raises serious questions of academic freedom."[237] McNair's promotion was restored, but the situation rankled the faculty all summer long.

Tom was especially upset by the attitude of McCrady. He was a former biology professor (1937-1948) understood to believe that women and blacks were genetically inferior to white men. He, therefore, would do all he could to keep both women and blacks out of the university for as long as he could. And yet he claimed to be a devoted Christian. On June 11, 1952, he issued the following statement.

> The action of the board of trustees was taken in a full
> session with 65 members present, including 13 bishops.

There was free and full discussion, and the final report was adopted by an overwhelming majority. None of us can know with absolute certainty what the ultimate solution of the many complicated problems connected with race relations in the United States will be. We can only pray that Divine guidance will help us to better judgments than we by ourselves know how to make. After as conscientious and prayerful a consideration of the subject as I was able to make, I feel deeply convinced that the action taken was in the best interest of both races.[238]

The piety and unctuousness coupled with the racism of the man disgusted the Govans.

The next move came in late July 1952. The Board of Regents held a special meeting to discuss and then respond to the theological faculty's protest. They "were unanimous in condemning the action of the faculty in taking this case to the press rather than to the Trustees through the Vice-Chancellor."[239] They noted that the action of the trustees on June 6 "had erected no permanent bar to the admission of qualified Negro students," and promised reconsideration of the faculty's request at the next trustees' meeting in June 1953.[240]

That is where matters stood officially for the rest of the summer. On campus, however, there were one-on-one and small group discussions among friends and colleagues about the issue, each person determining his or her position on the issue. All summer, rumors and facts vied with each other.

Arthur Ben Chitty, professor of history at Sewanee, described the divisions over the faculty's petition this way:

The protestors have received wide support from the general Church and they believed that expressions of the Lambeth Conference, General Convention, and Provincial Synod justify their position. Too, it must be recognized that the cause advocated by the theological faculty members is not without support at Sewanee. Many individuals—a majority of the seminary students, a considerable number of the college faculty and undergraduates and a number of residents—feel that bi-racial education is just and that segregation everywhere must end. In spite of this considerable sympathy for the abstract cause, the protestors have been roundly condemned on the Mountain.[241]

Many thought that the faculty's threat to resign was "too harsh," not only "unwise" but both "un-Christian and ungentlemanly,"[242] and that it blocked any revision of the attitude of the trustees.[243]

Chitty continued,

Life has been difficult for the members of the seminary faculty since their declaration of dissatisfaction with the action of the trustees on June 6. Their taking the protest to the public press was interpreted locally as disloyalty to the institution, and feeling against them mounted accordingly. In private conversation they [the faculty] have referred to "persecution" and "character assassination" as censure from their neighbors and from parts of the owning dioceses became more conspicuous. Support for their principle has been less vocal than condemnation for their action.[244]

Tom and Jane felt all of this conflict acutely. Their closest friends were suffering. They found themselves among a small, alienated minority in Sewanee. They had not made up their minds about the long-term future; it would take at least another year for them to decide. They would go to New York and then make a decision.

They knew that the faculty's decision to leave or stay would heavily influence them, but it was painful for them even to think about it. After all, Tom was a full professor with tenure and chair of the history department. Leaving meant losing his tenure, a terrible professional and financial loss. He loved the place. It was where he had met and married Jane, where he had converted to Christianity, where he had learned his profession, and where he had innumerable friends. It had nurtured him in every way, and he had counted on it to be a good place to live, better than most. Then he and Jane were surprised and disillusioned by all of June's events, the dishonesty and hostility of a trustees corrupted in part by racism and guided by what the Govans considered the deceit of Edward McCrady. Tom was forced to face the fact of the self-righteousness of Sewanee, its preciousness, its separation from the workaday world, harbored not just evil, but a special and dangerous evil, called hypocrisy. He was hurt and ashamed of the place, especially because it presumed to represent the Episcopal Church.

In August 1952, Tom hired a replacement, John Webb, to teach his classes, and in September, the Govans left for New York—shaken but together—to live at 10 Sheridan Square in Greenwich Village.

For four months the trustees refused to reconsider their decision. On October 6, 1952, Dean Brown and nine of the ten faculty of the School of Theology submitted their resignations to become effective in June 1953 at the end of the academic year. They began looking for new jobs. Thirty-five of the fifty-six first- and second-year students in the School of Theology began making plans to transfer as well, most of them to Virginia Theological Seminary which threw its doors open to them.[245]

Tom did not announce his resignation, and was buying time to weigh this difficult decision while in New York. He and Jane were grateful that the Tennessee state law schools and Fisk University were already desegregated.[246] But they especially enjoyed the brutal irony that the only other integrated educational institution in the state at the time, only eighty miles from Sewanee, was the Gupton-Jones School of Mortuary Science in Nashville. A school focused on death was desegregated; a school focused on eternal life was not!

9

New York: a Welcome Change of Pace, 1952-1953

America . . . is the result of a religious, not a moral idea, if by moral we mean dividing sheep from goats and what we mean by religion is the inclusive Fatherhood of God. For us "the people" means everybody [and that] distinguishes us historically.

Jacques Barzun

New York

The hustle, bustle, and anonymity of New York was a welcome relief from the relative intimacy and isolation of Sewanee. Theaters, concerts, museums, libraries, movies—all the cultural richness of one of the world's great cities—were at the Govans' disposal. Their modest means limited what they could do, but movies were everywhere, and they often attended Broadway and off-Broadway plays for just $2.40 a ticket. They saw Waiting for Godot, J. B., and Streetcar Named Desire. Each play touched deep places in them.

Tom was also a baseball fan, especially of the Brooklyn Dodgers when Jackie Robinson was in his heyday. Branch Rickey had signed Robinson in 1947 as the first black to play in the major leagues, but his signing was conditional: Robinson was not permitted to show his

143

feelings or respond to insults. His first year was tormented: he endured a petition to the management from his fellow teammates that he leave; the threat of a player strike in St. Louis if he were allowed to play there; constant racial insults from opposing players; knock-down pitches and spikes high on the base paths. He succeeded in keeping his hurt and anger under control, but he lost weight and nearly had a nervous breakdown. He survived, however, and at the age of twenty-eight helped the Dodgers win the National League pennant and was chosen Rookie of the Year.

By 1949, several other blacks were playing in the majors, and Robinson no longer had to restrain his emotions. From then on, he refused to endure any more racial slurs or taunts and became one of the most feared and respected players in the game.[247] By 1952, when Tom and Jane first came to New York, the Dodgers were on their way to winning the National League pennant for the third time. Robinson was at the top of his game, and Tom as a southerner with a special hatred for racism and special respect and support for the black struggle for equality, rejoiced in his success. Robinson was a winner, and Govan liked to see blacks winning in what had been a white world. On television and occasionally at Ebbetts Field, Tom cheered the Dodgers on.

It was as scholar that Tom most rejoiced in New York. Freed from the responsibilities of teaching, advising, and marking papers, and with full access to the libraries and other facilities of Columbia and Union Seminary, he was eager to progress with his primary purpose for the year. His goal was to consolidate his views on American history and test them against the wisdom of Reinhold Niebuhr at Union and Jacques Barzun at Columbia. He might make some progress on his biography of Nicholas Biddle, but for the time being, that was secondary.

Jane took care of the Govans' home, doing most of the shopping and housekeeping. Tom had his work, helped out with the heavy shopping, and around the house when asked. Although they both terribly missed their dachshund, they knew this was not the right time for another. Beyond the house, Jane gloried in the city and had plenty of time to explore and to drink in its richness. She spent hours in the Metropolitan Museum of Art, the Whitney Museum, and other galleries and museums.

Dear friends from the South, Lee and Cora Louise Belford, lived in the city as well. Lee was a fellow Episcopalian teaching religion at New York University (NYU), finishing his Ph.D. in religion at Columbia, and serving as associate priest on the staff of the Church of the Epiphany on the Upper East Side. He graduated from the University of the South in 1935. In World War II he served as a chaplain of the Fifth Marine Division, which led the attack on Iwo Jima. Cora Louise and Jane waited out the war together in Sewanee and became fast friends. Tom and Lee met for the first time upon their return to Sewanee after the war. They hit it off immediately, and soon found that they were kindred spirits both personally and professionally.

All four of them had similar ambivalent feelings about Sewanee. On the one hand, they loved it for its intimacy, its homogeneity, the mystique of the church, the university, and the South, all of which combined to nourish deep feelings within them. On the other hand, they were all free spirits living in a place that was tight, conformist, and even eccentric. In Sewanee, you could not step out of the norm; you could not be a free thinker. Both Cora Louise and Jane were strong women who evoked strong feelings in people. They had their own ways and opinions, and chafed in the Sewanee context. Neither was truly happy there. The place wore them down and they were glad to escape to New York, where they found the nourishment and the freedom they needed. Of course, Tom and Jane were nearer to Washington and Cotuit, the Ropers and Franny Schwab, so visits with them were more frequent.

The city had the double advantage of being a radical change, as well as a place where they could maintain their southern contacts. Tom and Jane had a constant trickle of family, friends and colleagues coming to or through New York. They put people up and socialized with old friends whenever the opportunity arose. Cora Louise remembers visits from old friends of Jane's: George Campbell and his wife, and from Sewanee Nancy Gailor and Trap Jarvey and his wife. Because they were free from the normal pressures of a university, New York was just the therapy they needed and they enjoyed their social life tremendously.[248]

145

Sewanee at a Distance

Sewanee was never far away. When the members of the theological faculty had business in New York, they always stayed with the Govans and kept them up to date on the latest news. The news generally saddened and angered Tom and Jane.

In the fall of 1952, "the school year seemed to open quietly, but before long, turmoil set in at the seminary." There were rumors circulating in Sewanee "attacking the professional competence and moral integrity of some of the School of Theology faculty members."[249] Tom believed that McCrady was behind the rumors, which "caused a strain on academic life, but also caused friction among the students. Some students were accused of being 'rumor spreaders' and 'carriers of information' against the faculty."[250] It was not, however, all rumor. McCrady fired Robert Grant, professor of the New Testament, on grounds of repeated public drunkenness.[251] Although there was disagreement over both the facts and the decision, Grant did resign in February and moved to the University of Chicago. "There were also charges against other faculty."[252] Chancellor Mitchell wrote to Allen Reddick, professor of church history,

> I suppose you are aware that you and McNair (Assistant Professor of Christian Ethics) have been reputedly linked in the drinking and other unseemly parties in which Bob Grant figured . . . I think you should know, if you don't already, that you have the reputation of one who drinks and carouses . . . My advice then is . . . that you do not consider the possibility of remaining on after this year.[253]

When McNair challenged Mitchell to substantiate the charges he had made against him, Mitchell denied having made them.

Govan was grateful that he was in New York during all of this, especially because most of the undergraduate students were as strongly against the theological faculty as he was for them, and dealing with them in class would have been painful and difficult. The School of Theology students, led by Duncan M. Gray, Jr. (later the Bishop of

Mississippi), were a different matter. On September 23, they voted on three resolutions: first, that they had "full confidence in the professional competence and integrity of the faculty": 59 yea, 2 nay, 15 abstentions; second, that they favored the admission of applicants . . . regardless of color": 71 yea, 0 nay, 6 abstentions; and third, that they were in "accord with the published position" of the faculty: 46 yea, 2 nay, 30 abstentions.[254] In other words, a majority backed the faculty and the rest showed their ambivalence by refusing to vote either yea or nay.

Then in October 1952, after four months of passionate debate, the theological faculty realized that the central Christian issues were never going to be resolved. On October 6, they formally resigned effective at the end of the academic year.

The news spread quickly, and the university had no alternative but to accept their resignations as of June. Once again, "The faculty, while roundly condemned on the mountain, received wide support within the Church and without." Nine Episcopal seminary heads came out against segregated theological education, and "the faculties of the three seminaries—Yale, Union, and General—also issued statements of support for the Sewanee faculty."[255] In New York, the Govans were among friends.

On November 13, thirteen of fifteen southern bishops of the Fourth Province, chaired by Bishop Edwin A. Penick, met to study the situation. Unanimously, they affirmed the Christian principle of desegregated education, but also accepted the need to consider "the time and circumstances of its application," and promised a report for the trustees of the university by January.[256] The trustees, however, voted by mail ballot not to meet again until June 4, 1953, thus purposely putting off the main issue regarding the admission of blacks to the School of Theology for another six months after the Penick Committee report was due. In the meantime, therefore, any new faculty recruited would have to accept their appointments with that issue unsettled. On February 9, McCrady announced the appointment of the first five faculty; they averaged sixty-two years of age, the youngest was fifty-two, and three of them came with no previous experience of teaching in a seminary.[257] They had obviously been hired because they supported the board of trustees' decision, not because they were the best teachers and scholars.

In response to this situation, John M. Krumm, Govan's friend and university chaplain at Columbia, fired off a critical letter to the editor of the Episcopal Church News, which said in part,

> In the opinion of many of us, no priest ought to accept any position on the faculty at Sewanee until the Penick Committee has reported and the response of the trustees to their recommendations has been ascertained.

> In the ranks of union labor, there is an ugly word for those who, in a strike situation, capitalize on the bravery and courage of others who fight for the workers' welfare. The word is "scab," and it has an uncomfortable relevance to the new situation at Sewanee.[258]

Pressure on the trustees continued to build. In February 1953, McCrady received a letter from the Very Reverend James A. Pike, then dean of the Cathedral of St. John the Divine in New York City, refusing an invitation to preach at the university's baccalaureate in June and to receive an honorary doctor of divinity degree. The letter was direct and full of irony. Pike wrote, "It is clear that the present faculty's stand is 'on the side of the angels' and I feel I must stand with them."[259] He also said that he had to refuse the degree because he could not accept "an honorary degree in White divinity."[260] This story hit the newspapers, and not only the Episcopal Church, but alumni and public opinion, forced the trustees to reconsider. "In response to Pike's withdrawal, the School of Theology Class of 1953, headed by Duncan Gray, wired him: "Congratulations on your defense of Christ's Church . . . . Faith can move Mountains.' They altered the current Eisenhower campaign buttons to read 'I like Pike.'[261] Most of the undergraduate seniors that year did not agree with him.

At their June 4, 1953 meeting, the trustees gave in and passed a resolution ordering the School of Theology admissions department "to give all applications for admission thereto sincere and thorough

consideration without regard to race."[262] A black student immediately
entered the summer graduate program, and another was accepted as
a junior in the fall.

For the theological faculty, their course was already set. They
reaffirmed their resignations and left for other seminaries. Several
went to Virginia, and some thirty-five students did the same. Bishop
Edmund P. Dandridge, the now retired bishop of Tennessee, who
had confirmed Tom in 1943, was appointed dean of the School of
Theology. As some wag put it, "It's hard to call a bishop a scab!"[263]

Tom and Jane were grateful to be in New York during this year of
conflict.

Kindred Spirits: Reinhold Niebuhr
and Jacques Barzun

Back at Union Seminary, one of the professional sadnesses of the
year was Reinhold Niebuhr's stroke in April 1952. He seemed to be
recovering during the spring, but his condition worsened during the
summer. He was unable to teach at all until the second semester, and
even then, taught on a radically reduced schedule.

Tom had particularly hoped to discuss with Niebuhr his most
recent book, *The Irony of American History*.[264] It had been written in
1951 during a time of Cold War frenzy when the whole intellectual
world, and in particular the university, was under attack from the
forces of extreme anti-Communism. President Truman had directed
that the hydrogen bomb be developed (1950), and had fired General
MacArthur (April, 1951). Alger Hiss had been found guilty of perjury
(January, 1950), and Joseph McCarthy had begun his witch hunts.
Niebuhr, in spite of his recent and increasingly bitter attacks on Soviet
Communism, had come under Justice Department and FBI
investigation for his long-term liberal stance toward the political left.
He had, after all, "belonged to, spoken for, or signed petitions for
countless left-leaning groups . . . [and was] declared subversive by the
Attorney General's office."[265]

In the midst of the furor, Niebuhr found the time and energy to
finish *The Irony of American History*, which Govan devoured as soon as it

was published. It focused precisely upon Tom's major concern: the meaning of American history and America's place in the world. Like Govan, Niebuhr was radically critical of Communism; like him also, Niebuhr was critical of American pride and self-righteousness but affirmed the pragmatic democracy of the United States because it divided and restrained power, while always seeking reform.

In his new book, however, Niebuhr insisted that the United States was more like the Soviet Union than Americans were willing to admit. Both countries believed they were seekers after justice, freedom, and the good society. Both sought efficient technical means of solving their respective nations' problems, but without the consent of the people. Both held the world hostage to the same hydrogen bomb.

Niebuhr did not see the United States as "the last best hope" of the world. He believed its history was proof of broken hopes and a denial of historical progress. He felt that the United States' record on freedom, equality and justice was, at best, mixed. The irony noted in the book's title lay in what he saw as the difference between American pretensions on one hand, and the realities of American history on the other. Niebuhr believed that this same irony was at the heart of the biblical message, which stated that human beings and institutions are responsible for their actions despite the inevitability of their sin and error. Life was also tragic, but not simply tragic, Niebuhr said, because we are not merely victims of historical determinism. Instead, we are free to influence history and pursue our destiny, and it is our freedom that makes human history ironic.[266] Both George Kennon and Arthur M. Schlesinger, Jr. were appreciative of this new, ironic interpretation of Niebuhrian "realism."[267]

Govan agreed but only up to a point. He applauded Niebuhr's rejection of the progressive model of American history held by many liberal and neo-Marxist American historians. He agreed that there was a lot more to American history than some form of economic determinism or some form of class conflict, like the conflict between enlightened liberals seeking reform versus privileged and well-to-do conservatives protecting the traditional status quo. He appreciated the sense of paradox and humor inherent in Niebuhr's concept of irony.

He rejected Niebuhr's close comparison of the United States with the Soviet Union. They were both great powers and were made up of human beings who shared a common human nature. But there, for Govan, the comparison ended. In structure, tradition, and spirit, Tom felt that there were fundamental and qualitative differences between the two countries. Marxist ideology, for example, insisted that human thoughts and behavior are determined by our physical context; American ideology insisted on personal freedom and moral responsibility.

He also rejected Niebuhr's tendency to drain off from American history any enduring or universal positive meaning for the world. This was, after all, the meaning for which Govan saw himself as a spokesman: the biblical meaning grounded in humility but abounding in hope that we can and must make progress in pursuing freedom, justice and equality, but when we fail, as we will, we are forgiven and charged with trying again and again. Govan saw in Niebuhr's view, by comparison, a despair that he felt was unworthy of a Christian. He longed to talk at length with Niebuhr about it.

The chance to do so did not come until the second semester beginning in February 1953, in a graduate seminar in social ethics. Niebuhr was struggling with a partly paralyzed left arm and slower, slightly slurred speech, which frustrated him because his mind was as quick and sharp as ever. His thoughts and ideas came flooding out faster than he was able to express them. But it was his lack of energy and resulting sense of powerlessness that upset him most and contributed to occasional bouts with depression. Although he was now more dependent upon his wife, Ursula, he was still actively embroiled in public affairs. Worried that Joseph McCarthy would gain a monopoly on the anti-Communist issue, he urged the death penalty for the Rosenbergs who had allegedly been spying for the Soviets. He even accused some of his left-leaning fellow Christians of being "fellow travelers."

Govan was disappointed by his lack of time with Niebuhr. This man was one of the major influences in his life, in his return to Christianity as a mature man and in his newfound biblical understanding of history as a mature historian. His debt to Niebuhr was huge, but it had all been secondhand through Niebuhr's books. Govan had clearly hoped to spend personal and quality time with his mentor. That he was largely denied this opportunity after many years of anticipation was a deep loss.

Happily, this was not the case with Jacques Barzun at Columbia. Barzun was at the height of his powers as a professor of nineteenth- and twentieth-century European history and culture. With eight books and twenty years of teaching behind him, he was not only a historian but also a social critic whose range covered virtually every facet of civilization. He was the enemy of specialization of the curriculum into a myriad of unrelated departments. This he felt tended to turn the university into a collection of professional schools. He also warned against the domination of all areas of knowledge by science. "The mind encloses science," he said, "not the other way around."[268] Govan was aware of Barzun's stature as a scholar through his books, which had covered such topics as race, freedom and the democratic experience, and the nineteenth-century Romanticists and Pragmatists, and higher education; and the false determinism of Darwin in natural history and of Marx in human history. He was eager to discuss these topics with Barzun. As luck would have it, that very year Barzun was working on a critical appreciation of American life, culture, and history, to be published under the title, *God's Country and Mine, A Declaration of Love Spiced with a Few Harsh Words.*[269]

Barzun's core convictions shine through the finished book, and it is clear that Govan shared them all. "Our minds," said Barzun, "should be able to hold two opposite ideas and use them both at once." To do so "strengthens judgement and gives action a surer touch. This principle secures the very point of government-by-discussion."[270] Govan agreed, and would add only that this principle validates government, whose powers are divided and limited by checks and balances. So, "contradictions co-exist and make valid claims that cannot be dismissed." To Govan, this was the very nature of truth and a key to freedom. He agreed with Barzun that too often people hide from contradictions and enter into what Barzun called "a cycle of illusion, disillusion and despair; which makes us embrace St. Thomas after Karl Marx, or nudism after Victorian petticoats; which replaces foolish sentiment with tawdry sex, and battle-and-king history with formless social studies; behaving in each phrase as abstractionists committed to a so-called idea instead of pragmatists keeping an eye on the ball."[271] It is better to be realistic from the start than disillusioned idealists.

Of reform Barzun said, "It consists in two parts. One is to keep pace with changing fact so as to conserve what we think good. The other is to spread, to generalize, whatever gains we make . . . . A social good cannot remain a good, it will fester, unless it is distributed as widely as possible. This is the meaning of equality—a deliberate undertaking to behave as impartially as we know how towards all men, not a silly and impossible measurement of their desserts."[272] Govan heartily agreed.

Barzun believed that America " . . . is the result of a religious, not a moral idea, if by moral we mean dividing sheep from goats and what we mean by religion is the inclusive fatherhood of God. . . . For us 'the people' means everybody . . . . [That] distinguishes us historically." Yet Barzun held that the moral attitude of criticizing and condemning corruption and evil is also necessary. "The thing condemned still fills a function and will need some sort of replacement. So, for example, we 'houseclean' our city political machines, we do not burn down the house."[273] Again, Govan agreed.

Barzun explained that he had been forced to give up orthodox Christian faith because of the narrow sectarianism of the churches which, he felt, excluded rather than included, condemned rather than forgave, was rigid rather than flexible, and rejected paradox and irony in the name of true doctrine.[274] Govan surely responded that it was for all of those same reasons that he was an Episcopalian. Whatever their theological differences, they shared the same spirit. Govan might have emphasized the universality of sin, while Barzun emphasized the responsibility of people to fashion their own lives, but they would have also accepted the other's view as also true. They could learn from each other.

10

"The Liberal and Conservative Traditions in the United States"

Unless freedom and equality are universal, unless all possess it by right, then none do.

Thomas P. Govan

During the spring of 1953 in New York, Govan had been preparing an address, "The Liberal and Conservative Traditions in the United States" (see Appendix 2). This address summarized his fundamental convictions about American history that had been forming over the previous decade. He was discussing many of the ideas with Barzun, and possibly with Niebuhr, but wanted to try them out in lecture form on a wide group of historians. Columbia University and the University of Virginia history departments responded with invitations for Govan to speak. He was delighted to accept.

In his lecture, Govan tried to correct what he considered to be a false understanding of the liberal and conservative traditions in the United States. The misunderstanding, he believed, was the result of myths about Thomas Jefferson representing the liberal tradition, and Alexander Hamilton representing the conservative tradition. These myths had been derived over the years, he insisted, from poets, philosophers, politicians, and especially from Progressive historians,

154

who had falsely used the two men as symbols of antagonistic class, economic, and sectional interests.

Jefferson, the "liberal," had become the symbol of the South, the West, the good rural life of agriculture and the frontier, and he was almost universally considered spokesman for freedom, equality, and democracy. Hamilton, the "conservative," by contrast, had become the evil symbol of urban, industrial and exploitative capitalism in the Northeast, the representative of aristocracy and authoritarianism. The differences were understood to be sectional, economic, and matters of class: South and West versus North and East; agrarian versus industrial and capitalist; rural versus urban; and democratic versus aristocratic.

This interpretation was based upon the false assumption that materialistic circumstances determine people's interests and behavior, and Govan responded to it exactly as he had ten years before in writing about the Civil War.[275] While not denying the existence of the materially based influences and interests, Govan insisted they were not the most important factors. The fact was, he said, that quite independent of these interests, people freely held ideas and beliefs, and it was these ideas and beliefs that motivated and guided their behavior. So, the real differences between Jefferson and Hamilton and the two traditions they represented, liberal and conservative, lay in their beliefs and ideas, in different political, philosophical, moral, and theological points of view, not in material circumstances.

Jefferson was the agnostic, rationalist scientist; Hamilton the brilliant, believing Christian pragmatist. Jefferson was the strict moralist, who divided people into good or evil camps; Hamilton was the humble moralist who believed that all people including himself were a mixture of the two. Politically, the liberals believed human beings were naturally good and therefore, they sought freedom without restraint for both individuals and groups. Conservatives, on the other hand, believed there could be no freedom for either individuals or groups without restraints. The universality of self-interest made restraints necessary. Freedom therefore required a strong federal government. However, government itself needed the restraints of a division of power and a reasonable balance of power (checks and balances). Govan said further that the liberal ideology, if followed, did not lead to freedom but to anarchy and then, in reaction, to totalitarianism. The conservative understanding led to moderate governments that could nourish true freedom.

Govan showed how historians and others since have misinterpreted Jefferson and Hamilton. The essay collection, *I'll Take My Stand*, published in 1930, was the perfect example of the kind of interpretation Govan opposed.[276] The scholars who wrote this series of essays contrasted the southern agrarian culture, for which they mourned, with the northern industrial urban culture, which they despised. Govan reminded these men that both North and South shared common European roots that made their similarities far greater than their differences. Historians Frederick Jackson Turner and Walter Webb argued that American freedom and democracy were actually produced by the rural and agricultural life of the American "frontier." Again, Govan argued that there were more similarities between the East and West than differences. He claimed that the real differences in economic interests were not between sections of the country anyway, but were within all of them—between those in all sections whose interests were in domestic markets and those exporters whose interests were overseas. Protective tariffs benefited the former, open markets the latter.

Morison and Commager's *The Growth of the American Republic*,[277] a two-volume American history textbook, first published in 1953 and studied by the next three generations of high school seniors and college freshmen, made precisely the mistake Govan was concerned about. They followed perfectly the myth about the liberal Jefferson and the conservative Hamilton, teaching that the real differences between the traditions were matters of economic, class, and sectional interests.[278] According to Govan, Morison and Commager were also insensitive about race: for example, beginning a chapter on the African-Americans in America, "And as for Sambo . . ." and then proceeded with their discussion.[279] Historian Charles Beard and literary critic Vernon L. Parrington also interpreted American history in economic, class and sectional terms as a conflict between honest southern and western agrarians and corrupt eastern industrialists and bankers.

Govan, on the contrary, argued that all of these liberals reduced political and moral conflicts to materialistic terms. To him, slavery, for example, was the real cause of the Civil War, as a moral, not an economic issue.[280]

This conclusion was of vastly more than incidental importance to Govan. While recognizing that Beard, Turner, Parrington, and Webb had been challenged and found wanting, Govan was deeply concerned that

> No one has challenged the whole corpus of their theoretical structure, the naive economic determinism that each of them, like the agrarians and new-conservatives, almost uncritically accepts, and their determination to ignore as unworthy of attention, the moral, the metaphysical, the theological debates about the meaning of freedom and equality that have constituted so important a part of their American history . . . .

> The important sources of division have actually been, first, the proper role of the nation in its relation with the states and individual citizens, and second the position of the Negro in the national society. The first of these debates is predominantly political, the second predominantly moral, but the majority of American historians have followed their teachers, Parrington, Turner, Webb, and Beard, by discussing the political differences as if they were moral, and dismiss the moral demand for freedom and equality of the Negro as a disguise for selfish and sectional economic ambitions . . . . [They too easily assumed] that their freedom and equality require the . . . enforced subordination of others and forget that unless freedom and equality are universal, unless all [people] possess it by right, then none do. The principles enunciated in the Declaration of Independence are not sentimental ideals. They are moral and

metaphysical truths rooted deep in human experience, and if they are neglected or obscured, the United States will follow the path of destruction through tyranny that so many other nations have taken.[281]

The essay, "The Liberal and Conservative Traditions in the United States," delivered in the spring of 1953, is in Appendices.

Tom had sent a copy of the essay to Jacques Barzun before going to Virginia to give his lecture. He included a letter, which read in part, "I want to talk all of these matters [the meaning of the terms 'liberal and conservative'] out with you because I have been trying to formulate them for myself in the backwoods [i.e., Sewanee] without opportunity for effective criticism, and they run all through my book on Biddle."[282]

Barzun responded to Govan while he was in Virginia by sending him an offprint article of his own on the same subject. It was waiting for Govan when he returned to New York. Govan had obviously had a good time at the University of Virginia and was pleased with the way his lecture was received. He was equally pleased and energized by Barzun's response to it. He wrote Barzun immediately on March 30, 1953:

> Your off-print was here when I returned last evening from Mr. Jefferson's university where I had given my paper on Liberalism and Conservatism to this History Club. [Govan referred to the Virginia history department as a club.] I am still full of it consequently and I cannot wait until I next see you to carry on at least one side of the conversation.[283]

Govan went on to say that he was surprised by Barzun's article, in particular, by some of the positive things Barzun had said about neo-classicism in relation to romanticism. This was a reference to the old liberal versus conservative debate, but now clothed in philosophical terms. Classicism was represented by Plato and Aristotle from the classical period of Western thought. Neo-classicism was simply a modern form of the same view: the belief that "human reason is the source of all human vitality and creativity."[284] Today, we might also call such persons "idealists" or "rationalists." Govan equated "neo-classicism with liberalism and . . . reactionism," meaning that liberalism was rational, logical, tended to be rigid, and was bereft of feeling.

By contrast, romanticism emphasized the natural impulses of the heart (spirit) and the body, and was full of feeling. Govan told Barzun that in his own mind he "had virtually equated romanticism with conservatism." Govan went on to agree with Barzun in praise of "romantic-conservative" thinkers in the West, like St. Augustine, St. Paul, Luther, Calvin, Edmund Burke, and Sir Walter Scott.

Just the day before, March 29, 1953, Einstein had made his famous statement that he could not "believe that God plays dice with the cosmos" and "that the theory of discontinuity and uncertainty, of the duality of particle and wave, and of a universe not governed by cause and effect, is an incomplete theory, and that eventually laws will be found showing a continuous, non-dualistic universe, governed by immutable laws, in which individual events are predictable."[285] By quoting Einstein at this length, Tom meant that the theory of uncertainty is incomplete precisely because the human mind is human and not divine; it is limited and therefore knowledge is limited and incomplete. Govan saw in Einstein's abhorrence of "discontinuity and uncertainty," and in the yearning for a deterministic universe "governed by cause and effect"[286] . . . a hidden (or not so hidden) idolatry. Einstein believed that God ought to be playing, not dice with His universe, but by Einstein's rules.

What he did say to Barzun about Einstein was that "this attempted return to Newtonian harmony and to the Medieval realists, particularly St. Thomas," seemed to him to be "neo-classicism" and that the conservative is always the critic of such attempts at system, "rational, non-contradictory system."

> The God of St. Paul, St. Augustine, and Luther—[that is]
> the transcendent harmony which has been revealed
> without removing the disharmony and incongruities of
> life and the universe—is almost necessary for conservative

critiques of the attempts to build a system of absolute truth in this life because they are idolatrous. Luther, in this view, is the conservative during the Reformation, rejecting alike the usurped certainties either of Pope or Council and the Scriptural certainties of Calvin, and never himself formulating a system which gave a competing certainty. So it is the liberal (in the nineteenth-century sense) who seeks certainty and rational system, laws that explain events, and it is the conservative in that sense who rejects systems and certainty as idols.[287]

The two men had also been discussing "human nature," Barzun affirming human goodness and Govan affirming human limitation and sin. "We have to retain the assumption that men are good," wrote Barzun, "for the simple reason that if we assume the reverse, we encourage the 'cops and robbers' notion of society [good guys versus bad guys], and every kind of social work [which recognizes imperfection and the potential for good in us all] becomes useless from the start."[288]

Govan countered Barzun by saying that:

> The danger in the assumption that men are good, it seems to me is that we will assume that cops are virtuous . . . [when in fact] cops are far more dangerous to freedom than robbers. The conservative suspicion of all men has its value not in connection with the wicked, the ignorant, or the poor, but with the rich, the intelligent, and the righteous. They are the ones with the power and greatness but interpret it as theirs alone, while the poor, the wicked, and the ignorant need to be shown something other than man's misery and wretchedness.[289]

Barzun replied warmly:

> Thank you for your good letter. I had no idea you'd fire back so soon, but since you say you'd been converting

the Jeffersonians down there by the winding wall [in
Virginia], I can understand why you felt in the mood for
a clean sweep!

As I see it at the moment, there are two things that need
clearing up—terms and psychology.[290]

The terms to be cleared up were "liberal" and "conservative" and
the psychology implied in each. The question that needed to be
discussed, continued Barzun, was the following:

What theory of government one adopts in order to arrive
at a point which . . . that theory desires as a goal, it being
understood that no perfection, but only an approximation,
is possible. Terms and psychology, then, you and I must
find time to discuss.[291]

It is certain that the two men did find time to discuss these issues.
Barzun truly made the year in New York for Govan; it was he who had the
breadth of cultural knowledge, European as well as American, that Govan
so deeply needed to tap and from which he needed criticism.

Spring 1953

Govan had a happy and fulfilling year in New York, but only for
one year—his grant money would soon end. His decision whether or
not to return to Sewanee was placed on hold because of the trustees'
delay in settling the desegregation issue. Tom needed to be settled
in some position. Throughout the year, he had been writing letters to
friends in history departments around the country about the possibility
of a visiting professorship. Any visiting professorship might develop
into what he needed most—a full professorship in a first-rate history
department. Tom's first offer was for the summer only at the University
of Virginia. He immediately accepted because, among other reasons,
it was close to the Library of Congress in Washington, D.C., where he
could continue his research on Nicholas Biddle.

In January 1953, he received an invitation from an old friend, Frederick C. Cole, academic dean at Tulane University in New Orleans, for a one-year visiting professorship to temporarily replace William R. Hogan. Again, Govan accepted immediately in spite of the fact that it would end his research on Nicholas Biddle for the time being. Even though the pay was small, this would give him a year's financial security. Later in the spring, Vice-Chancellor Edward McCrady called to ask if or when Tom was returning to Sewanee. Govan told him that he had already accepted a one-year appointment to Tulane, and that he had not made up his mind about returning to Sewanee.

Shortly after the Sewanee trustees' June 4, 1953 vote overturning their previous decision, Tom received a letter from a young English historian, David Underdown, who had just earned his doctorate at Exeter College, Oxford, asking about Sewanee. He had been interviewed for a position in the history department, and liked the sound of the department, but was worried that he would be coming into a university that was still segregated. Tom was pleased by the sensitivity of the young man and immediately wrote him back that he thought it would be fine if he took the job: the trustees had reversed themselves. He added, "You are a historian of seventeenth century England, and it would be good for you to experience at first hand some of the bigotry that was constant in that period and was present in Tennessee."[292] Underdown thought it was a wonderful letter, took the job, and had eleven good years teaching at Sewanee.

Tom's situation was frighteningly temporary, although he was grateful for the appointment. In his heart, he had resigned from the University of the South, which meant he had given up tenure, salary, and security. He knew it would not be easy to find another permanent position because he had not yet published a book, and because, as a full professor, he knew he could not call for full professor pay. His biography of Biddle was still in process. But the emotional tug of Sewanee was now gone. The Govans proceeded on faith and hope with their integrity intact.

Even so, the year 1952-1953 in New York was a wonderful rest and a profoundly nourishing and healing time for Tom. It was refreshed and ready that he and Jane left the University of Virginia in September, when summer school was over, and drove to their new home at 1316 Calhoun Street in New Orleans, and Tom began as adjunct professor of history at Tulane.

PART II

A New Birth
of Freedom

11

Painful Memories and Uncertain Prospects

I was too sensitive in regard to Sewanee to feel easy or free in Episcopal associations.

Thomas P. Govan

Grateful to Fred C. Cole, the academic dean, for his appointment at Tulane University and now free of the administrative responsibilities he had had at Sewanee, Tom plunged into teaching and advising graduate students. As he expected, his classes were hard going because the students, especially the undergraduates, were largely southern Jeffersonian "states' righters" and hostile to his view on American history. He needed Jane's support and comfort and happily received both in full measure. The shared pain of the Sewanee experience had drawn them together; their shared delight in New York had drawn them closer still. Now in New Orleans, they shared the worry over a temporary one year adjunct teaching job, the prospect of a peripatetic future, and very little money. But they were together, probably as never before.

Tulane is an urban university near the heart of the old city of New Orleans and next door to Loyola University. The city's culture and history, and its architecture and music are close at hand. The Govans found a small apartment within walking distance of the campus in a

167

mixed neighborhood of blacks and whites. Jane recalled, with more than a twinkle in her eye, that while Tom had a nice air-conditioned university office, she sweltered and was eaten up by chiggers in their small apartment.[293]

She missed the student contact she had had at Sewanee, and missed her New York friends and social life. Here in New Orleans, Tom would have his work, but she would have to find a new life. It would be dictated in part by her need to supplement Tom's small adjunct professor's salary. With her experience as a librarian in Sewanee, she soon landed a job in one of the best bookstores in the city. "One of the features of the store was two cats, Big Brother and Little Friend, who graced the shop window."[294] Jane still missed their dachshund, Judy, lost in the fire, so these two cats became her special friends. The job turned out to be a blessing and greatly satisfying to Jane. It made their lives in New Orleans economically viable.

One loss during this year was the Episcopal Church, which under normal circumstances they would have attended regularly, but could not. Tom later explained,

> I arrived in New Orleans at Tulane University in the fall of 1953 on a one-year appointment, I was too sensitive in regard to Sewanee to feel easy or free in Episcopal associations. Most of the people here, very rightly, have warm feelings, as I in part still have, towards the institution and place, and whenever informed that I had been there, they expected me to share in the enthusiasm. I would draw up and freeze, being unable to reply in their tone and unwilling to criticize and attack needlessly. My bitterness, my anger, and my sense of loss from Sewanee [was still very real].[295]

In self defense, Jane and Tom simply did not talk about the Episcopal Church, and stayed away from it. In effect this meant that they were cut off not only from many people who might have become friends, but from the Christian community which had been a major source of fulfillment in their lives.

By this time, at forty-six years, Tom had matured as a person and historian. It is clear that he was respected as a teacher and as a scholar. He was lecturing and being heard. He was writing reviews and articles, and they were being published.[296]

Rejecting "Sectionalism"

Tom was also a member of the central leadership of the Southern Historical Association of university history faculty. In 1951, C. Vann Woodward, then president of the association, had appointed him program chair for the 1952 annual meeting. Govan performed well and wrote up the proceedings of a successful meeting. Tom was not bashful about discussing his views, especially among friends, and clearly everyone on the association's executive committee knew what was on his mind. So it was no accident that he was asked to give one of the major addresses at the association's 1953 annual meeting in Jacksonville, Florida, from November 2nd to 4th. He chose the title, "Was the Old South Different?" He meant "different" from the new South and the rest of the country. Govan was going to be controversial. He

> . . . argued that slavery, rather than the incompatibility of capitalistic and agrarian economies, was the fundamental basis for the divisive feeling of sectionalism that culminated in secession and civil war. In accepting the results of that struggle, the restoration of the Union, and the ending of slavery, the South returned to its tradition and the concept of white supremacy which it shared with peoples of European origin.

This was his controversial point: North and South both agreed that blacks were inferior, and that they could be treated as such. In the South, they were denied the vote and confined to tenant farms. Only chattel slavery was denied. He said,

> The New South differed from the Old only as the latter part of the nineteenth century differed from the earlier

169

part. Most of the changes that occurred were merely
continuations of movements that began before 1860.
These alterations, in the main, reflect the economic and
intellectual revolutions in the world as a whole.[297]

He was controversial, but the session went smoothly and all present
were given cause to rethink their own views. The address was published
in *The Journal of Southern History*[298] and later in a book, *The Southerner as
American* by Charles G. Sellers, Jr. of Princeton University under the
title, "Americans Below the Potomac."[299]

"A New Birth of Freedom"—
What American History Is All About

During that first year at Tulane, Tom made a genuine effort to
finish the Biddle biography in spite of being so far away from the Library
of Congress. He knew a full-time full professorship depended upon his
publishing. By March, 1954, he had convinced himself that it was nearly
done and so began planning his next book. The new book would cover
the full sweep of American history and focus on the American attempt
to establish a social order that had as its principal purpose the
enlargement of human freedom—personal, political, and financial.
Govan applied for a $7000 grant for the next year, 1954-1955, from the
Ford Foundation's Fund for the Republic. He would call the book *A New
Birth of Freedom*, quoting from Lincoln's Gettysburg Address.

"The American Revolution," Tom wrote in his proposal, "had its
source in the Judeo-Christian tradition and the British development of
constitutional government." The Revolution "began in the eighteenth
century, but is still going on; and from the beginning there was a group
of political theorists who insisted that it and the traditions from which it
sprang were man's best hope, perhaps the only hope of establishing a
society which unites public strength with individual [freedom and]
security." Such a society was sometimes called "the American system."

"Beginning with Alexander Hamilton and continuing through
the administrations of James Monroe and John Quincy Adams, the
proponents of the American system of governmental direction,

support, and control of social and economic institutions and processes were in the ascendancy." They were Federalists who "acted upon the assumption that the United States was a single nation and that its citizens had complementary rather than conflicting interests. Their concern was the strength of the nation as a whole, which involved the protection and support of every individual, and the instrument they used was the national government (see Appendix 3).

The proponents understood also that human nature would make the achievement of their purposes very difficult. Alexander Hamilton at the Constitutional Convention had warned, "Give all power to the many [pure democracy], they will oppress the few. Give all power to the few [oligarchy] and they will oppress the many." Neither free individuals nor organized groups can be trusted with absolute power. Rather, "each must have power to defend themselves from the other;" that is, there must be a balance of power, if freedom is to be achieved.[300]

From the beginning "the intention of these traditional conservatives was misrepresented by their political opponents, who, motivated in part by ideology and in part by party interest, succeeded in defeating and reversing the whole [conservative] program under the guise of relieving the country from tyranny and exploitation." These "classical liberals" were most effectively represented by "Thomas Jefferson and his uncritical follower, Andrew Jackson. They believed that economic, social and political matters were controlled by natural laws with which men interfered at their peril, and that the government was best which governed least. They also believed that a pure democracy of the people would guarantee freedom for the people. They did not take into account, as the conservatives did, the power of self-interest and greed amongst ordinary people as well as the rich and powerful, which makes freedom so difficult to achieve.

"Their victory . . . was won in the name of the common people, but it opened the way for . . . exploitation and private tyranny" by individuals and groups. By the close of the nineteenth century, "the United States began to act [again] on the assumption that society could be free only when individual liberty was restrained and prevented from becoming despotic, while at the same time being protected and cherished."

"This return from anarchic individualism to a moderate program of social control" was resisted on the one hand by "the classical liberal (libertarians) who ignored the danger of the unrestrained individual," and on the other hand by the Marxian socialists who ignored the danger of the unrestrained state.

The conservatives remained aware of the hazards of both. "This middle position, however, has been valued and discussed less than its extreme opponents largely because of its very lack of certainty and finality" and because "it gives no promise of ultimate utopian harmony." It nevertheless "constitutes men's greatest hope of achieving a measure of security and freedom," because it is "an anti-deterministic, non-dogmatic, essentially pragmatic rather than positivist attitude." It "values both individual and collective action but remains aware of the dangers of both." Govan concluded his letter by saying "these conservatives relied upon older and more valid conceptions of . . . man and society."[301] By this he meant the biblical and English legal concepts that there can be no freedom or order without restraints.

This letter summarized Govan's view succinctly, but the book would not be written at this time. The work on the Biddle biography took much longer than he had hoped. He did not lose track of his ideas—they were later incorporated into a college text that he co-authored with his friends Forrest McDonald and Leslie E. Decker, finally published in 1972 under the title, *The Last Best Hope.*[302]

To Tom's distress, but not his surprise, no offers for a full professorship in American history appeared during that year, and by June 1954, he had not yet heard from the Ford Foundation. He appreciated Fred Cole's offer to extend his adjunct position at Tulane for a second year. The year would be his last at Tulane and then he would face an unknown future.

That is, except for one completely unexpected thing. The Episcopal Church called, asking if he might be interested in a full-time job working for the Church with university faculty. Tom immediately dismissed the idea. But soon he would change his mind.

12

Marking Time and Decision

I did not share [Govan's] religious views, although I respected them as I might respect a vegetarian's, but not a flat-worlder's.

Laura Roper

Summer Travels and New York: New Life in the Episcopal Church

For half the summer of 1953, Tom taught summer school at Tulane because they needed the money, but then they escaped the heat of New Orleans and headed North. Jane and Tom had several things in mind. The first was to check in with friends along the way, conspicuously avoiding Sewanee, about possible teaching jobs in the future. They also visited Tom's brothers, Jack and Roy, and their families in New Jersey, and then moved on to New York City and their old friends, Lee and Cora Louise Belford who happily took them in. Being in New York felt like coming home.

Tom and Lee talked about job prospects at NYU where Lee was head of the religion department. There were no openings in American history, at least for the present, but in the course of conversation, Lee and Tom discussed some interesting new developments in the life of the Episcopal Church nationally.

173

In 1947 the Episcopal Church was in the midst of a huge, new church-wide Christian education program to redress what was perceived to be the previous failures of the past sixty-some years since 1890. The Department of Christian Education had been created that year and funded under the leadership of the Reverend John Huess. The program immediately created The Church Teaching Series, six volumes published by the Seabury Press, covering the Bible, church history, theology, worship, ethics, and pastoral care. The books were hugely successful, selling more than 500,000 copies over the next twenty years.[303] Second, the Department developed an eleven-year curriculum for family and parish use with children. Third, it created a training program in Christian education for clergy and laity. Teams of three department members carried the program to all parts of the country, covering three quarters of the entire church. The program's focus was to integrate the insights of psychology about the learning process with the theological content being taught to bring about Christian conversion and change lives.[304]

The one area of education which was entirely absent from the program of the Department of Christian Education, however, was "college work," the work of college and university chaplains and their programs. Largely on the momentum generated by the Department, the General Convention created a new Division of College Work and placed it in the Home Department, not the Department of Christian Education because it considered the work primarily "missionary" rather than "educational."

College work was not new to the Episcopal Church. Before World War II there had been a number of full-time chaplaincies around the country, most of them in elite private universities such as those in the Ivy League. There had also been a number of part-time chaplaincies connected with parishes. The rationale for the work had been to protect youth nurtured in the church from what the church felt were the disillusioning influences of secular education. College students were seen by some as a crucial missionary field from which would come the future lay and clerical leadership of the church. At that time, the national church was not involved in supporting this work, so an independent organization, the Church Society for College Work, was formed for the purpose in 1930. This society raised money for the support of chaplains and lobbied the church on behalf of this "important mission field."

In the intervening years the number of chaplains had increased, but it was not until 1949, in connection with the church's Christian education program, though quite independent of it, that college work got its major new support. Roger Blanchard, later Bishop of Southern Ohio, was appointed director of the new Division of College Work, and was funded with a sizeable budget, much of it seed money for new chaplaincies. In a matter of ten years (1945-1955), the number of college chaplains tripled and the national budget rose into the hundreds of thousands of dollars. At its peak in the late 1950s, the department budget was over $1 million, and some 350 chaplains, over 100 of them full-time, were at work ministering to students.

Lee Belford told Tom that Blanchard also had another goal in mind. Clearly the faculty were at the heart of every college and university and had more influence on students than anyone else. Episcopal faculty were therefore better placed to be intellectual and religious interpreters to students than were the ordained chaplains who led worship. An adequate ministry to students called for a team of faculty working with every chaplain. There was also another need: faculty support for one another. The faculties and chaplains worked in an environment often hostile to religion, in which theological matters, on the whole, were dismissed as meaningless. The companionship and intellectual support of sympathetic fellow Christian peers was crucial. Govan's ears pricked up hearing this.

In 1952, just as Govan was leaving Sewanee, Thomas S.K. Scott-Craig, a philosophy professor at Dartmouth and a devout Episcopalian, was appointed the Executive Secretary for Faculty Work of the Church. Over the next three years, he traveled to every province of the church pleading the case of the chaplains and Episcopal faculty. He built a list of faculty, held meetings, and began the publication of the Faculty Papers (Christian apologetics papers interpreting and rationalizing the faith). Scott-Craig split his time between the road and his home in Hanover, New Hampshire, and spent only one or two days a month in New York City at headquarters.

Hearing this in 1953 was interesting to Tom, but academic. Belford, however, knew what he was doing talking with Tom. A year later this work would be anything but academic to Govan.

Vacation in Cotuit 1946

Tom with Franny Schwab

(left)Franny, Robert Hewick, and Jane
(right)Tom and Jane

176

Cotuit 1946

Tom and Jane

(left) Helen Brewer and Jane
(right) Tom

Friendships in Cotuit

Essential on the Govans' agenda that summer was a visit to Cotuit on Cape Cod with the Ropers and Franny Schwab. They had visited Cotuit almost every summer since 1946. Their friendships had deepened, were full of fun, and had the advantage of being

177

completely unentangled with the rest of their lives. They were just friends and completely mutual about it. Laura remembered a crazy ride with the Govans and Franny in the Ropers' "new bright-red convertible Chevy—with an irrepressible horn that went off spontaneously and scared the passengers more than anyone else on the road;" and a "memorably hospitable weekend in Cotuit with the Govans that ended with nothing left to drink but half a bottle of dry vermouth."[305]

For all of their closeness and common mind, there was one area over which they good-naturedly disagreed, and that was religion. Laura remembers "one night in Cotuit, when the Govans were staying with [them], Tom and I got into a hot argument over I forget what religious matter. He was a devout believer and I was an incurable skeptic. We hammered away at each other and finally, to clinch his argument, Tom shouted, 'It's right there in the Bible!' I said, 'Oh Tom, this argument's useless. We're at loggerheads." Jane piped up, 'You're not at loggerheads, you are loggerheads!' From then on Tom was known affectionately as 'old loggerhead.'"[306] That tag was a signal to him to drop the theology, and he graciously responded.

Another personal connection in Cotuit was Mack Schwab, Franny's brother. Schwab and Crosby Roper had been classmates at Harvard in 1931. According to Laura, they had met by chance as freshmen "moping along the Charles River" on their first night in college. They became lifelong friends. After college, Mack became a fervent Communist, to the disgust of his family. He was a G.I. during the war, stuck in Easter Island where he met a nurse, a lieutenant named Connie, whom he married after the war.

Tom liked Mack, despite his radical politics. He was always physically active, as Tom was not, ran in the District of Columbia marathon, played tennis into his 70s, taught Swedish walking which Tom had never heard of, and baked bread.

His primary interest was "in movies, even before they were taken seriously as anything but entertainment, and he became an accomplished photographer."[307] He worked all of his life in film and eventually taught in Oregon, worked for the Oregon Educational and Public Broadcast Services (OEPBS), finally as a producer-director of KOAC-TV in Eugene.[308] No doubt he and Tom argued politics, economics, and maybe religion. As the years passed, however, Mack's politics moderated considerably, a process to which Tom may have contributed, but never fully changed.

Twenty years later in 1974-1975, Mack was instrumental in getting Tom and his message on TV during the national bicentennial (see Chapter 28). He produced, directed and illustrated a twenty-lecture course on the meaning of American history, which turned out to be one of Govan's finest achievements.

The Govans returned to Tulane for the beginning of classes shortly after Labor Day.

The Challenge of the Church

In the spring of 1955, Scott-Craig's contract as Executive Secretary for Faculty Work was to expire and by mutual consent he returned to teaching. In December 1954, Roger Blanchard began putting out feelers for the names of potential successors for Scott-Craig. Govan's name came across his desk almost immediately. He was suggested by Scott-Craig, who had heard about Govan from Lee Belford at NYU and Craighill Brown, the former dean of the seminary, and from Richard Wilmer, former dean of the chapel at the University of the South. In addition, several members of the Church Society for College Work and the National Commission for College Work either knew Govan personally or knew about him. Govan had strong support from Albert T. Mollegen, professor of New Testament and Christian Apologetics at Virginia Theological Seminary, one of the most influential voices in the church.

All of those supporting Tom for the job did so because of his basic personal and theological stance as a Christian. There were several facets to that stance. First, like most faculty, he was a layman. Second, he was a university professor. Third, because he had not grown up in the Church and had become an adult member by choice rather than by habit. He had found his way into the faith by thinking and feeling, not inheriting it. Fourth, he saw religion as one aspect of the multi-faceted but unified and mysterious creation of God. Tom saw no conflict between religion and other academic disciplines or fields of knowledge. Religion was not, as was so often claimed in the academy, the enemy of free inquiry. Properly understood, it was, rather, the essential friend of all the other disciplines which reminded them all that their knowledge was partial, incomplete and never final.

Fifth, too many Episcopalians in the university had "built a wall in their heads between their religion and their professional work." Their religion was for Sunday, and covered issues of personal relations and ultimate meaning, but had practically no impact upon their professional thought, research, teaching or life. Most of them approved of this compartmentalization.

So from the Episcopal Church's view, Tom would be perfect for the job. For Tom, a lot of questions remained. He wanted a full professorship in early American history, but he was not going to get one until he had published his Biddle biography. That could not be finished without time off to complete the work. The dilemma remained.

In February 1955, church representatives, clergy and lay of the Episcopal dioceses of the South, the Fourth Province of the Episcopal Church, met in New Orleans. Roger Blanchard attended, as he did all provincial meetings, but this time he was present especially to meet and talk with Govan. Their conversations were productive. Tom had known about the job since his conversation the previous summer with Lee Belford, and he was, he admitted, very interested. But there was the problem of long-term security in the history profession which depended upon his publishing Biddle and for that he needed time. Blanchard assured Govan that continuing to be a historian would be part of his job. He encouraged Govan's continued participation in various historical associations, his lecturing, his writing of reviews and articles, and especially his completion of the Biddle biography.

Yes, there would be time for that too, but he wanted Tom to know that he was the Division of College Work's first choice for the job. That did it! Blanchard was offering him a chance to do important work and a chance to work on his book. Govan told Blanchard how ready he felt for work in a theologically-oriented setting for a change. Tom liked Blanchard and knew he could work with him. It was settled. He was ready to take the job if offered it and he said so.

Unlike Scott-Craig, Govan would move to New York and would have his office at headquarters at 281 Park Avenue South. When Govan asked Blanchard how he envisioned the job in practical terms, what it would entail, and what its direction should be, Blanchard's answer was, "We are hiring you to figure that out." They ended their meeting with a discussion of salary, length of contract (Govan insisted upon a minimum of three years, or if he proved "not to be suitable for the place," until he could find another job), benefits, and moving expenses. The security the Govans needed was now established.

The job offer was made official in March 1955. It included a salary of $7,500 without housing, but with moving expenses and a partial pension plan cost. The letter extended an invitation for Govan to attend an April meeting of the National Commission on College Work to be held in Estes Park, Colorado.[309]

Govan accepted on the same day he received the offer, and the National Council of the Episcopal Church confirmed his appointment to begin August 1, 1955.

13

A New Job and New Thoughts

Human knowledge, whenever it is taken as final, ends in deterministic doctrines, denials of human freedom, and all such determinisms, whether they be found in religion, history, politics, philosophy, ethics, chemistry, biology, or elsewhere must be denounced by the Christian as false.

Thomas P. Govan

Plunging In

In early September 1955, the Govans moved from New Orleans to New York City into an apartment at 81 Bedford Street in Greenwich Village, not far from NYU. Tom took on his new job as Executive Secretary for Faculty Work of the Episcopal Church. Suddenly here he was, in a brand new teaching role at the Episcopal headquarters, in the great city that he loved, and only a subway ride away from Union Seminary. He found the change exhilarating.

Tom was superbly prepared for his new job as both a theologian and a historian. For better and worse, he had known the Episcopal Church for some fourteen years, and he had taught American history for sixteen years, mostly at the University of the South, but also at Emory, Chattanooga, Virginia, and Tulane. He was thoroughly acquainted with many colleges and universities. Well aware that taking this job would mean returning to academia sometime later at a full professor's salary would be difficult, he nevertheless rejoiced in his new situation.

Jane was not so sure. She was feeling uprooted again and still without a clear future. How would Tom do in his new job? Would he be able to finish Biddle? When would he get the permanent full-time professor's position that he deserved and would give her the security she needed? On the other hand, she was deeply grateful for the understanding they had with the Episcopal Church which guaranteed Tom's position until he found a "suitable position," and that meant a full professor's position with salary and tenure. She was thrilled to be back in New York with all of its cultural richness. She would renew her passion for art in the city's museums. The Belfords, Lee and Cora Louise, were waiting for them. Finally, they were ready to find a new dachshund, a new "Judy" to be their companion.

Tom was immediately swallowed up by the job. Every morning he was at Episcopal Church Headquarters at 281 Second Avenue South by 8:00 o'clock for Morning Prayers and a staff meeting. From the beginning, Tom had a special sense of mission. He was convinced that the Anglican tradition held the key to the puzzle of how unity and freedom can be achieved among human beings in the nation and the church. He felt called to spread the word.

He began with very little sense of how his convictions could best be put into programmatic form beyond that created by Scott-Craig. He knew that his primary job at first was to listen, first to the Division of College Work and then to the faculty and administrators with whose ministry he was charged. He quickly learned that the focus of the division was upon "student work"—the chaplains and Episcopal students organized in Canterbury Associations—not faculty. He was grateful that the emphasis of the College Work staff was no longer on the old idea of the church as a "home away from home," but was being replaced by the concept of the church as a mission to provide Christian community and gain converts. From the start, Govan's vision was far broader than that. He believed that the church's focus should be upon a ministry that served the whole university: faculty administration, staff, and board of trustees as well as students. He also believed that the ministry was to be carried out not by chaplains alone and women assistant chaplains,[310] but by every baptized person in the university. He began gently suggesting these beliefs in the office.

In his first months on the job, Tom's vision led him to set up discussions on issues with as many faculty members, administrators, and chaplains as possible. In consultation with Blanchard and his assistant Louise Gehan, Govan planned a series of regional conferences, one in each of the eight provinces of the Episcopal Church,[311] at which he would speak and discussion would follow. His message—the story of his own intellectual and religious journey, which he called "Apologia Pro Vita Sua"—was fundamentally personal (see Appendix 1). That address startled and stimulated almost everyone who heard it. Here was not only a historian, but a man well-read in philosophy and theology, a committed spirit, and a warm person who was completely open in sharing his experience and his journey into faith. Through these conferences, Tom made many friends, provided genuine encouragement to many, and began the formation of a network of people around the country with whom he would work over the next five years.

That winter Tom also addressed groups of faculty and solicited papers from them for discussion. A paper entitled "The Stance of the Church in the University," written by a chaplain, stated that a "church is a holy institution with its own peculiar interests and concerns [i.e., for religion] that has relations with other institutions such as the [secular] university."[312] In front of a room full of colleagues, Govan questioned this identification asking, "Is the church not a body, an organism, whose members are united by the acknowledgment that the Lord whom they worship . . . is the Creator and Lord of all institutions . . . including the churches and the university?"[313] He stressed that Christians are members of both, agreeing that the churches as institutions have a rightful and useful role. But, he also asked, "are they [the churches] and the work they do any more intrinsically holy than the university and that which it does?"[314] Then, out of his own bitter experience at Sewanee, he said, "Where I have learned about hate, fear, and cruelty and the destruction these evils can cause is in my relations within the churches with those, like me, who call themselves Christians. It is there I have known, not theoretically, that when I would do good, I do evil, and have been aware of the continued need for me to say truly, 'Lord have mercy.'"[315]

A hush filled the room.

Tom continued. "The churches are not exempt from the evils of the world, nor from its goodness, but they are charged with the task of calling each, the evil and the good, by its true name, first within their own institutional life . . . and then in the rest of the world. They also have the responsibility of making their own members and others aware of the importance and complexity of these moral problems and of the dangerous tendency of all [of us] to seek simple and clear solutions and judgments." He went on to state that the Christian task is to be humble and to witness in the church, and out of it, to the Lord of all "as our redeemer and judge and as the source of all life and light."[316]

Tom also went on to discuss the way the doctrine of the Trinity (Father, Son, and Holy Spirit) was a model for good teaching and true education. Tom's experience was that too often teaching was the process of a knowledgeable teacher pouring knowledge into the minds of passive students; or worse, forcing it into the minds of resistant students. The assumption underlying Govan's analogy between the Trinity and teaching was that all communication is trinitarian, that is, a three-stage process. There is always a sender, a means of communication, and a receiver, and all three elements are dynamically related. If any one of the elements is left out, the whole process is broken. It is a trinity of elements in the unity of one process. In the Christian Trinity, God is the sender, Jesus is the means of communication, and people, inspired by the Holy Spirit, are the receivers.

Tom explained that like the Trinity, teaching is a unified, dynamic process. If the teacher does not have the knowledge or the spirit of the subject, if the students are not caught by the subject, the teacher and their spirit, then education does not take place. Govan said to teachers, "Remember that under God you are part of a trinity and your teaching will be deeper and better."

Govan proposed a number of possible reforms which could help in the incorporation of this trinitarian view of teaching: separate the teaching and the examining functions; give up rigidly-defined courses; and abandon the aim and practice of general education courses which "try to teach all students everything." General education, he believed, was wrong in principle because it was dictatorial: the teacher knows best.

In conclusion, Govan spoke out of his experience, described so fully in his "Apologia," of trying to be a scientist, a cool observer of facts. He had learned that this kind of teaching was a form of idolatry. The teacher plays God by claiming to have the truth, lacking respect for the ambiguity and complexity and incompleteness of truth, by claiming superiority to students, failing to respect them as persons and seekers; by claiming authority, in other words, which ultimately is God's alone. Facts are slippery, complicated, and changeable. Students are human beings: bright, creative, with minds of their own. Facts and students had humbled Govan as a teacher and taught him he was "merely a man." No longer could he be the "objective judge" of "faceless names in a gradebook," but a fellow seeker, always ahead of his students, and engaged with them in a living encounter with the material.[317]

Tom also called a group of college and university presidents and deans that year to discuss the church's work. He critiqued the university and presented the positive relevance of the Christian faith to its many conflicts and problems. In particular, Tom addressed the doctrine of original sin and the great commandment to love God and neighbor as oneself. He received mixed reviews on the paper, which for some was too prophetic and not practical enough.

In the spring of 1956, at the urging of Roger Blanchard, Tom presented an expanded version of that paper as his report to the National Commission for College Work, the advisory group headed by Bishop John E. Hines of Texas, to whom he was accountable. In large part, Govan's program during that first year was listening to and discussing with faculty and students. Tom published an occasional issue of Faculty Papers, featuring the writings of scholars and teachers on various aspects of the relation between doctrines of the Christian faith and the academic disciplines. He also continued to publish Faculty Notes regularly; and he extended ecumenical cooperation to the faculty Christian Fellowship sponsored by the National Council of Churches and its excellent journal, *The Christian Scholar.*

"Free To Be Merely A Man"

Through that first winter of Govan's work for the church, he labored on an essay that drew together his theological and historical convictions in one reasoned statement. He had a message for the Episcopal Church, particularly for Episcopal faculty, and he wanted it to be as clear and powerful as possible. As a theologically informed historian, he wrote from a single perspective that he believed had found expression in the English Reformation, the long English "revolution," which created a constitutional monarchy, and the American Revolution. That perspective assumed that the secular and religious spheres could not be separated because religious history is essentially a part of general history. Govan believed that God is God of all of history, not just some religious part thereof, and that without the religious perspective all of history loses its meaning. He hoped the essay would be published as the first Faculty Paper of his administration. He knew fundamentally what he wanted to say, but it was a struggle to work it out. The paper went through several readings and revisions.

The first version contrasted the Marxist approach to freedom and justice with that of England and the United States. (Marxists believed in the perfectibility of humans and of society but ended in dictatorship and oppression.) England and the United States did not so believe and achieved partial freedom and justice. The heart of Govan's argument concerned why this was so.

A second draft entitled, "The Historian and Human Rights," was written as a lecture and presented to a gathering of American historians. Govan delved directly into human rights: freedom of the individual, the freedom and equality of human beings, and the freedom under the rule of law. He showed how demonic each of those rights could become without the checks of the other two. The idea of the free individual, for example, came to include the right to do as you wished with your property. Thus, in the eyes of many, it became immoral for the state to interfere with slavery. In the United

States, this led to civil war; in Britain, it led to a "starvation and a suffering unparalleled in a country which was fundamentally rich and secure."[318] In France, Russia, and Germany, those in power used the idea of human equality as an instrument of complete tyranny. The rule of law can too easily become the rule of unjust law.

Govan added a fourth right: the inherent right to be "merely a man"—not a hero, saint, demon, scapegoat, or more or less than human, but "simply and merely a man."[319] This right spoke to the universal tendency of human beings to demonize those they disapprove of or dislike, and to exalt or sanctify those they approve of and love. The fact is, said Govan, that no one is really a demon or a saint. We are all merely human: that is, limited, fallible, sinners, who are not all bad but bad enough to need forgiveness, and not all good either, and therefore need to be criticized, corrected, forgiven, and redirected. This is the way we are. We all have a right to be allowed to be this way: merely human.

The English and American revolutions, once war was over, did not indulge in sanctifying and demonizing. Those revolutions were so conceived as to take into the account the frailties of human nature, not to demonize anyone. Far from trying to set up a perfect government upon clear and certain principles, they chose pragmatism and compromise, but compromise always with consent of the governed and under constitutional law that divided the powers of government (executive, legislative and legal) and provided a continuing principle by which the nation's life could be measured. Govan believed that the source of this spirit of compromise lay in the humility to recognize that God is God, and all human are merely humans.

The final version of the essay was completed and published by the spring of 1956, at the end of Govan's first year on the job. This essay, "Free To Be Merely A Man," is Appendix 4.

"Christian Freedom"

Once "Free To Be Merely A Man" was published, Govan realized that he had much more to say on the issue of true human freedom. He felt the need to be more explicit about his Christian theological convictions on the subject, so during the winter of 1957-1958, he wrote the two short statements, "True Freedom" (see Appendix 5) and "On Freedom II", and an essay, "Christian Freedom," which he no doubt used in addresses to university groups. These essays represent his most concise, full and even blunt, statements on the subject. Here the assumptions that underlie everything else he wrote are exposed and clear.

The enemy of freedom, Govan believed, was the human desire for certain knowledge and perfect political freedom and peace. Neither, he believed, was possible. This human desire for certainty and perfection was illustrated in various theories of scientific determinism (like David Ricardo's "iron law of wages" or Adam Smith's "invisible hand" in economics) that turned out to be not only far from perfect but also false. It was also illustrated by the political determinisms of the French and Russian revolutions that in the search for perfection utterly destroyed human freedom. It was illustrated in religion by the Roman claim of infallibility. Govan wrote:

> Some . . . have thought that the failure of these attempts to establish a perfect society through scientific socialism [Russian], liberal individualism [French], an absolute monarch or an infallible church [Rome] confirms the pessimistic conclusion . . . that it will always be thus to the end of the world (as Dostoyevsky's Grand Inquisitor put it). But this is not necessarily so.[320]

England and its successor, Great Britain, escaped this pessimism and found a real though imperfect freedom in its political organization and its religious establishment, neither of which, in the end, claimed absolute power or truth. The constitutions of the United States and of the Episcopal Church in the United States have followed this British example. With all of their limitations and failures, nevertheless, Govan believed these institutions had served God by not claiming too much for themselves. For the church, the only "perfect" freedom is the freedom of those whose sins are forgiven.

189

The Influence of
Frederick Denison Maurice

During Govan's first two years as Executive Secretary for Faculty Work of the Episcopal Church, one pervasive influence on his thought and work began to appear: the theology of Frederick Denison Maurice, considered by many scholars to be the greatest Anglican theologian of the nineteenth century. He re-interpreted Christian faith and the Anglican tradition in new and exciting ways.

Govan's interest in Maurice was fourfold. First, Maurice was a complete universalist who rejected the separation between the sacred and the secular. The God who created the world was Lord of both and head of the entire human race. The human race, therefore, is one family.

This kind of "universalism" got Maurice into serious trouble. He refused to commit either nonpenitents or nonbelievers to eternal damnation, rather leaving that judgment up to God. To conservatives who had a stake in the separation of the saved from the damned, this belief smacked of moral laxity and even heresy. Because the conservatives dominated the Church of England at the time Maurice lost his job as a professor of theology at King's College, London.

The second aspect of Maurice's thought that appealed to Govan was his attitude toward nineteenth-century culture. Unique among theologians of his time, he understood the new intellectual and scientific developments and had the theological insight to identify those that were idolatrous and wrong, and to reconcile those that were true, with the Gospel. He understood but rejected out of hand, for example, the harsh deterministic theories like Ricardo's "iron law" that kept wages permanently at a subsistence level making poverty inevitable; and Malthus' law that population always outruns the food supply creating inevitable starvation. He was infuriated by the scientific claim that people could do nothing to improve their situation. To the contrary, Maurice said, these laws do not determine the future. Rather, we have a moral obligation as human beings to act ethically against these negative tendencies and to change conditions for the better, and he insisted that we could.

Third, Govan found Maurice's attitude toward institutions a refreshing balance to Reinhold Niebuhr's "Moral Man and Immoral Society." Niebuhr had argued that only individuals are capable of self-sacrificing love; institutions at best are capable only of enlightened self-interest. While continuing to appreciate Niebuhr's, theory Govan learned from Maurice (as he already had from his experience as a historian) the opposite lesson: that institutions serve as essential restraints upon individuals and modify their behavior and their attitudes. Maurice believed that there could be no genuine human freedom without some sort of restraint. So very often it is not people but the institutions and the laws of society that are moral: thus, immoral man and moral society. As Govan would later write,

> Institutions are not organizations artificially devised by
> man . . . [but] principalities and powers of which Paul
> and the other apostles wrote, natural beings, corporate
> persons, children of God and like his other children
> angelic or demonic as they are obedient and disobedient
> to his commands. They must admit wrongdoing, if they
> are to be true servants, for . . . the evil be ever mingled
> with the good.[321]

Fourth, Govan found Maurice's analysis of the principles of education immensely helpful. Even though they were not directly applicable to the mid-twentieth century university scene, they clarified the issues for him.

"All principles and theories of education," according to Maurice, "could be classified under three heads—Spartan, Athenian, and Modern."[322] Spartan education taught self-restraint through discipline; Athenian education cultivated the human faculties through language and self-expression. The Modern era disseminated theoretical and scientific information. Alone, each of these approaches is not only incomplete but also destructive of the other two: discipline alone stifles self-expression. Self-expression alone destroys discipline. Scientific knowledge can provide no center of meaning for life. Christian faith, however, provides a ground for the healthy integration of all three. Maurice's conclusion, therefore, was that the church ought to be the one institution capable of properly educating the nation. That, of course, was practical nonsense to Govan. Not even the Church of England had succeeded in educating the nation, let alone the church in the pluralistic United States. Govan knew that the influence upon education that Maurice was talking about was sound and that Maurice's understanding would guide his work with the chaplains and faculty in American colleges and universities. The need for healthy influence of the Christian faith was, if anything, greater than ever.

Maurice provided the basic attitude and ideas with which Tom would approach his work with the Episcopal Church.

14

Church and University: Allies or Enemies?

The church and the university are not rivals. They are allies in a common cause which is described as the service and glory of God and the freedom of mankind.

Thomas P. Govan

New Initiatives

Govan's second year as Executive Secretary for Faculty Work (1956-1957) was momentous for him as well as for the church's mission in higher education. F. D. Maurice's theological "universalism" and the arrival of new colleagues who provided him great support made the year very creative.

Among Govan's new colleagues was Philip T. Zabriskie, a young, brilliant and creative chaplain at Amherst College, appointed by Presiding Bishop Henry Knox Sherrill. He succeeded Roger Blanchard as executive secretary of the College and University Division of the Executive Council. Zabriskie was officially Govan's boss, but was more a friend and colleague who brought with him from Amherst intimate knowledge of the student world. He deferred to Govan on intellectual matters, encouraged him in others, and always supported and cooperated with him.

An even closer and more important colleague to Govan, however, was Jones B. Shannon who served from 1957 to 1966 as the Executive Director of the Church Society for College Work (CSCW), an independent society concerned with all aspects of the church's mission to the university. "Jo" Shannon had been a highly successful businessman in Detroit, treasurer and then lay administrator of Christ Church, Cranbrook, Illinois, under Robert L. DeWitt. In his forties, Shannon went to seminary at the Episcopal Theological School in Cambridge, Massachusetts, and was ordained in 1952. He then served for five years as rector of St. Andrew's Church in State Park, Pennsylvania, and as part-time chaplain at Pennsylvania State University before coming to CSCW. He was a good administrator and fundraiser, but not a scholar, who nevertheless cared about education and the relationship of Christianity to intellectual life. He knew how to get things done.

New to CSCW, Shannon was eager to find fresh and untried roles for the Society. He and Govan immediately found they shared similar convictions and goals. They agreed that the Church's mission was not merely for students but for the whole university, that what the Anglican ethos stood for was not something narrow and sectarian, but universal and fundamental to the reform of higher education. They complemented each other beautifully: Shannon found in Govan the intellectual depth and expertise he needed; Govan found in Shannon the enthusiasm and managerial skills he needed.

Joint sponsorship of programs by both the Church Society and the Division of College Work would double the scope of what they could do. With Zabriskie and the support of the National Commission for College Work, Shannon and Govan would make new things happen. Their intention, as Govan told the commission, was to "initiate as broad a study as possible of the church, the Christian faith and the university, because all of us need to learn before we can teach, and the more persons we can involve in the enterprise, the clearer and more meaningful will be the results."[323]

Initially, they supported and helped publicize the high-level annual four-day Conference on Theology in Hartford, Connecticut, for Episcopal faculty. At these lectures, both Govan and Shannon made many new and important university contacts and friends.

Second, they reconstituted the Canterbury Associations on college campuses across the country, which up until then had been made up only of Episcopal students, and make these associations inclusive of all Episcopalians on campus, regardless of age, vocation or status: students, faculty, administrators, trustees, staff, employees, and chaplains.

Third, they launched a series of national study conferences to be held every other year. They brought together 450 students, faculty, administrators, trustees, staff, chaplains, and lay women chaplains from colleges and universities all over the country. These conferences would serve two purposes. The first was Christian education of the participants, and the second, as stated in the National Canterbury Association charter, would be

> ... to overcome the barriers that separate members of the Church and of the university community from each other within the existing structures of colleges and universities so that administrators, teachers, staff, and students may come to know each other as persons, not as categories, and unitedly engage in their common task of teaching and learning.[324]

To know each other as persons, not as categories and as "we" rather than "they," was a large order, but Govan and Shannon faced it directly. The purpose of the conferences was fundamentally one of reconciliation. "We need to come together," they said, "as a symbol of unity which both the church on campus and the university should have, but which neither possesses completely; and, second, because an experience of united prayer, worship, study, and discussion should be an aid in bringing about a more real understanding between the various and too often separated individuals and groups of the college community."[325] Three highly successful study conferences were held during Govan's time with the church in 1957, 1959, and 1961. They broadened the theological understanding of many Episcopalians.

Govan and Shannon wanted also to encourage among faculty more scholarly study of theology as it related to the various academic disciplines. This desire led naturally to a fourth initiative. They began summer schools for Episcopal faculty: a subsidized four-to-six-week period of guided study, reflection, and writing in the fields of theology and religion for twenty-five scholars. Govan was the director of studies; he and Shannon screened the applicants; Shannon handled the administration. As faculty, they recruited some of the best scholars in the church: Albert T. Mollegen, Robert Rodenmeyer, Elmer A. Vastyan, John B. Coburn, Stephen F. Bayne, Norman Pittinger, and others. Made possible in part by Shannon's successful fundraising, there was one school on the East coast at the Episcopal Theological School, Cambridge, Massachusetts, in the first year, 1958. Thereafter, there would be two; one on the East coast and another at the Church Divinity School of the Pacific in Berkeley, California. They had two foci: the chosen work of each scholar; and in-depth Christian study and worship with one's peers over an extended period of time.

The faculty attending these schools found them refreshing and informative. Fifty scholars a year was a small beginning, but immensely important. There were, of course, gaping holes in their program. Their central emphasis on the inclusion of all persons within the church and the university ironically took little notice of the then second-class citizenship (and in many places near absence) of blacks and women in either institution or their program.

A fifth initiative, primarily Govan's, became known as "The Church, the Faith, and the University Project." Govan formulated this initiative in the early spring of 1957 for presentation to and approval by Zabriskie, Shannon, and the National Commission for College Work. Govan was increasingly convinced that the church, and in particular, chaplains, Episcopal faculty, and students on the university campus, did not understand the fundamental conflict between the visions of the world held by the church on the one hand, and the university on the other. From the church's perspective, the world was God's world and all people were God's children. Therefore, education and learning existed to service God's purposes. From the secular university's perspective, knowledge was its own justification and to be true, it must be objective. Govan felt there was conflict here which needed to be clarified and diffused, and he was determined to educate both the church and the university. There was a deep need for discussion and an equal need for fundamental university reform.

Tom hoped that the issues could be raised by producing an authoritative statement of an Anglican theology of education. That statement would stand up to and challenge the various scientific and philosophical idolatries with which the university, and indeed the church itself and the world, was filled. In the back of his mind was a Declaration of Faith, not unlike the Declaration of Independence, which could serve as a standard by which universities could be evaluated. The project was funded jointly by the Church Society for College Work and the Division for College Work, and its findings would be published by Forward Movement Publications in time for consideration and approval at the church's General Convention in October 1958. The project was planned in three stages over a period of a year and a half.

The first stage, six months in duration, focused the issue and set the questions. The second stage entailed two colloquies of thirty of the best minds, academic and clerical, in the church. The colloquies were scheduled three months apart in October 1957 and January 1958, preceding General Convention by eight months during which the final document would be written and published for consideration by the Convention. Then, with an authoritative theological statement in hand, the church would proceed with its mission of self-education and the gradual reform of the universities.

It was a bold program, and Govan knew it. He knew also that it could not fully succeed, but he believed that being faithful and speaking out was its own reward.

"The Christian Faith, the Church, and the University"

The steps of the project were followed as planned, and after the preliminary meetings with chaplains and faculty,[326] Tom wrote his preparatory statement, "The Church, the Faith, and the University."[327] It focused first on the intellectual issues, and second, on the structural issues of university education.

First among the intellectual issues was the widely-held conviction that Christianity's doctrines and dogmas are the enemy of the university's principle of free inquiry. Govan agreed that the churches had repeatedly given credence to this conviction. He felt that the university needed to understand Christianity's great affirmation that people and the world are God's and that they are intended to serve God's purposes. The universities' knowledge was not their own, nor was it justified simply by their claim to objectivity or finality. In fact,

> whenever human knowledge is taken to be a final and true statement, [it] ends in some deterministic doctrine, some denial of the freedom of mankind, and all such determinisms, whether found in religion, history, politics, philosophy, ethics, chemistry, biology, or some other subject, must be denounced by the Christian as false . . . . To question these teachings is not to deny them [completely] but is to affirm that they are not the whole story, and we still have something to learn.[328]

By warning of this danger, Christianity was not the enemy, but the ally of free inquiry.

From the Christian view, the context of all human knowledge, like everything else in creation, is God's and God's purposes. The justification for knowledge is not in itself, but in its purposes and results. However objective it may be, knowledge still lies in a pragmatic and moral context "under God" and is justified or not by its usefulness and morality. What the church teaches is simply "the worship of God 'whose service is perfect freedom.'"[329]

The second aspect of Govan's analysis was centered on the university structure and its need for radical reform. His critique emphasized the contrast between the authoritarian but fractured university structure, and the united and democratic structure of the Episcopal Church and of the United States. In the university, unlike the church and the country, there was no room for "the consent of the governed"[330] and therefore true education was distorted or crippled.

Govan described the corporate structure of almost all universities as first

> Based on the enlightened [and thoroughly non-Christian] view that virtuous men (and what other kind would devote themselves to the holy vocation of education) could be trusted with absolute power.[331]

For example, the trustees are an unrestrained governing authority unaccountable to any person or group. They usually have title to the university's property, establish policy, govern the finances, and hire the president. They rarely meet or know the faculty, staff, or students.

That was the universities' first mistake. The second, in Govan's view, was their belief that "the effectiveness of corporate and individual [functions in the university] would be improved by an almost complete separation of trustees, faculty, staff, and students."[332] "The president is the employee of the trustees, not the elected head of the institution . . . . Upon him lies the basic responsibility of making the institution work, but the faculty and staff, who share this responsibility with him and upon whom he is dependent, have no voice in his election . . . . The usual result of this situation is suspicion, hostility, and on too many occasions, hatred."[333] The university thus is not a community of scholars, but a "corporation in which the employees who manage the enterprise necessarily control and dominate its operations and the other employees."[334]

The primary problem with this system of separation is that so much depends on personal relationships. As Govan wrote

> When the ties of personal acquaintance and love disappear, no constitutional provision brings them together to air their complaints, express their differences of interest and opinion and to compromise and conciliate one another so that necessary work can get done.[335]

Govan's solution to these problems lay in "a return to the political principles of Christian freedom as they have been expressed in the constitutions of the United States and of the Protestant Episcopal Church."[336] The university president "should be chosen by the votes of the entire adult community . . . not by the board of trustees alone."[337] If that were done, "faculty and staff could no longer pretend that they and the president represented distinct interests."

He knew well enough that "these changes would not result in a perfect university . . . . It would still be an arena in which partisanship, disagreement, and dispute were the dominant tone . . . but the university would be united and it would be free."[338] To Govan, freedom and democracy are the products of open disagreement, controversy, and compromise, not of peace and repressive uniformity.

According to Govan, the greatest improvement needed in the university was in the relationship of the teacher and the student. "As things stand, the faculty has the power and the responsibility to establish the curriculum, set academic standards, and ask the questions, write and grade the exams, and give marks to students. They wield almost absolute power over the students. As a result, despite the talk of 'the spirit of free inquiry,' . . . the most common characteristic of American students, whether they be freshmen or candidates for the highest degree, is their dependence upon the teacher for both content and interpretation."[339] Often they are involved "not in a common endeavor, but in a matching of wits. The student often has only two choices: conformity to the teacher's will or futile rebellion."[340]

Govan's suggestions for change were first to get the various elements in the academic community involved in discussion of educational policy: trustees, faculty, and student representatives. Then he would separate the teaching and grading functions of the university. He would "abandon rigidly defined courses in the name of flexibility and freedom for both the students and faculty."[341] He would do away with general education courses which "succumb to the idolatrous notion that unless [the university] teachers all students everything, they will not know."[342]

Lastly, Govan wanted the administration and faculty to insist that intellectual matters, not sports, fraternities, and social life, be the center of student life.

His conclusion for the church was that it had a fundamental responsibility to challenge the university with its obligation to reform and to define the nature of these reforms in a "declaration of independence" from its false educational values: namely, "the cult of objectivity," "the liberal absolutes of autonomous knowledge, determinative natural law, and its belief that [human beings] would be virtuous if only [they] were freed from institutional and traditional restraints."[343] The declaration, above all, would affirm that "the church and the university are not rivals. They are allies in a common cause which is described as the service and glory of God and the freedom of mankind."[344]

The first colloquy was held at the College of Preachers in Washington, D.C. in October 1957; the second at the Cathedral of St. John the Divine in New York City in January 1958.[345] Govan emphasized that the paper was prepared strictly as a "preliminary document." To that end, each page had a large three-inch right-hand margin for jotting down questions from the reader. The bottom half of each page was left blank for comments. The fact that it was considered a first draft for thought and discussion turned out ironically to be precisely its usefulness, making it alive and dynamic. It provoked discussion and continues to do so. By contrast, the final report, published by Forward Movement and commended to the church by the 1958 General Convention, sadly ended all discussion.

The colloquies could not agree on Govan's analysis, or his suggestions for action. Some members thought the proposal was misguided; some thought it was arrogant; some thought that the problems were too big to handle; some worried that the church's views could be too easily misunderstood. Many participants, however, agreed with much of what Govan proposed. The divisions among the participants were so great, however, their visions so different, their conflicting interests so strong, that the editor, Bishop Stephen Bayne, had a difficult time pulling them all together in his final report. In spite of some brilliant passages, the finished product read more like another preliminary document, a catalogue of opinions, and by its own admission, turned out to be "nothing more than a discussion." It was therefore essentially unchallenging, a discussion still needing resolution. It inhibited action because it implied that there was really nothing the church could do about the problem Govan raised: it was too big, and agreement about its resolution too difficult.

Following publication, it was widely distributed around the Episcopal Church. Sales were disappointing, no further discussion was stimulated, and most people who bought it put it on the shelf. Govan's paper, "The Christian Faith, the Church, and the University," by contrast, is still full of life and challenge and speaks today as clearly and powerfully as it did in 1957 and 1958. Being merely preliminary, it has never been published.

Govan was discouraged by the lack of interest in his report, but he was grateful to have his say. He was not surprised by his failure to achieve his ambitious goals. He had half expected the result to fall short. During this hard time, Jane was a huge moral supporter, standing with him and backing him up, as were all of his closest friends, especially Jo Shannon.

At this point Tom realized that he had done all he could for the church and he should refocus on his vocation as an American historian, complete and publish Biddle, and return to teaching at a university. The time for change had come, but it would be four years before he re-entered university life as a full professor. And that interval would be filled with struggle.

Two things, however, supported him during these hard years. His personal closeness to the leadership of the Episcopal Church continued to provide a wise and valued resource to him. Some were intimate personal friends who mattered deeply to him. Several of them, like Albert T. Mollegen, Daniel Corrigan, Jones Shannon, Michael Allen, and Robert DeWitt, were people he counted on and "lived by" until he died. The depth of these personal relationships lay, among other things, in a shared Christian faith.

The other constant support in Tom's life was a deepened Christian faith of his own, and regular involvement in the worship life of his local church, St. Marks-in-the-Bowery. Sometimes he would be up early on Sunday morning attending the 8:00 a.m. Eucharist with or without Jane, depending on her health. Usually they would attend the 11:00 a.m. parish Eucharist and sermon. He also was in the habit of praying more often and in a more disciplined manner than he had before working for the church, and he continued the practice. The words of the *Book of Common Prayer* were a constant spiritual resource upon which he counted. Three of his favorite and most used prayers concerned freedom. The first was the General Confession with its assurance of forgiveness and thereby freedom from sin:

> Almighty and most merciful Father,
> We have erred and strayed from thy ways like lost sheep,
> We have followed too much the devices and desires of
>   our own hearts,
> We have offended against thy holy laws,
> We have left undone those things which we ought to have
>   done,
> and we have done those things which we ought not to
>   have done,
> and there is no health in us.
> But thou, O Lord, have mercy upon us,
> Spare those who confess their faults,
> Restore though those who are penitent,
> according to the promises declared unto mankind
> in Christ Jesus Our Lord:
> And grant, O most merciful Father, for his sake,
> that we may hereafter live a godly, righteous, and sober life,
> to the glory of thy holy Name. Amen.[346]

The second was the Collect for Peace in the Morning Prayer service:

> O God, who art the author of peace and lover of concord,
> in knowledge of whom standeth our eternal life, whose
> service is perfect freedom;

Defend us, thy humble servants, in all assaults of our
enemies; that we surely trusting in thy defense,

may not fear the power of any adversaries; through Jesus
Christ Our Lord. Amen.[347]

The third was not in the Prayer Book, but was widely known and
used in the Episcopal Church:

O God, who art the light of the minds that know thee,
and the life of the souls that love thee, and the strength
of the wills that serve thee, help us so to know thee that
we may truly love thee, and so to love thee that we may
fully serve thee, whom to serve is perfect freedom: through
Jesus Christ Our Lord. Amen.[348]

15

Adrift with Feelings
of Despair

Let us [not] be afraid to witness to Him who is unbroken and
uncorrupted from out of our individual and institutional
brokenness and corruption, for we . . . are the persons whom He
loves and serves.

Thomas P. Govan

The Christian Historian

During his time working for the church (1955-1962), Govan remained in demand as a lecturer in the various historical associations where he was a member.[349] He gave a series of major addresses on American history, one of which was "Jefferson and Hamilton, a Christian Evaluation," given in 1956 at the University of Georgia in Athens. In this address for the first time as a historian, Tom was explicit in print about his Christian assumptions.

He had already covered much of what he had to say in his earlier essay, "The Liberal and Conservative Traditions in the United States," (see Appendix 2) but in that essay he had not identified what he meant by the word "Christian." Here he did, developing a carefully reasoned article relating Jefferson's and Hamilton's political philosophies to orthodox Christianity. He found Jefferson a heretic on four counts. First, he was an idolater because he worshipped individual freedom above God. Second, he was a Gnostic (one who believes in salvation through knowledge, gnosis) because he presumed to know the laws of nature (the science) which governed unregulated economics and pure democratic politics. Third, he was a Pelagian in that he believed like Pelagius that people were free to follow good or evil by their own choice and their own power. Fourth, he was Manichean in that he believed, like Manichaeus, that the world was a theater of battle between good and evil: the good to be found in rural agricultural world and the evil in urban industrial or banking world.

Hamilton, on the contrary, believed that all people were created equal. People and their institutions were sinful, governed in part by human "passions—ambition, avarice and [self] interest" and therefore neither could be trusted with unrestrained power. Humans were a mixture of good and evil. True human freedom, therefore, was limited freedom and must include restraints that came from government and law, checks and balances of power. He did not believe that the actions of individuals were determined by laws (natural or otherwise), but that individuals had enough freedom to make partial (though not perfect) decisions for themselves.

Hamilton was closer by far to orthodox Christian principles than Jefferson. Govan was at pains to show that these principles make for more realistic and therefore better government, a freer and more prosperous society. Govan believed that orthodox understanding, by taking self-interest and sin seriously, contained more truth about human life and history than any other. Those politicians and government officials who came at their work with Christian understanding were more likely to govern well than those who did not because they were more realistic.

What was true for politicians and government officials, said Govan, was equally true for historians. Those who came at their work from this view were liable to write more realistic and accurate history. The address was published a year later in *The Christian Scholar*, with comments from three historians: Arthur M. Schlesinger Jr. of Harvard University, Leonard J. Trinterud, Professor of Church History at McCormick Theological Seminary, and E. Harris Harbison of Princeton University.[350]

Schlesinger twice quoted the notes taken by Judge Robert Yates of Hamilton's speech at the Constitutional Convention to the effect that Hamilton believed "the rich and the well-born" would always govern well, whereas the ordinary people would not. Govan, responding in the next issue of *The Christian Scholar*, found it "very doubtful that Hamilton ever made" this statement. Quoting Hamilton's own notes and James Madison's notes, Govan made it abundantly clear that Hamilton believed in the universality of human sin. Therefore, no one group could be trusted with unlimited power, that each needed the power to protect itself from the others and to be a check on the others for the common good.[351] Govan concluded,

> Anti-Hamilton historians (like Schlesinger) have seized upon the (Yates) quotation because it justifies what they want to believe about his political philosophy. It has been quoted more frequently than almost any other statement attributed to Hamilton except his remark about the people being a great beast, but it certainly should never be used without at least indicating its source.[352]

Professors Trinterud and Harbison both criticized Govan's thesis, pointing out that Hamilton was not really an orthodox Christian in the full sense of the word, and that the word "heretic" was not helpful in describing anyone, let alone Jefferson.

In reply, three months later, Philip Zabriskie made two comments:

1. In his discussion of Christian orthodoxy, Dr. Govan is clearly not concerned with the whole gamut of Christian profession but here only with the Christian understanding of the root of evil and injustice. Christianity has always said that this root is sin, our sin, and not, at its root, social inequity, urbanization, ignorance, the sin of some other, or anything else. To exempt any group of human activity (including the Church) from sin is to make it an idol. This is that part of Christian understanding with which Dr. Govan is concerned. In relation to this, Hamilton describes life with a realistic appreciation of human selfishness,

which accords with a Christian doctrine of sin much more closely than Jefferson (whether or not Hamilton was in other ways much of a Christian). And such divergent philosophies or theologies have genuine consequences in political theory.

2. Dr. Govan affirms his belief in God's truth and his (Christian) conviction that no one man or group can be safely held to possess this truth or God's virtue. All of us are under sin: all need to be checked. This need is as important to democracy as its complement: all are under God's care; all need freedom and deserve to be heard. To omit the need for checks and the protection against anarchy is to invite totalitarianism.

Govan had a brief last word:

> I have little to add. If I wrote the things they say I wrote or attempted to do what they say I did, then the article did not communicate what I was trying to say. Another attempt would probably have no better results.[353]

The Trials of Nicholas Biddle

Since his departure from Sewanee, Govan's main effort as a historian had been his biography of Nicholas Biddle. That project was, as he later said, full of "woes and tribulations."[354] In May 1950, while still at Sewanee, he had signed a contract, sealed by a five-hundred-dollar advance, with E. P. Dutton and Company to publish the book if it was finished within sixteen months, by September 1, 1951. Nicholas Wreden, a senior editor at Dutton, was intrigued by the book from the start, believed in its importance, and felt it had a good chance of appealing to parts of the general public and historians.

That projected date of completion turned out to be entirely unrealistic largely because of Tom's involvement in the debate over desegregation raging through the University of the South. Govan was not able to concentrate on Biddle, so he missed the September 1, 1951 deadline with Dutton. Tom was depressed because he was forty-two years old and he had not yet published a book. He felt sure his professional future depended on Biddle's completion and publication.

Then came the fire and the near loss of the Biddle manuscript, followed by his escape for a restorative year in New York City. While at Tulane University for two years, he was somehow able to get going on Biddle again, finished the book in the spring of 1955, and immediately sent the manuscript to Dutton for publication.

By this time, however, two things had happened. In part because he thought the book was finally finished, Govan had decided that he could accept the position of Executive Secretary for Faculty Work of the Episcopal Church without worrying about his future as a historian. With the book published and his credibility established, he believed he would have no difficulty getting back into the history profession as a full professor.

But second, the administration of Dutton had changed. Nicholas Wreden, his strong supporter, had moved to Little, Brown and Company in Boston and so could not help him, but instead referred Govan to William Doerflinger at Dutton whom he knew was very sympathetic to Govan's project. Dutton's new president, Elliott B. Macrae, soon wrote back to Govan after reviewing the book to say that neither his editorial nor his promotion departments were enthusiastic about the book and suggested that Govan return the five hundred dollar deposit and send the manuscript to Wreden at Little, Brown. Wreden was delighted, and it was a foregone conclusion that after some editing and rewriting, Little, Brown would surely accept and publish the book. Confident that all was well, Tom and Jane left New Orleans in late July on a much-needed six-week trip through the West, only to find on their return in early September that Wreden had died unexpectedly in California.

Tom's heart sank! Here he was possibly without a publisher and just about to move to New York City to begin his new work for the Episcopal Church. The turn of events could not have been worse. The one bright light in the whole mess was Roger Blanchard's assurance to Govan that the Church would support him until Biddle was published. Little did he know what lay ahead.

On September 16, 1955, Govan wrote to Ned Bradford, the new

head of Little, Brown, commending the manuscript to him. Bradford and a number of readers found it to be more a biography of a bank than of a man, too financially technical, and rejected it as lacking appeal to the general reader.

That fall and winter of 1955-1956, just as he was getting started with the Episcopal Church, Tom tried several publishers without success: five rejections in a row. The reason most often given for turning the book down was its technical complexity and its lack of general appeal.

A sympathetic response came a year later. In October 1956, Govan wrote to a historian friend, Roger Shugg, now director of the University of Chicago Press, to ask if he might be interested in reading the manuscript. Shugg replied by return mail that he had "always believed in anything you [Govan] write and particularly in the importance of your biography of Nicholas Biddle" and reminded Govan that he had solicited the book in vain several years before when he had been with Alfred Knopf. Shugg went so far as to say, "one way or another, I hope we can publish your book in 1957."[355] That was a real boost.

Govan hastened to put the manuscript in the mail and wrote to Shugg on October 22, 1956 that he was aware that "many places need revision, restatement, and reorganization. The writing gets heavier as the book grows larger and larger," but that he needed help in deciding where cutting and restatement would be most effective. Then he confessed his conviction about Biddle and also his doubts about the text as it then stood:

> I am in the unfortunate situation of believing that Biddle was wrong, though understandably and reasonably wrong, only in his decision to continue the Bank under a state charter, but even this proved to be a mistake only because of a series of essentially accidental and unfortunate circumstances. I think, however, that my biased and prejudiced view is not sufficiently concealed and that the apologia would be more effective if I masked it by an apparent fair-mindedness in accepting as valid more of the criticism (of Biddle), and bearing down more

heavily on, instead of explaining away, the apparent
financial looseness of his management in the critical years.
The profits were so high between 1837 and 1839 that he
permitted extravagance—just as in recent years expense
account spending has been permitted to mushroom
throughout the whole corporate structure—but the
amounts were relatively so small that this careless
extravagance had nothing to do with the subsequent
failure of the bank.[356]

The book was on its way to a sympathetic publisher, but first
revisions and rewriting had to be done.

Forrest McDonald

Then in 1955, Govan met Forrest McDonald at the annual meeting
of the Southern Historical Association. McDonald was a twenty-nine
year old Texan, twenty years Govan's junior, brash, cocky, obviously
brilliant, a young historian "on the rise." Govan and McDonald
discovered they had a lot in common and very soon they had clicked
into a mentor-mentee relationship. McDonald recognized Govan's
massive knowledge of American history; Govan recognized
McDonald's extraordinary promise. Both were southerners and
conservative, revisionist American historians. Both despised the
current tendencies in American history writing: glorifying romantic
Jeffersonian anti-institutional individualism, supporting laissez-faire
theory in economics, believing agricultural life created virtue and
urban business life corruption, and affirming states' rights over
national unity as the road to freedom. Both were nationalists. Govan
was re-interpreting Hamilton and Biddle as workers for the common
good through whose policies everyone in American society benefited.
McDonald interpreted Samuel Insul, the utilities magnate who, like
Biddle, ended in disgrace. Both men were moderate conservatives
who flourished and then failed, ending unfairly in ignominy. They
knew their enterprises, the Bank and the utilities industry, were
necessary for the good of everyone in the United States. They shared

in part a common anthropology: both understood the universality of human self-interest and the capacity for evil. But, whereas Govan as a Christian believed even more in the human capacity for redemption, goodness, and self-sacrifice, McDonald would turn out to be more cynical.

McDonald was fascinated and impressed with Govan; he had never met anyone like him. And Govan, for his part was intrigued and impressed with this new, young historian. It would not be long though before their relationship became confused. At the time, McDonald was director of the American History Research Center (AHRC) of the Wisconsin State Historical Society. This organization was dedicated to helping historians edit and rewrite their work for publication and helping finance that process. McDonald had what Tom needed, and suddenly the mentor-mentee relationship was subsumed under the editor-writer relationship. Both men felt the tension in this change. McDonald read the Biddle manuscript, was impressed, but agreed with Tom that it needed "revision, restatement, and reorganization" and sent it out to a number of readers, including Ralph Hidy, a member of his board and a professor of business history at the Harvard Business School. The readers all responded critically but positively. In the spring of 1957, McDonald finally accepted the book on behalf of the AHRC, assigned one of his best editors, Livia Appel, to work on the revision with Govan, and began underwriting its cost. The younger man had become mentor of the older.

The verbal understanding was that the Center would assist in finding a publisher who would manufacture, promote, and distribute the book, and serve as a co-publisher with the Center. The Center would also have its name on the book and share the royalties with Govan. In effect, this made the Center part author and part publisher. Govan accepted this arrangement because he was desperate and trusted McDonald. It turned out to be a formula for confusion.

McDonald and Govan agreed that Roger Shugg and the University of Chicago Press would be their printing option when the time came. Livia Appel was a very helpful guide in the editing and rewriting process. Govan's special gratitude to both McDonald and Appel appears in his preface to the book.

Jane was apprehensive about the arrangement. She did not quite trust what she called McDonald's "immaturity." But Tom was delighted, in spite of the confusion. This help and encouragement came, it seemed to him, in the nick of time. He really might now actually get the book published. The Center's financial assistance was a blessing as well because working with an editor was costly and Govan's salary was small. Things were looking up.

Bray Hammond

During this period in Govan's career (1955-1962), he remained in demand as a reviewer of books in American history. Of the eleven books he reviewed, only one met with his enthusiastic approval, and that was Bray Hammond's *Banks and Politics in America from the Revolution to the Civil War*. It not only corrected the erroneous interpretations by historians of the American past, but provided practical guidance "for those who [will] make decisions about money and credit in the future."[357] Hammond argued that America is not divided between poor debtor farmers and rich creditor businessmen, as so many think. Borrowing was the practice not primarily for those in trouble but for those who make prosperous use of loans. "America has grown rich by borrowing."[358]

Above all, Hammond reinterpreted at length the roles of Hamilton and Nicholas Biddle, a subject dear to Govan's heart. Tom criticized Hammond only for his acceptance of the view that most of the political controversy between the Revolution and the Civil War was provoked by a "conflict of farmer and entrepreneur for dominance over American culture."[359] This, he believed, was the old misconception of American historians arising again. To be sure, political conflicts were provoked by rival political parties and by rival economic theories, but neither the farmers nor the entrepreneurs as groups were ever united on the issues. Each group was divided on every issue, and each group contained supporters for rival political parties.

Hammond's judgment on this question, however, had "little effect upon his treatment of the basic materials," said Govan. "What he has to say concerning the actual developments in the history of banks, money, and credit is . . . refreshingly honest, clear and hopeful."[360]

16

Nicholas Biddle, Tribulation and Triumph

It does seem to me also that I and my professional interests do deserve some consideration.

Thomas P. Govan

The Publication: "Woes and Tribulations"

All during his time with the Episcopal Church, Govan's primary concern as a historian was his Biddle biography. He was hugely encouraged by the interest of Roger Shugg and the University of Chicago Press. He received invaluable help with revisions from Forrest McDonald and Livia Appel of the AHRC.

The revision work took about a year and a half, and it was a painful business. Shugg insisted that Govan had to convince the reader that Biddle "was interesting, attractive, and important." Govan agreed, but "knowing this and being able to do something about it are quite different things."[361] He even suggested to Shugg that he might do two books: "the first a study of Biddle and the Bank War, centering on the political and economic ideas that were in conflict; and then a short personal biography to be published separately at a later date." In the first part he wrote, "I would make no effort to be neutral (honest

214

and accurate as I can be, of course, but writing actually a defense of the Bank, paper money, and credit, against Jackson and his agrarian nonsense), and in the second write of Biddle, the Nationalist, with the Bank as only the most important part of his nationalist views. I believe that by taking these new approaches, I could tell the story as an authority from outside, rather than doing as I have done in the present manuscript; that is to tell the story essentially in the words of the participants."[362]

With Shugg's support, Govan decided to stick with one book about Biddle as banker and nationalist, leaving out most of the personal and other sides of the man's life. The revision concluded a year later in the summer of 1958; the manuscript was mailed to the AHRC, read by their readers, and officially accepted for publication.[363] Govan heaved a huge sigh of relief; the job was done, or so he thought.

On September 24, 1958, with the approval of Donald Macrae at Dutton (contingent upon payment from royalties of the five hundred dollars owed them), Govan signed a publication contract with the Center. At that time McDonald told Govan that he had already begun negotiations on behalf of the Center with Shugg to have the University of Chicago Press manufacture, promote, and distribute the book, and that he had sent Shugg the revised manuscript. Shugg, in turn, passed it on to the members of his editorial committee to read. McDonald did not mention Govan's contract with the Center or the Center's desire to be co-publisher, to have its name on the book along with the University of Chicago, and share the royalties. Shugg had no idea of these parts of the arrangement, which lay in McDonald's mind.

McDonald's book, *We the People*, was published in 1958 and was an immediate success. Shugg and the University of Chicago Press published it precisely while Shugg was negotiating with McDonald and Govan over Biddle. And that was not all. *We the People* was published under exactly the same conditions that McDonald suggested to Govan, but never mentioned to Shugg: namely that the AHRC wanted to be a copublisher of the Biddle book, too, have its name on the book, and share in the royalties.

But why had McDonald not told Shugg about the Center's contract with Govan? And why had he not told Govan of his silence? Why this extraordinary disingenuousness? One wonders whether there had been conflict over the arrangement, that Shugg may have been "burned" and let McDonald know that he would never enter into such an agreement with AHRC again. But in that case, why did McDonald suggest the same arrangement to Govan? Could it have been his desire to impress Govan, to make himself and AHRC look super-competent and helpful?

Or perhaps it was simply a case of sloppy and irresponsible management and a preoccupation on McDonald's part with his own interests and future because at that moment he was riding high on the success of *We the People.* The book had made his name in the American history profession; he was "hot" property, and immediately job offers came his way.

In December 1958, at the American Historical Association meeting, both McDonald and Govan gave lectures on the theme of "Business Failures in American History." Govan spoke on "The Fall of the House of Biddle, 1841" and McDonald on "The Fall of the House of Insul [the utilities magnate], 1932." Both were previewing books.

At the meeting, McDonald presented Govan with startling news: he was leaving AHRC at the end of January 1959. He had accepted a position as professor of American history at Brown University.[364]

This was a shock to Govan because the final arrangements for the Biddle book still were not settled. Having trusted McDonald's initiatives and left negotiations up to him, Tom was now worried about being left in the lurch. Although Roger Shugg was still encouraging, "as certain as anyone . . . could be that the board [at Chicago][365] would accept the book for publication," he was ignorant of what was in McDonald's mind. There were no records in the AHRC files of these negotiations. Only McDonald knew the real situation. Govan had never discussed these arrangements with Shugg; nor did he know that McDonald had not told him.

Before McDonald's departure, Shugg called Govan to tell him that Chicago had accepted his manuscript, and that he was sending a contract for Tom to sign. Govan then called McDonald to ask him who, in his absence, could give the Center's approval to his signing. The gist of McDonald's response was "'that the affairs of the Center were somewhat uncertain . . . that its disposition, if any, had not been decided, and that he thought it would be entirely acceptable to everyone concerned if he (Govan) went on and signed the contract so that Chicago could begin work on the manuscript." Govan signed it in what he thought was the spirit of his contract with the Center in accordance with what he believed were the negotiations between Shugg and McDonald.[366]

In fact, by this time, in McDonald's absence, Clifford L. Lord,[367] director of the Wisconsin State Historical Society, the body sponsoring the AHRC, had designated his associate director, Donald R. McNeil, to take over the affairs of the AHRC. Govan was still uncomfortable about the situation in spite of McDonald's reassurance, so he immediately wrote to both Shugg and McNeil about what he had done on McDonald's advice. "Chicago wanted to begin work on the book," he wrote to McNeil, "and could not do so without a contract, so I thought I would speed things up by ignoring formalities. . . . I was acting on the advice of the person I thought still to be the responsible executive of the Center and in accordance with the will of the Advisory Council [of AHRC]."[368] In spite of these explanations, Govan knew that in his eagerness finally to get the book published he had been hasty. The upshot of all of this confusion was the extraordinary and embarrassing circumstance that Govan now had three signed contracts for the publication of the Biddle book: with Dutton, which had not yet been canceled because of the five hundred dollars owed them; with the American History Research Center, which had helped so much with the revisions of the manuscript and had a real stake in the publication of the book; and now a third with the University of Chicago Press, which had negotiated in good faith with both Govan and McDonald from the beginning.

"My own fault in all of this is plainly evident, regardless of the responsibility of anyone else," Govan wrote to Shugg, "and I hope that you and the present officers at the Center will help me in working out the mess in which I have gotten us involved."[369]

After talking with Govan, Lord wrote to McNeil, "Once again the departing machinations of our errant friend [McDonald] seem to be the source of the difficulties."[370] Later Lord asked McNeil to check with all those on whose manuscripts the Center had first publication rights, to see "what additional configurations Brother McDonald has made for the future of the Center." He had lost one manuscript, it seems, and "almost lost the Biddle. How much further did he go?" asked Lord.[371] He was upset with McDonald's mismanagement of the affair.

Trying to unravel the multi-negotiations, McNeil began to investigate. On February 26, 1959, he wrote Govan asking what his understanding of the Center's arrangement with the Chicago Press was.[372] Govan replied that he believed that "Chicago has accepted the manuscript for September publication, and if the Center remains in existence, its name will appear as it did on Forrest's [McDonald] book and it will share in the royalties according to the AHRC, not the Chicago, contract, but I . . . will be perfectly willing to go along with any procedure you suggest. What I don't want to happen is anything that would further delay the appearance of the book. It was to be finished originally in 1955, and if I told you all the woes and tribulations that I have already gone through, it would take at least two additional single-spaced, typewritten pages."[373]

The same day, McNeil called Shugg to discuss the arrangements. Shugg was shocked to hear about Govan's AHRC contract. This could not be. He immediately fired off a letter to Govan telling him to cancel it: "I hope you will proceed immediately to arrange with the Center for the cancellation of this contract by mutual consent, because any lawyer would remind you that you do not have a right to contract with us unless you have canceled any previous obligations to publish elsewhere."[374] He obviously was having none of McDonald's co-publisher and royalty-sharing ideas. "We stand ready to go ahead with your book, and certainly want to bring it out next fall; so please do this bit of paperwork right away."[375]

Negotiations proceeded, but the confusion and conflict remained: Shugg was clear about no co-publication with AHRC[376] and no sharing of royalties;[377] and McNeil, now taking on the mantle of AHRC's self-interest, was clear about affirming both, although he was able to find nothing in the AHRC's files to indicate any agreement between AHRC and the University of Chicago Press about either joint imprint on the book or shared royalties.[378] Govan was clear with both sides that he should not have signed "the contract with the University of Chicago without having the written permission of the

Center or a cancellation of the previous contract."[379] McNeil sympathized with Govan's position on the signing at least in part because, as he admitted, "the trouble with the Center has always been one of not maintaining business-like operations."[380]

McNeil then confused the situation further. He wrote to Govan and Shugg, "At the moment we [the Wisconsin State Historical Society] are negotiating with one of the leading Universities in the country [University of Texas] to take on AHRC, Inc. and to continue its publication program. We have offered the rights to the Biddle manuscript as one of the features of the negotiations. I have told Mr. Shugg who indicates that if the Center were solvent, the University of Chicago would not object to the publication of the manuscript by AHRC Inc."[381]

Shugg confirmed this. He evidently was willing to give up the book if that would expedite its publication. McNeil's letter continued, "If this institution [University of Texas], showing extraordinary patience with AHRC and extraordinary loyalty to Govan and his book, would take over the AHRC, Inc., it would want to go ahead with publication of the manuscript because of the contract we hold with you." In other words, Govan's manuscript, as property of AHRC Inc., would be sold with AHRC, Inc. to the University of Texas. McNeil concluded, "Either way, we should know very shortly as to who will publish your manuscript.[382]

On March 23, 1959, Govan wrote a letter that finally broke the stalemate. He addressed it to McNeil, but sent it first to Clifford L. Lord. If Lord approved, he was to send it on to McNeil. Tom made clear the moral case and his own strong desire for publication of the Biddle biography by the University of Chicago Press. Shugg's' integrity and dedication, above all else, to getting the book published, shone through this exchange. The spirit of this gesture was not lost on Govan and he wanted to make sure it was not lost on McNeil or Lord. He felt that Shugg and the University of Chicago Press were being misused. Govan wrote,

> What we need to do, I believe, is to consider the interests of the three [parties involved], the Center, the University of Chicago Press, and the author, not of any one of them

exclusively. But in this confusion, it is the Chicago Press that has been involved by the Center and the Author, jointly and separately, and is the party that should be our first consideration. The next face that must be considered is the Center and the money it has put into the manuscript and here I am ready to make any concession that you and the board of the AHRC thinks fair and correct regardless of contractual formulas. But it does seem to me also that I and my professional interests do deserve some consideration and both would certainly be better promoted by continuing the arrangement with the Chicago Press, an arrangement initially negotiated by the responsible officer of the Center.[383]

Govan had made his point. Without saying so, everyone agreed that Forrest McDonald had largely created the problem. They agreed that Roger Shugg had acted in good faith throughout; that Govan, however unwise and mistaken, had also acted in good faith; that there was a moral obligation to the University of Chicago Press and to Govan who was seeking reentry into the teaching profession. That settled it. McNeil and Lord agreed to withdraw the Biddle book as a part of their negotiations with the University of Texas. Now aware of the lack of candor on the part of McDonald about the meaning of the AHRC contract, McNeil wrote Govan on April 1, 1959 that "the Center has released you from the prior contract signed with it and has told Mr. Shugg to go ahead and publish the book. This is a statement directly to you releasing you from your contract with the Center."[384] In the end everyone had come around to making the publication of Govan's book their top priority and he repaid the Dutton advance. The University of Chicago Press would publish Nicholas Biddle on November 24, 1959.

That would be a day of great rejoicing and great relief.

Jane's Illness

Another crisis struck the Govans in October 1959 just a month before the publication date. Jane was diagnosed with breast cancer.

After many examinations and consultations, it was decided that she should have a mastectomy. Jane came through the operation in early November with her accustomed courage and honesty about how awful and how painful and draining it was, and her determination to recover fully. Needless to say, this emergency cast a pall over the joy of the book's publication. Tom began a long year of new responsibilities at home; they were still living at 81 Bedford Street, Greenwich Village. He now had to take care of Jane, and Judy II, their dachshund, shopping, and doing much of the cooking, while witnessing his wife's recovery and waiting for his career in teaching to once again become a reality.

Jane and Tom had been attending St. Mark's-in-the-Bowery more or less regularly for three years, but they hardly knew the new rector, J. C. Michael Allen or he them. When Jane was operated on, Philip Zabriskie, Tom's close colleague in the college and university ministry, called Michael to tell him that Jane was in the hospital with breast cancer. "Everyone loves her," he said, "but no one in particular. She's got to have a pastor. They've begun coming to St. Mark's. So, will you be her pastor?" It made sense to Michael; he went to visit her, which he continued to do regularly, bringing her communion, praying with her, listening, and just being a friend. The radiation treatments after the operation drained her strength again and again, until finally the treatments were over and she could begin the long road back to full vigor. It was a year before she was fully recovered, and even then she was weaker and tired more quickly than before. The announcement that she had a clean bill of health echoed Tom and Jane's rejoicing over the announcement of the publishing of Nicholas Biddle.

Publication!

In honor of the November 24, 1959 publication date of Biddle, Govan was invited to speak at 4:00 P.M. on that date to a gathering of the Historical Society of Pennsylvania. He chose as his title, "Nicholas Biddle, American Gentleman," emphasizing not only his banking career, but also Biddle's other gifts and qualities. Biddle had edited the literary journal *Port Folio* and the Lewis and Clark expedition papers.

In architecture, he was a leader of the Greek revival, and as farmer and manager of his country home "Andalusia," he was a keen observer and scientist. But above all Biddle was a "Renaissance gentleman," a Federalist of the old school, considered an aristocrat but with egalitarian convictions, a man of integrity, urbanity, and kindness. The occasion was especially pleasant for Govan because the invitation came from Nicholas Biddle Wainwright, a direct descendant of the "great man," director of the Historical Society of Pennsylvania and its library, which contained important pieces of Biddle's correspondence. Wainwright had helped Govan throughout the writing of his book, as a friend, liaison to the Biddle family, archivist, and enthusiastic supporter.

The initial response to Tom's opus was enthusiastic, but he knew that only time would signify the book's true place in American history.

17

Partial Vindication

He has written the thorough, devoted study of a man long left to neglect and misunderstanding but gaining at last the presentation warranted by his prominent and public-spirited career.

Bray Hammond

One of the things that Govan's study of Biddle showed was, as he put it, "that Biddle was an intellectual and that in competition with demagogues, like Andrew Jackson, for the approval of the masses, intellectuals always lose."[385] Govan might have to suffer the same kind of fate. He had lost out with the popular publishers, now he would lose out with the popular magazines. Sadly, but inevitably, the appeal of *Nicholas Biddle, Nationalist and Public Banker, 1786-1844* seemed to be limited to professional historians and economists. It was Tom's style that remained inaccessible, although its message continues to speak to the very heart of the nation.

So the commercial press did not review the book, as the general commercial publishers had not published it. Because it was not reviewed by *The New York Times, The New York Review of Books, Time* magazine, *Newsweek, Harper's,* or *The Atlantic Monthly* or any other general readership magazines, its message was not heard by the general public and has only, in passing, influenced high school and college text books and teaching.

> Biddle was respectfully and in many cases thoroughly reviewed by the academic or professional press. There were fifteen significant reviews in Govan's file (twenty-five references in all), many of them written by leading scholars of the day.[386]

Tom was especially pleased by a letter from Roger Shugg on September 9, 1963.

Dear Tom:

The Press is proud indeed that NICHOLAS BIDDLE, NATIONALIST AND PUBLIC BANKER, 1786-1844 is one of the 1,780 titles chosen by James Babb of Yale as a working library for the White House. We shall of course present a copy of your book to this distinguished and distinctive library of Americana.

Perhaps you will be interested to know that one out of every four books chosen was published by a university press and this Press shares with you the honor of placing thirty-nine titles in the White House.

> Yours sincerely,
> Roger W. Shugg

Bray Hammond's Review

The longest and defining review of Govan's Biddle biography was written by Bray Hammond in *The Pennsylvania Magazine of History and Biography*.[387] Two years earlier in 1957, Govan had enthusiastically reviewed Hammond's study *Banks and Politics in America from the Revolution to the Civil War*.[388] That book was doubly needed, Govan said, "first and most importantly . . . as a guide for those who will be making decisions about money and credit in the future, and secondly as a corrector of erroneous interpretations of the American past."[389] Hammond's understanding of finance was second to none.

Govan rejoiced particularly in Hammond's rejection of the great body of American historians who have "accepted a view of American History [which] divides the people into two groups, the poor farmers who are always in debt [and are defended by Jefferson and Jackson] and the rich businessmen who are creditors" [supported by Hamilton and Biddle]. According to Hammond, these historians failed completely to understand that most debtors were not poor farmers in trouble, but prosperous businessmen (and farmers) and business corporations getting rich by borrowing.

Hammond's one serious error, according to Govan, was to fall for the myth that it was "the conflict of farmers versus entrepreneurs for dominance over American culture, which provoked much of the political controversy between the Revolution and the Civil War." There was certainly political controversy, but not between farmers and entrepreneurs. The evidence, said Govan, indicated to the contrary that both groups were divided on most every issue, economic and political, and that they lined up on issues for reasons quite independent of their being farmers or entrepreneurs.

Three years later in 1960, Hammond returned the favor by reviewing Govan's book very positively, but not uncritically. Hammond traced through the whole course of historical interpretation regarding Biddle, referring especially to those who had tried to be fair to Biddle: Sumner in 1882, Cotterall in 1903, McMaster in 1906, Bassett in 1911, and Channing in 1921. All of these men were writing in the face of the overwhelming American folk myth, which portrayed Andrew Jackson as the democratic man of the people who, like Saint George, slew the dragon, "the Monster," as the Bank of the United States was called. Biddle was the scheming demon responsible for all of the Bank's evil machinations, which served the rich at the expense of the poor. Biddle was easy to criticize. "The Bank failed, and so did Nicholas Biddle, and it is by this failure that he has been remembered and judged."[390]

Biddle was a difficult man to defend, and yet, said Hammond, Govan had done it. He had written, "the thorough, devoted study of a man long left to neglect and misunderstanding, but gaining at last the presentation warranted by his prominent and public-spirited career."[391] Govan had the rare combination of qualifications needed to do the job: scrupulous honesty, complete mastery of banking and finance, an intimate knowledge of American history, a professional interest in writing this particular book, and passionate convictions about his subject which motivated his desire to make coherent order and meaning out of the "chaos of figures, statements, counter-statements, and vituperation" which the Biddle narrative entailed. He understood the need for central banking control, and the error of Schlesinger and other Jacksonian historians.

Hammond disagreed with Govan's complete exoneration of Biddle from culpability as a major contributor to the Bank's failure:

> Much as I admire Nicholas Biddle and little as I admire Andrew Jackson, the indiscretion and maladroitness of the one seem to me scarcely less evident than the pugnacious and almighty wrongheadedness of the other.[392]

In Hammond's judgment, Biddle should never have tried to continue after the failure of the Bank of the U.S. with the United States Bank of Pennsylvania. He should have retired in 1836 when the Bank of the U.S. was not rechartered but he was still revered.

Govan agreed, though he did not explicitly say so in the biography. He agreed with an emphasis very different from Hammond's. He admitted to Roger Shugg in 1956 that in writing the biography he "was in the unfortunate situation of believing that Biddle was wrong only in his decision to continue the Bank under a state charter,"[393] and wrong only in retrospect. Where Hammond called the decision indiscreet and inept (Biddle should have known that it was folly to challenge Jackson's political authority), Govan believed that he had a very reasonable chance of saving the Bank, and that he knew it. Hammond commented that Biddle "defied the political authority and invited disaster. In doing so he displayed courage, energy, intelligence, and patriotism; but he accomplished little beyond aggrandizement of his adversary."[394] True enough; that is what happened, but one can hear Govan responding, *Yes, but Biddle almost won.* He was right: in fact, he knew it. He showed courage not simply indiscretion; he showed intelligence and patriotism, not simply maladroitness. He failed, but it was oh, so close!

In the preface to the biography, Govan quotes an anonymous Persian chronicler:

> When a mortal's star enters the constellation of misfortune, fate decrees that all his undertakings shall have an effect opposite to that which he desires, and nothing can save him—not the most penetrating intelligence, nor the most extensive experience. His merits are annihilated by the rigour of destiny.

Govan then comments:

> This fatalistic statement of destined defeat is only partially true in this particular circumstance, and its truth is only true after the event. It obscures the closeness to victory that is hidden in Biddle's defeat, and what is best learned from the story is that the successful are not necessarily those who have the right of a matter or the losers those who are in the wrong.[395]

Hammond is left gently shaking his head, but does not regret Govan's enthusiasm or his judgment. His book would do much, he hoped, to overcome the myths about Jackson and Biddle. It also had a close bearing on the present: Biddle's "easy money program" to cure the ills of deflation and depression, Hammond reminded us, are used effectively for the same purpose in our own day. Govan would add it is so much more humane, and therefore better, than policies that may save banks but hurt so many of the people and their enterprises. Hammond ends his review with the comment that Govan "joins a succession of historians who, though they disagree on many things, demonstrate the real nature and importance of Nicholas Biddle's career and the honest statesmanship of his purpose."[396]

Clearly the book was a professional success of which all students of United States banking, of the United States Bank, of Biddle's life, and of Andrew Jackson and his administration must take note.

Further Reviews

Other reviews of Nicholas Biddle Nationalist and Public Banker, 1786-1844, however reflect a variety of views. The liberal-versus-conservative tensions persist among modern historians. The current liberal historians continue to sympathize with Jackson's antipathy to the Bank and his insistence that it was unconstitutional. They tend to agree that the Bank was entirely too autonomous and that its private centralized power constituted a serious threat to democratic government.

As Schlesinger had said in December 1946 in response to Govan's address on the Bank War at the American Historical Association meeting, "Such a concentration in private hands of control over the [credit] system was an anomaly in a democracy."[397] On the face of it, this claim had some justification. The system as it existed under Biddle depended upon one man. In someone else's hands and with different policies, the Bank's role as a national agency of monetary control could be betrayed, corrupted, or even destroyed and the national economy as a result thrown into crisis. The leadership of William Jones early in the First Bank's life and of Thomas Dunlap at the end, during the fall of the United States Bank of Philadelphia, illustrate this danger. The threat of Biddle and the Bank was never what Jackson and his liberal followers, including historians like Schlesinger, thought it to be: a threat to political democracy by some form of dictatorship imposed on the country by the president of the Bank. The real threat was the one Biddle constantly warned against: that destroying the Bank's power as an institution, a national agency of monetary control, would lead inevitably to the weakening of the national economy with all of the consequences thereof: depression and recurring boom-bust cycles. Govan's point, however, was not that the Second Bank of the United States was a perfect structure. It was simply that a national agency of fiscal control was necessary to the economy, that the Bank was such an agency, and that Biddle ran it as nearly perfectly as any man could under the circumstances, and that he did not deserve his fate.

In one of the reviewers'[398] most cogent arguments, the reader is reminded that the evidence upon which Govan chose almost exclusively to depend was made up of Biddle's voluminous correspondence and papers in the Library of Congress and elsewhere. Govan had been so impressed and convinced by Biddle's arguments and explanations of events that he had written an uncritical biography of the man, so uncritical that it was almost Biddle's own autobiography, with Govan as simply his stenographer. Jeanette Nichols, professor of American history at the University of Pennsylvania, added that, "it is difficult for any close student of a strong personality to avoid falling under his spell; but Govan let down his defenses when he decided he need go outside Biddle's correspondence only where it was necessary to check on its accuracy and to gain information about others."[399]

This sounds like a documented and sound argument, but it turns out that these reviewers have quoted Govan selectively. As Peter J. Coleman, professor of American history at Washington University said, "Govan's 'vigorous and persuasive defense of Biddle' is not merely a 'subjective analysis' on Govan's part," but "speaks from the historical record, not from the author's predetermination to render a 'not guilty' verdict against the President of the Second Bank of the United States."[400] Of that historical record Govan had this to say:

> The chief source for the study of the life and activities of Nicholas Biddle and of the operations of the Bank of the United States is in his personal and official correspondence. The Bank's records and general correspondence, with a few insignificant exceptions, were sold for pulp after its failure and liquidation, and this

fact has led to an element of distortion in all historical studies of the period. The loans and other activities of the Bank that were the official concerns of Biddle are almost the only ones of which there is any record at all, and these, particularly the loans to politicians and newspapers that, for obvious reasons, he personally handled, have received undue attention. The collections of Biddle letters and papers at "Andalusia," the Library of Congress, Princeton University, the Historical Society of Pennsylvania, and in the personal possession of Nicholas B. Wainwright constitute one of the prime sources of knowledge of the early history of the United States. From his youth on, Biddle preserved not only the letters he received but also copies or drafts of the letters he sent, and such was the variety of his interest and concerns that almost nothing that happened in the nation during his lifetime is not touched on somewhere in his correspondence. I have gone outside this correspondence only where it was necessary to check on its accuracy and to gain information about others.[401]

Govan had probed the only historical record available more deeply than anyone had before. Every reviewer agreed that this was the case, and they were universally grateful. But he had also understood Biddle and his view more deeply, more clearly, and in more detail than anyone else. The reviewers agreed but questioned significant parts of his judgment. Nevertheless, his portrait of Biddle "stands alone," said Richard P. McCormick, professor of American history at Rutgers: "It differs widely in important details as well as in total impact from previous delineations."[402] As an expert in banking and its history, Govan found himself convinced of the soundness of Biddle's motives and purposes, of his policies, and of his actions. He found Biddle's explanations more convincing than anyone else's, and he found the story as told by others in serious error.

18

Nomads

*We are in a desert and there is no water; we are in a winter that
does not lead to spring and we reject by disbelief the Gospel that
tells us we are wrong.*

Thomas P. Govan

By the spring of 1959, at the end of his fourth year as Executive
Secretary for Faculty Work, and having just completed his harrowing
negotiations over the publication of *Biddle*, Govan was getting restive.
He knew he was a historian, not a church bureaucrat, and that he had
to return as teacher and scholar to a history department, as he said, in
a "reputable university." He reported to the National Commission on
College Work that he had been actively seeking such a placement for
a year, but without success, and would continue his search. He now
knew that his Biddle biography would be published; he was confident
that it would be a professional success within the field of American
history, and that his name would be made within the profession,
making the search for a reputable job easier.

Govan reminded the Commission that it was understood when
he was hired that he would continue as Executive Secretary for Faculty
Work until a suitable opening for him in a university appeared. He
then raised the question with the commission of changing or even
eliminating the post he was holding. What were his reasons? For one

231

thing, great changes had occurred in the church's thinking about its ministry on campus. His work, after all, had affected the church's thinking, if not the university's. Very few of those involved in the work any longer "confused college work with student work." They recognized that the mission of the Church was neither to students alone, nor was its work and witness the exclusive responsibility of ordained priests.

The new view of the church's mission was carried out by all baptized Episcopalians on campus, students, faculty and clergy alike. As Govan had said, "each member of the church on campus, regardless of age, vocation or status is called to bear witness to the incarnate Word, the life which is the light of men."[403] The National Canterbury Association had been transformed accordingly. The purpose of this transformation was to "overcome [at least among Episcopalians on campus] the structural barriers that separate members of the academic community from each other, so that administrators, teachers, staff workers, and students may come to know each other as persons, not as categories, and unitedly engage in their common task of teaching and learning."[404]

Govan noted that he, and Scott-Craig before him, had brought important personal knowledge of the university to the church's national headquarters in New York City, but questioned the necessity of having a lay person in the post. "It is not easy to find an experienced teacher whose circumstances will permit him to take even the minimum required time from his professional work."[405] A three-year leave of absence is the most any lay faculty member could possibly get, yet even that was not long enough to become comfortable or effective in the job, he felt. To resign a faculty position, tenured or not, was risky. The church would have a moral responsibility to keep persons on until they found a position in a college or university, regardless of their competence or effectiveness. As a full professor of history, Govan was finding the search for a position extremely difficult. Govan felt that a priest with the right qualifications could do the executive secretary job just as well and without taking the heavy professional risk he had taken. The commission received the report with full seriousness and assured him of their support and of his position until he found a university position.

McDonald and Brown University

In December 1959, immediately after the publication of *Nicholas Biddle* and the favorable reviews, Govan, full of new confidence, began actively looking for a tenured history professorship. As a result of the book, he was known and recognized in a new way. He sent out a barrage of resumes and spread the news of his availability through friends by word of mouth.

Responses were not long in coming, but they were all for short-term visiting professorships. He knew very well that these responses might lead to what he so desperately wanted, and so was open to them all. The first came from the University of Oregon inviting him to teach the following academic year during the spring term, April to June 1961. A second invitation came from the University of California at Berkeley to teach that summer of 1961, July and August. He immediately accepted both, grateful to "get his oar in the water" again.

One of the friends he wrote to was Forrest McDonald, who by this time had been a full professor of American history at Brown University for a year, and had already had some influence in the history department. James Hedges, chair of Brown's history department, was going to be on sabbatical for the year 1960-1961; a substitute was needed to teach his large introductory American history course. McDonald could vouch authoritatively for Govan's quality as a historian. He even said once that Govan was "the only historian in the country who knew more about American history than he did."[406] He felt guilty no doubt about his part in creating Govan's troubles with the Biddle publication. McDonald spoke up strongly for Tom as a historian completely qualified to teach Hedge's course.

Govan's feelings about McDonald were mixed. On one hand, Tom recognized McDonald's brilliance and appreciated his obvious care and great respect for him and his work. McDonald and the AHRC had made all the difference in Govan's successful completion of Biddle. But on the other hand, Govan recognized McDonald's immaturity and tendency toward arrogance. He had been unable to keep himself and his concerns out of the negotiations on Govan's behalf and so, verging on disingenuousness, had confused the issue of publication terribly and placed Govan in a very difficult position.

Govan was inclined to be charitable toward McDonald, but Jane was not. She was furious about the Biddle confusion, and felt she could never trust McDonald again. She warned Tom about having anything to do with McDonald. Govan was in no position to quibble. He needed the job and they both knew it. So Tom wrote to McDonald that he would accept the position if offered.

The offer from Brown came in the spring of 1960, and Govan immediately accepted and applied for a part-time leave from his work for the Episcopal Church with whom he was still under contract until he had a full-time tenured position. Bishop Daniel Corrigan, head of the Home Department, and Presiding Bishop Arthur Lichtenberger, knowing Govan's desires, enthusiastically granted the leave. In September Tom received an official letter from Barnaby C. Keeney, president of Brown University, formally establishing both his appointment and his release in April to teach at Oregon, even though the Brown semester did not end until June. Someone else would be found to cover for him those last three months.[407] So now Tom had three jobs at Brown, Oregon, and California. Each of these appointments would give him wide exposure as a senior historian. But oh, how hard this uprooted nomadic life was for them, especially Jane. She felt lonely and upset facing another move. She was still recovering from her operation, but slowly. Tom had his job, but she had to tag along making new friends and finding things to do. All along they had been together in the big decisions: leaving Sewanee, working for the church, and now returning to academia. Their mutual need for support was one of the things that drew them together. Only McDonald divided them, and even then Tom knew she was right.

In September, the Govans moved to 76 Barnes Street in Providence near the university. As an adjunct (visiting) professor, Tom would earn between $2300 and $2400 from the university. Even with their $7000 from the Episcopal Church, they were scrimping.[408]

Except for Forrest McDonald, the Brown history department, including Hedges, was largely Jeffersonian and liberal, and not too sure they liked this new conservative addition in their midst. As a senior professor, but a new man in the department, Tom gravitated naturally to the younger teachers who were new and inexperienced, several of them on the tenure track. He had no power, but he could listen, suggest and advise. Several of them became close friends.

It did not take long for Govan's presence to be felt by the students. Both he and McDonald knew that he would be teaching the course from the "conservative" Hamiltonian view, not the "liberal" Jeffersonian one. This would be a considerable change from Hedges that presented Govan with a teaching challenge that both worried and exhilarated him. The Civil Rights Movement was gathering momentum and the southern states were resisting it on grounds identical to those they had used to resist giving up slavery. It was also true that racial prejudice was rampant throughout the country, North as well as South, East as well as West, and Brown University was no exception. Past history was radically relevant to the present situation. Everything Govan believed was again at stake, and he felt passionately about his mission to tell the true story of United States history and of the true meaning of the Civil Rights Movement.

Govan had a challenging first year with his students. He said things that were new to most and many did not like what he said. Among them, there was little question that he knew what he was talking about, and he made a dent in the popular Jeffersonian liberalism of the students. The December 2, 1960 issue of *The Brown Daily Herald*, for example, reported a lecture Govan was invited to give at "the sixth cultural affairs discussion at Phi Delta Theta fraternity." What he had to say was news. *The Herald* reported that:

> Jefferson, according to Govan, falsely assumed the States had compacted to form a union (the United States) as a result of the Declaration of Independence.

> To the contrary, said Govan, the foundations of the Union were formed before the states had a definite structure. The basis of union was first formulated in the First Continental Congress in which the colonies united to

fight for a common cause, and then later in the 1789 Constitution.

Jefferson also falsely assumed that the individual sovereign states had ultimate jurisdiction over the actions of the federal government, and that the federal courts did not have authority to interpret the Constitution for the nation and for the states. Govan said that Jefferson believed that freedom was dependent on the sovereignty of the states. Today, however, there is a sovereign state that is protecting a howling group of mad women shouting obscenities at a few six-year old Negro girls trying to go to school in Little Rock, Arkansas. That situation, he said, is the result of the [ideas and] work of one virtuous man [Jefferson] acting according to [his own] theory [of how] to protect the doctrine of (individual) freedom. The voice of the people is not God, Govan said, but (often) the voice of the devil seeking to destroy freedom. No one can be trusted to protect freedom without the support and restraints of law and of good training.

Challenging the Liberals Again

In November 1960 Govan was invited to lecture at the Southern Historical Association's annual meeting in Tulsa, Oklahoma. In a sense, as a southerner, he was "speaking to his own" fellow southerners, but his message would be one of devastating disagreement with most of them. The address was an updated version of his 1952 lecture at the University of Virginia and a summary of his course at Brown, "The Liberal and Conservative Traditions in the United States,"[409] revised, sharpened, and provocatively entitled "Agrarianism, Sectionalism, and State Sovereignty Denounced: a Refutation of Thomas Jefferson, John Taylor of Caroline, Andrew Jackson, John C.

Calhoun, and the Historians Who Have Been Misled by Their Teaching."

A report in *The Journal of Southern History* described the occasion as follows:

> The main attraction Thursday afternoon was a joint session of the American Studies and the Southern Historical Associations with the intriguing title of "The Southern Tradition: True or False, Orthodox or Heretical." (The room where the session was held was packed with more than 125 auditors). Thomas P. Govan of Brown University challenged the thesis that such agrarian leaders of the South and West as Jefferson, John Taylor, John C. Calhoun, and Andrew Jackson were the originators and defenders of the constitutional principles that have best promoted freedom and equality. On the contrary, Mr. Govan maintained that the true defenders of equality and freedom in America have been those in each generation who argued for national strength to promote, sustain, and protect the general welfare by restraining powerful and selfish individual groups.[410]

This was not the first time that Tom had spoken under dramatic circumstances, or spoken against the prevailing opinion. Nor was it the first time his fellow historians had heard this line of argument. But now the Civil Rights Movement was in full swing. Nine months earlier on February 1, four black college students in Greensboro, North Carolina, refused to move from a Woolworth's lunch counter when denied service. Since then, sit-in protests had spread throughout the South.

The southern states were universally resisting the Movement and the federal law beginning to support it, justifying their resistance on the old states' rights basis (earlier used to justify slavery and then white supremacy). The South, which in effect had "won" the Civil War after Reconstruction by reestablishing states' rights and white supremacy, was being challenged again. Liberal historians, literary critics, and other commentators—from the South, West, and even from the North—had been providing the justification the South needed by using the agrarian, sectional, and state-sovereignty arguments of Jefferson, John Taylor, Jackson, and Calhoun to support their resistance to the Civil Rights challenge. Govan reviewed the real history, the false meaning read into that history, and once more set the record straight.

The Southerner as American: C. Vann Woodward's Review

During the fall of 1960, *The Southerner as American*,[411] a collection of nine essays edited by Charles Grier Sellers, Jr. of Princeton University, was published. One of its key essays was by Tom Govan. In many ways the book was a rebuttal to *I'll Take My Stand: The South and the Agrarian Tradition*,[412] which had appeared thirty years before in 1930 and had tried to define the South as a section with a culture separate from the rest of the country; gentler and more civilized, less commercial. Sellers' book self-consciously sought to demolish this mythical past that had encouraged the South to stand apart from the modern world. It argued that southerners are and always have been first of all Americans, united with and like the rest of the country, and only secondarily separate and southern.

Govan's essay, "Americans Below the Potomac," wove two earlier essays together: "Was the Old South Different?" which said "no" to that question, and "John C. Calhoun: A Reappraisal," which found Calhoun's self-centered and separatist policies wrongheaded and a cause of the Civil War. This was the same theme about which he had spoken at the November 1960 meeting in Tulsa, Oklahoma, but with a slightly different emphasis: the fallacies of sectionalism. He felt strongly about this and had spoken and written about it often.

The book as a whole was favorably reviewed for *The American Historical Review*[413] by James W. Silver of the University of Mississippi. He wrote that Govan had rather thoroughly demolished the popular notion of two divergent, irreconcilable social and economic systems divided by the Mason-Dickson line: tariff, banking, and inflation-deflation issues transcended sectional loyalties; Calhoun's [separatist] economic policies [for example] were unsupported by a southern majority; and in 1850 Southerners considered themselves Americans economically."[414]

C. Vann Woodward, a southerner, an old friend and mentor of Govan's, reviewed the book for *The Journal of Southern History*.[415] He was a distinguished professor of American history at Johns Hopkins University. At the time, he was the recent author of *The Strange Career of Jim Crow* (1955), a ground-breaking book that denied the myth that southern culture was the source of racial segregation and demonstrated instead that formal segregation was the result of social and political forces in 1885, thirty years after the Civil War. In the process of his review, he quite unintentionally upset, hurt and angered Govan by suggesting that Govan had said that southerners were "merely Americans below the Potomac and even the Civil War and Reconstruction gave them no feeling of unity among themselves and difference from the rest of the nation."[416] What Govan actually said was very different. He had argued that the Civil War and Reconstruction had given them "a feeling of unity among themselves and difference from the rest of the nation," but that after the war they had given up that feeling of difference from the rest of the nation, because there was so much more uniting them with the North than dividing them.

Govan had described the United States earlier as "one society [North and South] which had been produced . . . by the [European] Renaissance, the Reformation, the Commercial, Scientific and Industrial Revolutions, Capitalism and Political Democracy."[417]

Feeling the strain he was under during that year and especially sensitive as a result, Tom fired off a letter to Woodward in protest. The incident was an example of how easily and inadvertently misunderstanding and misrepresentation can happen, and how sensitive scholars can be. Tom felt betrayed; and the review almost wrecked the relationship between two fine and steady men.

Govan had made a carefully nuanced point, and Woodward had misinterpreted it and made it into a blunt, over-simple incorrect point. What particularly hurt and angered Govan was that Woodward should have known better. He should have realized that on the issue of sectionalism, he and Govan had real differences, and for that very reason, he should have read Govan's argument with special care, but he had not. He had just not read Govan's article carefully and accurately enough.

Woodward immediately wrote to Govan and apologized. "You know, I hope that I would never consciously do you an injury and that I would be covered with shame to misrepresent anybody—consciously or unconsciously." On returning to the sentence of Govan's in question, however, he "was relieved to find that [he] interpreted the statement the same way and that if [he] had misrepresented [Govan], it was unintentional and in good faith." He then spelled out his thinking, which, without much doubt, Govan understood.

He ended his letter asking Govan how he could "put the record straight and remove from your mind and anybody else's mind the slightest suspicion that I would consciously misrepresent one of my oldest and most cherished friends." How the misunderstanding was resolved is not clear, though chances are that Govan wrote Woodward again, and Woodward finally saw the misrepresentation. In any case, their relationship was not broken. In a postscript, Woodward assured Govan that a permanent teaching job would surely turn up that spring (1961) and that "he would write the minute he heard of such a place."[418]

The Search for Work

In April 1961, the Govans temporarily moved from Providence to Eugene, Oregon, where Tom taught for three months, April through June. They liked the town and the university right away. They were welcomed with western hospitality; they found congenial friends; the climate was wonderful; Jane's aches and pains from her operation were reduced; and Tom's peers showed them both respect and affection. There were none of the tensions he had felt at Brown. Needless to say, Oregon was a real consideration for a long-term future.

One of Tom's primary preoccupations that summer of 1961 was the preparation of his five lectures on the theological meaning of American history for the third National Study Conference of the Episcopal Church to be held at Beloit College, Beloit, Wisconsin, from August 30 through September 6, 1961. This would be his major opportunity to spell out for the church his views on how the Christian faith in its Anglican form and the evolution of the English Constitution underlie the United States Constitution, its political and legal institutions, and are the basis of imperfect but very real freedom. He chose as his title the phrase, "A New Birth of Freedom" from Abraham Lincoln's Gettysburg Address.

It also happened that the second West Coast Faculty Summer School, sponsored by the Church Society for College Work and the College Division of the Episcopal Church, was being held at the Church Divinity School of the Pacific from the last week of July until the end of August. Tom's old friend, Jones Shannon, who was running the summer school that year, offered Tom a "faculty" position at the school. Tom accepted with the understanding that he had a major undertaking of his own to work on. So Jane and Tom moved from Eugene to the Divinity School in Berkeley and settled in for a quiet month before the Study Conference.

Where he would teach during the 1961-1962 academic year was not clear. Brown could not give him a full-time job that year because James Hedges had returned from his sabbatical and there were no other openings. The history department did take him on part-time to advise graduate students in history and to lead a seminar. In mid-summer he heard from his old friend, Lee Belford, from Sewanee and New York days, who was head of the religion department at New York University and had succeeded in working out with the history department a part-time adjunct professorship for Tom, with the hope that it would develop into something more. Govan gratefully accepted. For that year, the Govans had his church salary, a small stipend from Brown for work with graduate students, and a little more from NYU. Financially, they were barely making it.

The Govans returned to their Barnes Street apartment in Providence for the year exhausted from their travels. They enjoyed the town and the university and found it half as expensive as living in New York. But Tom would have to commute once a week for three days to New York, spending nights with friends or at the Episcopal Church Center at 281 Park Avenue South.

Tom's professional uncertainty, Jane's major surgery, their financial anxiety and near penury, and the physical strain of these peripatetic years were severely challenging, almost debilitating for the Govans. Even so, the courage and faith with which they were dealing with that strain showed in Tom's reports and letters to the National Commission for College Work. On the whole, however, except for a few close friends, the Govans kept their suffering to themselves.

19

A Final Year in Limbo, 1961-1962

The Christian understanding of history is the basic
affirmation of meaning and purpose in life, without which
there can be no history in any true sense of the term, or any
justification for its study.

Thomas P. Govan

Despite their insecurity, suffering and the necessity of waiting
and wondering for most of 1961-1962, some good things had happened
for the Govans. The previous summer of teaching at the University of
Oregon in Eugene had been stimulating, introduced him and Jane to a
place they liked very much—it was an extreme and welcome rural
contrast to Providence and New York—and he discovered that the
retirement age at the university was seventy rather than sixty-five as it was
at NYU. Given Tom's need for building up the level of his pension
benefits, he found this an attractive feature. His official church work was
winding down, but he was receiving full salary, such as it was. His university
work at Brown, although much reduced, allowed him to do what he
loved: work with graduate students in seminars and advise individuals.
Although the part-time appointment at NYU imposed a wearing
commute, it came with the tantalizing possibility of a full-time
appointment there the following year, 1962-63.

Segregation at Sewanee

There was one particular circumstance that fall rankled Tom and Jane concerning his old university, the University of the South in Sewanee. Its School of Theology had been desegregated since 1953, but the university did not follow until June 1961. In the process of those eight years, there had been a great deal of "foot dragging" over the issue, for which, Tom believed, Vice Chancellor McCrady was primarily responsible. Tom saw him as a torn man: on the one hand, a racist who wanted no change and gave ground only when he had to; on the other hand, a Christian who claimed to believe that all humans are equally God's children. He evolved into a "gradualist," who moved as slowly as possible. Govan fundamentally distrusted McCrady's claims to virtue.

The net result of desegregation at Sewanee was a trickle of blacks admitted into the university, mostly in the School of Theology. The Sewanee Inn and Claramont Restaurant, housed in buildings owned by the university and rented to Mrs. Clara Shoemate, still refused to serve blacks under any circumstances. The restaurant remained an embarrassment to both the university and the Episcopal Church.

In August 1961, the Episcopal Society for Cultural and Racial Unity (ESCRU), an independent society of the Episcopal Church dedicated to ending segregation and promoting racial unity, especially in the Church, challenged the university's policy of allowing Mrs. Shoemate to refuse to serve blacks, and threatened a sit-in. In response to ESCRU's threat, a group of faculty and students, black and white, from the graduate School of Theology and the school as a whole, staged a sit-in with the hope that Mrs. Shoemate would give in and serve all members of the university community. They hoped that "by proving that a Negro could eat at the Claramont, the threatened demonstration could be fended off,"[419] thus avoiding more negative publicity to the University of the South. Three faculty, one trustee, all white, and three graduate students, all ordained black clergy from South Carolina then studying at the university, sat in and were refused.

Then in September 1961, a group of Episcopal clergy members of ESCRU, black and white, carried out a sit-in at the restaurant, and when no change in restaurant policy occurred, returned in April 1962, to sit in for three more days. McCrady reiterated that the university disapproved of Mrs. Shoemate's policy, but could not and would not force her to change. Mrs. Shoemate was adamant, and so the clergy finally left unserved for the second time, but made a public statement condemning her actions and the university for tolerating her policy.

In response, the theological faculty of the university published a statement in the April 14, 1962 *Chattanooga Times*, which said,

> It is our conviction that the Christian faith and racial segregation are inherently contradictory. This is the common conviction of numerous persons and groups who over the years have worked for the elimination of segregation in the University of the South.
>
> In 1952, prior to the Supreme Court decision, the School of Theology was integrated. Since then the university has successively integrated the Summer Graduate School of Theology and the entire university structure, including the College, and the Sewanee Military Academy, together with such university-owned facilities as the Union Sandwich Shop and public concerts and plays. The university is now in the process of exerting its moral influence to bring about the elimination of racial barriers in the Claramont Restaurant and Sewanee Inn, a private business operated under lease in university owned buildings.
>
> These changes have been brought about essentially by internal pressures by the duly constituted authorities of the university, its trustees, regents, administrators and faculties. The Episcopal Society for Cultural and Racial Unity, on the basis of the same conviction and seeking

the same objectives, is employing tactics which in the Sewanee situation we believe ineffective and unnecessarily destructive. While we recognize that many difficult problems remain, we are grateful for the progress that has been made. Thus we will continue to attempt to be responsible in our local situation as we continue our determined efforts to bring about the elimination of racial segregation, here and elsewhere.

Govan was incensed and so drafted a letter to Edward McCrady that was intended to be signed by all the members of the Executive Council of the Episcopal Church. The letter was never completed or sent but expressed his central conviction:

> The priests who came [to the Claramont Restaurant] asking to be served, we believe, were the Church asking to be served, and when even the least of His children are refused, so also is He and His Church.[420]

On the evening of April 19, 1962, Govan had a long telephone conversation—Cora Louise Belford,[421] overhearing, called it "a shouting match"—with the Reverend C. Fitzsimmons Allison, a former student, a close friend and member of the School of Theology faculty. All of Tom's old feelings about the university reignited. He reverted to treating Allison as a graduate student, lecturing him. Next day he wrote the following letter to Allison:

> Dear Fitz:
>
> In our distressing conversation last night you did ask me to write the sort of statement I would like for you to issue and I have been presumptuous enough to comply.
>
> What I said, in love and sorrow, I meant and I was speaking with the assurance and certainty that I have most centrally learned from you. When we know that we have nothing

of ourselves, that adhering to the law in itself is of no value,[422] then we can, yea must, proclaim the law that applies to me as to you and to all other men (the law of love). Now to the statement that you and the others have written.

'It is our conviction that the Christian faith and racial segregation are inherently contradictory' is surely a Greek statement, not one based on a living faith in Him who said that "what ye do to the least of these, my children, ye do unto me;" who ordered us to love one another as He loves us;[423] and who judges His servants who hold on to their penny by burying it, most harshly.[424] It is by fruits that our work must be judged; and not once since 1952 [when the seminary was desegregated] has anyone in Sewanee produced any graceful, charitable fruits in this [desegregation] area. What has been done most reluctantly, and, I say it, deceitfully, has been done in response to external pressure or threats of pressure . . . .

'This is the common conviction of numerous persons and groups who over the years have worked for the elimination of segregation in the University of the South.' Greek humanists have convictions, but we serve a living Lord who judges and of whom we are properly afraid. We dare not separate ourselves from our brothers because in doing it we separate ourselves from Him who is the sole source of life, light, and knowledge.

To Tom, a Greek statement was a rational statement of conviction to be judged by the clarity and accuracy of its logic. But a biblical statement was a moral statement to be based on a living relationship with a living God who is to be obeyed or disobeyed. The truth or falsehood of a statement is to be judged not on logic, but on our behavior, its moral results. "By their fruit shall yet know them." We are to "love our neighbors as ourselves" and the faculty had not.

247

Therefore, their statement based on its immoral results was a "deceitful lie."

Govan's letter continues,

> In 1952, prior to the Supreme Court decision, the School of Theology was integrated.' This though factually accurate is, I insist, in implication a lie. The same harsh judgment applies to all the rest of the paragraph and to the first sentence of the next.

> I have read and reread this part of the statement seeking some foundation in truth (as contrasted with literal factuality) but I can see no way to interpret what you have said that makes it anything but entirely and utterly false. The sentence on ESCRU, though I believe it to be wrong, is not in itself particularly obnoxious, but in the context of your and your colleagues' claim to personal virtue, it is, to use another harsh phrase, nauseating.

> To turn from theology to history, we certainly learned from Chamberlain [who tried to appease Hitler] that licking the boots of bullies does not do any good. They interpret it as weakness, not an attempt at conciliation, and you strengthen their hand. If, as some apologists of Chamberlain maintain, but which I do not believe, he personally was buying time so that radar and the Spitfires would be ready, then the humiliation was necessary. But, in the situation at Sewanee at this moment, such humble licking of boots is not required, and here, though I can certainly be wrong, I speak with as much information and knowledge of the nastiness and hope as you.

> It may be that in this moment of crisis, I too should have a conversation with the headshrinker in Washington,[425] but then, if you reported what he said

accurately, he would probably tell me, as he told you, that my overwillingness to push into situations where I am not wanted along with the tears that I too easily shed, constitute evidence that I do care.

Jane joins in love to you, Martha, and the children.

Tom

The theological faculty responded to Govan's letter publicly in a letter to the editor of *The Living Church* (and other church periodicals) as follows:

Dear Sir:

On April 13, in a period of strain and excitement here at Sewanee, we issued a public statement that, as we now read it, did not convey what we intended to say. What we were trying to point out was that some progress had been made towards the elimination of racial segregation in the University of the South even though, at the moment we wrote, a group of Negro and white priests of the Episcopal Church were being denied service at the Claramont Restaurant on the university domain.

In our excitement, perhaps in our anger, we overstated the case and claimed for ourselves and the university a virtue we do not possess. In spite of our silence on the matter, we do remember that the trustees' action in June, 1953, permitting Negroes to enter the Theological School, was a reversal of the policy adopted the previous year, and that this reversal was in part brought about by the resignation of eight members of the theological faculty. This was one of the 'internal pressures' to which we referred in our letter, but we erred by failing to mention the heavy price paid by these men, our honored predecessors in the positions we now hold.

We also claimed too much for ourselves when we said, 'we will continue to attempt to be responsible in our local situation as we continue our determined efforts to bring about the elimination of racial segregation here and elsewhere.' We do pray that we will be enabled to act in this manner and for this purpose, but none of us, we know, has done what he should.

The university itself, though it has made progress for which we are grateful, has not done all that we claimed. No Negro has as yet been admitted to the college or the military academy, and the integration we referred to was an authorization by the trustees in June 1961, to admit qualified applicants to these institutions without regard to color or race. The Negro priests, who have studied at the Graduate School of Theology in the summer, we regretfully admit, have been subjected to numerous discriminations in the community, but most of these, we are happy to say, have been eliminated during the present year. This summer, those who attend will have the same privileges as the white priests.

Our charges against our brother priests, the members of ESCRU who came to Sewanee asking to be fed, also were overstated and uncharitable. We had requested them not to make such a demonstration, and when our request was disregarded, we were piqued, if not angered. What they did, we still believe, was unwise, but 'ineffective and unnecessarily destructive,' the terms we used, were too harsh. Our only defense is one we are not entitled to make, that we were replying in kind to what we considered their unnecessarily harsh statements about us and the university.

250

> Please pardon the length of this, our apology, but our
> earlier statement, we now know, gave an inaccurate
> picture.

The friendship, Christian commitment, and candor of Govan
and Allison made possible quite an extraordinary exchange and
a good result. The Claramont Inn was soon closed down. Govan
and Allison remained friends. This incident, however, revealed
Tom's natural tendency toward contentiousness, and the depth
of the pain he continued to bear as a result of his Sewanee
experience. Equally, it reveals the depth of his Christian
commitment and understanding.

The Christian Understanding of History

While in Providence, Govan was asked to lead a conference on
"The Christian Understanding of History" to be held at Packard Manse,
an ecumenical conference center in Stoughton, Massachusetts, on a
weekend at the end of January 1962. Faculty from the New England
area were invited to attend.

In the announcement of the conference, Tom expressed his
perspective on the subject more succinctly than ever before: Christian
understanding of history is not one interpretation or theory of history
among others, but the basic affirmation that human life and, therefore,
human history *do* have meaning, despite evidence to the contrary,
despite not being able to prove or fully understanding its meaning,
and despite the fact that all attempts to know "fully and for sure" end
inevitably in disillusionment and cynicism. His conference
announcement reads as follows:

> Christian commitment, the acceptance of Christ as Lord
> and giver of life, too frequently is thought of by Christians
> as well as non-Christians as an acceptance of a limiting
> and confining view, a prejudging of issues, and so not the
> proper attitude for a historian who must be free to follow
> wherever the facts lead. The Christian Understanding of

251

History thus is interpreted to be only one among many possible understandings of history, a rival of other religious and non-religious views.

If this be the true situation, no need exists for a conference of Christian historians on such a subject as the Christian understanding of history. Such a conference would call together like-minded men to better instruct them for their combat with others, and to provide them with more effective weapons of propaganda, and as such would only do harm.

But if the Christian Understanding of History is the basic affirmation of meaning and purpose in life, without which there can be no history in any true sense of the term, or any justification for its study, then the situation is different. A conference which has for its purpose the making of such a proclamation would be valuable to non-Christians and Christians alike, for the study and teaching of history is a frustrating and exasperating business, a vanity and striving after wind, as the Preacher said, for those who through history would know that which it is not given to men to know.[426]

The announcement was distributed widely among Brown University faculty and to other New England universities through the Packard Manse mailing list.

No one responded.

Govan was not surprised. He said that the people who might be interested in a Christian understanding of history were almost always thinking about it as "one among many possible understandings of history, a rival of other religions and non-religious views." That was precisely the view he wanted to counteract because to pursue it could only do harm by sharpening divisions. What historians need is an acceptance of what they cannot know and a living faith grounded not on their knowledge but on the reality of a living God. A conference to explore the plausibility and meaning of such a faith would be well worthwhile.

Govan believed that the word "history" was a synonym for the "Providence of God." That was the real issue, but no one understood it.

The conference was cancelled.

Last Report to the Episcopal Church

In what turned out to be his last report to the Commission on College Work of the Episcopal Church,[427] Tom articulated the temptation of both university faculty and clergy in the church to allow guilt and anxiety to overtake them. "We have closed our ears" to the Gospel and measure what we do by our own evaluation of our success or failure. "We pretend to a virtue we do not possess."

Our best efforts have not reformed either the university or the church. But our success is not the point, said Govan. We serve a God who loves us, the university, and the church, not as they should be, but as they and we are. Loving and serving as we are is enough because God loves and forgives us.

This was his final evaluation of his five years of professional work for the Episcopal Church. It reveals the passion of a man who had suffered a great deal over the previous ten years, but was not broken.

20

Security At Last, New York University, 1962-1967

Then Tom Govan, Eastered now,
south accented white man,
the burden of resisting hatred
heavy on his shoulders, a relief
of love warming his wrinkles
and white thatch,
read the lesson.

Will Inman

A Full Professor Again

In July 1962, James M. Hester, president of New York University, sent Govan a letter of appointment as full professor of American history, and Tom and Jane joyfully and immediately moved from Providence to an apartment at 3 Sheridan Square in West Greenwich Village. The steady urging of Lee Belford, the Govans' friend and chairman of the department of religion, and the very positive response of the American history profession to his book on Nicholas Biddle had finally had their effect. He was recognized at last as an important American historian, and being hired by NYU validated that. He resigned as Executive Secretary

254

for Faculty Work of the Episcopal Church, and a new period in the Govan's lives began. Life really was looking up.

Feeling better was long overdue. Tom had left Sewanee on principle; he had accepted his Episcopal Church job because he felt called to it, and his history career would be pursued from a biblical vision that almost no other American historian shared. Individuals might share pieces of his conclusions in particular areas, but none of his peers shared his unique theological position, which combined the Niebuhrian view of sin in the context of Frederick Denison Maurice's universalistic, Anglican view of God's Providence. He had been true to his Christian convictions, and it had cost him dearly. But now he would settle into his history vocation of teaching and guiding graduate students into the history profession, a part of his vocation he had missed terribly.

Jane Govan, age 59, in their apartment at
240 East 15th Street, New York City, December 1966

His gratitude and appreciation for Jane was unbounded. Her loyalty, support, and humor throughout that past decade, in spite of the tensions between them and his occasional bouts with depression, had been unfailing. He knew she was in fundamental sympathy with him on most things, and he was glad to be able to provide her with a more comfortable home and fewer worries about money. His salary was about $14,000 plus "perks." They felt secure at last.

One major reality of which they were reminded whenever they moved into a new home was the fact that they were still a household of only two; they were without children and always would be. Their great sadness was the main reason why their dachshund, Judy II, was especially important to them. She was good company and someone to care for. She had to be walked, washed, and taken occasionally to the veterinarian, and Tom helped with her care. But Jane went beyond that and several times had Judy bred; she brought up at least three successful litters during their five years in New York. Tom's enthusiasm for this repeated ordeal, as he put it, was "loyal but limited." He once wrote the David Underdowns, their friends now at the University of Virginia, whom they were planning to visit,

> our dog [Judy] is approaching her season which is a complicating factor in our plans at the moment, for Jane is determined that she is to be bred this time. Until this crisis is surmounted either by its happening or not happening—I'm not exactly sure which we are waiting for—Jane will not say yea or nay. I still hope she will come down with me and we certainly will plan for more than a day with you.[428]

Tom taught at NYU for five years, from 1962-1967, most of the time in four areas: United States history from the Revolution to 1836, the national period; the Civil War, its prelude and consequences; United States economic history; and southern history. His schedule usually called for one undergraduate and two graduate school courses, with accompanying seminars. He loved these seminars and their give-and-take with graduate students, but found straight lecturing to undergraduates far more of a strain because he was continually faced with students imbued with "liberal" Jeffersonian ideas that were in vogue at that time.

He often could not tell whether he was getting through to them. He was grateful for his graduate students: more mature and serious than the undergraduates, and because they were on the whole not from the South, more open to his view.

During his five years at NYU, the power of what he had to say was augmented by the events of the period, a mixture of hopeful signs and disastrous blows. The previous spring and summer of 1961 the Freedom Riders had protested segregation in interstate travel facilities. On October 1, 1962, a month after his arrival at NYU, James Meredith was admitted as the first black student to the University of Mississippi after a terrible riot. On June 11, 1963, the University of Alabama was desegregated when George Wallace finally gave in to the attorney general backed by National Guard troops. The next day the civil rights leader Medgar Evers was assassinated. On August 28, the March on Washington, 200,000 strong, was highlighted by Martin Luther King's "I Have A Dream" speech. On September 15 in Montgomery, a bomb blast at the Sixteenth Street Baptist Church killed four little black girls attending Sunday School. On November 22, President John F. Kennedy was assassinated in Dallas, and Lyndon Johnson became president. On July 2, 1964 an omnibus civil rights bill was passed, banning discrimination in voting, jobs, and public accommodations. On August 4, 1964, the bodies of three civil rights workers, Michael Schwerner, Andrew Goodman, and James E. Cheney, were found buried in Mississippi. Seven white men were later convicted of conspiracy in the slaying by an all-white jury. It was a volatile period.

None of this was lost on Govan or his students. They discussed these issues constantly, and Tom repeatedly placed these events in the context of United States history. He always reminded the students that the North and South together were one country and that racism, discrimination and injustice were national, not just southern, problems. Most of Govan's students agreed with him on these issues and were committed to the Civil Rights Movement. They learned history from Govan and the daily newspapers.

Vietnam, however, was another matter. Tom strongly supported the war; the students almost universally opposed it. As President Johnson escalated the war, and the draft came into effect, the Peace Movement grew accordingly and became a political force. Almost all of Tom's students considered themselves members of that movement.

Tom tried to make the case for the war. As a Democrat and a nationalist, he trusted the President to know more about the real situation than he or his students knew. As Harry Truman had carried out a "no-win, no lose" policy in Korea, so, Tom believed, Lyndon Johnson was doing the same in Vietnam. "Draw a line between North and South and hold it firm," seemed to be Johnson's policy. All attacks of the North upon the South had to be repulsed. Not until two years after the 1968 Tet Offensive in 1970, Johnson, under tremendous popular pressure, finally realized that the war could not be won and announced that he would not run again for the presidency. The war and, as a result, his presidency were considered failures. Only then did Govan, with his deep inclination to trust the judgment of federal authority, follow suit and change his point of view. It was painful to do so. Being wrong was hard enough. He felt sorry about that, but even more, he felt betrayed by the president.

Tom also lost credibility with his students over this issue, but won much of it back by being completely open and frank about how wrong he had been. They were impressed with a teacher who could admit he had been wrong.

Tom's mood at Christmas that year was darkened by his feeling about his old nemesis, Arthur Schlesinger, Jr., who was enjoying great popular success with *The Roosevelt Years*. In a letter full of sardonic humor that covered over genuine and long-term hurt, Tom confessed to a friend that any good feelings he felt professionally and in his relationship with Jane were overshadowed by

> my sheer envy of the money and fame that has come to
> Arthur (Schlesinger), Jr., whose book (*The Roosevelt Years*)
> even if it is good and which I hope it is not, I have resolutely
> determined not to read. Of course, like all my good
> resolutions, I will probably break it and if I do, I am
> determined to find the book wrong and mean-spirited
> somehow. You can see I am getting in the right spirit for
> Christmas.[429]

Schlesinger's success really hurt Tom. Envy was part of it, but even deeper was a sense of injustice—or was it failure? Tom knew he had American history right all along; he had spelled it out in *Nicholas Biddle* in 1959, and in numerous articles. Schlesinger in *The Age of Jackson* had been confused and wrong, and Govan had told him so (see Chapter 6). Then Schlesinger changed, admitted his errors and wrote *The Roosevelt Years*, which perfectly illustrated Govan's point. But Schlesinger made the money and received the accolades, not Tom. Yet, he knew that he had not gotten the word out as effectively as Schlesinger. He summed up his mood in a letter:

> Everything at the moment seems at sort of a standstill here, nationally and personally, an attitude of waitful expectancy almost as if we thought Godot was on his way. But maybe he will and maybe he won't. The mood will pass and when vacation is over, all things will begin again—I will be I, my things will be wet, to quote or paraphrase my own true poet [W.H. Auden, whom Tom knew slightly; they attended the same church, St. Mark's-in-the-Bowery].[430]

School vacations were always hard for Tom because his sense of his own identity was so entirely tied up with his vocation. When college begins again, "I will be I . . . my things will be wet." For Auden, "wet" meant alive, full of vitality and potential. Govan was "dry," deadened, and depressed, but hopeful. He knew Christmas was a fact, and the drought would pass.

Dwight McDonald

For Govan, one of the great pleasures of his return to New York (1962-1963) was meeting the radical journalist Dwight McDonald, then a staff writer for *The New Yorker* magazine. Govan had read his articles and come to respect his literary judgment. McDonald, for example, "deplored the dominance in American society of mass culture, which thrives not on aesthetic merit but on marketability," which pretends to respect high standards, but "actually degrades them and corrupts what is truly creative."[431] Tom especially appreciated his criticism of the updated language of the *Revised Standard Version of the Bible*, the permissiveness with new words and new meanings of older ones of *Webster's Third New International Dictionary*, and the pretensions of *Great Books of the Western World.*[432]

There is no record of how or where the Govans met McDonald, but clearly when they met, they liked each other,[433] found lots of common ground, and even discussed theology. McDonald wrote,

> Great pleasure meeting you and your nice wife and I enjoyed our theological talk (if my side can be so dignified). Theology, I find, is the only aspect of religion that interests me—I do love hairsplitting and argumentation.[434]

Govan had found a friend indeed. But there was more. They discovered that they both had written critical reviews of Arthur M. Schlesinger, Jr.'s recent book of essays called *The Politics of Hope.*[435] No doubt Govan had attacked Schlesinger's rosy liberalism much as McDonald had in years past. In any case, McDonald thanked Govan for his review and added,

> I only wish you had written more yourself and quoted less, because your last paragraph is so packed and rich— but maybe that's a good strategy.[436]

Tom was pleased, but when he read McDonald's review, he was filled with delight. McDonald had heard in Schlesinger's book "the intonations of a fashionable preacher blended with those of an ideological con man."[437] In *The Age of Jackson,*[438] McDonald said, Schlesinger had painted "a rosy picture of Jacksonian democracy" and mistakenly implied a parallel with Franklin Roosevelt's New Deal and won a Nobel Prize for it! Schlesinger claimed for himself the role of spokesman for what he called the "Vital Center," the liberal wing of the Democratic Party. Then Jack Kennedy was elected President and Schlesinger became a "Special Assistant to the President."[439] He was now, as McDonald put it, the "liberal prophet of Camelot." As McDonald pointed out, his introduction to *The Politics of Hope* sounded like "the triumphant chant of the prophet who, after seven lean years, sees his people liberated from the Egyptian bondage of the Eisenhower administration."[440] It was the pretension of the man that McDonald was lampooning, and Govan loved it.

Schlesinger's panegyric went on. With the Kennedys, Jack and Bobby, in charge:

> We no longer seem an old nation, tired, complacent and self-righteous. We no longer suppose that our national solution depends on stopping history in its tracks and freezing the world in its present mode.[441]

This was "the politics of conservatism—past memory" and we are done with it. Now,

> Our national leadership is young, vigorous, intelligent, civilized and experimental. We are the Sons of Liberty again. We have awakened from a trance.[442]

McDonald was puncturing Schlesinger's pretentious Kennedy balloons very much as Govan had in his review. In his letter to Govan, McDonald wrote, "I agree on your main points—and I even object to that hope-memory business [of Schlesinger's] in much the same terms you do."[443] They both rejected Schlesinger's thesis that memory of a glorious past is the source of hope for an equally glorious future. Govan had found a kindred spirit and it meant so much to him that he kept McDonald's letter.

St. Mark's-in-the-Bowery

Over time, both Govans became involved in the life of St. Mark's-in-the-Bowery Episcopal Church, where Michael Allen had been rector since 1959. They had been close to Michael ever since his visits to Jane in the hospital during that year. They were living close to the church, and they liked the mix of people in the parish: all kinds, well-to-do and poor, black, white, and Chicano, writers and artists. "W.H. Auden would pad across the street in his slippers going to the eight o'clock Sunday Eucharist."[444] But the parish was not at peace with itself.

For three years, Michael had been working hard to integrate a church that, as he said, "practiced every kind of segregation the Episcopal Church knew how to practice. St. Mark's had a 9:00 a.m. High Mass, full of families, many children, all black. The 11:00 a.m. service was low church Morning Prayer, all white, no children, many singles."[445] In his second year there he cancelled both services and replaced them with one 10:30 a.m. Liturgical Reform Eucharist.[446] The great majority of parishioners supported the move, and immediately it began to have the desired effect, uniting the parish in a new way, and establishing Michael's leadership.

In the next year "came the test," as Michael put it, just as the Govans began attending St. Mark's. The Civil Rights Movement had reached a crescendo in the summer of 1963, and Michael was bound to participate actively. The integration and health of the parish, he felt, required it. So he announced at the 10:30 Eucharist on the Sunday before July 4 that he planned to go to Baltimore on the Fourth of July to participate in a Civil Rights demonstration, and that he "did not want to go alone." Four parishioners, two black and two white, came up after the service and said they would go. The senior warden believed that "breaking the law" was going entirely too far, and "when they returned, he called a meeting of the vestry with the intention of firing [Michael]. The junior warden, a lawyer, announced at the beginning of the meeting it was not a legal vestry meeting, inasmuch as the senior warden had not followed the law in calling it, but suggested they might sit and talk informally. At the end of a conversation in which it was clear that the senior warden stood alone, the vestry voted informally to commend"[447] Michael and encouraged him to do it again in New York. "Then they asked the senior warden to write a letter to the congregation stating their position. The senior warden looked stricken, and then someone said that it might be easier on the senior warden if someone else wrote the letter, and he asked a black member to do so. Not long after that, the black man who had gone with Michael to Baltimore was elected senior warden."[448]

Two weeks later, Michael participated in a demonstration in New York sponsored by the Lower East Side Civil Rights Committee of which he was chair. He wrote that

> a group of Lower Eastside clergy and one social worker blocked cement trucks as they tried to enter the Rutgers housing project under construction for black and Latino tenants in a neighborhood where they were predominant. And yet not a single black or Latino was employed in constructing housing intended for them! We were protesting the City of New York's complicity in accepting segregated construction practices.
>
> We pled guilty to disturbing the peace rather than contesting the charge because under New York law a plea of guilty allowed us to make a statement on our own behalf.
>
> I remember the Summer day when we all walked into court backed up by the presence of our bishops. The judge in shirt sleeves and a loosened necktie saw us come in, looked startled, if not horrified, recessed the court, and then appeared in judicial robes to try a case that hit the front pages of the New York papers the next day! I read our plea from notes laid out on the pages of an open Bible, accusing the Mayor of New York City and his advisors of being the real criminals in allowing a housing project for racial minorities to be constructed by whites alone. And behind it all stood Tom, praying for us that day, advising us, inspiring us.[449]

Tom became a mentor for Michael Allen. He was appalled with his pastor's liberal Jeffersonian individualism and took him in hand to reteach him American history and the theological underpinnings of the American Constitution. Tom also went to work on Michael's theological understanding. Michael recalls one adult class in which Tom said that in the end there were "only two dogmas of the Christian

Church: the Incarnation and the Trinity. Anything beyond these two words belonged to 'doctrine' and were relative matters."[450]

Tom's mentor relationship with Michael was very hard on Jane. Her valued relationship with Michael began before Tom had even met him, and then along came Tom and "took him away." Jane, though very bright, was not a scholar or a theologian. Tom as a natural-born teacher did for Michael what he had done for countless others in the university and the church. Jane felt this deeply, and as a result, there was a sense of bitter competition between them, which she always lost. She could not compete with Tom as a mentor, preacher, or vestry member, so she set herself to work on the renewal of the church building, which was rundown and dilapidated. She had the artistic talent and know-how, and it was a way for her to stay engaged with Michael. But renovation was not a priority for Michael, and Jane's persistence irritated him. At one point he exploded at her, "We are not going to make a polished gem out of St. Mark's in the midst of a decaying community. We will be resurrected along with the resurrection of the community, and not before."[451] Jane, although hurt, patiently persisted and laid the foundation for a complete renovation of the church years later.

In the fall of 1965, Bishop Corrigan told Michael Allen that the World Student Christian Movement was meeting in Dallas on New Year's Day and wanted an ecumenical and contemporary Eucharist for that day. It could not belong to any one tradition, but had to be common and accessible to all. He asked Michael to find the writers and poets in the congregation to write that Eucharist. They accepted the challenge and met every other Tuesday evening for a year to celebrate the Eucharist according to whatever they had written up to that point. The St. Mark's Liturgy was used in Dallas.[452]

Tom was not a part of this process, but he was a member of the vestry when the parish considered using the new liturgy in the 1966 Lenten program. Tom insisted that it be used with the bishop's approval, so Michael wrote to request it. The bishop gave his permission in a beautifully backhanded way: he said it was "beyond his authority" to approve such a liturgy, thus signaling that it was also beyond his authority to deny its use. So the parish happily used the liturgy in their Lenten program.

In 1967, the national church published a proposed new liturgy as a possible replacement for the 1928 *Book of Common Prayer.* At St. Mark's, it turned out to be "such a disaster that it was killing [their] worship life."[453] It was then that Govan stepped forward to say they had no choice but to write the bishop and tell him what was happening and inform him that they could no longer use the 1967 liturgy, nor could they go back to the 1928 *Book of Common Prayer.* Their only choice was to use the St. Mark's Liturgy. Bishop Donegan gave his permission, faced as he was with so clean and non-negotiable a challenge. The next time he came to St. Mark's for confirmation services, they were using the St. Mark's Liturgy. At the end of the service, he exclaimed, "'Power to the People' with the rest of the congregation."[454]

Both Tom and Jane were immensely impressed with the creativity of the St. Mark's program. The parish sponsored and housed what became a flourishing arts program, which drew in many erudite and artistic sorts of people: Ralph Cook founded and directed Theater Genesis; the Poetry Project and the Millennium Film Project were also developed. Michael Allen encouraged and helped to fund it all. The discovery of this new church thrilled the Govans.

At Easter 1965, St. Mark's staged a drama of the Resurrection, which was televised live by CBS, truly an extraordinary undertaking. Afterward, Will Inman, one of the parish's poets, wrote a poem for the parish about the dress rehearsal, entitled "C.B.S. Channel Christ: or Rolling Away the Stone By Turning a TV Button: or Resurrection In Spite of Ourselves: or a Mystery of St. Mark's in the Bouwerie [sic]." It covered the entire Holy Week narrative, was long, full of humor, and quite wonderful. There were two references in it to Tom Govan. About a third of the way through the poem, there was this exchange:

> *And on another Wednesday*
> *After the film GOD NEEDS MEN*
> *When Tom Govan says*
> *'I love Him because He suffered*
> *and died for me'*

Bob (Hart) leaps like a young
Hart, crying
'F—Jesus Christ!'

> *'That would be a little*
> *difficult,' says Tom.*

Then later in the poem, Easter has come.

Then Tom Govan, Eastered now,
south accented, white man,
the burden of resisting hatred
heavy in his shoulders, a relief
of love warming his wrinkles
and white thatch,
read the lesson
> *antiphonally*
with Carroll Greene
> *darkfaced and*
> *collegevoiced*
>> *burying across electronic space*
>> *the myths of our aloneness.*[455]

The Govans felt engaged and fulfilled as Christians by St. Mark's and its rector as never before. They were at home, their hearts and minds were free and at rest there, life was authentic and full. God was a plausible reality. It was no wonder they wanted to be, and finally were, buried there.[456]

PART III

The Last Best Hope

21
Govan, the Controversialist, NYU, 1963-1967

The moral dimension of the historian's task, his inevitably acting for good or ill as the nation's conscience, as well as its memory, is both what I am interested in primarily . . . , and also that about which alone I am willing to write. Secondly, I want to argue the influence of ideas (Hegel, Freud, et al.) as well as that of physical, material forces.

Thomas P. Govan

During his NYU years, Tom was constantly embroiled in intellectual controversy, attacking "liberal" historians and their misreading of American history and then presenting his own "conservative" view. He waged these controversies in book reviews and articles in professional history journals, several of which are detailed in this chapter.

Carl Bridenbaugh's *Mitre and Sceptre*

One of the worst of the "liberal" historians in Govan's opinion was Carl Bridenbaugh, then president of the American Historical Association, a recent addition to the Brown University history department, politically a Jeffersonian "liberal" and religiously an anti-Anglican Congregationalist. His book, *Mitre and Sceptre, Transatlantic Faith, Ideas, Personalities, and Politics, 1689-1775*,[457] published in 1962, claimed that the Anglicans wanted bishops in the colonies in order to restore Anglican religious authority. "An Anglican episcopate was itself [automatically] an attack on religious freedom,"[458] he said. More than that, it was a move in the direction of establishing monarchy in the colonies, "mitre" leads to "sceptre," both of them the enemies of freedom.

Tom was angry about the book because he felt that Bridenbaugh's entire thesis was based upon "the Jeffersonian assumption that [political] freedom is to be established and protected only by republican polity, and where there is republicanism, there is freedom."[459] Govan disagreed and in the March 1, 1963 issue of the *Historical Magazine of the Protestant Episcopal Church* published a review entitled "The Historian as Partisan Prosecutor and Judge."[460] According to Jane, his review was "the only mean-spirited thing he ever wrote."[461]

Govan believed in a different source of freedom, namely constitutional democracy with its balance of power among three interests and functions: the diocese with its bishops, the local congregation with its priest, and the laity with their vote. Each was a check on the other two, and no one could permanently dominate. The result was a democratic church with genuine freedom, ordei and unity. Tom believed that placing absolute power in the hands of the local lay congregation would bring conflict and divisions to the church and militate against freedom, justice, and order.

The conflict between Govan and Bridenbaugh was an example of the old liberal versus conservative, republican versus federalist, Jefferson versus Hamilton argument. Govan thought it was a "bad book" and to show his disdain, quoted the Italian philosopher Benedetto Croce to the effect that historians who "bustle about as judges, condemning here and giving absolution there . . . are generally recognized as devoid of historical sense."[462]

Alan P. Grimes on Freedom and Equality

In reviewing American historian Alan P. Grimes' book, *Equality in America, Religion, Race, and the Urban Ministry*,[463] Govan wrote a powerfully perceptive commentary on the nature of equality and its relationship to freedom. Grimes argued for what he thought is an empirical human fact: that people are not created equal and that the claim of equality is merely a "pragmatic adjustment" made necessary by modern society.

Govan was morally incensed by what he considered to be a cynical view. "The drafters of the Declaration of Independence argued from a very different point of view," Govan said.[464] They argued from an article of faith, not a known fact, that "all men are created equal." This, wrote Govan, "is a moral affirmation of truth by a nation that restrains people in order that they and others may be equal and free." Neither articles of faith nor self-evident truths can be proven, but they are true, nevertheless, and can be standards by which a society is measured.

Govan's point was that when people are treated as equals in society, they will tend to become so. If they are treated legally as superior and inferior, then they are liable to become so as well. Govan felt that treating people equally is a moral commitment of the United States, never fully achieved. But that is what the American idea is all about and what American history bears out. One example is the reality of blacks' equality with whites. The crucial importance of equal education and equal opportunity—that is, treating blacks and whites as equals—is borne out every day. And the failure to treat blacks and whites as equals creates inequality. The moral imperative, said Govan, should not be trivialized and called a "pragmatic adjustment."

Eugene D. Genovese's
The Political Economy of Slavery

In the spring of 1965, Eugene D. Genovese published his well-known book, *The Political Economy of Slavery: Studies in the Economy and Society of the Slave South*,[465] which made his name. Govan thought the book thoroughly wrongheaded and pernicious. Govan did not acknowledge in his review that Genovese was a professed Marxist, but instead said Genovese defined "political economy" as a matter of "class struggle" between different "means of production" and then forced the facts into those categories. When the facts did not fit, Genovese simply altered them so that they would fit, and asserted the facts must behave as his theory prescribed. Govan, to the contrary, asserted that the "plantation owners . . . and other southern political leaders . . . were to be found on all possible sides in the party battles that divided the nation . . . [including] the congressional debates on economic policy."[466] The conflict Genovese saw between the pre-modern, pre-capitalist, planter-dominated South and the modern, capitalist North, each with different and conflicting views about man and society, Govan said, was a figment of his own theory. It was slavery, finally, seen as a moral issue, not a "conflict of world views," of "worlds," of "rival social classes or societies dominated by rival social classes,"[467] which was the source of the conflict between North and South. Govan's review was devastating. In the end, he won the day: Genovese gave up his neo-Marxism.

Arthur S. Link

"Agrarianism, Sectionalism, and Jeffersonian Democracy: a Moral Inquiry"

In July 1961, Arthur S. Link, professor of history at Princeton University and editor of Woodrow Wilson's papers, asked Govan to write an article for a book on American historiography being edited by Link and Rembert Patrick, professor of American history at the University of Florida and president of the Southern Historical Association. Govan was asked to follow a theme of his own choosing which would, in the process, introduce readers to "the main historical writings of [the federal] period" of American history: 1789-1837, Tom's specialty. He was glad for the opportunity. As it turned out, there were such differences and misunderstandings between Link and Govan that Govan finally withdrew from the project. In their correspondence about these issues, Govan reveals what he believed and stood for, why, and how.

Govan focused his theme on the conflict between the "conservative" Federalists and the "liberal" Jeffersonians of the period, and to contrast what the "conservative" historians of the 19th century (John Marshall, Richard Hildreth, and Hermann von Holst) said about that conflict with the "liberal" historians of the 20th century (Frederick Jackson Turner, Vernon L. Parrington, and Charles A. Beard). The article was intended to be a critical moral inquiry into Jeffersonian democracy and its sources, the very kind of inquiry which Turner, Parrington, and Beard tended to avoid and disparage.

Tom finished "Agrarianism, Sectionalism and Jeffersonian Democracy: a Moral Inquiry" and sent it to Link in late July. It was a careful expansion and rewriting of his point made at the Southern Historical Association in his address, "Agrarianism, Sectionalism, and State Sovereignty Denounced" two years before. Link, who had been in Europe, did not see it until September. Although he claimed to like the paper—as a good Presbyterian, he too was a moralist—he allowed that he did not "go in much . . . for what [he] called judgmental history,"[468] which was what he felt Govan had written. Link, by contrast, was inclined to be more objective and keep moral judgments to a minimum.

Link felt the real problem with Govan's paper was that it did not introduce the reader to the full range of historical writings about the 1789-1837 period. Link asked whether Govan could not "find some other common theme that would enable [him] to tie the loose ends together? . . . We do not . . . have an encyclopedic approach in mind, but must give far more attention to the leading current historians and their views."[469] Govan undoubtedly grumbled under his breath, "Yes, and they are all wrong!"

Govan was giving a series of talks at Clemson University when Link's September 7 letter arrived. He replied to Link five weeks later on October 17, 1962, thanking him but said he was surprised by Link's criticism. Govan explained: "I did deliberately confine myself in the text to those [historians of the period] I thought set the varied interpretations, intending to discuss in the footnotes the varied 20th century writers, most of whom are derivative in interpretation . . . . I was under the impression that what we were seeking to avoid was a catalogue of historians . . . and brief summary statements about what they said."[470]

When Link said in his September letter that "the historian's unique and most difficult task was to preserve the historical record in its integrity, that is simply to write as best he can about what happened in the past . . . but I applaud and read with pleasure when friends and colleagues do what you have done,"[471] Govan thought he was waffling and wanted to be doubly clear about his own point. He responded:

> The moral dimension of the historian's task, his inevitably acting for good or ill as the nation's conscience as well as its memory, is both what I am interested in primarily in my writing on historiography and also that about which alone I am willing to write. Secondarily, I want to argue the influence of ideas (Hegel and Freud et al) as well as that of physical, material forces.[472]

Govan concluded that he was "not adamant on details . . . but I am not willing to try some other theme, so if your decision is firm, I regretfully will have to withdraw."[473]

On October 27, 1962 Arthur Link tried again by asking Govan if there was "not some way you could accomplish your objective and ours at the same time?"[474]

Tom replied with a summary of his theme and how he planned to expand it. His concern was the need of students and of the nation as a whole, not merely to have "the facts," but to understand the meaning of history overseen by a gracious but moral and just God. To that end, he felt students needed to be exposed to the moral dimensions and implications of history to develop the ability to distinguish between right and wrong, and good and evil in that same light. Tom emphasized to Link that what free people believe and think matters more than the various physical forces that play upon their lives. "It's what they think about banking and the economy, for example, that matters," he said.

Link's concern was that Govan's article nonjudgmentally discuss all of the historians of the period 1789-1837 who were thought to be significant by the history profession at the time, regardless of their view. Govan replied that he could not do that; what was historically inaccurate had to be called inaccurate, and what was morally wrong had to be called morally wrong. He believed, for example, that Jefferson claimed dedication to the principles of freedom, equality, and justice, when, in fact, his attitudes and policies—materialistic, individualistic, anti-institutional, states' rights, and laissez-faire economics did just the opposite, creating division, lack of freedom, and inequality and injustice. This was no matter of theory or ideology, he said, because American history demonstrated these results. Down through American history, Jefferson's principles have been used again and again as moral justification for the very attitudes and policies that they destroy. Too many historians, like Turner, Parrington, and Beard, had followed precisely in Jefferson's footsteps. To deny this, Govan believed, was bad history and bad moral practice, and he felt bound to say so.

Link could not agree, but respected Govan and hoped to work out some compromise. Govan again suggested putting most of the historians Link wanted mentioned in the footnotes, but they could not agree on any solution to the dilemma.

Govan finally wrote Link on November 3, 1962, thanking him for his patience and consideration. "I believe, however, that our ideas about what students need are almost as far apart as our conception of what history is all about . . . . though we could come to an accommodation verbally, the contradictory beliefs would still be there . . . What I want to do is so obviously different from that which you want in the book that I think it only appropriate for me to withdraw with an apology to you and the others."[475]

One of the quite remarkable things about this correspondence was their civility, mutual respect, consideration, and patience, while still holding to their positions firmly. Tom ended the correspondence blaming himself for their misunderstanding:

> I heard in our discussions and read in your . . . letters only those things I wanted to hear and read, and it now becomes apparent that I misunderstood what was being said and written. I am not unaware of the difficult position I have placed you and the others in and can only say that I am truly sorry. But it is better, I think, to make the decision now

and submit to the inconvenience than for me, who always finds excuses not to do something I do not want to do, to have to say at this time next year that I have not done the article you wanted.[476]

Govan finished the article as he wanted it that winter.

Philip F. Detweiler

Three months later, on March 8, 1963, after Govan's friend from Tulane days, Philip F. Detweiler, had moved to Rice University and become the editor of *The Southern Historical Review,* Govan sent him the article. He did so, as he said, "with fear and trembling, though I believe what I wrote." He asked Detweiler to "agree with me even if you reject it, for I want to say convincingly what I have said."[477]

Detweiler replied later in the month, writing a devastating review laced with enough humor and self-depreciation to make it palatable. Tom gratefully revised and clarified the article, but for unknown reasons they never seemed able to agree enough on a final version to bring it to publication. The chances are that Detweiler, as a brand new editor, was not ready to publish such a polemical essay, written for historians about historians, and morally indicting some, at least three of whom were in high vogue and still alive. It could not have been easy for him to accept Govan, the moralist, who insisted that,

> Historians are not solely the custodians of the nation's memory, they are also keepers of its conscience, and on them lies the complex and difficult burden of seeking to distinguish right from wrong.[478]

Govan's point about the Jeffersonians was that although they had principles that affirmed freedom, equality, and justice, their attitudes and their policies denied and destroyed these very ideals which they sought.

Tom insisted that historians must not hide from this contradiction, but describe it for what it is. Jeffersonian arguments against federal action and national restraint represented "a low, sordid, selfish, and sectional spirit"[479] in the country. They have been used again and again as moral justifications for the immoral ambitions of special interests. They have been used to divide, and, in the Civil War, nearly to destroy, the country. It was the evidence of history, Govan believed, not merely theory, that proved Jeffersonian principles not only mistaken, but morally wrong.

Govan wrote with considerable passion because he believed that the attitudes and policies that had been in conflict between Federalists and Jeffersonians two centuries ago were still with us today, separating and dividing the American people—and American historians. "Local and selfish loyalties, social immaturity, groundless suspicions, and unfounded hatred and fears still do their harmful work," he said, "and most of the persons who are gripped by these [mental and emotional, not material] forces accept and advocate Jeffersonian principles."[480] He insisted that we must face the "moral question raised by [the constant] use [of these principles] throughout most of American history to perpetrate injustice, inequality, and the denial of freedom."[481]

"Those Mysterious Southern Agrarians"

Govan was very pleased when his article "Agrarian and Agrarianism" appeared in a new collection of essays edited by Charles Crowe entitled *The Age of the Civil War and Reconstruction*, 1930-1900. Tom's essay was the first to appear in the book in a section concerned with "Modern Images of the South." Crowe included it because it exploded the old sectional myth of the "agrarian South" versus the "industrial North." As Crowe explained in his preface to the article,

> The sectional conflict which reached a climax in the Civil War has been commonly characterized by schools of thought with distinctly different orientations as a struggle between the "agrarian South" and the emerging industrialism of the North. However, as Thomas P. Govan suggested in 1964, the explanation leaned heavily

on "agrarian," a term extraordinarily rich in ambiguity. If the word can be equated with "agricultural," it is too vague and general to be useful. The great majority of ante-bellum Northerners were also farmers. Modern Asiatic peasants, prosperous New Jersey truck farmers, Soviet collective farm managers, and quasi-feudal landlords of Peru can all be described as "agrarians." Obviously many definitions have been attached to the term. Several meanings are completely contradictory; others defended the South by reviving portions of the proslavery argument . . . . By making the South the major carrier of Jacksonian and Jeffersonian "democracy" and by describing the North as the seedbed of robber barons and the forerunner of industrial plutocracy, the dominant scholarly interpretation even characterized the slave owner as the defender of democratic values against the Free Soil and Republican challengers of "democracy!" In the days since the defenders of the "agrarian" tradition and the school of Ulrich B. Phillips dominated the intellectual scene, the context of interpretation has changed a great deal . . . . New perspectives for the study of white and black people were made possible by the decline of explanations which were tied to agrarian and plantation myths.[482]

Tom's article played a major role in the decline of agrarian and plantation myths. This was a sweet moment for him. For years, he had been warning his historian colleagues of the dangers in believing the myths they wrote about and in particular, the sectional myth, which pitted southern agrarians against northern industrialists. His point was finally being recognized.

"Was Plantation Slavery Unprofitable?"[483]

Govan's second republished essay was an old one dating back to 1942, entitled "Was Plantation Slavery Unprofitable?" published in *The Journal of Southern History*. It was now in 1966 included in *Pivotal*

Interpretations of American History, Volume I, edited by Carl H. Deglar.[484] By the word "pivotal," Deglar meant articles that forced "the study of American history to take a new turn."[485] He explained that

> As a result of the work of Ulrich B. Phillips, the unprofitable character of slavery became widely accepted among historians in the early years of the twentieth century. Among major modern historians, as Mr. Govan points out, only Lewis C. Gray disputed Phillip's view . . . . [I]f slavery was unprofitable, then the war that abolished the institution at a frightful cost in property and blood appears as a needless tragedy.[486]

According to Phillips, slavery would have dwindled away as a result of its own unprofitable weight.

Govan made two important points that permanently changed historians' understanding. The first was to redefine profit to include the lifestyle of plantation owners; and second, with this new definition in hand, was to examine the financial records of three major plantations and the national census reports of both 1850 and 1860. He came to the conclusion that historians "who have stated that slavery was profitable [i.e., Mr. Gray] are more nearly correct than those who deny its profitableness."[487] [i.e., Mr. Phillips and everyone else]. Deglar concludes that

> The importance of Mr. Govan's article is that it initiated a reappraisal of Phillips' position which has ended in an almost complete reversal in the judgement of historians on the subject.[488]

Govan's Concern for the National Economy: "Hamilton, the Bank, and the National Economy"

Ever since graduate school, Tom had been intensely concerned with the American economy and its relationship to the political history of the country. His knowledge of Alexander Hamilton and the Bank of the United States was well known and as a result he was invited to present a paper on "Hamilton, the Bank, and the National Economy"[489] at the December, 1964 meeting of the American Historical Association.

Govan was delighted to accept and wrote Alfred D. Chandler of Johns Hopkins University, who was chairing the session, that he "intended to discuss the debate over the function and purposes of the National Bank . . . with only passing mention" of whether or not the Bank was constitutional. This question, he knew, was "the main basis of opposition" to the Bank at the time, but that issue, he thought, had been thoroughly "kicked around and disposed of." It was "the Bank as the servant of the private economy, including most particularly agriculture, [which] needed examination." This had been "important to Hamilton," and it was important to Govan[490] because the financial processes of the country, as Hamilton and Govan knew, were fundamental to the country's political health, security, and freedom.

Govan suggested that Hamilton was at heart a soldier who realized that the colonies were losing the Revolutionary War, not by losing battles, but by having a losing, chaotic, and utterly inadequate economy. So Hamilton spent every moment that he could (away from his job as aide-de-camp to General Washington) to study economics and finance. He did so as his duty to the new nation. "It was only by introducing order into our finances—by restoring public credit, not by gaining battles, that victory would be won. The nation's troubles were more economic than military."[491]

First, Hamilton began a comparative study of the American and British economies. Soon he realized that those people with money to lend, "instead of having their profits enhanced through upholding government credit, frequently found it to their interest to undermine" that credit. Any financial plan that had a chance of working had to "make it the immediate interest of [those with money] . . . to cooperate with the government in support of a stable currency."[492] Following the English pattern, the plan he came up with was a national bank of issue.[493] Such a bank could "raise a vast fabric of paper [money] . . . on a visionary basis,"[494] namely people's trust that the paper would be repaid with interest. The Bank, when well managed, earned that trust, turned out to be fabulously successful, and made the country strong.

Second, Govan believed with Hamilton that those opposed to the bank, especially Thomas Jefferson and John Adams (who agreed with Jefferson on almost nothing but this one thing), were wrongheaded. Jefferson and Adams argued that the Bank was an aristocratic institution benefiting the rich, who could lend money and get interest without any effort, thus hurting the mass of the people, mostly farmers, who had only their labor or their produce to sell. Prosperity for the Bank and the rich thus meant adversity for everyone else. John Taylor of Caroline put it that "Increment of wealth to the one is diminution to the other."[495] Govan showed that these arguments were untrue and served the interests of the landed aristocracy, not the mass of the people, mostly farmers, and had its source in the ideology of large landowners, not in actual experience with the Bank. The reality, said Govan, was not that some get rich at the expense of the poor in a fixed and static economy, but that when the economy is dynamic and growing, everyone, rich and poor alike, benefit from it.

Those who opposed the Bank also accused it of stimulating "gambling, fraud, corruption and injustice."[496] Hamilton believed, on the other hand, that the cause of "avarice" in people was not merely self-interest and greed, but desperation in times of depression. To Hamilton, a healthy and stable economy that people could trust was the best way to reduce avarice and dishonesty,[497] because in a sound economy it would be more to one's advantage in terms of profits to be honest than to be crooked.

Third, Hamilton said, "The health of a state, particularly a commercial one, depends on a due quantity and circulation of cash, as much as the health of an animal body depends upon the due quantity and regular circulation of the blood."[498] A stable economy, therefore, is essential.

Fourth, Hamilton said, there is no necessary reason for a rivalry between landed and trading interests. Those interests are so interdependent that what is good or bad for one is good or bad for the other. The principle of cooperation in the economy is therefore more important than competition.[499]

Fifth, Govan and Hamilton believed it is an unhappy truth that banks are seldom understood or appreciated by the people because in good times they are not noticed and are taken for granted; only in bad times are they very visible and vulnerable to what is usually unfair criticism and blame.[500]

The article was never published, and the reason why is not clear. Remarkably, there were more than four thousand people present at the Association's meeting and the session on Hamilton and the Bank was only one among some four hundred others. So much material was produced that the report of the meeting in the American Historical Review could mention only the theme of the session, "The First Bank of the United States." Govan's address was not even mentioned, let alone his name and contents reported.

More to the point may be the possibility that in the minds of editors and publishers the focus on technical financial and economic issues placed this section of the conference beyond public interest. The omission may have reflected the bias of the history profession.

The Gallatin Project at NYU, 1965-1968

Tom had learned from experience that there was a bias among American historians against the financial world and its historical importance. He wanted to correct this perception, and New York City, as a world financial center, was the perfect place to begin. With his history department colleague, Vincent P. Corosso, Govan presented a proposal to the history department and then to the NYU administration for an "Albert Gallatin Institute for the Study of History and Development of the Commercial and Financial Communities in the City of New York."[501] During the last twenty years of his life, Gallatin lived in New York, was a leading member of the banking community, and played a major role in "shifting the country's financial center from Philadelphia to New York."[502] To name the institute for him was most appropriate.

The need for such an institute was clear. New York had been the financial capital of the country for a century and a half; it was as important to the nation as the political capital in Washington, D.C., "but what has gone on there in terms of day-to-day activities—as contrasted with scandals and moments of crisis—has been a largely unknown and untold story"[503] and has attracted few historians. Because "the language and thought patterns of the financial world are radically different from those learned and employed in the ordinary study of history,"[504] historians shy away from the area, with the result that important parts of American history are passed over in silence or are distorted. The business community then is left ignorant of its own past and the populace at large is left suspicious or even contemptuous of financial concerns. The proposal ended with the suggestion that one immediate and useful project for the Institute would be to complete the editing and publication of Gallatin's papers. Unfortunately, Govan brought neither the institute proposal nor the publication project to completion because of his move to the University of Oregon in the fall of 1967. The proposal still stands as an important challenge to NYU and to the history profession.

22

A New Discovery and a New Book?

As different kinds of law spring from different types of mind,
so too, as the centuries go by, they necessarily form different
types of men.

Quoted by Thomas P. Govan

A Job at the University of Oregon?

The spring and summer of 1966 was a turning point for the Govans. First, news of a full professorship in American history opening in the University of Oregon history department reached them in New York. Tom's heart leapt with excitement; he immediately gathered the necessary papers and applied for the job and then steeled himself to wait for a reply.

The Govans were more than ready to move out of New York and settle down somewhere else for Tom's last ten years of teaching. They realized that they were aging and that retirement was on the horizon. Tom and Jane were about to be sixty, and knew they did not want to retire in New York. The city was, as Jane put it, "ungodly expensive," and everyday living involved too many difficulties and left them with too little financial flexibility. They longed for their own home in a more rural and less expensive area, a home on a plot of land containing a lawn and room for a flower and vegetable garden. The Govans had been much taken with Eugene and the university back in 1961, but of special importance to them now was the fact that the university retirement rule was set at seventy years of age, whereas NYU's was set at sixty-five. Five more years on salary would mean much to them.

Then came a surprise invitation from Oregon to come again to Eugene and teach in the summer session from June 8 through August 15, 1966. Tom was thrilled. He remembered with pleasure that summer of 1961, when he had last taught at Oregon—he had earned the friendship and respect of the history faculty, especially some of the younger members for whom his gifts as mentor were a new and much-appreciated experience. Tom could not help believing that this invitation was a sign of real interest in his application. Maybe the department wanted another extended exposure to Tom to make sure that he was the person they really wanted.

The Govans had a good summer at Oregon. Nothing official was said about the job, but the grapevine via his friends was very positive.

Then in early 1967, he was invited to Oregon again, this time by the history department to give his sample lecture as a job candidate. He was thrilled, not only because he wanted the job, but also because he was "on the scent," as he put it, of a new idea that he very much wanted to test out on his colleagues. He was excited about it because he believed that he had hit upon a new and deeper interpretation of the sources of political, social and religious English freedom.

The Common Law and English Freedom

Govan had been thinking about the basis of English Common Law for over a year. His question was how much influence had the Bible had on the development of the Anglo-Saxon Common Law (that is, the general and ordinary law of the country), which was later passed along to Anglican theology at the time of the Reformation?

Govan's educated guess was that during the Anglo-Saxon period, the most important influence on the church and the Common Law of England was the Bible. The Anglo-Saxon kings—Alfred, Edgar, Edward the Confessor, and others—were all devout Christians, who heard the Bible read weekly, sometimes daily, in the normal course of worship, and may well have modeled the embryonic constitution and Common Law of pre-Norman England on the law of the Old Testament prophets as codified in the Book of Deuteronomy and, as put into practice by Josiah, the reforming king of Israel.[505] In any case, "their point of view," said Govan, "was entirely Hebraic."[506] By that he meant that English law, like that of Israel before it, was based on the conviction that God was the true King of the nation and the Commandments, later expanded by the Old Testament prophets and Jesus, was to be the fundamental basis of the common law of England.

The idea that the Old Testament had influenced the common law was there, at least by implication, in the writings of William Blackstone, the great eighteenth-century historian of English law.[507] It was also there in F.W. Maitland's work in the nineteenth century[508] and in the work of a handful of other historians since. Maitland even says that the earliest written law—and that had to be in the Anglo-Saxon period—has already ceased to be primitive; it is "already Christian, and so close is the connection between law and religions, that we may well believe that it has already undergone a great change" from primitive times.[509] His implication is clearly that Christianity and the Bible had already heavily influenced it. Govan believed a good case could be made for this, even though proof positive was not possible. As Govan described it, the common law had grown gradually within the untidy history of pre-Norman England. It had evolved in response to local needs, the need for order, the need for a modicum of fairness in adjudicating conflicts, but above all, to set the rules of property ownership and of business transactions. "This strange, untidy, ever-growing and changing collection of customs, traditions, charters, judicial decisions, statutes, and proclamations," wrote Govan, "[was an] almost unique body of law, which is the source from which has been derived[510]

> 'the Englishmen's' ideals of political life and freedom; the general capacity for self-government, the general English willingness to trust to this and to make it a basis of public policy; the balance of the English character, its

sobriety, its dislike of extremes, its lack of vindictiveness; its hatred of arbitrary power, of government by police methods, of judicial processes in secret; its suspicion of official efficiency . . . As different kinds of law spring from different types of mind, so too, as the centuries go by, they necessarily form different types of men.[511]

Here is an indirect, subtle kind of influence heading toward increased freedom and in the process, creating a people, who, having had a taste of freedom, wanted more.

The Common Law as it developed in England was pragmatic, nonperfectionistic, and grew on the basis of precedent. What had been done before should be changed only if conditions demanded it. Because Common Law grew out of the experience of people, it had no pretensions to virtue. But, as William Montesquieu said, it had a purpose: England was

. . . a land, perhaps the only one in the universe, in which political and civil liberty is the very end and scope of the constitution.[512]

Govan believed that the influence of the biblical faith had an important hand in bringing this about.

The year 1066 marked a turning point in England. William the Conqueror brought with him into England both Roman civil law and the religion of the papacy. The civil law was based on reason and the classical Justinian Code, which was orderly, theoretical, grounded in and deduced from universal principles, and stood in stark contrast to the messy, pragmatic, practical historical precedent of the Common Law. There were three principles of the civil law: to live honestly, to hurt no one, and to render to everyone his due. Govan granted that these were sound and noble ideals, and following William Blackstone, he accepted "the usual equity of the Civil Laws' decisions."[513] But there were problems. In the first place, the Civil Laws were too general; and they were not flexible enough to properly guide complex legal decisions. Based on national principles, they also had a tendency to be doctrinaire, rigid, unchanging, and unable to take extenuating circumstances into account. Authoritarian Norman kings administered them. So, there was consistent conflict between this Norman law and the flexible law of English precedent.

William also brought the Roman Church law and doctrines of the papacy into England in a new and very direct way. From 1066 until the Reformation in the sixteenth century, the papacy and the curia completely dominated the Church of England's life and thought. As church historian David Little would write,

> So long as the Church of England owed its primary religious allegiance to the Pope, so long as it remained a branch of the Roman Church, the full development of self-consciously independent institutions was impossible. The Church's doctrines and practices were controlled by the Curia, and the Church had its own legislature and courts, shaped and informed not by common law, but by Roman canon and civil law.[514]

The Common Law of England, however, survived the threat of the Roman civil law. The lawyers and judges of England simply refused to allow Roman civil law to displace their Common Law and its long history. William and his royal successors were forced to accept an uneasy and uncomfortable partnership between the two. The spirit and attitude of the Common Law survived as the dominant legal influence in the country. As Govan put it,

> In the centuries between the Norman Conquest and the Reformation the English laity (in particular, the lawyers and judges) resisted the efforts of bishops and clergy, many of them foreigners,[515] to subject England to the precise, clearly defined, and universal precepts of the Civil Law; they were, in fact, challenging the fundamental teachings of the classical minded church to which they, like all other western Europeans, almost unquestioningly belonged.[516]

One indication of the Common Law's power was the fact that Pope Innocent forbade the clergy to read the Common Law because its decisions were not founded on imperial constitutions, but merely on the customs of the laity. The Roman Church claimed the same logical correctness, "the same finality and consistency" for church law "as that found in the Civil Law," that is, "the inerrant infallibility that, according to scripture, belonged exclusively to God."[517]

Against this the English argued for

> . . . a different understanding of man's knowledge and truth that was historical rather than philosophical in nature, personal and ever-developing, not conceptual and static, Hebraic not Greek; and . . . when justifying the separation of the Church of England from the Church of Rome [at the Reformation] adopted this national point of view.[518]

They would insist on their right to continue to search for the truth that lies just beyond reach.

William Blackstone wrote that during this period, the Common Law had

> . . . vigorously withstood the repeated attacks of the Civil Law; which established in the twelfth century, a new Roman Empire over most of the states on the continent, states that have lost, and perhaps on that account, their political liberties; which the free constitution of England, perhaps upon the same account, has been improved rather than debased.[519]

Clearly, Blackstone believed that English freedom was a product of its legal history.

When the Reformation came, the Common Law was there, ready to be one of the major supports for and influences on the reformed Church of England as well as the new independent nation. The Reformation would be regarded as a return to the past, really to the Anglo-Saxon tradition, "a vindication of the rights of the

Crown . . . against usurped jurisdiction by the Papacy."[520] It rested on twin pillars: the supremacy of the state over the Church, and the legitimization of that supremacy "by divers sundry old authentic histories and chronicles,"[521] which made up the Common Law.

The Common Law emerges as the source and champion of English freedom and in the process, teacher of the church. Govan often said that God does not work only, or even primarily, through the church.

But how true was this description of English history? Most historians believed that the Common Law tradition had not actually been the source of English freedom, but that the English thought it had been. They saw that the break with Rome at the Reformation had "created a need for new authority and set [the English] in search of self-authenticating institutions and urged on them the belief that no segment of their common life, including the Church of England, needed to rely on anything but their own sovereign past."[522]

As David Little said in 1966, "It was . . . the English Reformation which stimulated the creation of what has aptly been called 'an ideology of historical consistency' or 'a fiction of continuity.'"[523]

Govan knew this argument and he knew, for example, that most of the work of Sir Edward Coke, from Elizabeth's reign to the Long Parliament, illustrated it. Coke was constantly reinterpreting and rewriting the Common Law so as to make it a powerful instrument in opposing the Divine Right of Kings claimed by James I. He was making new law while claiming it was the old.

Conclusive proof was hard to provide for either of these views to the exclusion of the other. But Govan felt justified in holding on to his view since the other side could not prove him wrong and the circumstantial evidence seemed to be heavily on his side. He held on to his view that at the time of the Reformation the Common Law influenced Anglican theology more than theology influenced the Common Law.

This is the point, however, at which Govan's argument goes deeper than those of any other historians—before or since. In fact, it was the first point he made in his lecture, and it is fundamentally moral and theological. He began by reminding his audience that Henry VIII and all of those who supported his break with Rome did so largely for self-interested and reprehensible motives. Henry wanted to divorce and remarry. He wanted his own way. The Pope refused to approve, so Henry separated the Church of England from Rome, and established a national church with himself as the head. All his ministers, except for Thomas More, but including Thomas Cranmer, the archbishop of Canterbury, went along with Henry, not because they approved but in order to save their own necks. Thomas More lost his. These men could, therefore, make no claims to virtue. They were not good men, and they knew it.

The same thing was true, Govan pointed out, of the prophet Isaiah who knew he was a "man of unclean lips and dwelt among a people of unclean lips;"[524] of King David, an adulterer and murderer; of Peter who betrayed his Lord three times; and of St. Paul, who wanted to do good and could not, and instead, did the very evil thing he did not want to do.[525] That was Govan's personal experience, especially from Sewanee, and his relationship with Jane and her mother. Human sin, he believed, was pervasive.

Archbishop of Canterbury Thomas Cranmer knew this imperfection was a universal human condition and saw to it in the new 1549 *Book of Common Prayer* that the entire nation, including the king, began their daily worship with the General Confession: "Almighty and most merciful Father, we have erred and strayed from thy ways like lost sheep."[526]

As Govan wrote,

> It was the admission of wrongdoing, not its avoidance, according to the biblical writers, that freed men from the burden of sin, that enabled them to be obedient to God of whom it is said, 'His service is perfect freedom.'[527]

Confession was then followed immediately by the Absolution. God forgives his people and sets them free from guilt and anxiety, and calls them to new life. Isaiah was a man of unclean lips, but he knew it and was forgiven. When God asked, "Whom shall I send, and who will go for us?" Isaiah was able to answer, "Here am I, send me."[528] Isaiah became a prophet; Peter and Paul became apostles; Thomas Cranmer became a martyr; none of them good, but all repentant, forgiven and therefore, free and able to answer God's call.

These biblical stories were all about liberation, about freedom, about change and new life. Micah had asked, "What does the Lord require of you?" The answer lay not in virtue, but in humility; not in perfection, but in the recognition of imperfection. It lay in "doing justly, in loving mercy, and in walking humbly with our God."[529] Ironically, then, it was in the permanent human need for repentance and forgiveness that Govan found the source of true human freedom, personal, social and political. It is fundamentally a moral and theological source carried in part by an imperfect Common Law and an imperfect Church of England.

Tom's lecture particularly stimulated one young graduate student. He was upset. He questioned Govan's entire theory, but most of all his seeming reification of "history" as the major actor in the process. Tom answered bluntly, with a little grin, "If I said God did it, you wouldn't believe me."[530] The young man asked for a copy, which Tom sent him as soon as he returned home to New York. The young man later responded,

> You spoke of having a 'scent' . . . I think that perhaps you have several [scents] and that you have not distinguished them one from another. Some of the problems you touch on have been under consideration for a generation or more now—by better historians than [William] Blackstone. If you came out of the barn with this chapter as it now stands, you would be shot down before you get your wheels off the ground.[531]

Despite a disclaimer that he was no "expert, just a young feller whose ox had been goosed (or gored)," the young man asked twenty-seven questions, made thirteen comments, most of them critical, and suggested a sixteen-book bibliography for Tom to read. The young man had the grace, however, to end his letter appreciative of Govan and depreciating of self:

In summary, a most stimulating paper. Thank you much
for allowing me to read it and for inviting these remarks,
which another may think totally misguided.[532]

Tom guessed that the student was reflecting a view that he had
considered self-evident until he heard Govan speak: that the Common
Law was not actually a source of English freedom, but that the English
thought it had been. And certainly God could have had nothing to do
with it.

There is no further record of Govan's response, but he could
have referred to F. W. Maitland's *The Constitutional History of England*
and his many other sources.[533] They provide a great deal of evidence
that supports Govan's position. Maitland, for example, says
unequivocally, that the English kings, Ethelbert (a contemporary of
Justinian and his Code) in 600 CE, Ine in 650 CE, and Alfred in 690
brought together and published "sets of law" for their kingdoms,
written not in Latin, but in English.[534] Maitland also reminds us that
England in the seventh century was "already Christian," the king served
under God. For example, King Ethelred's coronation vows were
threefold: to keep peace; prevent robbery and injustice; and
"command justice and mercy in all judgement."[535] That sounded like
Saul, David, or Solomon in Israel.

Maitland's point was that all of this law was entirely English and
that the "influence of Roman jurisprudence was hardly felt."[536] In any
case, Govan made only very slight changes in the text of his lecture
while his conviction on the issue continued to grow stronger in
successive years.

In 1975, nine years later, Govan wrote a history of the Anglican
Communion and what it stands for as a part of the bicentennial of the
American Revolution for the Episcopal Church. It was published that
year as a Forward Movement pamphlet under the title, "The Rejection
of Denominational Idolatries." In that essay, he is explicit about his
conviction that it was the common law that influenced the church in
the direction of freedom, not the other way around. God, he believed,
was much involved.

A Welcome Book Contract:
A New Birth of Freedom

In the late summer of 1961, Govan had delivered a five-part lecture series entitled, "A New Birth of Freedom" at the Episcopal National Study Conference in Beloit, Wisconsin. At the close of the conference, approximately one thousand copies of the lectures had been distributed in bound, mimeographed form, and in the spring of 1966, Robert Amussen, a young editor at Bobbs-Merrill, Inc, read one of these copies. Amussen attended St. Mark's-in-the-Bowery off and on and had met Govan there; they had talked at St. Mark's and he had asked to see a copy, and was fascinated by it. Here was a new theological angle on American history that Amussen believed needed to be widely known and would sell. He showed it to Lawrence Grove, the editor of Bobbs-Merrill, who agreed. In short order, Tom had signed a contract to revise and expand the lectures into a full-length book, but while working for the Episcopal Church, he had been unable to bring it off. At that time, of course, he was also struggling to finish his Biddle book. So getting back to this book again gave him a lift, and as the new academic year opened, he began work on it in earnest.

As he later wrote, however, the "task was more difficult than he had expected it to be." On the one hand, there was an immense amount of research to do. "It required knowledge of the political, legal, and theological background of the English Reformation and the development of the English monarchy, the founding and growth of the American colonies, their quarrel with the mother country, and the national history of the United States." As he said, the story was complicated and "would not easily work itself out."[537] Again and again, he found himself bogged down with masses of paradoxical detail and confronted with new ideas needing verification. Govan kept in touch with Grove, who never ceased to be encouraging, and finally in late February 1967, he delivered Chapter 1, "The English Background." It was an expanded and rewritten version of his lecture at the

University of Oregon from the summer before. Both Amussen and Grove read it and liked it. Grove wrote

> I am constantly thankful for historians who are lucid and scholarly. Gentlemen historians do not carry much weight anymore, but professional historians aren't ready to take on the role of teacher to the history reading public. I look forward to reading more as you get into hotter water. I hope you will keep us informed along the way, so we can schedule publication with some sense of reality.[538]

They were especially "pleased" they said to see that he was "off the hook," that is, not stuck any longer and now getting things down on paper. In fact, Govan was still "on the hook," and very discouraged about it. Sadly, he never got beyond that first chapter. He could not give the book the focused effort and attention it required. The confirmation of his appointment at the University of Oregon came through in January, and he and Jane became completely preoccupied with planning their departure, buying a house in Eugene, and the prospect of a secure, new beginning.

Tom was distressed that he never did get the book written because he truly believed it would have been his magnum opus, expressing his deepest and most important convictions about life and American history. The first chapter by itself offers a feel for the direction he would have taken.

A New Birth of Freedom

"The English Background"

Govan opened his first chapter with Abraham Lincoln who, in his second inaugural address (1865), saw the Civil War as the judgment of God upon the nation, North and South, in which the offense of slavery had taken root. Judgment was God's business. Our business, on the other hand, was to "judge not that we be not judged." Lincoln understood his presidential vocation to be an instrument of God to finish the war, to purge the offense of slavery, but then "with malice towards none and with charity for all . . . to bind up the nation's wounds . . . and to do all which may achieve a just and lasting peace."[539] That was Lincoln in 1865; he was thoroughly biblical.

Govan, writing a hundred years later, during the Civil Rights Movement and a desperate war in Vietnam, insisted that the truth of a hundred years ago was still true today.

Then he turned to the thought of Frederick Denison Maurice. His point, said Govan, was that wherever and whenever in national life, God was dethroned in the name of the king, the church, the nobility, or the people, then judgment inevitably followed and freedom was destroyed. The king, the church, the nobility and the people are "under God" and must not forget it. For that reason, Maurice opposed the divine right of kings, the infallibility of the pope or church, an unchecked aristocracy, or an unchecked democracy. He affirmed the mixed government of Britain with its checks and balances, insisting that as long as the king, the nobles, the church, or the people confessed that they had a vocation and ministry under God and were not merely seeking power for themselves, then freedom, peace, and justice could prevail. He claimed for the Reformation, the liturgies and formularies of the Church of England (not the church in its actual life), the denial of all forms of sectarianism, and the affirmation of universal human fraternity as children of God.

Next he argued that most of the founders of the United States understood their task as a calling, undertaken on behalf of not only this nation, but also the world; Lincoln called this nation the world's "last best hope." The issue was whether a nation which affirms freedom, justice, and equality for all, and which achieves both freedom and security for its people, is possible. Can such a nation be maintained?

The answer was and is twofold. Yes, it can, the founders said, but not perfectly. The nation would need constant reform. The primary function of the Declaration of Independence and the Constitution, therefore, was to establish standards and principles of judgment by which individuals and groups could measure their actions, as well as order and guide those actions. Reform, by appeal to the basic affirmations of these documents, was the point. This was the form of government for which Alexander Hamilton fought. It was intended to be a continuation of the form and spirit of British government, which Lafayette, Washington, Montesquieu, and William Blackstone called the "best government in the world." And Govan agreed.

Undergirding all of this were the formularies of the Church of England that, unlike most Reformation churches, was founded not over a theological dispute, but over a personal and political controversy. Here Govan stated again what he had said earlier at the University of Oregon. The English reformers were men who knew their own corruption and fallibility during Henry's VIII's wild reign. They knew they were sinners who needed to say the General Confession daily, repenting not only as individuals, but also as responsible members of society: the nation, the church, and all the rest. For, as Govan said,

> Institutions are not organizations artificially devised by men . . . (but) principalities and powers of which Paul and the other apostles wrote, natural beings, corporate persons, children of God, and like his other children angelic or demonic as they are obedient and disobedient to his commands. They must admit wrongdoing, if they are to be true servants, for . . . (as they said) the evil be ever mingled with the good.[540]

The point of all this, said Govan, was that

> the moral ambiguity of the conduct and the cause of the English reformers was thus an advantage rather than a defect. It prevented them from attributing to themselves, their nation, or their church, a perfection and virtue that no man or institution has, as the way was left open for them and for others to demand and seek continued improvement and reform.[541]

Govan then claimed that the Common Law tradition had been the teacher of the pre-Reformation Church and had laid the groundwork for the Reformation and the Elizabethan Settlement.

Finally, Govan recognized that England was not able to live up to the real meaning of its traditions or its reformations. That took years of history, and it did not come by conscious decisions of good men, but rather by the repeated conflicts among very imperfect men. Through it all, however, the "free constitution of England was," as Blackstone said, "the source from which the nation balanced what was right and wrong, what would work and what would not. It sought a balance between order and freedom, stability and change."[542] In the end, civil and religious freedom became a reality, and

> by coincidence, certainly not as a part of a plan, the place where religious diversity [and freedom] was first recognized and established was the colonial dominions of America.[543]

To that story, he was planning to turn in his second chapter. Although Govan never completed *One Nation Under God,* his Deems Lectures in 1975 told most of that story.[544]

23

Home At Last, The University of Oregon, 1967-1977

Our mutual, but conflicting certainties are tearing the nation to pieces, as England in the seventeenth century was, by virtuous men in possession of the truth, and I guess the only thing to do is to pray that out of these struggles and conflicts, as in those, His cause, that is the cause of truth, freedom, justice, and equality, will be advanced.[545]

Thomas P. Govan

The Move to a New Home in Eugene, Oregon

The year 1967 was a joyous and daunting year for the Govans as they were about to make the final major move of their lives together. Tom had received an offer to come to the University of Oregon as a full professor of history with tenure, a salary of $20,000, "perks," and retirement at age seventy. He later learned that the appointment had been approved by a unanimous vote of the history faculty.

They had been waiting and wanting to return to Oregon. This was a dream come true and a great blessing. At last, Tom had a secure position until retirement in a place where they could afford to own their own home. He had left the security of tenure at Sewanee fifteen years earlier in 1952. Since then, it had been a long and sometimes painful journey, but he had to admit infinitely worth it. He had stood for what he believed and had served his church and historical vocations as faithfully as he knew how. His integrity was intact.

Finishing up at NYU, closing up their New York apartment, making the move and getting started at Oregon became his priority. At NYU, Tom had his regular courses to teach and quite a few graduate student theses to see through, either to a finish or into the new year, when his advising would have to be done by mail. As for owning a house in Oregon, the Govans could afford neither a downpayment nor a normal mortgage, but through the generosity of a New York friend were provided with a low-interest mortgage loan.

The house they chose at 3170 Nob Court was not far from the university, in an attractive suburb, where the house lots were approximately an acre, and the streets were contoured to the land. This meant room for a garden, privacy, and an open feeling of living in the country. The house was on a rise and facing west, so they had a long view toward the western horizon and the sunset.

On the first floor, facing the street was the living room with a fireplace and dining area, a kitchen, a lavatory, and a study for Tom. Upstairs were two bedrooms and a large bathroom. Because the house was built on the side of the rise, the basement in the back looked out over the lawn and gardens. It consisted of an attractive sitting room around another large fireplace, a mud room and gardening area near the back door to the garden, and a storage room. By October, they began to settle into the new home they already loved.

Part of Tom's initial responsibilities at the University of Oregon were to help team-teach a large two-semester undergraduate course on the "History of the United States," and teaching two graduate courses, "American Economic History" and "The Early National Period in United States History." In addition, he had a group of graduate students for whom he became thesis advisor. Within a year, Tom was appointed director of graduate studies for the history department.

A letter from Tom in December 1967 revealed him in high spirits having left his depression behind.

> I have wanted . . . for all these months . . . to write you
> about how wonderful Oregon is and how well things
> have turned out. We have bought a house with a
> wonderful view, a comfortable one that has plenty of
> room, and we hope that you and Ellie someday will
> come this way.[546]

Tom and Jane could not believe they were suddenly over sixty. "You must say 'No, no, no, it can't be so,'" he wrote a younger friend. "But it's strange that I, like others who have reached such an age, cannot believe it."[547]

In addition to age, circumstances had conspired to bring, as he put it, "A breath of reality into our Eden." He wrote his friend, Michael Allen,

> The extra bedroom has turned out to be a most useful
> part of the house, certainly temporarily and perhaps
> permanently, since Jane's twelve-year-old nephew, Tommy
> Dickson, has had to come to us. His mother [Nancy,
> divorced from Jane's brother, Thomas Hyde Dickson,
> who had later died] is in very bad shape with severe
> depression and illusions or delusions, of secret enemies
> who were bugging her house. She is now in a hospital,
> which is a relief, because we feared on the basis of calls
> and letters, that she might take more drastic steps. If it
> turns out, as it may well, that he stays on with us, then
> pray for two elderly persons confronted with the task of
> living with an adolescent in this most difficult time. I truly
> am frightened at the prospect, even though, as a historian,
> I do know that boys do grow up into being men in spite of
> it seeming impossible for them to do so.[548]

The boy stayed with the Govans, but it was not long before Tom and Jane realized that neither of them could handle him; he was too disturbed and rebellious. They were overwhelmed and wrote to a younger friend,

If you have ever seen a perplexed elderly couple, it is us. He is a nice boy, but a boy. If you have any words of advice, please forward them, for we do need help.[549]

The friend gently replied:

I am quite new at being a father, so the only advice I can offer on the 12 year old is tender love and care. As a teacher of this age, I can say, they can be difficult. This is a tender age and a teacher must count ten before reacting to what they do. Nevertheless, I am sure you and your wife can solve any problems the youngster has. I do not have to repeat in this letter the respect and love I have for the both of you.[550]

At this point they were ready to consider alternatives. Nancy was better, so Tommy returned to live with her, at least for the time being. The Govans felt badly about their failure, but were relieved. As the winter departed, their spirits rose. Tom wrote:

The weather has been magnificent; spring has been with us for almost six weeks and only occasional rainy days. . . . With the enthusiasm of a new convert, both Jane and I, as refugees from asphalt, have spent more time than we should working in the yard. I am digging in the dirt, as unbelievable as it may sound, and have built frames for espaliering sick trees, sprayed against bugs, and built paths—but now it looks that rain will come back again and enable me to return to work.[551]

Tom's feelings about the university were mixed.

The department has its problems, but, on the whole, is less torn with dissension than most. But what is strange is the exact reversal of my role from NYU. There I could reach students and gain their respect, but not my

colleagues as a whole. Here, at least during the first quarter, my teaching has been a complete bust [the students were not "getting it"], but my colleagues admire me tremendously. Both things, I hope, will come to an even keel. I know I am not as bad as the students have found me to be and on the other faculty side some of my meanness will come out.[552]

Thomas Payne Govan at the University
of Oregon 1967-1977

Tom knew his irascible side all too well. He did not suffer lazy and uninterested students gladly. The Oregon students were not as savvy about life as the New York students had been, and so found him obscure and difficult. Of course, they had never heard his message before. They found Govan's use of words like "conservative" and "liberal" were confusing. He refused to tell them what *he* wanted, but instead encouraged them to consider what they wanted out of the class. Although he would tell them what he believed and expected them to listen, he also insisted that they explore and think for themselves.

The faculty, on the other hand, appreciated his conciliatory and conservative attitude.

The late 1960s were troubling times for the United States, including the social unrest over civil rights and the Vietnam War, a major preoccupation for Tom as a citizen, a Christian, and historian. Blacks had rioted in Newark, New Jersey in July 1967. The federal government's Kerner Commission reported that the nation was moving toward two societies, one black and one white, separate and unequal. Martin Luther King was assassinated in April 1968; Robert Kennedy in June. A majority of Americans supported the Civil Rights Movement and were horrified by these events.

Stanley Feldstein, a former graduate student of Tom's at NYU, sent the Govans an audio recording of King's speeches. Tom replied gratefully:

> The King record came and we have relived all our sorrow, anger, and bitterness, but I remember what Robert Penn Warren once said about the 'powerful, painful, grinding process by which an ideal emerges out of history' and am somewhat reconciled, though no less regretful, at the seemingly needless cost.[553]

What Robert Penn Warren called the "process," Govan believed was somehow the Providence of God. He ended:

> Jane joins me in best wishes and we are both anxious for you all to see the place and Eugene.

> Affectionately, T.P.G.[554]

Tensions within the University of Oregon, 1968-1969

In the spring of 1968 after the assassination of Martin Luther King, Jr., near the end of Govan's first year at the University, "racial issues loomed larger on the radical student agenda than in any other year, temporarily overshadowing emphasis on war, governance, cultural styles, and economic conditions." The issue of instituting a Black curriculum headed the list. Jack Maddex, a graduate student at the time and now a professor of American history, told the story.

The outgoing but very "progressive university president, Arthur Flemming, appointed a 'President's Committee on Racism' in the university to which he co-opted the leaders of the Black Student Union (BSU), radical faculty whom 'the black students recommended and a few prominent university administrators who were uncomfortable with the majority's activity style and policies." The recommendations made by the committee were "quite unrealistic, but they mirrored the sense of social crisis and the urgency of justice that many . . . felt" at the time. As it turned out, however, the recommendations "hadn't even been filed in most of the offices to which [they] had been circulated."[555] The uncomfortable administrators temporarily had their way.

Maddex wrote in 2002:

> The History Department Tom Govan had joined in 1967 exemplified the 'generation gap' of that time. For the most part, the eight full professors were men of about Tom's age, who appeared (to their younger colleagues) stodgy and traditional. Some of them had been active in the 'Old Left' of the Depression era, but that did not prepare them for 'New Left' emphases and styles. The five associate profs were more aggressively 'professional,' more alert to the institution-building potential that baby-boom budgets promised. The assistant profs, whose number had swelled to about 11 in just a few years of heavy hiring, were young, flexible, and more responsive to recent trends (though not, as a group, extremely left). Some issues in the department meetings divided the faculty along approximately generational lines, to everyone's discomfort. The youngsters would cast almost half the votes in a typical department meeting—but the members they were threatening to outvote were the ones who would make the

decisions on their tenure. The recent record of assistant profs getting tenure was discouraging; one or two of them were already 'lame ducks' that spring.[556]

The Black History Issue

In 1968-69, Oregon recruited a cohort of 75 black students who augmented the ranks of the existing black student population. They contributed much to black campus activism. It became clear that more courses relevant to these students would need to be designed. Kenneth Porter, a distinguished senior member of the Oregon History Department, decided to offer an undergrad "American Negro History" course. According to Maddex, "Porter was an eminence whom the newer black history scholars were consulting on difficult matters of fact, but he had taught the subject only in grad seminars and in part of a quarter of his American Social History sequence. It was in the winter quarter that he taught it, and 'program' advisors directed their advisees, many of whom were militant and/or academically struggling into it. The experience resulted in very negative feelings between Porter and those students."

In the spring, Val Lorwin, who was a European economic-social historian, suggested a course called simply "Black History." No effort was made to include black students in the development of the curriculum until Maddex let his black student contacts know about the meeting. A significant delegation "crashed" the department meeting, occupying places around the table before any of the faculty arrived.

According to Maddex,

> Bill Hanna, who was near the end of his ill-starred term as Department Chair, played his usual role: reactionary, confrontational, and politically inept. He asked the 'Negro students' to leave the meeting. They replied that they were Black, not Negro and asserted their right to a voice. After about 2 minutes of sharp exchanges, Hanna declared the meeting illegally constituted, and dashed out of the room. I don't

remember that any other faculty member left with him. Some (particularly younger) faculty members hoped for some dialog about curriculum with the student activists, while other (particularly elder) ones considered themselves captives in an illegitimate situation but weren't going to be chased off their turf. Tension was high because of intrafaculty as well as faculty-student differences. In the choppy discussion that ensued, Tom Brady (then an assistant prof in his second year on the faculty) articulated the medieval principle, 'Let the one who has an interest be heard,' and (soon afterward) assumed the chair of what we subsequently called the 'illegal meeting' of the Department.

Maddex continued:

Several faculty members persuaded the students that any discussion should focus not on their complaints against Porter's course, but on general considerations and future possibilities. Tom Govan came across as one of those in the conciliatory camp, interested in discussion for future improvement. Some of the students were suspicious of him. Willie Triplett, the BSU president, had been in Tom's survey section, and cited it as an example of Eurocentrism. 'You told us that Columbus discovered the world,' he said to Tom. Tom said Willie had misunderstood him because 'you didn't hear me; you slept' during his lectures. Willie considered it unfair to bring up such a personal matter. But he found Tom a considerably more constructive critic than Porter, who told him 'I do not care whether you are the president of the Black Student Union, or Eldridge Cleaver himself.'

After considerable discussion, Lloyd Sorenson (a full prof who had been silent till then) proposed that the History faculty and the BSU should (separately) prepare

307

proposals for future black history courses, and delegate three representatives from each side to meet as negotiating teams to seek agreement. That enabled [them] to fine-tune the wording of his 'illegal motion,' and take an 'illegal vote' on it. Tom Govan offered common-sense suggestions on the negotiating process, and the majority of the faculty present agreed to present that proposal to the next legal department meeting. A conservative minority disapproved, but eventually resigned themselves to playing an obstructionist role within the process.[557]

Govan's Plan

Tom took the lead in planning the African American history curriculum. According to Maddex, the potential for ruinous confrontation was high at that point. Although some of the senior Europeanists had taken conciliatory stances at the meeting, and most of the junior faculty were so inclined, most of the professors in American history were senior faculty who appeared to range from conservative to downright intransigent. Without Tom's leadership, it would have been very difficult to adopt any proposals about courses within American history against their opposition.

Tom seemed to be the only one among us who was drafting proposals with a view to negotiation and eventual adoption. But he drafted, and redrafted. At one point he was even contemplating two course sequences: one on the history of white racism in the U.S., and one on the history of black people in the U.S. He eventually designed a sequence with the latter as primary focus, but prominently including the former as a theme. His eventual proposal was for a three-term course sequence covering the subject chronologically. He envisioned the course as a team effort: two faculty members, a grad assistant— and three paid black student assistants recruited by and from the BSU, to assist fully in course planning, discussion group leadership, and grade assignments. (It was the Sixties!) He planned (though he wouldn't state it in any document at that point) to reserve a considerable majority of the slots in the course for black students. This was an interim plan, to be accompanied by an earnest effort to recruit a new specialist in African American history.

Tom didn't seem to care what kind of attack he was courting from his colleagues, especially the ones who were of his own age and in his own field. After a conversation with the (much younger) Department Chairman, he said, 'I wish he'd a taken a swing at me— because, old as I am, I'd have beat the s[***] out of him.'

Tom proceeded to lobby colleagues, particularly the younger ones, for support of his plan. The department appointed a committee to draft negotiating proposals for a department meeting. The committee meetings were difficult. Two of the members drafted a pretty limited proposal, and Maddex submitted a minority report based on Tom's plan. Radical though Maddex was, he was finding the confrontation stressful. Tom kept reassuring him: "Damn it, Jack, we've got the votes."

The department voted to substitute, and then adopt, the minority report as the faculty's negotiating offer. According to Maddex

At the negotiating session, the Black Student Union representatives came in with a plan for lots of new courses and faculty, but readily accepted the Department's offer as a big gain they could actually get. Tom enlisted the support of the incoming department chairman (Stan Pierson) for the considerable department resources it would require. Some additional resources came from the University administration, but I don't know whether [maybe] Tom was also lobbying with the administration to get those. Given the political pressures then, he probably didn't have to.

Maddex continued,

> Tom knew that he and I would have to be the two faculty members in the team to teach the year-long course in 1969-1970. That was kind of a surprise to me given our personal and ideological differences. But we began to gear up for it during these same weeks. At the time my wife and I lived about six blocks up the same hill from the Govans. So, in evenings in that spring of 1969, we would go by to talk with Tom about the issue and the ongoing plans and politicking. We would walk into their house to find Tom and Jane reading *The Autobiography of Malcolm X*, Carmichael & Hamilton's *Black Power*, and other books of that sort. Having been current on radical matters till about the time of the Selma March, they knew that the situation had changed drastically since then, and they were working to get abreast of the Black Consciousness-Black Power scene. As usual, Tom expanded his horizons to encompass new realities while relating them to the familiar landmarks of his own worldview. A few months later, I heard him, in an argument about the value of book learning, urging a 'program' grad assistant to learn 'the lesson of Malcolm X.' That lesson, for Tom, was Malcolm's learning (in prison) that expanding his library and his vocabulary would be the necessary way to achieve the revolutionary race leadership he sought."[558]

That August of 1969, with a wry sense of humor, Govan wrote to Michael Allen describing his efforts:

> I have this summer become "an educator," involved for the first time in such things as "lesson plans" . . . at the university . . . We had a confrontation with the

black students in the spring and out of it I have had to begin preparation of a Black History course with a white graduate student [Maddex] and two black undergraduates . . . [This] will be the first time in my long years of teaching that I have ever been even outwardly systematic.[559]

Team Teaching

Maddex continued:

In 1969-70 Tom and I, with the team constituted by his plan, did team-teach a three-quarter sequence on Black American History. We covered the chronology in the first two quarters, and zeroed in on themes of current interest in the third, which was the tumultuous spring quarter of 1970. The actual implementation didn't live up to our dreams. One of the major themes of Govan's view of history was that liberal planners' idealistic visions would always get wrecked by the world's stubborn realities. In this instance, he would get a chance to go through that experience himself. It was an exhausting year, but we all learned much out of it in many different ways. We did familiarize many students with a history they claimed but still needed to learn, and engaged with them in a lot of burning questions with which they were wrestling in the social conflicts that were raging. In 1970-72, Sheldon Avery (while completing his dissertation with Kenneth Porter) taught the sequence. Others have taught it since then, through many changes of its name, number, and description.

My experience of team teaching with Tom Govan (whose arrival as a senior colleague had originally felt threatening to me) had many highlights. In the course of his historical discourses, Tom would weave in everything he thought about. I heard him describe to students the terrible effects of smoking. Though an unbeliever, I enjoyed his frank recognition of divine agency in his history lectures, complete with casual statements of what the Lord's reasons were in the particular event. Students would come up to me after his lectures and ask, 'Did he say that God prevented Union victories until the Union took up emancipation?'

When Tom gave his concluding lecture in the team-taught course, in spring 1970, the campus and much of the society and culture were in a turmoil that felt revolutionary whether it really was or not. Tom began the lecture just carrying on the narrative, but in covering recent years wove it into a conclusion that reviewed the long history of racial oppression and African American accomplishments. Before long he was talking about America as an entity with a divinely given mission. He portrayed it all as symbolized by the cross-shaped pattern of the main public buildings and monuments in Washington, D.C. As he covered in succession the points of that cross, asserting the essential symbolic role of each one, he must have seen me grinning from ear to ear, foreseeing the stumbling block that lay ahead of him. When he got to the last point, he frankly acknowledged that 'then they went and spoiled it' by filling that spot with a memorial to 'my great enemy, Thomas Jefferson.' Undaunted, though, he went on to relate American's revolutionary mission with the new revolutionary aspirations that were in many students' minds then. 'I don't know whether there will be another revolution,' he concluded, implying that he could see both a case for revolution and a case against one. 'But if there is one,

I hope that it will be a revolution founded on the
American ideals of freedom, justice, and equality.'[560]

Maddex concluded, "I don't remember the other sentences that
framed that one, but that stated his basic conclusion, and his other
words beautifully accentuated and elaborated that conclusion."[561]

Trouble in the Episcopal Church

In the meantime, the state of the Episcopal Church nationally
did not improve. It had been in a deepening crisis since 1967 when
Presiding Bishop John E. Hines, in response to riots in the U.S. cities,
called on the Church to set aside a portion of its annual budget to
support grant programs, which would empower people living in urban
ghettos "to stand on their own feet." Empowerment meant putting
money at the disposal of ghetto groups to "set, pursue, and achieve
their own goals." This project was called The Special Program by the
Church. Never before had the Church established such a program
and clearly it was controversial and risky. From the start, the Church
was divided about The Special Program. Some saw it as a liberal
political move that was flagrantly outside of the church's mission;
others saw it as a profound act of Christian obedience. Many
Episcopalians were distressed and reacted by withholding their
financial support to the Church. That in turn created a sudden
reduction of the national Church budget and by 1970 the necessity of
laying off staff, many of whom Govan had known well and cared about.
This led to the resignation of a number of key people in leadership
positions.

The first to resign, on June 30, 1970, was the Right Reverend
Stephen F. Bayne, Jr., former bishop of Olympia in Washington state,
who had written the 1958 report, "The Christian Faith, the Church
and the University." Later he became executive secretary. He was also
the former executive officer of the Anglican Communion worldwide,
and then the first vice president of the Executive Council of the
Church and Deputy for Program. He was a gifted man, loyal to the
presiding bishop, who left to teach at General Theological Seminary

in New York City. The second to resign was the Right Reverend Brooke
Moseley, former bishop of Maryland, currently the director of the
Overseas Department of the Episcopal Church, who became the
president and dean of Union Theological Seminary in New York City
after his resignation.

Warren Turner, treasurer of the Episcopal Church, and a close
friend of Govan's, resigned, not so much over the racial issue, as
over the empowerment issue. As treasurer, he felt he could not go
along with Hines' Special Program which was giving up
accountability for a great deal of church money by giving it to
urban groups about whom the Church knew little, and this he felt
was irresponsible.

Govan essentially supported Hines and the Special Program and
so was disturbed by these departures. He wrote to Turner:

> It was not just the lack of money, though that is bad, but
> the almost simultaneous departure of you, Steve [Bayne]
> and Brooke Moseley and their decisions to retire behind
> the massive walls on Ninth Avenue and Morningside
> Heights.[562] My own retreat, first to academia then to the
> province [Eugene, Oregon] gives me no ground on which
> to speak, but are we giving up? Have we been beaten?[563]

Implicit in these questions was whether everything he had given
his life to academically, politically, and religiously, namely freedom,
equality, and justice under God, was being deserted by the very people
he had counted on most. This was another crisis for him personally as
well as for the Church.

> I sometimes feel that Time [magazine] was right in 1961
> when on the cover of the Easter issue they present the
> Munch painting called *Angst* with the frightened man on
> the bridge cowering with covered ears and then again on
> the early March issue of *The New Yorker* just this year [1970],
> Steinberg's cover saying "Nothing, Nobody, Nowhere."

I am not actually as low in spirit as all this sounds, but it is strange how on all sides we seem to be closed in without any capacity to break out into creativity, except ironically, through the exploration of a totally dead moon within what seems a lifeless universe.

The students, even the non-radical ones, are convinced they are going through a meaningless performance and it is almost impossible to break through the walls of indifference, boredom and rejection.[564]

This was a pretty gloomy letter, full of self-reproach, illustrating in himself the "Age of Anxiety" of which W.H. Auden had spoken; but Govan ended by writing

And yet outside there is a glorious spring, a resurrection has again occurred, and there may be one for me, as I hope there is for you.[565]

For Govan hope was a matter of the spirit. When he was downcast, he never sought a clinical diagnosis or treatment. External circumstances, physiological and psychological explanations were low on his scale of interpretation because he felt the spirit lives largely beyond such interpretations. He understood despair and fear to be a loss of spirit, a loss of faith and hope, even "being possessed by demons," which Jesus could cast out. He did not deny psychological or physical or circumstantial explanations, but denied their determinative power over his spirit, which for him remained free, and for which he felt responsible, whatever his highs and lows.

24

Family Life in the 1970s

Well, as usual the argument was over something like the railroads
during the Civil War. Jack knew it all, from knowing nothing!
And Gilbert knew it all because he was older and he had read
more than Tom. And Tom knew better than either of them because
they were stupid.

James Bunnell

By the academic year 1971-1972, Tom's position in Oregon's history department was well established and his teaching was going well. Tensions within the department were much reduced in part because of Tom's moderation and sense of humor, but the real cause lay in his and the younger history faculty's willingness to work with the black students on the one hand, and the students' growing confidence in them as understanding allies. Tom's team teaching plan was working and everyone was relieved. Tom and Jane continued to be delighted with their home and were, as Tom had said, at peace with each other.[566]

Shortly after Thanksgiving, their dear friends Cora Louise and Lee Belford invited them to New York for the Christmas-New Year's break. Now able to afford such a trip, they joyfully accepted. They spent their time around Christmas in the city visiting old friends at the Episcopal Church's Second Avenue headquarters, at New York

University, and at St. Mark's-in-the-Bowery, where they basked in the beauty of the Christmas midnight service.[567]

And there were family to see across the river in New Jersey. By 1972, Tom's mother had died. His sister, Carol Tucker, had looked after her in Atlanta ever since his father, Will, had died thirty-two years before. Carol was at last free to retire from her job as a comptroller at Oglethorpe University, sell her house, and move to New Jersey to be near Jack Govan and his family. Jack's wife, Natalie, had also died and he had moved in with his daughter, Kathie, and her husband, René Monges, in Haworth, New Jersey, some eighty miles northwest of New York City.

Jack's apartment was on the third floor of the Mongeses' house, where he lived separately from the rest of the family. He also contributed a great deal to the upkeep of the house, providing, among other things, a houseman, Robert Johnson, who had worked for him ever since Kathie had been a small child. Robert did odd jobs, and even babysat for Kathie's children, ages two to twelve. Robert was a key person in the household, and during the week, always stayed through dinner. "Uncle Jack" also hired the Mongeses a full-time maid named Bea.

Jack, Kathie, and René invited Tom and Jane, along with Carol and her daughter, Betty Conn, to dinner mid-week between Christmas and New Year's Eve. As usual, there was plenty of liquor available. It was a party, and as often happened at family parties, it became a family ruckus, this time over plans for New Year's Day. It had been agreed that Robert would have the day off because he had a long-planned engagement. Kathie was giving a brunch for fifty people, and Bea had agreed to help New Year's morning, provided she could have that afternoon off. Betty Conn described what happened.

"At the dinner table—this is just four days before New Year's Day, remember—Uncle Jack leans back and says, 'Bea has to work that afternoon. She cannot work that morning, because I have invited Carol and Betty and three others over to have black-eyed peas and hog jowl.' Clearly Uncle Jack had a good deal to drink.

"Kathie said, 'Daddy, please! You just can't do this to me. I've invited fifty people over for brunch, a big crowd.' Bea was crucial because Robert wasn't going to be there. Well, they wrangled all during dinner, and Kathie got more and more upset. And Mother (Carol) and Betty kept saying, 'We don't need black-eyed peas and hog jowl. And if we must have them, we can cook 'em ourselves.'

"And Uncle Jack said, 'No, she's my maid and I pay her salary and she is going to . . . . ' You know, it got to be that kind of thing. And whenever that kind of thing happened, René always stayed out of it and let them figure it out. So they reached this impasse. And Tom got involved as the go-between. Robert was there, and Tom got on the phone and talked to Bea. Negotiations went on all through the evening. The children were coming in, getting ready to go to bed. And there was all sorts of confusion about that. Neighbors came in, and they were still arguing. Tom was still trying to get it settled. He said to Betty, when he finally got it settled—he came over to sit in a chair by Betty—'Whew! It finally got settled. I've been involved in all kinds of family arguments, but this is the first one in my whole life that involved black-eyed peas and hog jowl.'

"Going home that night, Mother (Carol) said to her, discreetly—Uncle Jack was driving, of course, and Uncle Tom was in the front seat—she said, 'You know, Tom never has any money. He borrowed twenty dollars from me to give to Bea. He'll never pay it back . . . he never does.' She said it so sweetly, but there it is! They all call Carol 'Miss Priss.'"[568]

And that was the Govan Christmas and New Year's of 1970-1971!

Family Stories, Early 1970s

Betty Conn told another story about Uncle Jack and his sons, who were much like him. She was visiting for the weekend in 1972-73 along with her sister Kate, and Jim Bunnell, who were down from Andover, Massachusetts. "The whole dinner conversation at this restaurant involved what it cost to replace telephone poles in various counties and states. This came up because all of them had totaled so many cars and knocked over so many poles that even their mother, Carol, knew the details. 'No,' she would say, 'you're all wrong about that, Jack; it was this way.' With Jack and arguments, alcohol was often involved."[569]

Jim Bunnell, a brother-in-law and close friend, thought, "Tom was aware of the connection between booze and a lot of these family arguments. What bothered him was not the booze, but that anyone was bothered about it" or thought it was the cause of the arguments. It was just there, and "he expected you to accept it" as a given.[570] Tom would argue that the Govans were a clan, the clan was close, and it was not booze that caused the arguments, at least not always; it was just the competition and the insecurities of the clan members. And "when they were together, they were 'thick as thieves' and they fought like thieves. Alcohol only occasionally made it worse—that was all."[571] Tom grew up in a generation for whom drinking was socially expected and normal, even "smart," a generation who tended to deny alcoholism as an addiction or disease. Tom's lifestyle reflected that.

An example Jim cited occurred at the Bunnell's home in Andover, around 1973. Gilbert, Jack, and Tom were all there and eventually got into a ferocious argument. Jim later related:

> Well, as usual, it was [over] something like the railroads in Georgia during the Civil War. I know nothing about American history—European history is my field—and I wasn't about to get into that argument. But, Jack knew it all, from knowing nothing! And Gilbert knew it all because he was older and he had read more than Tom. And Tom knew better than either of them, because they were stupid. Tom felt that Gilbert was 'pulling big brother' on him and got furiously angry with him. Both men were bruised by the incident. The next day, I asked Tom, 'Why argue that way with Gilbert?' And Tom said, 'It's just brothers. Arguing that way is just brothers.' . . . Tom could get angry, but it did not last long, especially with Gilbert.[572]

Home Life with the
Govans in Eugene, 1973-1975

Tom Govan and Laura Roper in Eugene,
Oregon circa 1972

Sarah Bunnell, Jim's daughter and Tom's niece, lived with the Govans in Eugene for two years, 1973-1975, during her freshman and sophomore years at the university. She loved their neat, modern house with its basement room looking out onto Jane's garden in back and the first floor living room with huge picture windows overlooking the whole valley to the West. She found it was a pleasant house to live in. Sarah also got to know Tom and Jane and their lives from the inside. Their daily routine, as she described it, was very similar to the one they had followed in their Sewanee days. Tom, an early riser, would get up first and Sarah would wake to the smell of coffee, "the strongest coffee on the planet earth!"[573] Tom would drink the whole pot except for one cup for her. As she went down the hall to get her cup, she would inevitably smell his cigarettes, too.

Elinor W. Crocker, John Crocker Jr.'s wife, Tom Govan
in his morning wrapper, Jane D. Govan, Sarah Bunnell,
the Govans' niece

By this time, the Govans had two dachshunds, Fritz and a third Judy. Fritz would accompany Sarah down the stairs in the morning. Tom would usually be in his old bathrobe and have on an old pair of brown shearling slippers. Jane was "a big bathrobe person, and she would keep him well-stocked with them." By the time Sarah got downstairs, Tom would be finished eating his cereal of shredded wheat and be in the living room reading, coffee and cigarettes in hand. He and Jane read everything and were up on all the latest books. Tom read a lot of history and theology, but also enjoyed poetry, novels, and other works. He was interested in what Sarah was reading and read them, too. They kept a constant turnover of books from the library. Sarah was fascinated by the volume and variety of the books in the house. "Just coming into their living room was an education. They didn't watch much television, but did have a portable TV, which they tucked away in a cupboard when not using it. The one thing they would never miss was "Upstairs, Downstairs" on Masterpiece Theatre . . . . They were both addicts!"[574]

Jane would get up in the morning whenever it suited her, early or late. She'd "come down in some robe looking elegant," have her coffee and cigarettes and sit and read.[575] The newspapers would come, and the three of them would devour *The New York Times*, *The Atlanta Constitution* a day late, and the local paper. When it was time, Sarah would ride her bicycle to the university or catch a ride with Tom.

If they were home for lunch, there would be "Coca-Cola in the bottle and some kind of really deep, dark bread with some sort of incredibly delicious deli-sliced meat, intense mustard, and more coffee; in summer, iced coffee."[576] Then Jane might work in the garden and send Tom out on an errand.

Fall was a special time. The Govans had a small orchard of magnificent Worsley Delicious apple trees that Tom kept pruned. The fruit was large and tasty. At harvest time, Jane would send everyone she could find, including neighbors' children, up those trees and fill the garage with apples. The Govans had two refrigerators full, but the apples overflowed onto shelves and into boxes. It was fun for everyone.

Jane Govan in her garden, Eugene, Oregon, 1974

And there was Jane's garden. It was not a big and bursting garden that "you could feast on. It was rather like a hundred little exquisite nibbles, like miniature strawberries growing by the path, a little of this here, and of that, there."[577]

Tom and Jane were very social in part because she was gregarious and so enjoyed the role of hostess. If they had people in for lunch, it had to be a pre-planned event, because lunch, on the whole, was too early in the day for Jane. Later in the day, however, was another matter. Sarah called her "a magician, socially facile and fluid and effortless."[578] She could throw together quickly the most incredibly elegant, simple, delicious, fun, entertaining meals, dinners, and gatherings, either planned or impromptu, if someone dropped by at the right time of day. Jane could whip it all together. At least once a week, the Govans would have guests, mostly history or other faculty Jane liked. The men were usually Tom's colleagues and occasionally came over without their wives. The women did the same, dropping off a book or recipes or potluck food. "There was a lot of coming and going, sometimes for five minutes, or fifteen, and sometimes they would stay and have a cocktail. It was always cocktail hour" at the Govans, but mostly around sundown.[579] They drank good bourbon whiskey: Jack Daniels, Virginia Gentleman, or several other brands. They would have at least two, maybe more. "No one got drunk, but they certainly did drink."[580]

Sarah remembers thinking that her Aunt Jane was sort of a "druggy," because "she had one heck of a medicine cabinet. She looked really healthy, but she had had her problems; scar tissue from her mastectomy and dreadful arthritis. Her hands were so gnarled."[581]

Despite physical incapacities, Jane did a great deal of handiwork. Sarah spent many evenings transferring designs onto needlepoint canvases, so that Jane could needlepoint Matisse pillows for the living room sofa. She did one for the church that was "stunning."[582]

Another dynamic of the Govans' social life was the fact that people found Tom fascinating intellectually. "Living with Uncle Tom," Sarah said, "was like living with Socrates or someone!"[583]

"These men would sit around the room listening and talking. Sometimes, they'd be at his feet on the floor. And some of them would get into loud heated discussions with him. Uncle Tom loved that. He did not ever seem threatened by another person's opinion. He knew exactly where he stood. He had a coherent point of view, which I didn't really understand. Often I would say something and he'd make it clear that he thought it was baloney, but he wouldn't say why. So I never really understood a lot of what was on his mind. I really loved him. But there was a barrier. I never got too close to him. I couldn't; he was too high above me. I couldn't communicate with him, because I didn't want to waste his time.

"He never resented my not having conversations with him. He was just fine. I could go and read or look through their art books or stare out that living room window with him and just be completely at peace. Sometimes he would cackle, just laugh aloud at what he was reading."[584]

"Sometimes he was willing to interact with you on a level that was just wonderful." One night in the routine of washing the dishes after dinner—Sarah would wash and Tom would dry—they began talking about a Shakespeare class she was in. Sarah began telling him about a soliloquy in Hamlet, during which Polonius says to his daughter, Ophelia, "Above all else, to thine own self be true and it must follow as the night the day, thou canst not then be false to any man" (Hamlet, I, iii, 78-80). Sarah said, "The next thing I knew, he erupted, which he could do easily. I wasn't really used to that. It took me a while to figure out that he wasn't just mad at me. But he'd just lose his temper and slam the pan down, and the next thing I'd know, we would be in some heated, fun discussion about something I was reading, usually Shakespeare. And he'd be smiling the whole time. I found him completely fascinating. He'd explode and call me a 'damned fool' and 'if I believed this or that, I was a damned fool.' That night, for example, he bellowed at me that Polonius was an old fool and what he said conflicted sharply with Jesus' two Great Commandments. The trouble was that Polonius was presenting a partial truth as though it were the whole truth—which it was not. Because being true to yourself very often means primarily that you will be false to your neighbor."[585]

Jane was less direct than Tom on literary issues, especially moral issues, and she was less intellectual; but she certainly held her own with him by being up on current literature, art, architecture and theater. And she was determined to educate Sarah. "She would do things like buy tickets to special events, for example to a special series of classic films, like O'Neill's *The Ice Man Cometh*. They would get all dressed up and Tom would put on a tie and his best jacket. But it was primarily through the books she encouraged us to read and discuss with her that she influenced us intellectually."[586]

The Govans went to church more or less regularly at St. John's Episcopal Church in Eugene. It was a homey church, and Sarah sometimes sang in the choir. Tom was licensed by the bishop to preach every month or so. Only once did Sarah hear her Uncle Tom preach a midnight Christmas Eve service. She wanted to go more often to hear him, but her Aunt Jane discouraged it. This seemed to be a pattern: Jane did not want Sarah too close to Tom. She was Jane's friend first, and Tom's second, and Jane did not want that reversed.

Sarah enjoyed going to church with them partly because they were not compulsive about it. She thought going or not may have depended on what had gone on the night before. There was a party or a gathering at least once a week at the Govans, usually informal. As Sarah put it, "They just excited these other people and there was always somebody's house to welcome them."[587]

"On Sundays, sometimes, when we did not go to church, Aunt Jane would be in her wrapper until two or three in the afternoon. On Sundays when we did go to church, there would be a luncheon somewhere with friends or colleagues."[588]

Jane did a lot of baking. Often on weekends she would put Sarah to work on the preparations for some big baking project, whether it was pies, breads, or getting ready for Christmas. Jane made "the best fruit cake I ever had in my whole life," Sarah said. "And it was spiked."[589]

"I really remember those times around Christmas. We were in church a lot then, because I was in the choir and we were singing all over town. There always was their Christmas party. Everybody showed up. People, all kinds of people, from the history department, from the church, from town, everywhere. Aunt Jane made a feast with fruit cake and Uncle Tom and I made the eggnog. It was an all day thing to make that eggnog. It was out of this world. In these enormous bowls, we beat, I don't know how many, egg whites, and cream, and ice cream, and Jack Daniels by the bottle. It was a big Christmas party and they had a big Christmas tree in the living room and had to move furniture around to make room for it. The party was loud and got raucous. I remember the next day, nobody got up until about three in the afternoon!"[590]

One year there was also a big Christmas party at the home of a colleague, Tom Brady, who had just returned from Salzburg. He and his wife, as Sarah put it, "were prone to not having as wide open and heavy-duty a drinking kind of party as the Govans, so it wasn't quite as rowdy, and I don't remember anybody 'sleeping in' the next day. Everybody was talking about the political scene over in Europe. And their whole house had this little old Salzburgian look and feel about it from all the things they had brought back. Tom Brady could get really loud and argumentative, and he would get on a scream with Uncle Tom. They'd yell and scream back and forth, but he was kind of nice to me and he was kind of funny. But what I most appreciated about him was that he would play 'Royalty' with Aunt Jane. It was a card game she loved. Uncle Tom didn't seem to like the game much more than I did and we would both try to get out of it, but Tom Brady would come and spend hours playing with her—screaming and yelling and carrying on. He would fight her tooth and nail, as if they were going to fight to the death over who was going to win. They could do this over and over without hurt feelings because they were such close and trusting friends. They would be drinking, you know, and it was all in fun. It would start after dinner and just keep going. Uncle Tom would either be watching the news or doing whatever he wanted. He didn't sit around and play with them.

"I did a lot with Aunt Jane and I didn't mind because she was fascinating to me. I had a feeling that I ought to listen to her, because when I was growing up, I had heard a great deal from Mom and Dad [Kate and Jim Bunnell] about Uncle Tom and Aunt Jane and they would talk in reverential or fond terms. And then my grandmother [Carol Tucker], whom we called 'Tukkie,' loved Uncle Tom more than her other three brothers. He was the one she would call if she needed help. So, before I went to live with them, I always [had] heard a lot about Uncle Tom and Aunt Jane; they would be either wonderful and hilarious stories or good stories. It wasn't until after I'd been with them and come back home that we talked about some of the other aspects, the negatives. So I was pretty open to them. And Aunt Jane talked quite a bit, actually. And she'd always have some project going, so she'd have me cooking, doing needlepoint, whatever. She didn't make me, but there were things I could help her with and they were fun. I took her orders pretty well. You know, I went into the army afterwards and I think I got completely ready for it. Aunt Jane was my first drill sergeant.

"She opened me up to a certain phase of modern art, Monet, Matisse, and that generation. She had a good art library and we talked at great length about some of those pictures, and Uncle Tom would pipe up about them sometimes. He had opinions about them, too. They both really loved art, so that was fun."[591]

Jane did all she could to turn Sarah into the person she wanted her to be. She tried unsuccessfully to set her up with dates. She told her what her best colors and styles of dress were. Naturally there was some friction between them, but Sarah was remarkably appreciative. She might resent being pushed around "but you know," she would say, "Jane's taste was impeccable. She was a brilliant decorator. She had a real sense of beauty, and she could create a beautiful room inexpensively. Aunt Jane picked the patterns that she thought would look best on me. And we sewed them out of gorgeous material that Aunt Jane and I bought."[592]

Jane did the same with Sarah's education. Sarah "tended towards English and theatre and art, but was steered away from history by Aunt Jane."[593] Jane did not want her to fall under Tom's spell or influence. "I was a little cross about it at the time, but it turned out all right because none of the history courses grabbed me."[594]

Sarah summed up her experience by saying, "I came away from two years with them with the clear impression that Aunt Jane provided for Uncle Tom a place where his colleagues could come and sit at his feet. She made them feel completely welcome. She would wine and dine them and set up occasions for him. She had such an easy way about her that she made it easy for him. She was really good at it."[595]

25
Govan's Intellectual Work, 1967-1975, University of Oregon

What I am arguing against . . . is the view that economic decisions are made for economic reasons . . . Men's moral and political ideas are always more powerful.

Thomas P. Govan

The major intellectual hurdle facing Tom Govan in his first years at the University of Oregon was his inability to proceed with his dream project, *A New Birth of Freedom*. So he did the next best thing by working on shorter more feasible projects, carrying on with what he had always done: book reviews, correspondence, and short articles.[596]

Robert W. Fogel on "The Economics of Slavery"

During that first year at the University of Oregon, Govan corresponded with Robert W. Fogel, a young professor of economics at the University of Chicago who had written a long paper on "The Economics of Slavery" in 1965. Fogel's methods stressed quantification and statistics as a means of checking and establishing factual information. In particular, they were a means for exposing and

328

correcting the errors of traditional historians about slavery. He had read Govan's article, "Was Plantation Slavery Unprofitable?" in Carl N. Deglar's collection, *Pivotal Interpretations of American History,*[597] and recognized him as one of the few historians who would understand and appreciate what he was trying to say. Fogel was, therefore, eager to seek Govan's critical comments. In September 1967, he wrote Tom who, in response, gave Fogel a short course in the economics of slavery. First, he questioned Fogel's assumption that "the demand for cotton and other commodities" governed their price. He wrote Fogel that the credit and money supply were the primary factors which determined the price of cotton and other commodities, not, as Fogel thought, the supply and demand for cotton itself. The primary issue was whether money was cheap and abundant. "Men buy when money is available in expectation and hope . . . . The high price for land and slaves in the late 1850s, for example, is not proof that men who started new farms . . . did not see and feel the developing crises. Most of them did, but they either had money or could borrow it (money was cheap and abundant) and so they used it."[598]

Second, Govan insisted that the selling of slaves was not an "industry;" it occurred only in hard times.

Third, it was not worn-out land that sent farmers West, but primogeniture. The oldest son inherited the eastern land; the younger sons had to go West for theirs. For that reason the number of towns and cities in the West grew faster than those in the East.

Fourth, slave owners did not rent out their slaves primarily for profit, but out of "public concern and [often competitive] patriotism for the purpose of supporting 'internal improvements,'" that is, public works that would benefit the whole community: the building of bridges, roads, canals, and railroads.

Fifth, slavery was never supported or opposed because it was profitable or unprofitable. The issue for both sides, pro and con, was always moral in nature. The defenders of slavery believed white civilization would be destroyed if the slaves were freed. Even those opposed to slavery believed that when freed, they would have to be colonized elsewhere.

Sixth, slavery would not have died of stagnation. On the contrary, the slave states "boomed and busted" like the rest of the nation. Slavery made no difference.

Govan agreed with Fogel's criticism of Eugene D. Genovese and other historians who wrote from a Marxist view. Their analyses were simply not borne out by the evidence, in detail or in general. Genovese, he said, was "more of a philosopher than a historian, more interested in what [he thought] should be than what was."[599]

Tom made two final points in his correspondence with Fogel. The first:

> What I object to most seriously about your whole approach is its substitution of logic and mathematics for historical investigation. Life is not logical or mathematical. These are tools, not determinants, and should be used, not worshipped. There are too many unknown and unknowable variables to enable us to substitute theory for fact in regard to the past—though I value the effort to gather accurate statistics and to use them. But the statistics need to be about actualities, to the extent that we can ascertain them.[600]

Second, on October 17, 1967, he wrote:

> What I am arguing against, I think, is the view that economic decisions are made for economic reasons, that there is an 'economic man.' Men's moral and political ideas are always more powerful, in part because of the complexity of the economy and of each person's relationship to it. For example, in my own inconsequential position, I am both a debtor and creditor, a taxpayer and a parasite living on tax-payers, a consumer of goods and [as a history professor] a supplier of a service, and, more importantly than all these, an ideologue with strong convictions in favor of that view of society which emphasizes the complementary aspects more than the

competitive in the national economy. So I am a protectionist (when dumping from outside is a danger), an internationalist (when someone would try to save our own situation by dumping abroad), a moderate inflationist, a despiser of the superstition about gold, and a believer in the possibility of managing, within limits, the credit and money supply nationally and internationally, etc. etc. These are the factors which influence my decisions and why, at the moment, I am in favor of the Governor of Oregon's reluctant decision to recommend a 3% sales tax. But, as I sit here, I cannot decide what it is that has led me to the decision. I do not think it is my change of situation—I supported Rockefeller's sales tax in New York when I was neither a homeowner or a public employee—and yet I am deeply concerned by its costs to the poor.[601]

In a sense, I guess, as a historian, I am almost a nominalist or existentialist, concerned with the individual and the particular, though knowing that dealing with fact at such a level is both impossible and meaningless. Perhaps what I am really desirous of is that historians though concerned, of necessity, with the general rather than the narrow particular, should make it apparent that they know the particulars exist.[602]

Fogel was very much a man of the particulars, who counted individual bits of evidence to verify general "facts." He, no doubt, agreed. There the correspondence ceased.

Six years later in 1974, Fogel's article was expanded into a full-length book that caused a tremendous public uproar.[603] Fogel seemed to be defending slavery. Using a vast amount of data, he had concluded that slavery in the pre-Civil War South was neither a stagnating influence on the economy, as some claimed, nor the vicious and brutal business depicted by the abolitionists. It was, on the contrary, an economically efficient and highly lucrative system for producing cotton, and slaves, who were generally treated well, were diligent, hard working, and had internalized the Protestant work ethic of their masters. Good treatment of slaves, after all, was as much or more in the slave owners' interest as bad treatment. On average, slavery was a benign paternalism.

This view of slavery, of course, undermined the orthodox image of a vicious slavery that brutalized, dehumanized, and destroyed the slave. On the contrary, said Fogel, the slaves on the whole, withstood the brutalizing psychological effect of a tragic condition with great fortitude, maintaining their religion, moral values, family loyalty, and work ethic.

The furor and outrage over his seeming defense of the morality of slavery was not lost on Fogel. Nor was the fact that critics found "numerous lapses in scholarship, errors of fact and breeches in the elemental rules of quantification."[604] So in 1989, Fogel produced a second book with the intention of setting the record straight.[605] Although he omitted some earlier truth claims, he sought to correct some errors and defend his major conclusions, but make it absolutely clear that he despised the immorality of slavery, and stressed that slavery had been abolished precisely because its claim to moral legitimacy was untenable and bankrupt.

In 1993, fourteen years later, along with Douglas C. North of Washington University, Fogel received the Nobel Memorial Prize in Economic Science, honoring his way of "applying economic theory and quantitative methods" to history.[606] Govan, always skeptical of Fogel's approach, would have found extreme irony in this honor.

Adlai Stevenson: a Study in Values, a Review

Govan wrote at least nine book reviews in 1968. One of the best was his review, *Adlai Stevenson: a Study in Values* by Herbert J. Muller,[607] who was the "liberal academic intellectual" about whom Govan had written in his 1956 Faculty Paper, "Free to Be Merely A Man" (see Appendix 4).

Stevenson, like Roosevelt, had been forced by the realities of the twentieth century world to give up his youthful Democratic dreams of a better society, governed by "virtuous men, ruling themselves with a minimum of public restraint and expenditure." Both men changed and adopted the far more realistic belief that all humans and all human institutions are corruptible, influenced by their own self-interest. Therefore, they need to be restrained. They came to believe that freedom, justice, and equality, as well as national prosperity and strength, can be established only by a government that has the power to instruct and restrain all individuals and groups and the material means to provide for the common defense; in other words, to believe in the existing government of the United States.

For all practical purposes, Muller had been forced to make the same change of view, for the same reasons, and Govan gives him credit for that. The trouble, Govan found, with Muller's view was that "he disowns traditional Democratic policies but not the easy distinction between good and evil on which they are based." He continued to think in black and white moral terms, of "good guys" and "bad guys," good morals versus bad morals, of which he, Muller, was the judge.

It would never occur to Muller, therefore, to question the appropriateness of Eisenhower's Moral Crusade[608] for the reason that it was self-righteous and based on the false assumption that pure morals exist and we are the ones who have them. But he has no trouble criticizing the personal "moral character of most of the General's associates."

> He also criticizes Stevenson for not always conducting himself according to the pure standards of his enthusiastic academic admirers, particularly his work as ambassador to the United Nations.

Muller does not seem to understand that the position Stevenson held at the U.N. was by nature imperfect. Every day he had to make decisions between lesser and greater evils, between U.S. national interests and those of other nations. Moral perfection was completely impossible and irrelevant.

And "It never seems to occur to [Muller] that the Scriptural injunction, 'judge not that ye be not judged' is wise advice for historians and biographers (and repentantly, reviewers [like Govan] as well)."

Muller's most telling comment on Stevenson was this:

> The political figure most admired [by Stevenson] was that self-confessed but repentant sinner, Abraham Lincoln, who based his hope for a better world on the conviction that unworthy men, acting from unworthy motives, could and did (during the Civil War, for example) accomplish good through government.

Stevenson had learned from Lincoln. Muller had not.

Once a Slave: The Slave's View of Slavery[609]

Govan took on two other important intellectual projects during his first year in Eugene, both concerning slavery. The first was mentoring former NYU student Stanley Feldstein through his thesis on the slaves' views of slavery. It was an important project because it would bring out of almost total obscurity some five thousand narratives of slavery, written or dictated by the slaves themselves. Feldstein's intention was to present "only what these narratives say about slave life and the institution." He was not claiming to write a history of slavery, or even to tell the "true" story of slavery. Feldstein's story was to be only about the narratives and what they said.

Both Govan as teacher and thesis adviser and Feldstein as the student and writer struggled. Feldstein was under an NYU thesis deadline of October 1968. Govan desperately wanted the thesis to be absolutely first-rate because it would fill a gap in historiography by telling a very different story of slavery from the likes of Eugene D. Genovese with his neo-Marxist bias, or Robert W. Fogel with his "objective" and statistical bias. It should be published and Govan would write the introduction.

In January 1968, Govan began reviewing parts of the first draft. His reply to Feldstein was not encouraging.

> Dear Stanley,
>
> I will not do anything to put you in a good humor but get right down to business. You are doing what I did not want you to do, writing this to please me and not yourself, and in so doing have not told a story. You are not writing a history of slavery, but a study of what the slave narratives say about slavery, and you have to get outside the narratives, organize their general story, and then tell it, using what they said as illustration. I have presumptuously written two pages to illustrate what I mean . . . .
>
> Your first chapter should thus be on making slaves of human beings. Then a second, on how it worked, which it did by the evidence of the slaves themselves! Their acceptance. Then perhaps would follow a description of life on the farms and plantations, the actual working of the system as seen by the slaves. Then what led some to break away. Then a general summary of what slavery appeared to be to the slaves.

At that point, Govan offered some pastoral care:

> Do not be discouraged by this response of mine. Go back to your thesis proposal and see how you told what you were going to do. I had hoped not to have to do this with you, but it seems inevitable. Every manuscript that I have seen that is at your present stage is very much like this. But you must remember that everything you say must begin with a clear indication that this is what the narratives say. A general statement of your method of working will not suffice. It must be made clearly apparent in every paragraph.[610]

Feldstein's long reply indicated that he understood Govan's point: namely that he had to write his own story of what the slaves said about slavery, using their narratives as illustrations. He must follow his own "central story thread," Govan said, and thus order what the slaves said in his own way.

But Feldstein's feelings had been hurt by Govan's letter. They were good enough friends, though, that he could say so.

> I must be truthful and tell you that I was hurt by your reaction. But you are the expert and I know that I must take direction from you. I will do my best to satisfy your guidance.[611]

Govan's immediate response was also full of feeling, but urging that they must be more objective if the job was to get done well.

> We must not be sensitive with each other, we cannot be defensive in our attitude, or else we cannot communicate. I, for example, was hurt by the statement, 'But you are the expert and I know that I must take directions from you.' In my view, I am not the expert, nor the director. I am a critical and concerned reader, enthusiastically hopeful that you can make your story what you want it to be, and seeking only to be of help.[612]

Govan went on to discuss Feldstein's difficulty with repetitions, with his failure to provide transitions, with paragraphs not centered on one subject.

More of the same came in Tom's next letter to Feldstein, again offering a pastoral care approach:

> Please don't be discouraged, each writer, everyone of us, has to undergo the same experience, not once but hundreds of times. We know the material and what we want to say, but we forget that our reader does not. He needs to have things pointed out to him; he

cannot know what we are doing unless he is told and retold but in such a way that he is not aware that he is being told and retold.[613]

On March 11, Govan reacted with more satisfaction to Feldstein's revised text. On the 19th, Feldstein was again expostulating about the incredible strength of most slaves under oppression. Although some were broken and dehumanized, made into near-animals, many more maintained their humanity, their feelings, their pride, and their values under horrible conditions—"What strength there is in men!" Tom responded,

> Somehow, you must let your admiration for those who could not be broken shine through without making it too explicit. In other words, take pride in the unbroken spirits who continue to live and struggle in the midst of completely degrading conditions. You have done this already, but don't let your hostility to the oppressors and the oppressive situation be the only theme.[614]

Four months later in July, in the midst of a relatively positive letter, Tom included a paragraph that was devastating about a new chapter Feldstein had sent.

> Even in your present mode of approach, your story is disorganized and repetitious—you have not thought through what you were going to tell your reader, or if you have, you have not prepared him for what he is to be told.[615]

And in August:

> You have totally ignored the problem of transition from section to section and most of the time from paragraph to paragraph. There may be a logic to your organization, but it is not made explicit in terms of story development.

You are writing a story of what the narratives say about
slavery and this story must be told.[616]

Finally, the thesis was completed and Feldstein received his Ph.D.
in history. The following year, 1970, William Morrow and Company
accepted it for publication[617] and Govan was asked to write the
introduction,[618] which he did with great pleasure, and in it said,
"everything he had wanted to say about slavery."[619] Govan traced the
despicable history of slavery in the United States. One of his major
points, which he had made back in 1940, but which had not been
generally accepted by historians, was that after the Santo Domingo
insurrections, fear of blacks became far more influential than the
desire for economic profit in motivating slaveholders to defend slavery
and want to make it a permanent institution. This was when, because
of fear, southern opinion began claiming that slavery was the sole
means by which the two races could live together.

Another point in the introduction concerned the opposition to
allowing slavery into the northern territories of the West: it was not
just anti-slavery sentiment that was the source of it, but anti-black
sentiment among whites who wanted no blacks in the area at all, slave
or free. The irony of this was not lost on Govan.

Govan then went on to focus on the treatment given slavery by
modern, so-called "objective" American historians. Some were outright
racists, like the followers of William E. Dunning and Ulrich B. Phillips,
but not many. Most of them heartily disapproved of slavery, but "as
objective, detached, and uninvolved scholars" could not, on principle,
allow their disapproval to show. In the attempt to avoid "partisanship"
or "making an easy distinction between good and evil, right and
wrong," in itself a praiseworthy objective, "their writing became morally
neutral"[620] about slavery itself.

Wanting to preserve "objective" neutrality, they came to "distrust
and ignore" all sources which they felt were "partisan and self-
interested propaganda, not factual description," especially all of those
narratives written or dictated by slaves "who passionately hated" slavery
and were used as abolitionist propaganda. "So prevalent was the
distrust of these accounts," said Govan, "that historians of slavery almost

entirely ignored them, turning instead to more neutral sources,[621] and after a time their very existence was forgotten."[622] So the history of slavery had been terribly distorted. Feldstein's book was an attempt to put the record straight. Every instrument of cruelty, Govan said, was used for the purpose of "obliterating the mind, crushing the intellect, and annihilating the soul" of the slaves, but they refused to be crushed. In spite of terrible circumstances, the slaves, in most cases, maintained "their humanity and their humaneness" as well.[623]

Govan rejoiced in these narratives as the real truth about slavery, truth that helps people feel and share their feelings, truth without which true objectivity would be lost.

Govan's Biographical Sketch of Nicholas Biddle, 1970-1974

In the fall of 1970, Govan received a request from Professor John A. Garraty of the Columbia history department to write a sketch of Nicholas Biddle for the *Encyclopedia of American Biography*.[624] Tom agreed, and Garraty sent him a contract, including a "factual summary" and evaluation of Biddle, both of which were intended to be helpful. Govan's heart sank when he saw them: clearly Garraty knew nothing about Biddle and had not bothered to consult Tom's book.

Govan nevertheless wrote a sketch and sent it in well before the August 1 deadline, but with a rather curt cover letter containing a number of caveats.

> Dear Jack,
>
> Enclosed in my sketch of Nicholas Biddle, which I could not quite confine to the assigned 700 words. To tell the story even in briefest outline, I had to rely entirely on assertion. What I say is true, but, of course, no one but me really believes it.[625]

One can almost hear Govan adding, "And that means you too, Garraty." In all probability, Garraty did, out of ignorance, go along with the prevailing anti-Biddle view and no doubt Govan wanted to shake him up a bit. For this reason he said he had to violate Garraty's further instruction to give only one biographical reference. Govan gave his own very favorable biography, *Nicholas Biddle: Nationalist and Public Banker* (1959) as "the best reference," and added rather pointedly that his positive judgment of Biddle was supported in whole or in part by the works of Catterall (1903) and Redlich (1951), Smith (1953), and Hammond (1957). Because the prevailing view of Biddle was far more unfavorable, and because Arthur M. Schlesinger Jr.'s *The Age of Jackson* represented that unfavorable view, he felt it was only fair and necessary to include Schlesinger's book as a second reference, in spite of the fact that Tom completely disagreed with Schlesinger and believed his book to be fundamentally wrongheaded.

Govan knew that he and Garraty might be so far apart on the issue of Biddle that he should give Garraty a way out. So, wrote Govan, "You have been given (by me) ample reason to cancel our agreement, and if you choose to do so, I will understand."[626] Govan ended his letter with more pointedly negative remarks.

> I have also rewritten "the factual summary" since that seemed easier than to correct its errors of both fact and interpretation . . . . I have paid no attention to [your] . . . explanation of the crisis of 1837 since, in my opinion, it is totally wrong. [Whoever wrote it] . . . does not understand the operations of the banking system, believing, for example, that notes of South Carolina banks could be used in payments in New York, and is completely baffled by a bill of exchange. Such is econometrics—confusion confounded but stated with an air of absolute certainty.[627]

Govan was irritated by Garraty's seemingly willful ignorance of Govan's long-published views on Biddle, hence this terse ending to a defensive letter.

The article that Govan sent focused on the critical importance of a central banking system to the nation, and on the fact that Nicholas

Biddle both understood that importance and, between 1823 and 1839, directed the operations of the Bank of the United States brilliantly in the service of both the federal government and all of the economic interests of the country.

In bitter irony, Govan concluded his article with a negative quotation from William Cullen Bryant, a partisan Jacksonian editor and poet, a quotation that was so flagrantly biased and personal an attack on Biddle that the reader, Govan hoped, would catch the irony and understand how unfair and wrong it was. Bryant reported that Biddle died "at his country seat, where he had passed the last of his days in elegant retirement, which, if justice had taken place, would have been spent in a penitentiary."[628]

To Garraty's credit, he did not cancel the agreement, but recognized the soundness of Govan's view. He quite rightly felt that Govan's article was more a sketch of the Bank's history than a biographical sketch of Biddle.

Three years later when the *Encyclopedia* was finally being readied for publication, Garraty and Govan agreed to revise his article, but only slightly. It was published in the 1974 *Encyclopedia* and survived unchanged in the second edition published in 1996. Govan had made his point that the major significance of Biddle's life was his management of the Bank: brilliant, sound and utterly honest. He sought to serve the common good of the country and in so doing very much represented the wave of its future.[629]

26

The Struggle To Get His Message Out

*I will argue that the nation, as an organic person, is subject
to the same temptations as individuals and that in America,
as in England before it, the nation, not the church, has led
the struggle to accomplish what history has led us to assert:
that is, that freedom, justice, and equality are the aim and
purpose of its laws.*

Thomas P. Govan

Alexander Hamilton and His Adversaries

Although he had lost confidence in his ability to finish *A New
Birth of Freedom,* Tom's desire to produce another big book kept gnawing
at him. As a result, in 1968-69 he "turned back," as he put it, "to another
uncompleted project, a study of Alexander Hamilton and his
adversaries."[630] He knew, of course, that except for Forrest McDonald
and a very few others, he was largely alone among American historians
in his views about Hamilton, Jefferson, and American history.
Nevertheless, the project seemed plausible to him because he had so
much of it already written by the spring of 1970. "One of these episodes
in this latter study [had been] completed," he wrote, "but not submitted

342

for publication and several others were in rough draft."[631] It is not clear from his papers what episode was completed and which were in rough draft. It is clear that without doing any new writing at all, he had an immense amount of Hamilton material already on paper, albeit in a scattering of lecture notes and articles written over the previous twenty-five years. They included the following:

> Chapter 1:" The Principles of Freedom: the Hamilton-Seabury Debate"(1935-7)
>
> Lecture notes: "The Miracle of Funded Debt" (1935-7)
>
> Lecture notes: "The Enemies of Banks and Banking" (1935-7)
>
> Lecture notes: "Jefferson's Moral Crusade, 1789-1801" (1935-7)
>
> Chapter 7: "The Rich, the Well-Born and Alexander Hamilton" (1949)
>
> Chapter 10: "The Liberal and Conservative Traditions in the USA" (1952) (see Appendix 2)
>
> Chapter 15: "Jefferson and Hamilton, a Christian Evaluation" (1957)
>
> Chapter 16: "A New Birth of Freedom" the Beloit lectures, which contain a great deal of Hamilton material (1962)
>
> Chapter 17: "Agrarianism, Sectionalism, and Jeffersonian Democracy, A Moral Inquiry" (1963) (see Appendix 8)
>
> Chapter 18: "Hamilton, the Bank, and the National Economy" (1964) (see Appendix 7)
>
> Chapter 19: A New Birth of Freedom, "The English Background" (1966)
>
> *(All of these are in unpublished and/or early draft form.)*

Another Hamilton article would come later in 1975, "Alexander Hamilton and Julius Caesar, a Note on the Use of Historical Evidence." Most current American historians were Hamilton's adversaries, and Govan found himself still having to defend Hamilton against anti-

Hamilton scholarship. He had done so in 1950 in his article, "The Rich, the Well-Born and Alexander Hamilton."[632]

In "Alexander Hamilton and Julius Caesar, a Note on the Use of Historical Evidence,"[633] Govan was contending with what he considered the unmistakable "tendency of historians in the prevailing anti-Hamilton climate of opinion to accept uncritically discreditable evidence about him in the writings of his political opponents."[634] In this case, historians Dumas Malone, Julius Boyd, and Douglas Adair all accused Hamilton of approving of Julius Caesar and wanting to be the American Caesar, literally an American dictator. They made their accusations on the basis of secondary sources, whereas the evidence from Hamilton's own writings suggests just the opposite. Govan believed these historians must have been aware of Hamilton's writings, which express his negative views about Caesar, but were "not convinced by what they read." Govan simply wanted historians to "apply the same critical standards to the writings of (Hamilton's) political opponents as they did to his own."[635]

Unhappily, nothing came of Tom's hope to write the Hamilton book either. In spite of his determined resolutions, he could not bring the project off. It seemed that when working alone without the stimulation of conversation with others, his confidence in his writing was easily undermined. This, in turn, contributed to his tendency toward depression. When feeling down, Tom probably drank more than he should, and that only made things worse.

There were also external circumstances that interfered with his work. Tom knew he was a cause of tension within the history department. He agonized over the Vietnam War and was shocked when the National Guard shot and killed four people at Kent State University. The Episcopal Church was in crisis.

Despite the flagging book project, there were some good feelings. On December 22, 1970, he wrote,

> It is a beautiful day and personally, I am very happy. Jane is feeling well, my classes did not go too badly, and by the way, William Morrow is publishing a book in January by one of my NYU students, Stanley Feldstein, entitled *Once*

a Slave, to which I wrote the introduction that says what
I have wanted to say about slavery.[636]

It was a bittersweet time. He had again lost the dogged
determination that alone can produce a big book.

The Last Best Hope, a History of the United States by Forrest McDonald, Leslie E. Decker, Thomas P. Govan[637]

The major diversion in Govan's intellectual life in 1970-1971,
however, came from Forrest McDonald. There are some indications
in Tom's files that in 1969 he may have contacted Forrest to collaborate
in bringing off his proposed book, A*lexander Hamilton and His
Adversaries,* as he had done earlier with *Nicholas Biddle.* Govan knew
McDonald was among the only historians who shared his views about
Hamilton. He knew McDonald well enough to appreciate his
sometimes-brilliant insights, but also to feel completely confident
and comfortable about criticizing and correcting McDonald's errors,
in particular his tendency toward cynicism about people and events.

McDonald deeply respected Govan and could accept his criticism
and correction. But it was Jane Govan's strong opinion that getting
help from McDonald was a temptation to Tom, a crutch he knew he
should not need to use. She was infuriated by the idea of their
collaboration because she distrusted McDonald, believed he was self-
serving and would use Tom for his own benefit. She blamed McDonald
for the near derailment of Tom's Biddle biography, and feared that
McDonald was capable of doing it again with the new project. Jane was
convinced that Tom should focus only on his own ideas and what he
had to say.[638] She had more confidence in Tom than he did in himself
at the time. What Jane did not fully understand and what caused
some tension between them was Tom's lack of energy and confidence.
The contact between Tom and Forrest, if it was actually made, did not
lead to a book about Hamilton, almost certainly because of Jane's
hostility toward McDonald, but it may have led to another project, this
time on McDonald's initiative.

In the fall of 1969, McDonald, then at Wayne State University, and Leslie E. Decker, a fellow historian at Oregon, were completing an American history textbook for high school students and college freshmen. The first draft was ready, and because of the earlier relationship between McDonald and Govan, and Govan and Decker's friendship at Oregon, both men agreed that Govan would be the ideal person to review their book.

Larry J. Wilson, the history editor at the time for Addison-Wesley Publishing Company in Reading, Massachusetts, arranged the contract. That November, Wilson sent chapters nine through fifteen to Govan for comment. One month later, a letter from Govan arrived on Wilson's desk, containing twenty-four single-spaced pages of commentary, ninety-five separate and numbered comments, many of them paragraphs of up to a hundred words. His comments ranged across the board, from pointing out and correcting errors of fact, interpretation, understanding, judgment, and logic (where two statements contradicted each other) to overstatements (some of them irresponsible, in Govan's opinion), the use of inappropriate language, statements not warranted by evidence, things left out that ought to be left in and vice verse, passages that were too long, out of order, and so on. Most of the comments seemed to be aimed at McDonald who was obviously the chief author. Altogether, the comments demonstrated Govan's complete mastery of the period.

Govan's letter to Wilson summarizes his overall reaction to the manuscript.

Dear Larry,

The attached 24 pages of notes probably tell you more than you want to know but I wanted to have them on paper. I have been overly careful in those areas where I have some knowledge, but it does seem to me that Les and Forrest have relied too much on their memories and secondary sources.

I find much of the tone of the book objectionable—they seem to me to equate realism with cynicism—and are much too free with epithets instead of description. They overstate the negative side of almost every individual.

But in spite of all my criticisms and reservations, the manuscript, it seems to me, contains within it the materials for an important and useful book. It plows new ground in many areas—most important of all, it is unique among American texts in that it attempts to describe the European influences that have played such an important part in the history of the United States. They also deal seriously with the actualities of economic development—not telling them from the political side alone—and have avoided the simplistic cliches of conventional works.

They deal with history in a serious way, but since the work is so fresh and brings in so much unusual information (information that most teachers, to say nothing of students, will not have encountered previously) that I think their readers will need much more aid than is now supplied.

My concern with the book as a teacher and a historian lead me to both violent applause and condemnation. They have tried to tell what actually occurred, what the influences were, and this effort can only be praised. But the net effect of their mode of speaking is to cheapen and vulgarize. They raise the moral questions, but do not treat them seriously, though in their own moral statements they recognize that the good is always mixed with evil, disinterest with interest, and yet most of their explanations of actions concentrate on selfishness and self-interest.

I, of course, am going over the manuscript with Les in even more detail, but if you have any questions about my views or anything else, do not hesitate to ask.

Sincerely, T.P.G.[639]

Larry Wilson replied in December that Govan's review was "superb and exactly what he had in mind when he had asked [Govan] to do it." Other readers confirmed many of Govan's responses to the manuscript, and as a result, "serious revision" would be necessary, and Wilson would be "negotiating with the authors in this regard."[640]

The negotiation led to an almost total restructuring and rewriting of the book, which could only be done by including the critic and his criticisms in the project. The only solution was to make Govan a co-author, and he knew it. Govan found himself operating with confidence again, and to great effect. The dialogue, the arguments, the agreements with McDonald and Decker galvanized him. On the one hand, Tom was thrilled. On the other hand, he was stuck and knew that, too: unless he became co-author with McDonald and Decker, there would be no textbook. The book's potential was too important not to pursue, both in content and for Tom personally. He agreed and spent all of 1970 and most of 1971 completing the book.

Needless to say, Jane's irritation and hostility toward this second collaboration exceeded that of her reaction to the first. She blamed them both for it. Added to her distrust of McDonald, she felt Tom's Hamilton book was now permanently doomed. And she was right.

Her understandable anger showed a lack of understanding that Tom felt he needed. Jane did not want to face what Tom had begun to realize: he did not have the energy or the ability to focus alone for the long blocks of time that would be required to write the Hamilton book. He was superb and confident in collaboration, but not on his own.

In a December 1970 letter, Tom wrote

348

This has been a hectic fall. I most unwisely agreed to co-author a textbook that was already written but needed revising and polishing. I had read it for the publisher before, but it was not until I got into it seriously that I learned how much needed to be done. No wonder our Ph.D. candidates have such a terrible time with their examinations when so-called senior scholars make such egregious errors and are sure that they are right. The most flagrant example was a paragraph on the financing of the War of 1812 in which five statements were made—each one wrong.[641]

Jane's worst worries about the project came true. McDonald and Decker used Tom's wisdom, knowledge, and expertise, but never adequately gave him credit for his crucial role in recasting the book and making it a useful venture. "Tom walked away from the project," as Robert Berdahl put it, "pretty much empty-handed; the book, though good and useful in many ways, did not sell very well, so it did not make any money, and Tom had given up what Jane thought he should have been spending his time on [the Hamilton book]. I think he understood that he wasn't going to get the Hamilton book done, and the collaboration with McDonald and Decker was a kind of reason for not keeping at the Hamilton project. And because Jane did not see it that way, there was tension."[642]

Nevertheless, working on *The Last Best Hope* was a fulfilling experience for Tom because he had put his indelible mark on a major new American history text. It said much of what he wanted to say on the subject. Even if he never completed his own "big book," once again, he had had his say.

In the end, Govan's collaboration on *The Last Best Hope*, the title he had suggested for the McDonald and Decker text, did more than just give him his say: it revived his confidence in himself as a historian and inspired him to return with new concentration to his own book, *A New Birth of Freedom*, which he had abandoned in the spring of 1968.

In 1971, in an application for a year's fellowship leave from Oregon for the purpose, he described what that experience with McDonald and Decker had done for him:

> The detailed examination and revision of a text covering the same time period and problems, which is now completed, has renewed my interest and restored my confidence. I now see my way clear to complete a revised and expanded version of my [1961] lectures by the spring of 1973.[643]

He realized that he needed a full year off to begin that project and applied to the Ford Foundation for a fellowship for that purpose.

This Nation under God: Theological Reflections on American History

By 1974, Govan's intention had become more explicitly theological and more focused in his mind. He changed the title from *A New Birth of Freedom* to *This Nation Under God*, still a quote from Abraham Lincoln referring directly to national history, but now a pointedly theological interpretation of that history.

The first chapter, "The English Background," had laid the foundation for the book, stating the theme and tracing its development through the establishment of the first colonies. Now in the summer, fall, and winter of 1971-1972, he proposed finishing the second and third chapters, for which he had completed all of the basic research. They would "describe the establishment of the other colonies, their relations with the mother country down to 1763, the Revolution, and the adoption of the Constitution." The six remaining chapters, four through nine [were] to be written during a fellowship year (April 1, 1971-April 1, 1972). They would deal with the following time periods and subjects:

> Chapter 4: The political, social, and economic conflicts down to the administration of Martin Van Buren.
> Chapter 5: Slavery as a moral and social, as well as economic, problem and the Civil War.

Chapter 6: The nineteenth-century abandonment and partial reassertion of government authority.

Chapter 7: The United States as a world power down to the depression of 1929.

Chapter 8: The response to the Depression, communism, German national socialism, and Japanese expansion.

Chapter 9: The crisis of faith and confidence that has followed the victory in World War II, which involved the entire world.[644]

In making his application, Govan asked several friends to be references. One of them was Paul Ward, an old friend and Executive Secretary of the American Historical Association, former president of Sarah Lawrence College, a historian of early England, and a fellow Episcopal layman. Govan had written Ward a letter about the purpose of his book, including a brief introductory summary, which he intended to use as part of his application. In the letter, he said

> My purpose is to use Biblical theology as a clue to the understanding of the whole course of American history, its achievements and its failures, not its founding alone. I will also attempt to show that the English and American constitutions and laws are "demythologized" versions of Biblical teaching, and that history (a "demythologized" name for God's will and providence) through circumstance, more than the conscious desires of men, has provided the motive force for whatever improvement has occurred as well as being responsible for the backsliding and failure.
>
> I also will argue that the nation, as an organic person, is subject to the same temptations as individuals, and that in America, as in England before it, it, [the nation] not the church, has led the struggle to accomplish what history (God's will) has led it to assert, that is, that freedom, justice, and equality are the aim and

purpose of its laws. These assertions, though honored frequently by their breach, do have a positive effect, and it is they which have protected the nations from such tyrannies as resulted from the French and Russian revolutions.

What I am seeking to guard against is the perfectionist illusion, which, when found wanting as it always is, leads to nihilism and despair or to withdrawal from life and society. You and I have talked of such matters though not in these specific terms, both our experiences in academic life confirm them, and I am grateful for your willingness to serve as a reference in regard to my application.[645]

In the application, he said:

The study should lead me to a deeper understanding of the current crisis, for Americans, along with others, have lost not only faith in God, but also belief in man. They expected improvement, some perfection, but when men and nations continue to be wicked and oppressive, to engage in war, and to ignore such problems as poverty, urban decay, and pollution, they lose all confidence and hope. They cannot accept the fact that freedom, justice, and equality are not easily achieved or maintained, that their costs are heavy in terms of sacrifice, and that those now alive, like their ancestors before them, if they would seek improvement for themselves and their fellow-men, must be prepared to submit themselves to what Robert Penn Warren has called "the powerful, painful, grinding process by which an ideal emerges out of history."[646]

27

Govan, the Teacher, 1967-1978

From him I learned how to look at history, what questions to ask of it, and most of all, how to teach it. And I remember his passion and idealism.

John McElligott

Being a Historian: Not a Job but a Calling

Tom had written that his teaching at Oregon that first year had been a disaster. The student course analysis booklet the next fall, however, told another story. Tom was encouraged and quite pleased with a blurb in that booklet about his graduate course, "History 492: Early National Period of the United States." It read:

> HST 492 is not listed in the 1967-68 U. of O. Catalog, so you will have to guess what the course's objectives are. Or, maybe you can find out more about it by playing Twenty Questions (is it animal, vegetable, or mineral?) with the professor or with the course alumna. [sic]

One student reports that the course is the "first one I've had as a grad student that has come up to my expectations." Another student says it is "a good course if you are willing and interested in independent work—offers questions to be thought about, but the student must find his own answers."

No reading is specifically assigned. Independent study is encouraged: each student "having his own reading and work projects." Generally, the students approve of the loose structure of the course.

For the most part, students are enthusiastic about Professor Govan's lectures. "The anecdotes, diversions, and comparisons with present day situations" are appreciated by one student. Another says that "the interpretations of all aspects are enlightening and relationship among topics is good." But one student points out that "Sometimes, the instructor's points were not made clear—he takes for granted sometimes that the students are following him."

Most of the students polled would probably agree with the student who says, "There is always a definite confidence that the professor is very much qualified in his knowledge." Another student says, "Dr. Govan is not of the Ding-Dong school of education—he does not try to encourage bright faces or 'experiments' . . . . He is a teacher, a thinker, not a methods expert; . . . he would undoubtedly flunk education classes, but that is why he is a good teacher." Similarly, another student says of Professor Govan: 'Receptive to meaningful questions, but not receptive to stupid questions. . . . It may be in relation to that last statement that two students commented on the "feeling of uneasiness" that exists in the classroom.

Not one pollee said that he would not recommend the course. The following advice, offered by one of Professor Govan's students, might be worthy of consideration: "The course should only be taken if the student is experienced in independent research. If the student prefers structured courses, I would not advise him to take this one." (The University of Oregon, 1968-1969)[647]

In other words, Tom was treating his graduate students as what they were, graduate students working toward an MA or a Ph.D., not undergraduates. They were expected to choose their own research and pursue it. He would respond carefully and in detail to their work. All the while, he would be lecturing and leading discussions on the Hamiltonian (conservative) tradition and its conflict with the Jeffersonian (liberal) tradition in American history.

Among Tom's papers are numerous examples of his work with graduate students, especially those writing Ph.D. dissertations. Clearly he depended more on the student's motivation than on teaching methods to get his points across. He concentrated on the content of the history, what he believed had happened and why, presenting always a view that he held with both the passion of true conviction and an equal awareness that there was more to learn. When the students caught the excitement and conviction that permeated his teachings; when they were able to respond to a man who treated being a historian not as a job, but as a calling; when they realized that his passion was for truth and that he took very seriously the moral and theological implications of people and events, then, if they were caught by his spirit, Tom's classes were both a joy for him and his students.

When students rejected or rebelled against his teaching, however, they found themselves rejecting and rebelling against him; he and his teaching were one. He was as patient as he could be, especially when the students' questions and reactions were serious and honest, but he could be hard and cutting in his response. When the students were fundamentally disinterested in anything more than marks and what they imagined Govan wanted them to "cough up" on exam papers, the class could be a disaster. If the HST 492 student report is any indication, it seems in that first year, his classes may have reached more students than he had thought. Tom was a firm taskmaster on students' papers. He insisted always that the writer decide what he wanted to say, tell the reader what he was going to say, and then say it, backing up each assertion with evidence from history (not merely with a theory of history), then telling the reader again what had been said and what the reader should have learned.

A good example of Govan's impact on his graduate students was Stanley Feldstein, the author of *Once A Slave*, for which Govan wrote the introduction. At NYU "most professors got up in front of the class with a set of notes and began lecturing. You could ask questions when he stopped to light a cigarette or perhaps at the end, but that was about all. And you sat there with a legal pad and took notes. For the most part, they were teacher-dominated classes."[648]

Feldstein explained why Tom's approach was so different:

> He would begin asking questions, assuming you had read the material, and if you asked questions, he would answer them, sometimes at length. He told the class that he might not know as much as other historians, but he understood it better. That is what he meant: you can read all that factual stuff, but he wanted you to understand it. He said, 'I could get up there and give you a factual lecture, but why waste time? You can read all that in a text book. Why take thirty pages of notes in class, commit it to memory, and then take an exam?' Three or four weeks before the final exam, he would give us the questions, say, six of them. You could choose any three, but you had to know your stuff and be prepared. This was new, and some students left the class. I came back. A friend said, 'Keep coming, you'll learn.'[649]

Feldstein was so thoroughly convinced by Govan's approach and ideas that he replayed them on his doctoral exams, and during his orals argued with the examiners. As a result he did not do well. When he asked Govan why, Tom replied, "You became me, instead of being yourself." The examiners didn't like it that Feldstein had followed Govan in rejecting "sectionalism" and insisting that race and slavery were what divided the country.

Jane's advice to Feldstein was to treat the examiners like friends and have a discussion. Tom added, "If you know it, tell them. If you haven't read it, tell them so, but add that you are aware of it. And remember 90% of your effort in preparation is wasted because they're only going to ask you about 10% of what you know."[650]

Tom continued to be thesis advisor to a number of Ph.D. candidates from NYU, and correspondence with these students is revealing. We have already seen Govan, the taskmaster, at work with Feldstein on *Once a Slave*.[651] Another was Stephen Channing who, upon Govan's advice, went from NYU in 1965 to the University of North Carolina, where he did graduate work under Fletcher Green— constructing his dissertation around the idea that "fear of the Negro" was the deepest cause of southern secession from the Union in 1861. In 1968, while still at work on his thesis, Channing wrote to Govan:

Dear Prof. Govan:

Two years ago I sat down and tried to write a letter to you expressing my sense of obligation to you. I spoke about the experience of writing that seminar paper at NYU on the effect of the revolution in Santo Domingo on American slavery. I wrote of your excellent advice and encouragement when I decided to leave NYU for the South. It was your seminar, and the really exciting experience of working with you in it, that persuaded me to work in Southern history, and to come to North Carolina.

I have worked very hard since coming here . . . . Every time I sat down to write a seminar or term paper, every time I wrote a verbose, turgid, or worst of all, boring paragraph, I thought of your criticism. You could taunt,

357

and could even hurt, but inevitably your criticism was
correct and invaluable. Since gaining some proficiency
in the literature of Southern history, I have come to
respect you even more, as a working historian in your
own right. Time and again, I have wanted to write to you
and express my feelings of admiration and indebtedness,
but to tell the truth I suppose that I was intimidated by
you, and I never could express my sentiments just the way
I wanted to, so the letter was never written.

As for my dissertation . . . I am working under Joel
Williamson . . . He is an imaginative and warmly sympathetic
advisor, and I am glad that he was here, particularly since
Green was no longer taking on new Ph.D.
candidates . . . With what I hope was not foolish boldness,
I elected to write on the secession of South Carolina, from
Harper's Ferry to the ordinance of secession. I will spare
you a lengthy discussion of my thesis, except to say that fear
of the Negro, a dread of insurrection, and fear of the
consequences of emancipation was the essential,
preponderant cause of secession. Do you see your hand in
this? I hope so, for my paper on Santo Domingo (at NYU)
was an important prelude to this work.[652] The standard
historical interpretation of secession in the 1960s, under
the influence of Charles and Mary Beard, was that
economics and the conflict between agrarian and industrial
societies, rather than slavery and race, were the real
underlying causes of secession.

Govan took pride in the fact that he had been the first to put the
fear thesis in print back in 1940.[653] Responding to Channing's feelings
of intimidation, he replied that he envied those who, like Williamson
and Green, could be warmly sympathetic. He had just been through
a grueling round of personally reviewing twelve student papers; he
had not been particularly warm or sympathetic: the session had been
"grueling for me as well as the victims. But each of us," he

philosophized, "is stuck being what he is, I guess. At least I am unable to reform, and it is heartening to learn that it is sometimes helpful."[654]

In May 1969, by prior agreement, Channing asked Govan to read and comment on his thesis prior to his rewriting it for Simon and Schuster, who was interested in publishing it. Tom's reply was a nine-page, single-spaced, detailed commentary and criticism, some of it biting, but ended as follows: "Stephen, I have made numerous small suggestions on a number of [your] . . . pages. But nowhere have I indicated what I feel [about the whole]: that you have done a superlative job and written it most effectively"—pointed and occasionally sarcastic comments, but most importantly, the overall compliment. Channing's book was published as *Crisis of Fear* and thanks to Channing, Govan received a small stipend of one hundred dollars for his labors. Channing went on to teach at the University of Kentucky and was promoted to associate professor of history in 1970.

More gratitude came his way in from a teacher at the Dwight Morrow High School in Edgewood, New Jersey, who had been a student of Govan's at NYU. He wrote a touching letter to his old professor:

Dear Dr. Govan,

I've been trying to write a letter to *The New York Times* this morning to express my grief, and my concern over the recent death of Dr. King, and I've found that possibly you, more than any other individual, are responsible for helping me to crystallize my thoughts. I have a long way to go before I can articulate them as well as you, but I must honestly say that my "moral conversion" started approximately four and a half years ago in your class when you spoke of how unrestrained individualism leads to tyranny. I have been trying to find the words to say how the unchecked portrayal of force as a good will lead to violence; of how we all pulled the trigger in Memphis because the assassin thought that he would be a hero in the eyes of his society, and I now realize that you have led me to draw these conclusions because you have made

me conscious of my responsibilities to my fellow man
through your teachings of Kant, Camus, Heidegger,
Hamilton, and the Bible.

Once again, professor, thank you. Sincerely,

J. Lewis Shapiro[655]

The following year, several dissertations from NYU came Govan's
way. One was a proposal and first chapter from John F. McElligott, a
former student. He was in a state of panic because he was dissatisfied
with the chapter, but paralyzed over how to improve it. He had left
himself only two weeks for each of the remaining chapters, and he
was desperate. He wrote to Govan:

> As for its lateness, I have no explanation. I work on the
> thesis every day, but produce very little. I don't seem to
> concentrate very well any more. I am suffering the physical
> symptoms of anxiety neurosis which my family's physician
> claims dissipates my energy. It seems that after studying
> Darwin so long I am developing his illnesses. Much worse
> off than I, however, he wrote *The Origin of the Species.*[656]

As for himself, McElligott was still determined, but getting nowhere.
Govan responded positively to what the young man had done, but added
the advice that McElligott needed to provide his readers with a "prefatory
explanation" of why they were being told all about Darwin, his struggles,
and the massive changes in understanding that Darwin was introducing.
Then Govan burst into a deep and rollicking bit of long distance pastoral
care. He knew all about this kind of writer's block and panic firsthand,
and the self-doubt and depression it can bring. He wrote

> Now as to your personal difficulties. You need to go to an
> exorcist and get rid of the demons, self-created most of
> them, that you are permitting to interfere with your work.
> Their name may be legion, John McElligott, or Tom Govan,

but hunt for a herd of swine, and banish them somewhere near the ocean so they can be drowned.[657] Why be anxious? God provides! Damn it, believe the stuff you have written or quoted. We are infantile needing support and protection from the one we seek to kill, so why be bothered when you find this to be true?[658]

Your demon, however, may be of a different kind. It may be called the end of the summer, or a chapter every two weeks. If the imposed discipline of the deadlines and daily work is useful, continue to observe this self-imposed rule of life—but if it interferes, then throw it out. Go out to the beach, get drunk, take days or weeks off, and finish the thing during the coming year. You are doing a substantial job, wrestling with a real and difficult problem, and if this chapter, like the thesis outline, is a sample of your work, then you are handling it better than most.

I am looking forward to additional chapters because my curiosity has been aroused. I will work as fast as I can but do not feel that you are under pressure from me of any kind. And if you take one year more than you planned, what the hell, the bomb has not yet, and may not be, dropped. With these glad tidings, I close,

Cordially,
Thomas P. Govan[659]

Ten years later, in March of 1979, just after Tom's death, McElligott wrote Jane from Eastern Illinois University, where he was teaching history:

Dear Mrs. Govan,

It was only today that I learned of Professor Govan's passing and I felt compelled to write you to extend

361

my sympathy and to express the respect that I have long held for him.

I wrote my doctoral dissertation under him from 1965 to 1973. In my tardy progress towards that degree I had many teachers, most of them good ones, but he was by far the best. I looked forward to every class and hated to see the hour end. From him, I learned how to look at history, what questions to ask of it, and most of all how to teach it. And I remember his passion and idealism.

I have never written a letter like this before and I hesitated to write this one. It seems almost senseless and sadistic to write letters praising the dead to the one most bereaved. One would think they could only exacerbate the sense of loss the closest ones must feel, for I have no words to ease your pain or to reconcile you to your loss. But I think the end of a life leads one to examine it. To decide it was a meaningful and worthwhile life makes the death more acceptable. You can determine that far better than I. I can only offer my small testimony. He was a great teacher who inspired a host of students. He taught us so many valuable things. Now I am a teacher and everyday I teach my students what he taught me. His words and ideas now come from my mouth and I only hope I have just one student (he had many) who will want to teach the next generation what I teach him. I would love to tell my students that the best of what I have to say comes from my teacher, but Professor Govan always told us to attribute nothing to him; to take complete responsibility for what we say ourselves, but I would like you to know that what he learned and thought and puzzled out is being taught in classrooms all over this country.

Sincerely,
John McElligott[660]

In the 1970s, Govan received a steady trickle of letters from his "disciples" as one student calls himself. Typically, they reported on dissertations finally finished, Ph.D.s in hand, teaching posts pending or secured, and personal family news. One NYU student wrote:

Dear Professor Govan:

I am pleased to write you that it is now final. NYU has seen fit to grant me the Ph.D. degree. With this step behind, I want to thank you again for your help and encouragement.

It has been my experience, as student and beginning teacher, that something about Academia keeps teacher and student at intellectual arms-length. Whatever the reasons, most teachers do not make time to exchange ideas informally with their students. Among my most pleasant and stimulating hours at NYU were those spent with you in that kind of conversation that seems to me the most important relationship of teacher and student.

It is therefore with some regret that on your departure I seemed to be resisting your attempt to have me write a suitable opening paragraph. I believe that when I resumed work on the dissertation two years later, what you were trying to show me became clear.

Also, any earlier regrets that I did not select one of several topics of my choosing (and that you were quite willing to accept) completely vanished as I learned more about Hamilton. What an amazing human being! The young Hamilton, particularly, seemed able to pierce to the heart of a subject with unerring skill. He was a man of spirit who flung himself, sometimes recklessly, into the excitement of living.

I am aware that you would not agree with the
interpretation that developed as the dissertation
moved along. Some of my emphases are indicated in
the Introduction, Table of Contents, and Conclusion.
I am taking the liberty of sending you Xerox copies of
these sections under separate cover.

I leave an important piece of news for last. I will be teaching
at Paterson State College in September. I feel very fortunate
to be so well placed, especially with the present market.

I hope you are well and have a pleasant summer. With all
good wishes.[661]

Another letter came from a former student, now an associate
professor of history at NYU. She had been seriously injured in an auto
accident, and Tom had written an encouraging letter offering her all
the help he could give. She replied, "Thank you very much for your
letter. Many of your disciples have been inquiring about you, and I am
pleased to learn that everything is all right—despite the usual
confusion that can be expected in a university at the present time."
She went on about her own difficult year: "After being treated—or
mistreated—by several physicians (whose eyes lit up when they
learned I was involved in litigation as a result of being hit from the
rear by a tow truck)," she went to a public rehab hospital for help. She
had two job prospects, but because of her need for physical therapy,
she would have to live in a large city. So the prospects seemed
unpromising. She had just heard that she would not get tenure in the
NYU history department, in spite of the fact (she discovered later)
that the history faculty had not voted on the issue. Also Rutgers
University Press was reading her dissertation on Godkin, and she had
given them Govan's name as one who had read it. Finally, "I have been
doing some writing," she said, "although my doctors warn me that my
back muscles are too weak for me to do any lengthy work. If any of it
turns out to be worthwhile, I would be delighted to make use of your
kind offer to look at it . . . I really appreciated hearing from you."[662]

In 1981, two years after Govan's death, his niece, Kate Bunnell, was reading a Fourth of July op. ed. article by Jeremiah V. Murphy in *The Boston Globe.* He had written about how whenever he saw a Memorial Day parade, he would find himself "thinking of Gettysburg and the brave men in the awful heat of July in a small Pennsylvania town." He ruminated that:

> Perhaps it began for me immediately after World War II when I was a University of Virginia student and enrolled in a history course entitled, "The War for Confederate Independence." The course was taught by a middle-aged Georgian and I figured that I would get the old propaganda pitch. But I was wrong.

> The professor said Mr. Lincoln was absolutely correct and that he made concession after concession in order to keep the Union together and to avoid a bloody civil war. On at least five occasions, in that one-semester course, a young man from Virginia or South Carolina or Mississippi would stand up, his face pink with emotion, strike a pose of military attention, and then angrily shout at the professor: "Sir, you are a liar!"

> Then they would march out of the classroom and they would always slam the door. The professor would just stand there with that little grin on his face. It really was quite a course.

Immediately, Kate recognized the teacher, the course, the opinion, and the "little grin on the face" of her Uncle Tom. She continued reading Murphy's article:

> Those feelings about Gettysburg and the price we paid came again a few years ago when I was teaching a Boston University journalism class as a part-time instructor. The

topic was covering speeches, so I picked the Gettysburg Address, because it is concise and brief and beautiful.

It was delivered by Mr. Lincoln in November 1863, when he dedicated the Gettysburg cemetery for the brave men who had fallen there five months earlier. Today it is a national shrine.

So I would read the speech aloud and the students would take notes, but the words spoken aloud got to me again.

"Now we are engaged in a great civil war, testing whether that nation, or any nation so conceived and so dedicated, can long endure. We are met on a great battlefield of that war. We have come to dedicate a portion of that field, as a final resting place for those who gave their lives that that nation might live."

Those words haunt me, as they have haunted millions of Americans down through the years who have read them or heard them spoken aloud.

Through Jeremiah Murphy, they haunted Kate too, and in them she felt the passion of her Uncle Tom. She knew he had been teaching at Virginia right after World War II, so surely this must be him. She wrote Murphy to ask if the teacher had been Govan. Murphy replied immediately, "I am all but positive your uncle was my professor in that long ago Virginia history class . . . . He certainly had that little smile and Georgian accent. He was also a damn fine teacher." His influence was still felt thirty-six years later.[663]

Another letter referring to that same time just after World War II when Tom was at the University of Virginia, came from a young historian in Tuscalooga, Alabama. It arrived just before Tom died.

366

Dear Tom,

... I have thought quite often about our sessions in the
Age of Jackson Seminar at UVA and the help you gave me
in my first outrageous attempts to cope with Sam Smith.[664]
I guess it always takes a while for you to realize how much
you have learned without really being aware of it. I guess
I have never mentioned it to you. Somewhere along the
line I have acquired a vast respect for language and
structure, and even though I have trouble using them
effectively, I think that this was one of the many things I
got from you. We graduate-type students are appreciative,
even though it takes a few years for the lessons to sink in.

It is Friday noon, but I cannot say thank God. Two
committee meetings and I must get ready for at least one
of them. Keep the faith, kid.[665]

After Tom's death, there was a flood of letters to Jane from his
former students. One from Ira Cohen at Illinois State University spoke
for them all:

To this day, I find myself using materials and ideas
that he first exposed me to. He was, perhaps, the only
teacher I had in graduate school who genuinely made
a difference to me.[666]

The most powerful and revealing statement about Govan as a
teacher came from William Robert Ellis, Jr., now rector of Trinity
Church in Bend, Oregon, who was a student at the University of
Oregon from 1973-1977.

I met and got to know Thomas Govan in the fall of 1973
when, as a freshman, I took a class with him on radicalism
in the 19th and 20th centuries. The thing that impressed

me incredibly about Govan was that he began, literally in his very first lecture, by saying that basically the libertarian ethic, as noble as it might be in conception, fails and fails utterly. And then, he went on to give the reason for the failure and quoted the Confession from Morning and Evening Prayers, in the 1928 Prayer Book, pages six and twenty-three. And, of course, he quoted it in its entirety up to the "miserable offenders." And this was the first time in my life, in spite of the fact that my dad was a preacher, that I had heard a person present a truly integrated political and religious philosophy. I had never seen a person for whom religion was not simply a series of beliefs, nor simply a way of acting, but informed every aspect of himself and his world and his own place in it. Govan's political philosophy arose, obviously from his religious convictions, rather than the other way around. You cannot understand Tom Govan at all without understanding that . . . and being thoroughly familiar with the 1928 Prayer Book. To understand him you have to think in those terms.

But, of course, he scandalized many of the students, for whom obviously the university was a place to get away from the strictures of religion. He got some questions about that, which he really dispatched summarily.

But anyway, throughout the course of the whole term . . . what came out, of course, was his great devotion and admiration for Alexander Hamilton, and his equally great scorn for Thomas Jefferson. And his belief about Jefferson was that he failed to understand human nature and himself as a victim of it, so far as he was a slave owner, as well, as in a lot of other ways. And Hamilton did understand. Govan was fond of pointing out that Jefferson, the great champion of the common man, was a slave owner, while Hamilton, the elitist, was the first attorney for and charter member of the New York Society for the Manumission of Slaves. So, in the course, he made these comparisons. There was a great deal more substance to his point than that, but the point always in the background was that we are inherently self-interested and that Hamilton understood this and that the only way to build a decent and just society is to take into consideration the fact of human sin. And to ignore it is to invite disaster. And that's how he critiqued the libertarian ethic from its first earliest stages, which we saw in the Virginia and Kentucky Resolves, through the Nullification controversy in the 1830s, through the Civil War, through the radicals of the late 19th century (Emma Goldman and so forth), all the way up through Vietnam.

So it was in that course that I met him and became incredibly impressed with him; because not only of the marvelous integrity with which he approached his own subject, but the thoroughness with which he integrated his political and religious understanding into a consistent and unified presentation. I really thought that was quite wonderful.

He was a very humble person, and I believe he never really knew what a powerful speaker he was. And if he did understand it, he couldn't quite believe it. I don't think he realized how impressive he was to people like me, because there were larger numbers of people who dismissed him, I think, as just an old man. And to them, as a result, he seemed dogmatic.

Govan smoked compulsively during his lectures. Smoking was still okay in the classroom in 1974-1975. He smoked all through. And the last class I had with him, he would not actually light up, but just hold it in his mouth the whole time, trying not to smoke. It was always Pall Malls. There was a certain self-consciousness about his presentation that suggested that he was kind of nervous and not sure of how he was being received or how his work was being accepted.

He was really a very sensitive person who spoke from his heart. Periodically, he told stories about this. There was one he told about his living and working in the South as a teenager. There was some kind of meeting being held where he worked, and he was assigned to the front door. And this large and very impressive black man came in for the meeting and wanted to leave his hat and coat in the cloak room. Govan realized that he was in the presence of a man vastly superior to himself, not just in size and stature, but in presence, and Govan, not knowing what to do, said, 'I think you had better go round to the back door.'[667] His point was: how can we allow a society like that to develop in which a person like me could be allowed to speak to a man like him in those terms? There was something just fundamentally wrong with a system that could allow that. Govan also told stories from his own experience at the University of the South. At Oregon, Tom was always one of the few faculty members who was consistently noticed.

Reading papers with him was an interesting process. He would have us come in and talk them over in detail, and even when he was critical of a paper, and mine deserved a lot of that, especially the first few, he would never privately in his office say anything but what was supportive and constructive, like "This point could have been stronger." And he would correct my grammar. He'd think with me about "how this could be said better" and how "it might have been punctuated differently." He cared about language.

And when I went to seminary and went to the pre-seminary conference and was asked to describe my conversion experience, I invariably referred to my experience with Tom. Tom explained me to myself and he explained my position before God in so compelling a way that I found he had converted me. I had always known God was there, but I never had known quite why. Tom explained why. There really is something in the soul of man that cries out for redemption. And things in the world and in my life began to make sense: the cry for redemption in personal life; the cry for freedom, equality, and justice in the political and social realm. And these two were intimately interrelated. I've never seen any analysis of the human condition that had anything like the cogency and urgency with which he spoke.[668]

28

"Radical America, the Continuing Revolution," 1971-1976

These truths are true no matter how often they are ignored or denied . . . not as accurate descriptions of what has been achieved, but rather as guiding principles . . . standards of judgment to which appeals for improvement can be made.

Thomas P. Govan

The American Revolution Bicentennial Commission, 1971-1972

In 1971, Govan was ready to take a year off to write his great book, the culmination of his life as a scholar, teacher, and theologian—for that is what *One Nation under God* would have been—when suddenly a new and exciting diversion appeared. On November 3, 1971, he was appointed with nine others to the American Revolution Bicentennial Commission of Oregon by Governor Tom McCall. Their mission was to plan a year-long, statewide celebration of and educational program about the American Revolution.

Govan was tremendously pleased by the appointment. It was an opportunity for him to influence the direction of the commission's work, something he considered an authentic part of his vocation as a historian. Little did he know how all-consuming it would become.

The monthly meetings were sometimes tedious—dealing with minutia and mechanics—but at every one, the so-called "Heritage 76" segment of the commission's work came under discussion. "Oregonians," the charter said, "will be asked to recall their heritage. The Declaration of Independence, the Constitution, and the Bill of Rights will be explained and understanding increased by displays, contests, and printing of the documents. Educators and students will conduct seminars on the higher, secondary, and upper elementary school levels throughout our school system, public and private." Tom approved, but as usual, his vision was broader and deeper than this. For the time being, he kept quiet.

During the 1972 commission meetings, Govan's voice began to be heard and his historical and moral authority appreciated. As the leading historian on the Education Committee, he was asked to write an introduction and historical outline of a course of study on American history, for schools and for the general public. It would be sponsored by the Commission and taught by qualified teachers at every level. Tom responded the way an evangelist might welcome an invitation to lead a camp meeting. He was being asked to do something he very much wanted to do, and he knew he had the message they most needed to hear. The course would, he suggested, "set forth the permanent meaning of the Revolution and its continuing influence."[669]

His excitement over this opportunity was only half of what he was feeling. There was also a deep sadness because he knew he was repeating an old pattern. Once again, he was being diverted and had an excuse for not writing his book, which he knew should be his primary task. Here was a public enterprise concerned with the same issues and history that he knew he could complete, especially when surrounded by and in collaboration with people who welcomed his leadership and his ideas. Tom rationalized his decision to stop writing by thinking that the work of the Commission, which he hoped to lead, would reach more general readers than his book ever could—a program that turned out to be one of his finest educational achievements. In any case, *One Nation under God* was never heard of again. Very probably, he put it away for good.

In his address to the commission in November 1972, Tom proposed a program that would have as its purpose to clarify the universal significance of the principles of the Declaration of Independence, the Constitution, and the Bill of Rights, and to emphasize how difficult the principles are to achieve. "More was involved in the [revolutionary] struggle than the overthrow of the British rule."[670] The real issue at stake, then as now, he said, was what people believed about freedom, human rights and the purpose of government. "All men are created equal," according the Declaration of Independence, and "they are endowed by their Creator with certain inalienable rights," and "among these are life, liberty, and the pursuit of happiness," and "to secure these rights, governments are instituted among men, deriving their just powers from the consent of the governed."[671]

This was the generally held faith of Americans during the revolutionary period. In his Commission address, Govan argued that "much of the doubt, disillusionment, and cynicism in the contemporary world [with regard to this faith] is the result of a misunderstanding of the function these truths are intended to serve,"[672] and his program's aim would be to clear up these misunderstandings.

> These truths are true no matter how often they are ignored or denied, but in an imperfect world made up of imperfect men, they never have been, perhaps never will be, completely established in the conduct and law of any society or government. They have value, nevertheless, not as accurate descriptions of what has been achieved, but rather as guiding principles, aims to be sought, and standards of judgment to which appeals for improvement can be made.[673]

They expressed the hope and intention of the nation. Tom's comments were addressed to those liberal idealists—

especially some historians and political radicals—who saw no hope of achieving the country's ideals through reform and insisted that their only hope lay in radical change, even "revolution." Usually, the idealists supported schemes socialist in nature. Others were so upset by the injustices, inequalities, and the lack of freedom in the United States that they had given up and became quite hopeless and despairing. Still others were simply cynical because they believed that "arbitrary, inequitable and unjust power [was] a permanent characteristic of all societies."[674] Still others cynically wanted power for themselves and were willing to use any means to achieve it. Many gave "lip service to the principles of freedom, equality, and justice,"[675] but denied them by their actions.

The result of these despairing and cynical beliefs "has been to discredit not only the words [freedom, equality, and justice], but also the realities they represent in the minds of people everywhere."[676] Those who believe and affirm these principles are "dismissed [by the cynics] as hypocritical propagandists or idealists, unaware of the real nature of the world."[677] Govan believed these negative attitudes were as dangerous today as ever and needed to be counteracted because they fueled "revolutionary" ideas.

Govan also wanted to make clear in his presentation how incredibly difficult it was to establish and maintain freedom, justice, and equality in society. He quoted Robert Penn Warren, "who described the four years of fratricidal [civil] war that ended slavery in the United States, as an example of 'the powerful, painful, grinding process by which an ideal emerges out of history,'"[678] but Govan applied it also to "the entire history of the continuously frustrated but persisting effort by men to establish and maintain a society in which they would be free to seek equal justice for themselves and for all others."[679] The American people needed to be reminded of both the difficulty and the extreme importance of seeking constant improvement. People will never achieve perfect and equal justice, but they can never afford to give up trying.

Govan also pointed out that the origin of this effort to achieve perfect and equal justice was "to be found in the ancient world, in the writings of the Judaic prophets [who called on the people to repent of their sins and to 'do justly, love mercy and walk humbly with thy

God.'[680]], and the Greek and Roman philosophers, who called for just and rational reform, but only rarely in succeeding centuries have freedom, justice, and equality been embodied in the institutions and laws of established governments."[681] The British and American governments proved to be the exceptions. In 1776, the American statement of ideals by themselves was not enough. The colonists had to resort to revolution to establish a new government in order to preserve the freedom, justice, and equality they had enjoyed under British rule. Since then Americans have continued to seek what they know will never be attained completely, perfectly, and finally—a free and just society. We believe, however, that reform and improvement can be achieved through "the powerful, painful, grinding process" of history that Warren described. Slavery lasted for some ninety years after the Declaration of Independence and illustrates "how difficult it is for [people] to be willing for others to share that [freedom, justice and equality] which they demand for themselves."[682]

"Many in the United States," Govan concluded, "think there should be a quicker and easier way to achieve these ideals, but none has ever been found." For whenever men in charge of government are "given power to define what is evil and rectify it permanently, to make practice conform completely with theory, they seem unwilling to use it for this end. Instead, they use their power to gain their own ends, suppressing or eliminating those who disagree or disobey, and the struggle for freedom, justice, and equality has to begin again."[683]

After he finished speaking, Tom handed out a brief annotated outline of the specific subjects and time periods the course might follow. His proposal was unanimously approved. In January 1973 Govan was elected permanent vice-chairman of the Educational Committee.

A Television Course: "Radical America, the Continuing Revolution," 1973-1976

Donald S. Bryant, director of the Oregon Educational and Public Broadcasting Service (OEPBS) was present at the November 1972 Commission meeting and heard Govan's presentation. He was captivated by its different and deeper interpretation of the meaning of American history. Two years later, he wrote:

> As I listened to him, I concluded that he had gotten the business of revolution together better than anyone I had ever heard or read previously. I suspected that he knew his field so well that every time he spoke, he delivered an excerpt from one of the campus courses on radicalism in American history. I thought how great it would be if we could channel all that knowledge and dedication into a televised course. I didn't pursue the idea, however, because production people talk disparagingly about what they call the 'talking head' technique, and I didn't know what else you could do on camera with a guy who'd been delivering history lectures to college students for 40 years.[684]

By 1973 Govan as vice-chairman of the education committee had been instrumental in setting up various lecture series in schools, colleges and public forums in almost every community in the state. He had also been exploring funding possibilities, primarily from the National Endowment for the Humanities. Then suddenly Mack Schwab from Cotuit days reappeared in Tom's life and their lecture series took a creative turn. As Bryant described it:

> Well, a year ago last spring [1973], Mack Schwab, one of our producer-directors at KOAC-TV was getting ready to retire, and I asked him if there was anything he'd like to put on video tape by way of a 'swan song.' Mack answered that there was a man at U of O who had a lot to say about revolution, and he'd sure like to get him on tape, with plenty of accompanying visuals; that is, slides. That was it, and so Tom and Mack set about to produce a twenty-lesson television course, 'Radical America, the Continuing Revolution.'[685]

Although Mack still held his communist opinions, he had mellowed over the years, grown amiable about his politics, and was able to maintain friendships with many vehement critics of the Soviet Union, including Tom.

Thomas P. Govan in front of the Declaration of Independence which appeared on the cover of the July 1976 issue of *The Hungry Eye*, the monthly magazine of the Oregon Educational and Public Broadcasting Service.

So they were friends who respected each other and agreed to disagree on the true meaning or "revolution."[686] Their collaboration was a credit to the flexibility of both men. Mack was thus responsible not only for Tom's opportunity to give his television lectures, but worked hard with him to make them alive and effective. It was a meaningful collaboration for both men and a nice conclusion to their careers and friendship.

Bryant continued:

> If you've viewed that course (we've aired it twice) [so far], you know that Mack lifted hundreds of slides from paintings, photographs, illustrations, maps, and other graphics, to reinforce the key concepts expressed in Govan's lectures. For example, when Tom said that 'radical' isn't a bad word, but simply means getting at the

roots of a matter, Mack put up a slide of a bunch of beautiful red radishes! When any historical personage was mentioned, up went a slide portrait. There must have been a slide every thirty seconds in some of those lectures. The technique kept both your eyes and ears busy.

The course is a good one . . . . We think it's about as good as anyone could do with lecture material and a shoestring budget. You can't do the 'Ascent of Man' with twenty reels of tape and a few rolls of film for making slides.

The closest Mack came to an extravagance was the reproduction of an excerpt from the Declaration of Independence—you see it on the cover.[687] Mack made a slide from a picture of the original document and then projected it on to paper on the back wall of the set. He hired an artist to copy over the enlarged script, changing only the s's to a modern style in order to assist the reader. When he submitted the bill he apologized for spending the money. Actually, the artist's fee was a pittance, and the excerpt was a great idea; it provided additional visual continuity throughout the twenty lessons.

Well, that's what the cover is all about[688]—the American Revolution Bicentennial, about a great teacher of American history, and about a great artist and great guy, Mack Schwab.[689]

The half-hour lectures were publicized ahead of time as a regular course-for-credit at the University of Oregon, open to anyone who signed up for it. The instructions read: "All students taking this course for credit will be given an open book examination on the text of the lectures. Those taking the examination only, and passing it satisfactorily, will receive a grade of C. Those desiring a higher grade will read three of the books from the [sixty-six book] reading list and submit a four-page, typewritten, and double-spaced report on each."[690]

There is no record of how many people actually took the course, but it was one of the first attempts at long distance education. It was broadcast several times and thousands saw it on TV. There was also considerable demand for the text; some two thousand copies were produced and copyrighted in 1976 by the OEPBS. The twenty lectures of "Radical America, the Continuing Revolution" are in the Govan Archives.

Tragically, by the time the station was asked for a copy of the tapes (1995), they had disintegrated as a result of poor storage conditions and station policy of not keeping film after a few years.

29

Freedom in State and Church: The Deems Lectures at NYU, October 1975

Life is to be lived, not controlled, and [our] humanity is won by continuing to play in the face of certain defeat.

Thomas P. Govan

"We Hold These Truths; the American Credo"

$\mathbf{B}$y the fall of 1974, Govan and Schwab had finished filming the television lectures. In October, Govan received a phone call from his old friend, the Reverend Dr. Lee A. Belford, professor of religious education and a senior faculty member at NYU, asking him to deliver the Deems Lectures at the university in October 1975. Belford knew about the television lectures and wanted Govan to condense them into three forty-five minute addresses, and suggested that they might be published.

The Deems Lectures were endowed in honor of the Reverend Charles Force Deems, a distinguished New York theologian-historian, who died in 1893. It was a prestigious series, intended to deal with some aspect of "the relationship of science and philosophy with religion."[691] Since 1899, there had been twenty-four lecturers including F.S.C. Northrup, John Baillie, William E. Hocking, John Macmurray, Hendrick Kramer, Henry Sloan Coffin, Austin Farrer, and Emil L. Fackenheim. Govan would be the first historian in the series, appropriately lecturing on American history during NYU's bicentennial celebration. Govan immediately agreed and suggested "We Hold These Truths; The American Credo" as a title.

In February 1975, Govan wrote to Belford:

> I hope to point out . . . the theological sources of the American effort to establish and maintain freedom for all the people, including slaves, and to see that effort as a precedent for the rest of the world.[692]

The following fall invitations were sent to a small number of invitees. The event was publicized in the university and open to the public. On October 14, 15, and 16, 1975 at 8:00 p.m., in the Bobst Library on the Washington Square campus of NYU, Govan delivered his lectures. His goal was to spell out the meaning of the American Revolution. In his lectures, he spoke directly to what he perceived to be the doubt, cynicism, and disillusionment, which he felt had been creeping deeper and deeper into the hearts of the American people ever since World War II. He believed the country had lost its faith in God and so had fallen into cynicism and despair. People could no longer believe in the American creed: "We hold these truths to be self-evident." Without a sense of God's providence in American history, and with an awareness of their own inability to raise life above its tragic realities, Americans were also losing faith in the meaning of service and sacrifice and were becoming frightened and selfish. Volunteerism and charitable giving, for example, were both down. The current political reality did not help; Nixon had been president for two years. He had brought a half-million U.S. troops home from Vietnam, yet the war went on. The U.S. was increasing its bombing, mining harbors, and had invaded Cambodia. The Peace Movement was at its height, and the nation's campuses were in an uproar. With the passion of true conviction, Govan sought to raise the spirits of his audience and to light the fires of hope and courage in their hearts again.

Govan wanted to convince Americans once again to recognize the universal and eternal truths of the Declaration of Independence, no matter how often ignored or denied. He argued that dogmatic statements of truth are essential, even though the truths they express can never be fully realized by imperfect people in an imperfect world. The Declaration nevertheless committed Americans, as Govan expressed it, to "continue the struggle for a victory that can never be won."[693] In fact, it is in the struggle that Americans become human beings. "Life is to be lived, not controlled," he said, "and humanity is won by continuing to play in the face of certain defeat."[694] To keep trying with humility and hope, that was the point.

Govan also discussed the historical process by which the thirteen British colonies in America became the United States of America and how it was not an intentional process. Rather inadvertently, it had come about, as it were, by accident, through a variety of circumstances and decisions, the results of which no one planned or could have foreseen. Humans were involved in the process, but not in any determinative way. For example, the attempt of King James I to maintain control of the colonies entirely independent of Parliament by means of royal charter, ironically gave the colonies a degree of freedom and self-government that could not have otherwise been had. With equal irony, these charters became a part of the British "Constitution" which the colonies cherished and under which they flourished. Finally, it was on the basis of this constitution, including the royal charters, that the colonies rebelled against Britain who, by its oppressive behavior, had betrayed its own constitution. Another example is the fact that the smaller and weaker of the two defeated the larger and far stronger, a most improbable outcome.

As a theologian, however, Govan could not say that this outcome was merely accidental or merely inadvert because God's Providence was mysteriously involved. Through the process of history he believed God's will was somehow being expressed. He wanted to emphasize that it was God's intention that Americans have freedom, equality, and justice, and that they be models for the rest of the world. He based this conviction partly on the biblical injunction to humans to repent and be forgiven. He also referred to the *Commentaries on the Laws of England* by William Blackstone, in which he discussed human rights as an expression of God's will for people generally. Blackstone's views were fatefully echoed by Thomas Jefferson in the Declaration of Independence.[695] Somehow in spite of all the human forces of resistance, God was bringing about that freedom, equality, and justice, however limited.

The English Foundation

Govan continued by detailing the English laws under which the colonists lived and how these law evolved. They were not the products of political theories, like those of Thomas Hobbs or John Locke, he said, but products of "the powerful, painful, grinding process of history." That history began with the Anglo-Saxon Kings, included the Norman Conquest, Henry VIII and the Reformation, the "divine rights of kings" claimed by James I and II, Charles I and II, the republican experiment of Cromwell, and finally the Glorious Revolution of 1689 and the beginning of constitutional and limited monarchy. "The mixed government of England, with its combination of monarchy, aristocracy, and democracy"[696] was reproduced in the colonies with their various combinations of "a governor, an advisory council, and an assembly elected by the people."[697] This structure was "not perfect, nor was it intended to be," but it did provide government by which people could seek to "establish and protect the rights of all" to life, liberty, and the pursuit of happiness."[698]

> Only a few in America or England, during the period of colonial settlement, thought that government should have [these purposes]. Most wanted liberty (political and religious) for themselves and their particular group, not for others. Another half-century would have to pass before this fundamental article of the Declaration (of Independence) . . . would be

generally accepted, at least as it applied to all white subjects of the King. This acceptance did not come easily.[699]

Great Britain, as the result of this history, became the only nation in the world at that time whose constitution and government made political liberty its primary purpose. That liberty achieved in England was shared by the colonies.

The Colonies as Part of the British Empire

Govan went on to describe the changes taking place in the seventeenth and eighteenth centuries that directly affected the American colonies and ultimately led to the Revolutionary War. Most important was "the balance between order and liberty"[700] achieved by Great Britain's mixed government, which combined the apparently contradictory principles of monarchy, aristocracy, and democracy.[701] Leading scholars of the time, Blackstone in England and Montesquieu in France, agreed that England was the freest and best government in the world.

This balance was shared by the colonies in a federal-type empire that had developed over time, not according to any rational theory or conscious aim, but simply in response to commercial, political, and other circumstances. As members of this empire, the American colonists were subject to two sets of laws, one political, the other economic. First, there were the royal charters that granted them considerable self-government in the form of local assemblies, subject only to the generally benign supervision of a local governor and finally to review by the Privy Council in England. Second, they were subject to Parliamentary regulation of trade within the Empire. Both of these were relatively relaxed and supportive for years, and the colonies recognized their constitutionality and flourished under them.

In 1689, William and Mary increased the strength and prosperity of the empire by excluding all foreigners from shipping and trade within it, thereby eliminating competition and providing the colonies with huge commercial opportunities. Growing tobacco was forbidden in England, for example, and various subsidies and preferential tariffs were instituted as well. The most important source of England's imperial prosperity was the financial revolution begun by William and Mary in 1689 "by the creation of the Bank of England and the funding of the national debt."[702] Up until that time, national debt "had been considered a burden that reduced the current ability to spend."[703] The Bank of England and the funded debt changed all of that. As Govan described it,

> These innovations, as if by magic, transformed spending in excess of current income into a source of national wealth. A funded debt, like gold and silver, provided a safe foundation for an increase of credit that was the equivalent of an increase in the money supply . . . The funded debt along with gold and silver, were used as the capital of a national bank empowered to issue circulating banknotes redeemable on demand in [gold and silver] . . . Buyers and sellers would use these paper notes as readily as gold and silver so long as they retained confidence in the ability of the issuing bank to redeem them, and the principal virtue of such currency was its capacity for almost indefinite expansion without arousing doubt and distrust.[704]

This new process "raised imperial prosperity to ever higher levels, and Great Britain, including its colonies, became, not only the freest, but also the wealthiest nation in the world."[705]

The American Revolution

All was well between the colonies and Great Britain until 1763 when Britain finally won the French and Indian War and wanted to consolidate the Empire under its control. At that point, the Parliament began claiming an authority over the colonies which up to that time had been exclusively the king's. The colonies recognized the authority of the king over them because he had chartered them in the first place and had granted them freedom they had had for at least a century. Ironically, in the eyes of Americans, it was the British Parliament, not the American colonies, who were breaking the law and acting like revolutionaries. It was Parliament that was upsetting the previous arrangements and laws of the British Empire.

When the Americans resisted Parliament, they were charged unfairly by Britain with "being republicans seeking independence."[706] Nothing could have been further from the truth. The vast majority of colonists were convinced monarchists who desired to remain in the British empire and were fiercely loyal to the king. All of their arguments right up through the Declaration of Independence were "founded on the constitution of the British empire as it had developed through history."[707]

Not until a year after Lexington and Concord, when the king officially declared them American rebels, did the majority of colonists feel they would have to declare their independence and establish a new nation. When they did, they modeled that nation on the British system, without the monarchy.

The Declaration of Independence and the Constitution as Creeds

Govan concluded his lecture series by focusing on the meaning of the Revolutionary War. "The nation through its reaffirmation of the principles of the Declaration of Independence in the Constitution," he said, "assumed one of the traditional functions of the church. It established a standard, a principle of judgment, by which national [state] and individual actions could be evaluated. When these fall short, as they always do, improvement can be demanded through appeal to these basic affirmations."[708] To this day, the Declaration and the Constitution still fulfill the role of a creed. They have always motivated those who seek equal justice and freedom for themselves and for others. Whenever Americans have made progress in this direction, it has required a strong and active federal government, as was the case, for example, with Lincoln and the Civil

War, Theodore Roosevelt with big business, Franklin Roosevelt with the New Deal, and even Lyndon Johnson and his Great Society. Govan's final judgment was that despite tragic failures

> . . . to achieve freedom, equality and justice in our society, grievous though they be, this nation is still more nearly free, more nearly just, and more nearly equitable than almost any other that has existed on earth. The principles on which it was founded continue to be true, regardless of their abandonment in most of the world.[709]

In summary, his message was that when people give up their faith in the providence of God, which our American history demonstrates within the seeming inadvertence of history, then they turn to their own theories, scientific, philosophical, political, and economic into dogmatic certainties, and try to impose them upon one another. Thus, order, freedom, equality, and justice are confounded and risk being lost. The great thing about the Declaration of Independence and the Constitution is that they commit us to a struggle for victory (of freedom, equality, and justice) that can never be fully won, but must be continually worked toward.

Even while Govan's faith and conviction shone through these lectures, he was not happy with them. He said that "the audience in New York though small was generous but still I do not quite like them [the lectures]. I tried to cover too much, to squeeze too many ideas and too much material into too short a time and too small a space."[710] Nevertheless, the written lectures brought his historical, philosophical, scientific, political, and economic ideas together in a theological-historical statement more succinctly than ever before. Sadly, they were never published, presumably because he preferred it that way.

In spite of his doubts about his lectures, Tom had a wonderful time at the party beforehand. Many friends from the 1950s, when he worked for the Episcopal Church, were there. He wrote

> It was a joyous reunion not only for us but for them, since they seldom see each other in New York.[711]

"The Rejection of Denominational Idolatries," A Plea for a New Birth of Freedom in the Church

In preparation for the bicentennials of both the United States (1976) and later of the Episcopal Church (1989), the General Convention of the Episcopal Church, meeting in Louisville, Kentucky in late September and early October of 1973, appointed a bicentennial committee. Part of that committee's responsibility was to oversee the publication by the Forward Movement Press of a series of pamphlets on topics related to the bicentennial celebration. Several thousand copies would be distributed throughout the Episcopal Church and would appear for sale in the tract racks of churches all over the country. The editor was Govan's old friend from Sewanee, the Reverend C. Fitzsimmons Allison, now rector of Grace Church in New York City. It was Allison he had chastised for the theological faculty's continued passive collusion with the racial policies of the University of the South. He knew and understood Govan's view and together they hatched the final long essay that Govan wrote before he died, "The Rejection of Denominational Idolatries," published in 1975.

In this essay, Govan tells the story of Anglican Church history from the beginning in fifth-and sixth-century Celtic England through the period of the American colonies, and then picks up the history of the Episcopal Church in the United States from its formation in 1789 to 1975. His essay is a critique of proud sectarianism and a call for a humble spirit of flexible tolerance. The Church in 1975 was struggling with the development of a new *Book of Common Prayer* and the question of the ordination of women. Govan keenly believed that the historic attitude and teaching of the Anglican reformers of the Church of England and of the founders of the Episcopal Church could be an immensely helpful and authoritative guide, so he set out to teach its history and its humility.

For one thing, the rule throughout the history of both churches, English and American, had been that "doctrine was immutable and was limited to the Apostles and Nicene Creeds. Everything else was a matter of discipline and was variable, including the words through which the unchangeable truths were expressed" and, of course, the interpretation of these words.[712] Matters of discipline include such matters as the proper form of church polity, ministry, and worship; who is eligible to be called to the ordained ministry; the position of women in the church; the position of gays, the church's teaching on abortion, and so on:

> Profound changes in almost all aspects of life have occurred in [the] two centuries [of the Episcopal Church's life] . . . . Some things have not changed, however, and perhaps the most significant of these is the temptation to all to be certain [we] alone possess the truth. The warnings were against individual and corporate idolatry.[713]

> Following the Church of England, the Episcopal Church has utterly rejected claims to inerrancy, infallibility, and other forms of denominational idolatry . . . . [714]

> All that the founders of the Episcopal Church were willing to claim, like the English reformers three centuries earlier, was that their particular forms had historical precedents, that they were not forbidden by Scripture, and that their usefulness was confirmed by reason and experience.[715]

Govan was emphasizing the humility and the flexibility of this nondoctrinaire view. He went on to say that:

> Warnings against individual and corporate idolatry found in the Scriptures and reaffirmed by the English reformers and the founders of the Episcopal Church, thus, have not lost their usefulness. They are needed as much as ever . . . . [716]

because the Church is torn by division over many issues of discipline.

The historically established authority of the Church to take action [on all of these issues] is unquestionable.[717]

But, as the 1662 Prayer Book puts it:

It hath been the wisdom of the Church of England to keep the mean between the two extremes, of too much stiffness in refusing, and of too much easiness in admitting variation . . . of things advisedly established.[718]

Challenges to the Church's authority have been made repeatedly on grounds other than the two creeds. Only recently, a schismatic Episcopal Church has been formed on such grounds. And some Episcopalians are rejecting gay marriage, the ordination of gays to the priesthood and especially to the episcopate on the same grounds. If Govan were alive he would be reminding us that the Creeds do not pass judgment on the issues. He urged that we learn and obtain guidance from the moderation and the humility of both the English reformers and the founders of the Episcopal Church[719] in dealing with such challenges.

30

The Final Years, 1971⁻1979

Historical study, the academic life, was not simply a profession for Tom; it was a calling. It was a way of thinking, and in so far as it guided his relationships with people and institutions, a way of living.

Stanley Pierson

In June 1971, at age sixty-five, Tom was eligible by university rules to retire.[720] He was feeling awful because he had a terrible case of the flu and would gladly have retired that year if he could have afforded it, but he could not. He and Jane were living so close to the line that Tom needed to continue to teach.

Retirement in 1971 was not an issue because in 1967, when he had first come to the university, it was agreed that so long as he was healthy and performing his duties well, Tom could continue by contract, one year at a time, for another five years until the end of the fall semester in 1976. The history department wanted to keep him on and did not even consider searching for someone to replace him and, quite literally, no one could.

On June 6, 1971, the Dean of the Faculty Harry Alpert wrote Tom that "because of the highly specialized nature of your assignment at this time, the president, Robert D. Clark, deems it to be in both the university's interest and the public interest to continue you in full-time employment for the academic year 1972-1973" at a salary of $20,000.[721]

Thomas P. Govan at the time of his retirement, 1977

Tom would receive the same letter in each of the four successive years. Before Christmas in 1976, he retired and became emeritus professor of history. For one last time, Harry Alpert, now vice-president of the university, wrote Tom an official letter:

> We wish by this action to acknowledge our appreciation for your valuable contributions to the University as a dedicated teacher, productive scholar, courageous exponent of innovative perspectives on American history, and active contributor to the well being of the University community. You have truly earned the esteem and admiration of many colleagues and students.
>
> I should like to take this occasion to express our deepest

thanks for your nine years of dedication and loyalty to the University and our fondest wishes for many years of joy and happiness in retirement.

Sincerely yours, Harry Alpert[722]

It was true that he had served the university well. Through his television lectures, *Radical America; the Continuing Revolution,* which were shown several times. Also in the previous five years, he had given the Deems Lectures, "We Hold These Truths," at NYU, and he had written the booklet, "The Rejection of Denominational Idolatries," for the Episcopal Church's Bicentennial Committee.

In the fall of 1976, he wrote

> It is hard to realize that this is my final year, but I am looking forward to release from the classroom. I was spoiled in New York by teaching only graduate students, but this term I have two large undergraduate lectures and it seems to me that I cannot reach them.[723]

Before Christmas that year, he gave his last lecture. On December 20th, he turned in his final grade report, his last act as a teacher. "I feel like a grammar school student on the last day of school."[724]

Tom was honored being appointed speaker at the mid-year commencement exercises. It is not clear what he spoke about, but it was perhaps a version of his bicentennial message directed toward the crisis of the moment. Nixon was gone; Gerald Ford was president and had just pardoned Nixon. The evacuation of Saigon had been completed, millions of dollars set aside for the relief of South Vietnamese refugees, and 140,000 refugees were flown to the United States—there was much to talk about.

On January 4th, the Govans left the fog and rain of Eugene by car and headed south toward Mexico, where they intended to spend six weeks or more of complete rest and vacation. On the way, they would impose on various friends, including the Corrigans at Santa Barbara. Not until late January would they cross the border.[725]

Daniel and Elizabeth Corrigan were special friends of the Govans. Dan had once been the Episcopal bishop of Colorado, but for years he had been head of the Home Department of the national Episcopal Church, including the seven years Tom was Executive Secretary for Faculty Work. He had technically been Tom's boss, but actually was a colleague, friend, and staunch supporter. Corrigan was one of the church's great preachers, as Tom was one of its great teachers. As couples, they were extremely close and had a warm and happy reunion.

In Mexico, the Govans took their time. They relaxed on beaches, absorbing sun; they slept and when they were rested, they traveled the country, exploring historical sites and museums, basking in the culture and history of Mexico. Both were especially "fascinated by the pre-conquest story. Our greatest joy was in the National Museum of Anthropology, which is the most beautiful museum we either had seen."[726]

On March 17, 1977, Tom wrote that they "had just returned to Eugene from darkest Mexico" brown and rested. "I am getting restless now that my retirement is three months old," he said, "and next week will begin writing some of the things that I have been mulling over these past years."[727] As though he had not been doing so for years! But there was more to be done. Unspoken was the regret, deep regret . . . that so much had been left undone. However, he said,

> It is lovely to get up each morning with the whole day before you to write a while, then read, and as the days grow warmer, to get out into the yard for weeding and other destructive activities.

> We hope, next year, to come east in the fall or spring . . .[728]

Cancer

In the fall of 1976, Tom began to realize that there was something physically wrong: he was having abdominal discomfort. When he saw his local doctor, he was referred to specialists in Portland. The following January, Tom was diagnosed with cancer of the colon, necessitating radical surgery and a colostomy. He was operated on in Portland. The cancer had spread to his liver and was so embedded that the doctors could do nothing to help. All they could offer was chemotherapy to prolong his life.

The day after the operation, Bob Berdahl, having heard the diagnosis, visited Tom in the hospital. "When I walked in, Tom said, 'Bub'—he always called me Bub—'if anyone thinks I'm going to quit smoking now, they are crazy!'"[729]

Allowing Tom some post-operation time to heal, the doctors then administered a course of heavy chemotherapy and sent Tom home, where he learned to cope with the colostomy. Tom resigned himself to the ugly discipline of light chemotherapy and went on with his life. He now knew he had no more than a year or two left.

Few of his friends knew the truth about Tom's situation, and in April 1977, there was no mention of it in his most revealing letter to me.

Dear John,

It seems that each time I write you, it is on a notable day. Today, the fifth of April, Jane is seventy and if I were not the same age, I would be thinking about a divorce. Fortunately, neither she nor I have learned to act our age, so we may still work it out together . . . .

I hope the writing is beginning to go for you. Let me see the things you are doing. My own has not started yet, but I am working around to it.

This is a beautiful spring day. The garden needs weeding and if I do not get out this afternoon, it will be a week before I can get to it, since I have to go to an orthopedist's office tomorrow to have a 'Deuben's contraction' [Dupuytren's contracture] attended to . . . . My little

finger on my right hand has almost doubled over and he
will have to cut it loose.

We hope to come east in the fall and will surely see you
then.[730]

Thanks largely to steady, light chemotherapy, Tom's condition
remained more or less stable for a year. He was able to do some work,
but he never made it back East.

In January, 1978, Albert T. Mollegen, New Testament and
Christian Ethics professor at Virginia Theologian Seminary, who had
originally suggested Tom for the Faculty Work job back in 1955, an
old friend and collaborator, responded to Tom's bad news:

> Thank God you and Jane had the good trip East [for the
> Deems lectures] . . . I ain't giving up on you two coming
> here [to Goodwin House, an Episcopal Church-sponsored
> retirement home in Alexandria, Virginia] to read the
> Washington Post and discuss world issues at mealtime
> and over a Jack Daniel's or Virginia Gentleman.[731]

> Most of my life has been spent with men and . . . Tom
> Govan [is among] the ones I love best . . . I simply am not
> going to give up this host of sinners to cancer or the devil.
> There is something everlasting about such friendships.

> I remember writing Jane once when I was in an airplane
> and she had a mastectomy [that] I was praying for her
> and [was] with you two, feeling nearer to God in the
> clouds. Jane wrote me an answer and a good one. I return
> that good answer which she may not remember: "To hell
> with cancer and Idi Amin and Caligula and all the
> daemonic powers. We are Christians of a sort and 'Jesus
> is Lord.'" OK? OK!

> Molle[732]

That same month, Tom received an invitation to lecture at the first annual Midnight Sun Symposium at the University of Alaska, Anchorage. The overall subject was "Theories of Representation," grist for Tom's mill. He would speak as a historian by profession, but also as a philosopher-theologian deeply interested in language, metaphor, symbols, myth, faiths, facts, experience, memory, and history, all under God. The symposium was scheduled for May and Tom was determined to be there because he had his message to deliver. Despite the colostomy, he made the long trip and fully participated in the conference. Several months later, Stephen Haycox, associate dean of the University of Alaska, wrote "everyone is still talking about your thoughts."[733] Tom came back exhausted.

Jane later wrote:

> During all this time, we had trust and confidence in our doctors, and they rewarded us with truth and candor and with human kindness and affection.
>
> We had a year of grace—time to gather our resources, spiritual and personal. We found that we had more blessings than wounds to count. We learned more about the value of life than the fear of death. We had faith and an abundance of love and kindness from friends and acquaintances. We had some joyful companionship as well as times of stress and anxiety.[734]

Despite the treatments, "there were a lot of good times that year," according to Berdahl. "We would drop by and have a drink with them. Tom was usually in good spirits."[735]

On July 29, 1978, the Govans read in *The New York Times* that their beloved St. Marks-in-the-Bowery had burned the day before. Important renovation work was being done at the time and the fire had been started probably "by the heat of a welding torch."[736] The building and tower had been gutted but left standing. The Govans were shaken and hurt by the news, especially Jane who had put so much of her energy into the restoration work being done there. They saw pictures of the roof in flames. The organ was destroyed, the inside plaster and outside stucco ruined, windows blown out, the belfry clock destroyed, and the bell cracked. It was a disaster.

In subsequent days, Bishop Paul Moore and the Reverend David A. Garcia, rector, both spoke brave and hopeful words about a complete rebuilding and restoration that would soon begin. The life of the parish went on unabated in borrowed facilities. In fact, over the next five years, two and a half million dollars would be raised from foundations, corporations, churches, individuals, and even government groups, and the entire church and parish house were restored and the churchyard and cemetery renovated. This was made possible because St. Mark's-in-the-Bowery was registered as a national monument, something Jane had lobbied for in the mid-1960s. Later Jane made a significant contribution in memory of Tom. For the moment, however, they were downcast.

The End

During that same summer, Tom had to return to the hospital for more intensive therapy.[737] Bob Berdahl and others took turns driving the Govans to Portland and back many times. "Tom was pretty good" despite the ravages of his treatment. When the results became too bad, he was switched to cobalt treatment. In the fall, "it became obvious that Tom was losing strength."[738]

By early January, he had experienced prolonged pain in his liver.[739] Jane later wrote,

> We were told that he 'had about a month' to live. We were offered the faint possibility that a little time might be gained by returning to the Portland hospital for [more] intensive chemotherapy. We thought about it overnight and elected to see it through at home if possible. Our doctors supported our decision.[740]

This was a desperately hard time for Jane. Tom was "quiet and stoic," but she "began to lose her grip," finding it "next to impossible to talk with others without weeping."[741] But that was temporary. She soon got hold of herself.

That was when Jane began calling close friends to let them know the end was near. Several flew to Eugene in January to see them. Michael Allen and I were among them. Laura Roper was there more for Jane than for Tom, and Jane knew it. Michael Allen and I had come as much for ourselves as for them. Tom was exhausted but willing to try to summarize his faith and views in taped interviews with me. He was as sharp as ever intellectually, but was so weak and drugged with morphine and his voice was so husky that we gave it up after a few tries. For us, it was both a wonderful and happy time of reminiscing and an agonizing time of feeling for Tom's suffering and facing our own imminent loss.

The next day Michael and I had a reassuring visit with Jane. She later wrote "I am relieved of tension and anxiety after talking with you about what happens [after] Tom's death. I woke up knowing exactly what my wishes were. When you told me to consult my comfort, I was free to do that."[742]

That same day she spoke with the rector of Eugene, Oregon's St. John's Church about a memorial service for Tom, and received approval for a hospice fund in his memory. She recruited friends to help during Tom's final days, and decided that Tom would be cremated and later buried at St. Mark's-in-the-Bowery, New York. She spoke to the Ropers about making living arrangements for her later on at Goodwin House in Alexandria, Virginia. It all came clear.

One night Tom, who was upstairs in bed attended by one of his faithful friends, was heard crying out at one point, at the top of his lungs, "I'm coming, Jesus, I'm coming." We all laughed and then stopped. Although we were tempted to think this outcry harkened back to Tom's pre-Anglican days, on second thought, we realized that was not true. This simple, direct, and personal conviction that Jesus was there waiting for him was very much a part of the mature life of this highly sophisticated theologian.

Other friends and acquaintances wrote appreciative letters to Jane and Tom. After Michael Allen returned home, he wrote all that he had not been able to say in person—there had never been quite the appropriate amount of privacy during his visit. Jim Govan, Tom's nephew and Gilbert's son, wrote him in thanks for a visit Tom had made to see him and his wife during one of the most difficult moments in their lives:

> As long as both of us live, I will remember that kindhearted trip you made to us in Tuscalooga . . . No one before or since has done anything so loving for me. When Carol [Tom's older sister] was here, we talked one night about all the things we owe you, Tom. They were far too numerous for us to cover in four hours, but I hope you know what a profound influence had have had on all our lives, how different they would have been if you had not been our kin and our friend, and we love you for it.[743]

Jane described the end:

> By late January, Tom was too weak to go to the doctor's office for his weekly [chemo] injection, and our doctor began coming here as he had promised long ago. The same fine nurse from the Home Health Agency, who had carried both of us through Tom's convalescence from surgery last year, came to us again. Those two good people told me what to expect and what was to be done for Tom to keep him as comfortable as possible. It was then that I reached a depth of fear; a fear of my own inability to take care of him, of my ineptitude, lack of experience and shaky nerves. I was consoled by being told by the doctors that no one 'could do him any harm now' and that I should give up my reluctance to lean more heavily on the friends who wanted to help. Our young friends, who had given and offered help for a year, formed themselves into an organized group to help us both. One of the women took full responsibility for organizing all the schedules and shifts, got in touch with people who wanted to help and let them know what they could do. Other friends

who had nursing experience and full or part-time jobs came here in their free hours and took turns sleeping here. For more than two weeks, while Tom was actually dying, there were always at least two extra people in the house during daylight hours and more than that at night, sleeping in shifts and taking turns of active duty. Nor was I left alone; I could sleep a little, knowing that someone would call me.[744]

One of those present for the last week of Tom's life and for several weeks after his death was his niece, Kate Bunnell, who helped in every way, including keeping the family and close friends informed about the situation. She thanked Jane later, saying "I will always be grateful to you for giving me a chance to share Tom's last week with you and your friends and to stay with you for several weeks afterward."[745]

Jane's letter went on:

> ... Our doctor continued to come and give guidance and moral support to all of us. The medication was increased or changed to keep Tom comfortable, and pain was always under control.
>
> He was not too heavily sedated to know each of us and was rational most of the time. He had no food for two weeks before he died and later was unable to swallow even liquids. Hypodermics were used when he could no longer swallow, and it became a question of waiting until his strong heart wore out.
>
> This was a tremendous experience for all of us, and an extremely valuable one. I will always be deeply grateful that Tom could die at home with people he loved and escape the tubes in a hospital. This was truly love in action. I learned that death is just another part of life, and it was wonderful at the very last to be able to ask friends to leave me with Tom alone.

402

He died within fifteen minutes after they left us . . . just
could breathe no longer.[746]

The date was Monday, March 5, 1979.

The memorial service in Eugene was scheduled four days after
his death on March 9 at 4:30 P.M. at St. Mary's Episcopal Church. The
Reverend Duane S. Alvord, rector for the past six years, presided.
The service followed the order of The Burial of the Dead, Rite One
in the Proposed *Book of Common Prayer*. After the opening sentences, "I
am the resurrection and the life, saith the Lord," those attending
sang "O God Our Help in Ages Past." The readings from Isaiah, the
Psalms, and Revelation emphasized the compassion and love of God,
which transcends death. After singing Luther's great hymn, "A Mighty
Fortress Is Our God," the rector read from the Gospel of St. John,
Chapter 6: "For this is the will of my Father, that everyone who sees the
Son and believes in Him should have eternal life; and I will raise him
up at the last day."

The gospel was followed by prayers, one of which was a prayer of
thanksgiving for Tom's life, which Jane and I had worked on together.
Read by the rector: it rehearsed his life, his qualities as a person, as a
scholar and teacher, and his contributions to the church, to the
university, to all of us, and ended:

> We give thanks for his life and his love. And we give
> thanks even for his death: for sadness met without
> surrender, suffering accepted without self-pity, weakness
> endured without defeat, and death faced without
> despair.
>
> And finally, O God, we thank thee that he is at home at
> last with thee; and free—free at last!
>
> We pray through Jesus Christ our Lord. Amen.

The Lord's Prayer was followed by the Intercessions, and the
Commendation:

Into thy hands, O merciful Savior, we commend they servant Thomas. Acknowledge, we humbly beseech thee, a sheep of thine own fold, a lamb of thine own flock, a sinner of thine own redeeming. Receive him into the arms of they mercy, into the blessed rest of everlasting peace, and into the glorious company of the saints in light. Amen.[747]

Then, the rector led a quiet recessional out of the church to the Guild Room for a reception.

A memorial fund was established in Tom's name at St. Mary's "to help on a non-sectarian basis in the care of the terminally ill at home or in hospice."[748] His way of dying gave a real boost to the hospice movement in Oregon as a whole.[749]

Two days later, Sunday, March 11, a second memorial service was held at Grace Church, New York, where the Reverend C. Fitzsimmons Allison, a former teacher at the seminary in Sewanee and an old friend of Tom's was rector.[750] It was a wonderful service, small, intimate, and alive with shared affection for Tom. Jane was exhausted and did not travel across country for the service. Some of the Govans' East coast friends were able to be there, including his brother Jack and his sister, Carol Tucker, and a niece, Betty Conn. Many friends may not have heard about it until later. Fitz Allison wrote Jane:

Dear Jane,

We had a lovely service here. Tom Pike officiated,[751] John Crocker read his tribute and Lee Belford complemented it with a most gracious appreciation of Tom's "contentious" reputation. I was especially moved by that aspect, as I believe that any commitment to truth is going to be viewed by many less committed folk as contentiousness. Perhaps it is a self-serving interpretation for myself, but I share with Lee and many others an admiration for the very thing in Tom that often made others uneasy.

Tom's niece [Betty Conn] read a lesson as did Suzanne Reid[752] and Cora Louise Belford.[753] We held it here at Grace Church because St. Mark's has not recovered from its tragic fire, and we did have Tom Powers, the organist who was at St. Mark's when you were there, playing the hymns.

Afterward everyone was invited up to our Rectory, and we had a good time being able to greet old friends and recall so many poignant times in our lives. Fleeta and Isabel were there,[754] as well as Van Bowen, Phil Zabriskie, Arthur Chitty,[755] and many more. Suzanne had me read your letter to Harriet Price.[756]

Enclosed is a tape of the service. I am sorry it is not a more professional job, but I believe you can get the gist of what is said and a sense of the celebration in the service of Tom's life and our common faith.

Everyone wanted to know when you will be in this area. Do let us know.

With the warmest love always,

Devotedly,
Fitz[757]

The burial of Tom's ashes at St. Mark's-in-the-Bowery did not take place until April 29th, nearly two months later. It had been agreed that after Easter, when the rush of Holy Week was over, and Michael Allen could be in New York from St. Louis, it would be a good time to have the service. Michael had unavoidably missed the two earlier services.

Michael and his wife, Priscilla, arrived in New York on Thursday night, April 26th and were visiting with Steve Facey, the St. Mark's parish administrator and manager, when Lee Belford called to ask if on the 29th the church would be free for the burial. It was free, and Michael would be the officient. This meant a lot to Michael because, as he said, he had not been part of the service either in Eugene or in New York.

He later described the service to Jane:

> We gathered, the Belfords, the Coopers, David and Migdalia Garcia (the rector of St. Mark's and his wife,) Steve Facey and Bob Amussen (on Sunday) at four. Bob and Steve opened the vault.[758]

> I felt more comfortable using the new (1979) Prayer Book, Rite Two . . . . We read the opening sentences responsively: 'Everyone the Father gives to me will come to me. I will never turn away anyone who believes in me' . . . . We then read Psalm 46: 'God is our refuge and strength': Psalm 90: 'Teach us the number of our days that we may apply our hearts to wisdom': Psalm 121: "I will lift my eyes to the hills."

> Then, as Bob lowered Tom's ashes into the vault, tied to a long black cord, I read the committal itself and then on to the prayers . . . . I found myself almost unable to go on and had to cut down the prayers.

> I felt so clearly that he was there with that funny quizzical smile . . . . It was a precious moment for me, burying Tom, precious because it declared closure for me, and I needed that. [759]

The obituaries were many, from Oregon and New York in the North, and from Atlanta, Sewanee, Nashville, and Chattanooga in the

South. They spoke about where Tom had studied and taught, emphasized *Nicholas Biddle* as Tom's one major scholarly work, and included his World War II histories, his co-authorship of *The Last Best Hope*, and his bicentennial TV lectures.

The University of the South student news bulletin had a beautifully inaccurate report of Tom's career and funeral service; in the margin Jane had written, "Wrong, of course!" Their comments about Tom as a teacher, however, were right on target.

His reputation was one of

> a challenging teacher and colleague. The tutorial which
> has been offered to history majors for the past thirty-five
> years is his monument at Sewanee.[760]

Tom would have liked that. Jane's comment in the margin was, "This is true."

A fund in Tom's name was started in the History Department to be used for the support of research by untenured faculty and advanced doctoral candidates. A memorial gift and the planting of a tree in his memory was given by Mr. and Mrs. Ross E. Jackson, a faculty colleague and his wife.

There was another monument to Tom that would have surprised him. His nephew, Thomas James Tucker, who loved Tom as his uncle but had been rather critical of him for not living up to his full potential as a productive scholar, set up, with his brother-in-law, a $1.5 million endowment at the University of the South in memory of three people, one of whom was Tom. Its purpose was to make attendance at the University of the South financially possible for students who were the first in their families to go to college. That would have pleased Tom immensely. For all Thomas Tucker's criticism of Tom as a weak and lazy scholar, he still had admiration for what he stood for. He used to say of Tom, "He doesn't make the cut," but the endowment would seem to belie that.[761]

Jane received countless letters from friends, colleagues, and former students of Tom's. Among them were letters from Senator

Mark O. Hatfield, Tom McCall, the governor of Oregon, and R.D. Clark, president of the University of Oregon.

Two letters that meant much to her were from old Ministry in Higher Education stalwarts of the Episcopal Church, Albert T. Mollegen, retired from Virginia Theological Seminary, and Bishop Daniel Corrigan, retired from the Church headquarters in New York. Mollegen wrote:

> I'll say nothing and everything at the same time. I am a believer as you two, you and Tom, are.

> No two Christians of my sort are more beloved by a great host than you two.

> Embedded on eternity is Tom's monkey-like grin which Ione [Mollegen's wife] so loved when he said to her, when I was lecturing, "Here come those damned pigs!" [Mark 5:1-23][762] and now [you] come to Goodwin House.

> I have so many friends whom you will love and who will love you . . . .

> I think you know that the tears which stain these sheets are shot through with joy. I am privileged to have loved and to love Jane and Tom.[763]

Seven years later, in 1986, Dan Corrigan was still grieving. After having heard from Jane, he responded:

> Dear Jane,

> Your present lovely letter is another experience of what has been happening a lot to me recently. It follows a whole night in which I was visited by the presence, one after another the apparition of those whose going away

was occasioned by Death, moving out of my world, or
[those whose going was occasioned by] rending conflict
which left us bitterly separated. The GRIEF is the shade,
the abiding presence! Papa, Momma, Grandma, Aunt
Mary, Uncle John, etc. The teachers who opened worlds
both great and microscopic; the friends who became
enemies yet now . . . are together again (How crazy we
were to let that ÷ [division] of opinion separate us!) Some
still in the flesh, fleshy yet shaky, can be found and
reconciled, just as eager as we to be together again. What
a great gift is GRIEF=Death and immortality.

Say to Ginny [Shannon] and John Crocker and any other
shades of days gone by you may encounter that we
remember. At the heart of the matter "Do this in
remembrance of me" has many dimensions including
the Communion of Saints.

I must not go on day dreaming like this—so pray with me
that something like La Casa Gonzales will always be
around.

With love and gratitude, Dan[764]

Besides letters to Jane, there were also two statements about Tom,
which speak volumes about his life. The first is from an appreciation
of Tom prepared by Stanley Pierson, a close friend and chairman of
the history department, for the next faculty meeting after Tom's death.
Among other things, he said

Truly, Tom Govan was primarily a teacher; it is as a teacher,
I believe, that he would wish to be remembered. And the
many tributes that came from former students across the
country during his final illness testified to the continuing
impact of his teaching. Historical study, the academic

409

life, was not simply a profession for Tom; it was a vocation, a calling. It was a way of thinking, and in so far as it guided his relationships with people and institutions, a way of living. In scholarly debate, he was often cantankerous— at times outrageously dogmatic; but he took great joy in the give and take of the contest and few who engaged in such exchanges did not come away enriched by the encounter. His work, his life, was informed by strong religious convictions; he believed that understanding never emerges of itself from the facts—that only by means of a perspective, a point of view, a faith, could understanding be gained. This, I believe, was the source of his power as a teacher, not only of his students at many universities, but as a teacher of his younger colleagues at the University of Oregon.

Tom Govan had something of the courtliness, the charm, and the special gentleness of his southern heritage. But he was also a strong and passionate man. He was a radical in the real meaning of that term— one who goes to the root of things. At crucial moments in his life, his passionate radicalism surfaced. In 1952, when the Board of Trustees at the University of the South refused to integrate the institution, Tom resigned his position as tenured professor and chairman of the History Department in protest. For this "rare and remarkable act of civic courage," as one of my colleagues express[es] it, Tom paid a heavy price professionally. It was five years before he regained an academic position.

We are saddened by the thought that he did not live to complete his projected work on Alexander Hamilton. For Tom possessed a rare, and perhaps unique, understanding of the historical origins of the American

experience. . . . It was through a study of Hamilton that
Tom had hoped to demonstrate the ways in which the
English legal and religious traditions entered into the
making of the American nation.

We—his friends—will miss him greatly, both as an
adversary-partner in scholarly debate and as a warm and
open human being.[765]

The second statement was from Robert M. Berdahl in a letter to
Stanley Pierson's wife, Joan, who was preparing notes for an editorial
to be published in *The Register Guard*, Eugene's leading newspaper.[766]
He wrote that Thomas P. Govan

[w]as never inspired by careerist ambitions; he was
guided by his conscience and his sense of where he
could best serve. This is what kept him teaching at
Sewanee despite offers to move to more prestigious
institutions elsewhere. It is also what led him to resign
a tenured professorship, in a rare and remarkable act
of civic courage, when Sewanee refused to integrate
its seminary in 1952. His desire to serve led him to
leave, for a time, university teaching and to delay his
own professional advancement, when he went to work
for the Episcopal Church. He has consistently put his
own self-interest aside for what he considered a more
important task.

He is rare among contemporary historians in a
number of ways. First of all, history is not merely a
profession for him, it is a calling. History is under his
skin, shaping the way he thinks and believes. Second,
his historical vision has always been shaped by a
theological perspective; likewise, his theology has been
informed by his historical understanding. He has

understood the human capacity to corrupt all institutions, no matter how well they are devised nor how high their principles. [His point of departure is the first sentence of the Introduction to the 1549 *Book of Common Prayer*: "There is nothing by the wit of man so well devised or so sure established which in the continuance of time hath not been corrupted."] But what is truly remarkable is that despite that propensity to "screw up," as he so eloquently put it the other day in a taped interview with John Crocker, he has never been pessimistic about the future or about man's capacity to do good. His historical perspective joins with his Christian faith to stress the restorative and reconstitutive powers of the human spirit.[767]

Jane's Final Years, 1979-1991

Jane Govan's conflicting feelings of terrible loss (she and Tom had been married for thirty-nine years) and the huge relief that the struggle was finally over were mediated by the knowledge that she had done all she could to help Tom and had lived through the past year and a half well. Jane had made it possible for Tom to die at home with dignity and surrounded by friends. In so doing, she and their friends had been a model of hospice, which would grow into an important movement in the Eugene area and change attitudes toward death and dying. All of that made her feel good.

There was much to be done. Jane answered letters, thanked the many friends who had helped out, formalized a hospice fund at St. John's Episcopal Church in memory of Tom, and began to pursue her plans for the future. It was not long before she contacted Goodwin House, the Episcopal retirement home in Alexandria, Virginia, as Albert T. Mollegen had been urging. Word came back that there would be an opening in the fall.

Jane followed someone's advice by taking a one-room rather than a two-room apartment in order to save money for travel. Almost immediately, she regretted it. The room was entirely too cramped and felt like a prison. Sometimes it drove her crazy and made her depressed. Jane had made her decision, however, and was stuck with it. On balance, the move would be a good one. Jane would be secure and looked after and lots of friends would be within reach. Besides Mollegen, "Bobs" and Warren Turner were there, and Laura and Crosby Roper were nearby in Washington.

Her old friend from the Episcopal Church days in New York, Suzanne Reid, flew out to Eugene in September and drove Jane in her car, loaded to its limit, back across the country to Goodwin House. Jane moved in with all the essentials that would fit into her new quarters. The rest she gave away to family and friends.[768]

By far, the deepest understanding and clearest picture of Jane's life between 1979 and her death in 1991 comes from Harriet Price.[769] Harriet had met the Govans at the 1959 National Canterbury Study Conference in Colorado Springs while she was a student at Northwestern University. In 1960, Harriet, Jane, and Tom were appointed Episcopal Church representatives to the World Student Christian Federation Conference "For the Life of the World," in Strasbourg, France. Harriet naturally "fell under their wings,"[770] and they became close. Harriet was drawn to Tom's theological side because he made sense to her, but being a woman and more of an artist than theologian, she gravitated even more to Jane.

"I was a girl," she said. "I was different from the rest of you [men]. Jane and I would stay up until all hours discussing literature. There weren't enough women around. She did not get her share of the pie and it hurt like hell; she was pretty clear about that."[771]

Their relationship grew over the years, but flourished after Tom's death. Only then could Jane fully accept that Harriet cared about her in her own right. As she said, "Jane never really knew how I loved her; she always thought that Tom was the one getting the attention."[772]

Even after Jane's move east from Oregon, Harriet made a special effort to be close to her. Now married with children, Harriet took her family down to Virginia from Maine to visit. "It was wonderful. She loved our children."[773] From then on, Jane considered all the Prices "family." The bond between Harriet and Jane grew very deep. "Come to find out," Harriet said, "I was born just at the time (in 1940) that Jane was due to give birth to the only child she was ever pregnant with."[774] Harriet was now Jane's daughter and Jane, Harriet's mother.

Jane went to visit Harriet in 1983, right after Harriet's father had died. "She came up to Southwest Harbor and spent a couple of weeks with us. We had a St. Bernard (old and sick) whom we knew we had to put away. And Jane said, 'I want you to do it while I'm here, before I go home.' So George and I took the beautiful animal to the vets and came back at noon. We came in the door and George said, 'What about a bloody Mary?' 'Yep, that's a good idea,' Jane said. 'And now I want to tell you why I wanted to be here. Our dog [her dachshund Judy] died in the [1952] fire [in Sewanee]. And this is a much better way to die, and I couldn't bear to leave until it was done.' That was the thing about Jane; she felt things, she remembered, and she could make decisions."[775]

Goodwin House was a mixed blessing for Jane. On the one hand it kept her constantly involved with people, but her one-room apartment made entertaining more than two people virtually impossible. Although she was a gourmet cook, she found that cooking more than breakfast created smells that would last for days because of the poor ventilation in her room. More often she ate meals other than breakfast in the dining room. On the other hand, she loved gardening at Goodwin House almost as much as she had in Oregon. It was a good excuse for her to get outdoors. She was also quite self-sufficient.

Jane had always been an avid reader and her time at Goodwin House was no exception. Typically, she gave sage reading advice to her friends. Harriet Price remembers Jane recommending books as varied as *Time and Again* by Jack Finney, and Eva Fige's biography of Monet, *Light*, and of course the writing of Flannery O'Connor.[776]

Jane Dickson Govan soon after Tom's death circa 1980

On a par with her love of books was Jane's profound love of art and her belief that all great art "in one sense is religious art," because all true beauty is ultimately of God.[777] Her artistic sense was broad and impeccable, including especially the biblical and liturgical work by Matisse, but also Australian art and the Mola art of Panama. During Tom's time working for the Church in the late 1950s, Jane rejoiced in the opportunity to organize two exhibits of twentieth-century religious and liturgical art for Church conferences. She always kept Tom up-to-date on the best of modern art and now, with the National Gallery so close, she could easily stay abreast of current developments.

Jane had her troubles with health. There was the mastectomy in 1959. At Goodwin House in her seventies, she had occasional vertigo, which originated in arthritis of the neck and spine. It would come with tension and leave when she was once again "calm and free."[778] In 1984, Jane had "temporal arteritis," an inflammation of the temple arteries, a condition that threatens eyesight. Dr. Erickson, a "house doctor" whom she loved, looked after her and understood what a struggle it was for her to take care of herself alone. In 1985, Jane thought she had gone through a kind of nervous breakdown. Very likely it was a bout with depression. Harriet Price, who knew a lot about depression from experience and study, helped Jane considerably by coaching her through these spells.[779]

The Chapel in Goodwin House, Alexandria, Virginia.
Jane gave the simple cross over the altar in memory of
Tom.

With all of her trouble, however, Jane never lost her sense of humor. She wrote Harriet about her Christmas shopping. She had ordered by telephone "some pop-up sponges for neighbors and six glasses for myself."

> The biggest Boy Scout I have ever seen was helping
> [us] with packages [at Goodwin House] before
> Christmas and brought up to me a package the size of
> the old wardrobe trunks. It had to be kept in my
> apartment until after Christmas—no room [in
> storage] downstairs. They had sent me 6 times 6 glasses
> (because they came in 6 packs). I had to tell them
> there was no space to keep them, nor would I live
> long enough to break them![780]

Later in the spring, Jane wrote:

> My day you don't want to know about so I won't tell you!
> I can't sleep . . . to bed at 2:30 A.M., awake at 5; hang on
> until the vampire from the lab came to take blood at 7;
> then, weak and hungry, went down for breakfast,
> reasonably dressed. Ate a field hand's breakfast—hot in
> my clothes. Back to find [the] a.c. [air conditioning] not
> working (awful day)—so the maintenance man had to
> come. Then the weekly maid, then 2 visitors because a
> crack in the door (I'd cracked the front door open for
> ventilation). Phone [rang] every time I went to the
> bathroom, calls I haven't answered. Had to go to the
> nurses for something else. Came back, phone ringing—a
> 'visitor' on the way up to surprise me—never showed—
> wrong name. Phone constantly, telling one another we
> have a.c. or we don't have—I have to call maintenance
> for mine. AND HOW ARE YOU?
>
> Love, Jane[781]

In one letter, there was one of Jane's classic but poignant remarks that "waiting for a TV part was like waiting for a liver transplant."[782]

In another letter that reflected Tom and Jane's relationship, she wrote:

> Almost mid-night. Tomorrow is Dec. 22, and the 48th
> Anniv. of Tom's and my wedding—the "winter solstice"—
> as Tom answered once when I asked, "Do you know what
> day this is?"[783]

Jane once wrote to Harriet about her marriage with Tom:

> I live with (and on) many happy memories of Tom. I
> believe now (as I did in troubled times) that when we got

separated, crossed-up, into enemy camps, we were at least for that spell of time, somewhat out of our minds— It's probably fatuous for almost anybody after a long marriage to believe it was all good, open and honest. Maybe I'm perverse, but again there's a value in knowing. I know we let each other down; I know we gave each other trouble; I know we managed to be miserable sinners in lazy and inactive ways, and yet seeing many of the facts of life together gives it even more strength, and gives me pleasure now.[784]

And later she wrote about her faith:

My whole life has been hit or miss—and I know tonight as I knew in 1959 that I've hit more than I've missed. I know the date because it was the night before that cancer surgery. I tried to pray (thinking I'd known how all my life)—and what came out loud was "Thank you, God— it's been good." That's still it—about Tom and everything else.[785]

Jane was a devoted Episcopalian who spent regular time saying her prayers and often attended the mid-week Eucharist in the Goodwin House Chapel. She donated the Celtic cross that hangs over the chapel altar in memory of Tom. As a member of the Church of the Resurrection across the street from Goodwin House, she regularly attended Sunday worship and contributed the flowers on the high altar on the first Sunday in January in memory of him.

In April 1991, Jane had a stroke, which left her very weak, partly paralyzed, and almost without speech. Harriet recalls the uncanny timing of that event. Back in 1959, after her mastectomy, Jane had urged her to keep up with breast cancer technology, which Harriet had done. And "wouldn't you know, I ended up having a mastectomy, too, and it came just when Jane had her stroke. I always used to say to Jane, 'I will come to be with you,' and here she had a stroke and I couldn't do anything about it. So there was Laura Roper (Jane's old friend) totally deaf. She visited Jane three times a week at Goodwin House. And, of course, Jane couldn't talk and she was too weak to write.[786] I think of these old friends almost completely unable to communicate. So Jane died without my being able to get to her. I did send a friend with a tape I made for Jane. I told her what had happened and why I couldn't come. She understood. It really affected her. Then she asked for a glass of sherry!"[787]

Laura admitted that "communication with Jane was difficult to say the least: I am profoundly deaf, she was unable to write and so weak that she couldn't raise her voice. I did most of the talking, there— told her news, gossip, etc. that I thought would amuse or interest her. She was perfectly clear-headed and responsive and sometimes I could catch what she said. Once, for instance, when I'd done something for her, she said: 'I'm appreciative.' I took Franny (Schwab) Heuick to see her, and they had a very satisfactory meeting, being old and loving friends. The last time I saw her, she was clear-headed but very weak. Once I found her in the hall lined up with the other patients in her wheelchair with her head on her knees. I asked if she wanted to be straightened up and she indicated yes, so I set her up and we had a short visit. So far as I know, she was never confused, except perhaps just after the stroke. She had a very kind and empathetic nurse, who was with her when she was dying. I was in California visiting my son."[788]

Jane died on June 3, 1991 at the Goodwin House infirmary at the age of eighty-four.[789] A memorial service was held a week later in a full Goodwin House Chapel with the chaplain, the Reverend Robert H. Andrews, presiding. Jane's body was cremated and sent to St. Mark's-in-the-Bowery, where her remains were buried four months later in the churchyard vault beside Tom's on October 8, 1991 at 3:00 PM.

Some fourteen people attended: Michael Allen and I, old friends Suzanne Reid, Evelyn Fortna, and her son, Ned (Jane and Tom's godchild), two McNairs, Ruth E. Kinsey, Jane's nurse; and five old acquaintances from St. Mark's dating back twenty-five years. In the early 1960s, thanks largely to Jane's initiative, the parish launched the Preservation Youth Project, which recruited, trained, and hired local unemployed youth and put them to work around the church, and Jane had known them all. They had designed, contoured, and restored the ancient west churchyard around the grave vaults with a mosaic of paving stones and appropriate plantings. Present at her burial were Stephen Facey, the parish administrator and four members of the original project: Carlos Garcia, the youth leader at the time and three of his "boys," now all in their thirties and forties.

We met in St. Mark's parish house because the fire-damaged church was not yet restored. We joined in reading the Burial of the Dead from the *Book of Common Prayer* followed by a Requiem Eucharist, gathered around a moveable altar. I celebrated and Michael Allen preached. "It really is true," Michael said, "that in Jesus, God has a place prepared for us where there is no pain, no tears, just rejoicing with all of those we love." We passed the bread and wine one to another, around the circle, and then went out into the church yard for the burial of Jane's ashes. Nearby a farmer's market was in full swing and the rumble and busyness of the city were very much with us. The vault, number 23, already had Jane's name on it, just below Tom's. I read the burial words:

> In sure and certain hope of the resurrection to eternal life through our Lord Jesus Christ, we commend to Almighty God our sister Jane; and we commit her body to the ground; earth to earth, ashes to ashes, dust to dust. The Lord bless her and keep her, the Lord make his face to shine upon her and be gracious unto her, the Lord lift up his countenance upon her and give her peace.[790]

Michael lowered the ashes, tied on the end of a ribbon, down deep into the vault and all of us said, "Amen."[791]

Then we shared wine and cheese and lots of wistful, happy talk.

Epilogue

This book has been the story of Thomas Payne Govan's life: a southerner who, with his wife Jane, rebelled against the southern tradition of racism, against the South's pride in the lost cause of the Civil War, and the myth of a pastoral and agrarian southern past superior to the rest of the country. In the process of this rebellion, he became first a "liberal with socialist leanings." As a budding professional American historian and economist during the 1940s and 1950s, however, he was forced by what he was learning to change radically and to become a Hamiltonian conservative in government and finance and an Episcopalian Christian in philosophy and religion.

On this journey he was almost alone among his peers because his religion was not separate from his work as a historian, but informed it. As one of his students said, "his religion was not simply a series of beliefs, nor simply a way of acting, but informed every aspect of himself and his world and his own place in it. So, his political philosophy arose, obviously from his religious convictions rather than the other way around . . . . You cannot understand Tom Govan at all [as a person or historian] without understanding that."[792]

When I first met him, I recognized a kindred spirit who spoke to my life as a Christian and as an American, and combined these two influences in a marvelous way. Govan believed that the "self-evident truths" of the Declaration of Independence were articles of faith which in turn were the moral and theological basis of the new nation. The founding fathers believed that law, politics, and economics were not separate and distinct from ethics and religion, "governed chiefly by . . . utility, convenience, gain or power." Rather, all governmental authority was obliged to respect certain general principles of reason and nature, "established by God; [thus] the state and the law are to be essentially organs of right and justice."[793]

The working out of these principles in our American history, however, has not been a simple matter. Govan repeatedly described what Robert Penn Warren called "the powerful, painful, grinding process" of history through which the English and Americans had arrived at these religious and political convictions but have only partially realized them. He emphasized the fact that we never would realize them completely, but that we are obligated as human beings to keep trying.

Govan was, as a result, the enemy of all rigid fundamentalisms, whether secular, economic, and political (such as Communism, Fascism, Socialism, doctrinaire capitalism, or libertarianism), or religious and theological (such as Christian, Jewish, or Islamic). And in all cases he believed the "separation of church (synagogue, mosque or temple) and state" must be maintained because that separation is necessary to neutralize fundamentalism and promote true freedom. Neither church nor state can be allowed to dominate the other.

The most dangerous conflicts in our world, as well as in our country, unfortunately are fueled by these fundamentalisms: by their shrill and hostile claims and counterclaims, their violence and their cruelty. So, Govan's story is important. It is the narrative of a mature historian who has told us who we are as human beings and as Americans, and what our country is and must be about: namely, a continual Rebirth of Freedom.

APPENDICES

A Selection of

Govan's Essays

Referenced by Chapter

1. "Apologia Pro Vita Sua," see Chapter 2
2. "The Liberal and Conservative Traditions in the U.S.," see Chapter 10
3. "A New Birth of Freedom," see Chapter 11
4. "Free to Be Merely a Man," see Chapter 13
5. "True Freedom I," see Chapter 13
6. "Agrarianism, Sectionalism, and State Sovereignty Denounced," see Chapters 11 and 18
7. "Hamilton, the Bank, and the National Economy," see Chapters 10 and 21
8. "American Slavery," see Chapter 24

Appendix 1

See Chapter 2

Apologia Pro Vita Sua

Whitinsville, Massachusetts, Fall 1955
Thomas Payne Govan

In most instances the faculty members in our colleges and universities need help, for theirs is a lonely and desperate existence, more so all the time, for nowhere else, it seems to me, is the feeling of the uselessness and pointlessness of effort as strong as it is among devoted, concerned college and university teachers. They feel lost under the hordes of uninterested, poorly prepared students they are being forced to deal with, and, at the same time, many of them who began their own studies with superb confidence in the adequacy of their methods and techniques to find right answers, have found this confidence gone as in their more mature years they plunge deeper into the mystery, the unexplainable, the unknowable that surrounds us all. For this reason I have decided to begin this session with a paper based upon my own experience in the hope that it will provide us with an introduction to the discussion to follow of what are the needs in faculty work and how they are to be met.

My talk this morning will be in a sense an "Apologia Pro Vita Sua" because it has occurred to me that as I begin my new work with Christian faculty members that it might be valuable to stop and examine the steps which brought me to the realization that I, as a historian and teacher, was a Christian and, more specifically, an Anglican. The way I took was the way which opened to me, and was not necessarily the only way or a way that anyone else could use. But it was my way, and I have dared to think that you whose concern it is to bring faculty members to the realization that they too are Christian might find something usable and useful in the story.

As I try to think back through the veil which hides my childhood from me, it seems that I cannot remember a time when I was not a skeptic; awed and frightened by the mysteries of existence, the world, other people, and myself, but dissatisfied with the apparently easy way in which these frightening mysteries were explained away by those around me. I wanted answers, but was given only comforting words; and did not realize that the purpose of these comforting words was to affirm the existence of the fundamental mystery of the human situation, not to dispel it. It seemed to me that the explanations offered were fairy stories, similar to and of the same quality as the story of the stork as an answer to where I came from and how my birth occurred, or of Santa Claus to explain the origins of the gifts and toys which appeared at Christmas.

I began to believe that I was almost alone in my fears and concern; that all others were indifferent; and that they were not afraid because they lacked the courage to compare their explanations with the mysteries they pretended to explain and find them wanting. The church and its ministers to me were the most guilty. They were the most certain, and their explanations the least believable, particularly as I became a little older and learned something of science and mathematics. Here was a system of knowledge that was exact and precise, based upon evidence and measurement, that gave definite answers. These words, it seemed to me, were truly comforting. The mysterious lost part of its frightening and awesome character as I became convinced that it was merely lack of knowledge, not the unknowable; and I knew too little to understand that beneath the massive structure of scientific and mathematical knowledge there was an abyss of meaninglessness and nothingness; that this vast framework had been erected upon a line of faith called axioms or assumptions which had no foundation, no proof, no evidence to substantiate them.

I was at this stage when I began the professional study of history. I had almost forgotten the mystery which surrounds us and intrudes into the center of our being. I no longer asked or concerned myself with fundamental questions, at least I tried to avoid them, and it was only infrequently that involuntarily they would intrude themselves into my mind. Each time the awe and fear reappeared and I was uncomfortable, so I strove to banish them to the realm of the undiscussed and unthought of, where, to my way of thinking, they properly belonged. As a beginning student of history (this was a long time ago in the early 1930s) I was a scientist, a believer of fact, and I interpreted my task to be the use of scientific procedures to find out exactly what happened in the past and then to record it. I strove to free my mind from all preconceptions, all prejudice, all thought, and to become what would be, in effect, an investigating and recording machine.

This phase was very brief,[794] and lasted, as I now remember it, only through that part of my introductory study which concerned itself with method, for I soon learned that though almost two whole generations of American historians had given lip service to this point of view, their work belied their professions. If the facts were capable of being ascertained and recorded exactly as they occurred, then historians should be agreed, but in my reading I soon found out that in no single instance had any two historians examined the same evidence and arrived at an agreed set of facts. And each time that I began to struggle to learn what happened in any particular episode in the past and went back to the original sources I found what appeared to be serious and invalidating errors in all that had been previously written. At first I thought that these disagreements, these omissions, these errors were merely the fault of the individual historians, who, for reasons that were unexplainable, had failed properly to use the method that had been developed, and that my investigations and writing would not have the same weaknesses. But then, and this was the most disheartening part of the business, when I began to write, I found that I could not reproduce on paper the vision of the past in all its accuracy and fullness that I had seen while conducting my investigation. The words, sentences, and paragraphs did not fit the

427

reality as I had seen or imagined it, and what I wrote seemed different from what I had originally thought. Facts, singly established, changed their character and form when combined with others, and all were subtly modified and distorted when transmuted into words.

I began to find that instead of being an investigating and recording machine, as I had planned, I had become a child again playing with a game box in which the facts were little round balls to be manipulated into holes and held there while the rest were brought into a similar position; but that now the balls and the holes did not retain their shape and position. Each time I would have it seemingly completed and all in place, everything would change and all would have to be done over again. Facts were not the answer, for facts were not so simple as they appeared to be. Forty-nine facts, as I soon learned, could add up to a complete falsehood if the fiftieth was unknown or deliberately omitted, and if the fiftieth were found and included, then there was always the fifty-first.

These difficulties and defects that I found in the method that I had been taught disillusioned me with my teachers, but my conviction that the world and man were explainable in terms of themselves remained unshaken. I still believed that history, properly studied, could give permanently valid answers not only concerning what happened in the past, but also for the present and the future; that what was wrong with man and society was a lack of knowledge and understanding of the natural laws that governed them; and that when this knowledge and understanding were acquired, the problems confronting man and society could be solved. I had misunderstood my task, or rather, I had been misinformed; for the historian could not find the laws which governed man and society merely by gathering the facts and inducing almost semi-automatically from them their coherence and meaning. Instead, he first had to find what the laws were, and then the facts would cohere and confirm.

I turned in my reading from narrative accounts of what happened to the books that concerned themselves with the interpretation and meaning of history, and here I came to complete despair. I had always been what I considered to be a liberal, a skeptic concerning the value of accepted institutions and beliefs, but not concerning the fundamental purpose and meaning of life. I had accepted without question or doubt the assumption that the new, the modern, the contemporary was better than the old, and that in some automatic fashion the human mind was slowly freeing itself from the superstitions that had enchained it in the past. Spengler's *Decline of the West*, which challenged my naive belief in simple and automatic progress, came as a distinct and unwelcome shock to me. His assertion that all societies, including our own, were subject to the same biological laws that governed individual life seemed irrefutable and, without wishing to do so, I was forced to believe that the western world, having passed through the periods of infancy, youth, and maturity, was now in its final and inevitable stage of decay and death.

Spengler's pessimistic conclusions were confirmed by my reading of Henry Adam's "Letter to the Teachers of History in America" in which he used the second law of thermodynamics to prove that the world and man were condemned not to growth but to continuous decline; that through increasing entropy the ultimate fate of all that existed was cold, cheerless, static and perpetual night. Before reading Spengler and Adams I had always assumed that the liberal, the scientific view of society was optimistic, that it was the old and discredited view of man as a fallen creature, condemned by a jealous God to toil and sweat that was pessimistic. But now I had to change my opinion, for as I went back into the liberal tradition I found not life, hope, and joy, but harsh and irrevocable natural laws dooming man to inevitable famine, plagues, and wars. Malthus, Ricardo, and James Mill, unlike as they were in many aspects of their economic and political thought, were united in their belief that man could do nothing to improve his own situation economically because economic affairs were governed by laws. The iron law of wages was one and that concerning population another, which would have their way regardless of what man wanted or tried to do.

I began to read Jefferson, whom I had always regarded as a spiritual forefather, in the light of my new understanding and to my surprise he was not as optimistic as I had hitherto thought. His statements to Madison that American freedom and democracy were the products of the free land and great natural resources of the new continent began to have a new meaning, particularly when the corollary is considered which said that once we became crowded together in cities as they were in Europe we would eat upon one another as they did. His equating of the good society of virtuous men with agriculture and his dismissal of city dwellers, artisans, and craftsmen as sores on the body politic now had a different sound as I began to realize that I was an urbanite, living in an urban community and the people whom I wanted to help to a better society were in a similar situation.

The period of which I am writing was the early thirties, the Depression years, and I could not believe that the situation in which we found ourselves was without a remedy. The liberal tradition, however, not only had none, but also said very flatly that the way things were was the way they had to be, that the Depression with its unemployment, its starvation, its death was a natural and normal way to rid ourselves of surplus population; that if this decrease did not occur, it would have to come through additional wars, new plagues, or general starvation. Spengler was right. We inhabitants of megalopolis had no choice but to eat one another until the whole society died and through natural processes another was born.

My search for comfortable words through science and natural law had thus ended in failure. There was no comfort in a philosophy and point of view which doomed all human struggle to defeat and assured me that the only outcome of life was death. I had for many years accepted this as my personal fate and prided myself on my willingness to accept it as a testimony to my personal courage, proving that I did not have to use the crutches that sustained other men, but I was unwilling to accept this conclusion as it affected mankind and the generations unborn. They, in spite of all, I felt certain, would live, but to sustain this hope I had to have a new philosophy, a new science of man, for that which I had originally substituted for the old and the discredited, gave not hope, but despair. This new philosophy and its science of man was, of course, there waiting for me in Marxism, which took the same materials that had led Jefferson, Malthus, Ricardo, Mill, Adams, and Spengler to enunciate a deterministic philosophy of death, and from them wrought a new synthesis promising life.

Marx, like most other social observers who based their conclusions upon what they called science, considered himself to be exclusively naturalistic. To him, life, consciousness, thought, memory, and all other vital and mental phenomena were aspects of matter and capable of being explained and understood in terms of themselves. But his point of view was more agreeable to me as a historian than those of the liberals because Marx honored the past as a necessary period of preparation for a glorious and perfected future while most of the enlightened observers of the 18th, 19th, and 20th centuries despised the past as a long era in which the virtuous but ignorant people had been victimized by self-interested kings, nobles, and priests. I too had come to honor and love the past and had been forced to realize through my examination of the correspondence of hundreds of men who had lived in the 18th and 19th centuries that they were brighter, better-informed, and more intelligent than I. But the problem remained to explain why it was that able, intelligent, and disinterested as they in many instances were, they had not been able to create and hand down a better world for us to live in. Marx had an answer to this dilemma also. They had not been able to do other than they did because they were acting under the influence of the laws of history and society, and these laws had their origin not in the consciousness of men, but in the means of production, in the economic organization and processes developed by the society, and so the men in any particular era had been unable to transcend the circumstances in which they lived.

Many of the difficulties which had previously bothered me as a historian were thus explained away. The facts which I and other historians had tried to deal with were not facts at all. What we had been doing was to examine consciously the conscious records left by men who themselves were unaware of the laws and forces which governed their actions. We were bound to get confused and contradictory answers, just as men had done in regard to falling bodies before Galileo explained the apparent varying speeds by an analysis of the countervailing forces. There was a uniformity and regularity behind the confused appearance of reality; so that now I had the clue, the proper method, I could begin to ascertain what really happened in the past. The time was now about 1935, I had finished my master's degree, had taught for a year, and was beginning my work for the doctorate. I was in the South and my chief concern was with its economic and political situation, relatively so much worse off than the rest of the country, and I determined to examine the circumstances in the early 19th century which had produced this result.

Marx himself in his articles on the American Civil War in the *New York Tribune* had provided the terms and the fundamental analysis. The war was not fought for political or moral reasons. Slavery and states' rights were not the issues. The war was a revolution in which a rising bourgeois class in the capitalistic North had thrown off the restraining shackles imposed upon its growth and development by a feudal, agricultural South, and, as part of the historical task, had accomplished the final emancipation of that part of the proletariat which was held in bondage. The way was now open for this new class, in its proper time, (which, in 1935 did not seem so far off as it does in 1955) to seize power in the final and perfecting revolution.

I was writing a thesis and time was short so I selected as the proper unit for my study the subject of banking and the credit system in my native state of Georgia in the period between 1810 and 1860. I was involved in this task for the two years between 1935 and 1937 and strange and, from my point of view, unpredictable things were happening in the world around me as I centered my attention on the preceding century. The essentially pragmatic administration of Franklin D. Roosevelt, acting with courage, confidence, and intelligence, had begun to restore the American society and economy to a sound and healthy condition not by the destruction of individual liberty, but by a new birth of freedom. Internal peace and the rule of law was brought back into the country by a strengthened and invigorated government which protected the right of industrial labor to organize, provided useful work for the unemployed, increased the income of farmers, and restored profits and security to industrial, commercial, and financial enterprises.

This result did not make sense to me. The crisis, a natural and predictable result of the laws of capitalism, should have created a revolutionary sentiment in the minds of the exploited workers and farmers which in truth would so frighten the bourgeoisie that they would throw off the liberal disguises which masked the fact of their rule and resort to a naked and unlimited dictatorship. The United States, Great Britain, France, and the other capitalistic countries should, it seemed to me, follow the path established by Hitler and Nazi Germany, but they did not and I could not understand why. A similar problem was confronting me in my research on the early part of the nineteenth century. The United States in 1837 was also in the grip of an economic crisis with a large internal and external debt, and this crisis, like its successor in 1929, had been brought about by a mixture of domestic and foreign pressures. Observers in 1837 had blamed the crisis on Andrew Jackson and the financial policies he had forced upon the country in his war upon that massive and powerful private monopoly the Bank of the United States, and what was bothering me was the realization that I was beginning to believe that these observers were right.

I did not want to be forced to defend the actions of a wealthy and aristocratic Philadelphia banker against Jackson, the spokesman and tribune of the people, but in June, 1837, Nicholas Biddle, the head of the Bank of the United States, realizing that he could not collect what was owing to the institution or pay its foreign and domestic debt unless something was done, used the great power of the institution to protect and restore the national economy that had been wrecked by the mistakes of the political administration.

The surmounting of these two economic crises one hundred years apart could not be adequately explained in Marxian terms of class struggle. Biddle and Roosevelt both inherited wealth and both determined at a very early age to devote themselves to the public service, but when the opportunity came they rescued the whole country and its economy, not one segment or class. Both talked not of the conflict of economic interest between manufacturers, workers, merchants, bankers and farmers, but of their mutual interdependence, and how if the farmer and worker could be made into purchasers, manufacturers and merchants could sell. Each of these wealthy public leaders believed in order and the rule of law, but both valued freedom; and they found that individual liberty could not be maintained except in a society in which government and its institutions were strong enough to restrain not only the weak and numerous, but also the powerful few.

I was forced to begin a reexamination of all my beliefs about the American political and economic system and the figure who soon began to take a dominant position was the man I had considered to be the arch-spokesman for special privilege, a defender of monarchy and all its evils, and one who had tried to fasten upon the United States all the inherited weaknesses of the British Constitution. His name, of course, was Alexander Hamilton, and I began to read with a new vision what he had said in the Constitutional Convention and in his private correspondence about the nature of man and society. Take all men, he once said, and what are they governed by? Their passions and their interests. He quoted David Hume, who said that in devising a government we should consider all men to be knaves and governed by their interests; and later Hamilton warned that if all power were given to the many, they would oppress the few. Similarly, if all power were given to the few, they would oppress the many. So that in any proper form of government, each, the many and the few, must be possessed of power to protect itself from the other.

This view of man and society seemed dimly familiar to me but I was reluctant to accept it. It meant the abandonment of all hopes of a perfected society in which perfect men lived in permanent peace and harmony. If all men were governed by their passions and interest, if all societies and governments could be corrupted, then so was I and so could be the utopia which Marx and I envisioned. Something of the sort was happening in the Soviet Union and I began to realize that perhaps Hamilton was right after all.

The old and inherited principles and institutions were not without merit or use, particularly those of Great Britain and the United States, which, admittedly imperfect and in constant need of change, did provide an opportunity for men of courage, capacity, and intelligence to work towards the solution of problems without fear of what would happen to them if they failed. Not having the correct principles of social organization nor the aim of a perfected society, they could go about meeting needs to the best of their ability. I did not know what was happening to me or my beliefs about history, politics, and economics, but obviously something was. I was no longer a liberal or a Marxist and the only name that I could apply to myself was that of pragmatist, a historian who judges men and institutions by their fruits, their usefulness, not their logical consistency nor their expressed purposes.

This is still my position, though I have changed the name. As a historian I am seeking to know, to understand, and to evaluate the past, but always I realize that I will not know or understand completely or evaluate with exact justice. Through all my wanderings and doubts, however, one conviction has never wavered or been lost and this is the firm belief that life is meaningful and has purpose. I always remained confident that bad as things appeared, all hope was not lost, and that mankind would, to use Faulkner's phrases endure and prevail. In my ignorance, I once again thought I was alone for all other men, it seemed to me, knew what was the truth even though frequently the truth they knew did not set them free, but rather enslaved them.

I have now come in my time schedule to the years between 1939 and 1942, very consequential years between the outbreak of war in Europe and that day in October when my friends and neighbors most politely asked me to defend them. I was teaching at a small Episcopal college for accidental reasons and as part of the community participated in the daily and Sunday chapel services. These breaks in the routine of teaching were a welcome relief as they provided a brief interval in each day for quiet thought in pleasantly formal surroundings, but for many months I thought they were and could be no more than that. I would, on occasions, pick up the *Book of Common Prayer* to take pleasure in the magnificent cadences of its prose and once for no particular reason that I can remember began to read its preface written in 1789 in Philadelphia, just two years after the Constitution of the United States was composed there.

"It is a most invaluable part of that blessed liberty wherewith Christ hath made us free," the preface begins, "that in his worship different forms and usages may without offense be allowed, provided the substance of the Faith be kept entire; and that, in every Church, what cannot be clearly determined to belong to Doctrine must be referred to Discipline; and therefore, by common consent and authority, may be altered, abridged, enlarged, amended, or otherwise disposed of, as may seem most convenient for the edification of the people, according to the various exigency of times and occasions." This paragraph startled me as did the final one which said, "And now, this important work being brought to a conclusion, it is hoped the whole will be received and examined by every true member of our Church, and every sincere Christian, with a meek, candid, and charitable frame of mind; without prejudice or prepossessions; seriously considering what Christianity is, and what the truths of the Gospel are; and earnestly beseeching Almighty God to accompany with his blessing every endeavor for promulgating them to mankind in the clearest, plainest, most affecting and majestic manner, for the sake of Jesus Christ, our blessed Lord and Savior."

There was something familiar in these words, reminiscent of something I knew very well and after lunch in my office I took down the records of the Federal Convention and turned to a speech made by Benjamin Franklin on the final day which requested all there to accept and sign the Constitution. "I confess," Franklin said, "that there are several parts of this constitution which I do not at present approve, but I am not sure I shall never approve them: For having lived long, I have experienced many instances of being obliged by better information or fuller consideration to change opinions . . . which I once thought right, but found to be otherwise. It is therefore that the older I grow, the more apt I am to doubt my own judgment, and to pay more respect to the judgment of others . . . In these sentiments . . . I agree to this Constitution with all its faults, if they are such; because I believe a general government necessary for us, and there is no form of government but what may be a blessing to the people if well administered, and believe further that this is likely to be well administered for a course of years, and can only end in despotism, as other forms have done before it, when the people shall become so corrupted as to need despotic government, being incapable of any other. I doubt too whether any other convention we can obtain may be able to make a better Constitution. For when you assemble a number of men to have the advantage of their joint wisdom, you inevitably assemble with those men, all their prejudices, their passions, their errors of opinion, their local interests, and their selfish views. From such an assembly can a perfect production be expected? It therefore astonishes me . . . to find this system approaching so near to perfection as it does . . . Thus I consent . . . to this Constitution because I expect no better and . . . I cannot help expressing a wish that every member of the Convention who may still have objections to it, would with me, on this occasion, doubt a little of his own infallibility, and to make manifest our unanimity, put his name to this instrument."

I wish I could say to you that the resemblance in tone between the Preface and Franklin's speech, the latter of which had seemed to me to be a complete statement of my own beliefs about history, politics, and life, was the effective cause of my awakening to the realization that in my struggle to understand and make sense out of the past I had finally come back to the tradition which I thought I had abandoned in my youth; but I cannot. This realization came, however, in the same years from the reading of Reinhold Niebuhr's *The Nature and Destiny of Man*, which sent me back to the Prayer Book, to the General Confession, the Collects, the Creeds, and other formularies, and to the understanding that finally, through the Grace of God, I, who had wandered for years in a far country, had been led back to the truth which frees instead of enslaves and found the words that in moments of doubt, despair, and torment are truly comfortable. I had found confirmation of my fundamental belief that life and history had meaning and purpose; that my search though never to be ended, was useful, and that man, though he sought to destroy himself and his neighbors, could through Love and Grace, not only endure and prevail, but also be redeemed.

Appendix 2

See Chapter 10

The Liberal and Conservative Traditions in the United States[795]

Thomas Payne Govan

Thomas Jefferson is best remembered as the American who wrote that "all men are created equal," and that "there are rights which it is useless to surrender to the government, and which governments have yet always been found to invade. These are the rights of thinking and publishing our thoughts by speaking or writing; the right of free commerce; the right of personal freedom." He has been rightly enshrined as one of the nation's heroes, and his words, as one side of the truth, must be believed and praised. They are key affirmations in the American tradition, and, as such, have performed a useful function in preventing the too easy establishment of false orthodoxies or permanent class and caste distinctions.

They are not, however, the whole truth, and Jefferson, if followed too closely, leads to pessimism, because to him democracy and self-government were accidents based upon a particular material circumstance. Americans could govern themselves, he wrote to Madison, only "as long as we remain virtuous; and I think we shall be so, as long as agriculture is our principal object, which will be the case, while there remain vacant lands in any part of America. When

438

we get piled upon one another in large cities, as in Europe, we shall become corrupt as in Europe, and go to eating one another as they do there." Later he said, "I consider the class of artificers as the panderers of vice, and the instruments by which the liberties of a country are generally overthrown," and again that "The mobs of great cities add just so much to the support of pure government, as sores to the strength of the human body."

These harsh and dogmatic judgments concerning the character of the urban populace were not in contradiction to Jefferson's words in the Declaration of Independence. The equality there affirmed was that of the creature at birth, when, according to John Locke's sensationalist philosophy, the mind and character of all men were malleable blank tablets to be written upon by experience and education. Virtue, vice, and the inequalities and differences which subsequently appeared were thus the products of individual life and training.[796]

Jefferson, without being false to these fundamental assumptions, could write, "Those who labor in the earth are the chosen people of God . . . whose breasts He has made His peculiar deposit for substantial and genuine virtue. . . . Corruption of morals in the mass of cultivators is a phenomenon of which no age nor nation has furnished an example," and then conclude that "generally speaking, the proportion which the aggregate of other classes of citizens bears in any State to that of its husbandmen, is the proportion of its unsound to its healthy parts, and is a good enough barometer whereby to measure its degree of corruption."

Alexander Hamilton agreed with this denunciation of the morals of the urban groups. "Your people, sir," he has been quoted as saying, "are a great beast." He likewise believed in the fundamental equality of men, but the basis of his belief was different. To him, not a member of any church but a thoroughly Christian thinker, all men were equal because each was a sinner and there was no health in him. As early as 1775, he quoted with approval David Hume's maxim "that in contriving any system of government, and fixing the several checks and controls of the constitution, every man ought to be supposed a knave, and to have no other end, in all his actions, but private interest."[797] In the constitutional convention he stated in one speech that "most individuals and all public bodies" are governed by the "passions of avarice, ambition, interest," and in another, "Take mankind as they are, and what are they governed by? Their passions. There may be in every government a few choice spirits, who may act from more worthy motives. One great error is that we suppose mankind more honest than they are. Our prevailing passions are ambition and interest; and it will ever be the duty of a wise government to avail itself of the passions, in order to make them subservient to the public good; for these ever induce us to action."[798]

Hamilton could not, therefore, agree with Jefferson's exemption of the cultivators of the land from the corruption which was inherent in all men. He also thought that the problems of government were more complex than did Jefferson, who once said, "Only lay down true principles, and adhere to them inflexibly." Hamilton, on the other hand, stated in the Constitutional Convention that "We are now forming a republican government. Real liberty is never found in despotism or the extremes of democracy, but in moderate governments. Those who mean to form a solid republican government ought to proceed to the confines of another government. As long as offices are open to all men, and no constitutional rank is established, it is pure republicanism. But if we incline too much to democracy, we shall soon shoot into monarchy.[799] The difference of property is already great among us. Commerce and industry will still increase the disparity. Your government must meet this state of things, or combinations will in process of time undermine your system."

The liberal and conservative traditions thus found opposing spokesman in Jefferson and Hamilton at the beginning of the American republic. Jefferson, in theory not in action,[800] was almost the archetype of the liberal in politics, theology, and philosophy. He was a many-sided and attractive man, interested in all the manifold experiences of life. To each he brought an inquiring and open mind which would discard any cherished belief that seemed in conflict with new evidence. No old and established dogma had authority with him. The result of this attitude, however, was not an optimistic philosophy of human freedom, but a materialistic and despairing determinism. The liberals of the period of enlightenment, trusting too much in the powers of right reason, made themselves and other men the slaves of uniform natural laws which they thought underlay the conflicting appearance of the world.

Jefferson became the spokesman in America for the point of view which said that economic enterprise was governed by natural laws with which man interfered at his peril. The wisest policy for any government was to leave all economic activity unregulated, uncontrolled, undirected, because that government was best which governed least, stating in justification "that were it made a question, whether no law, as among the savage Americans, or too much law, as among the civilized Europeans, submits man to the greatest evil, one who has seen both conditions would pronounce [it] to [be] the last; and that the sheep are happier of themselves, than under the care of the wolves."

The wolves, of course, were not the proper guardians of the sheep, but neither were the natural laws of Ricardo and Malthus, the one limiting wages to the bare cost of subsistence, and the other dooming mankind to eternal famine, pestilence, and war as a remedy for an inevitable overpopulation. Hamilton repudiated these deterministic doctrines and refused to accept a definition of men which separated them into two classes, the sheep and the wolves. He knew that man, unrestrained by customary (not natural) law and tradition, was more often a wolf than a sheep, and that anarchy was inimical to human freedom, because it leads by reaction to tyranny.

Another danger to liberty for Hamilton was the unrestrained authority of an individual or a group, for, as he said, "Give all power to the many, they will oppress the few. Give all power to the few, they will oppress the many. Both therefore ought to have power that each may defend itself against the other." Like Burke, he advocated the principle of the British Constitution because he believed that through it alone could public strength be united with individual security and freedom. Power in this government was unlimited, but it was divided between a monarch and two legislative bodies, one the changing representatives of the people and the other the permanent representatives of the aristocracy, because none of the three was virtuous and all had to be distrusted.

Both Hamilton and Burke predicted that the French revolution would end in tyranny because it was based upon the postulate that ignorance and neglect of the rights of man were the sole causes of oppression and corruption in government, and, having defined these rights and guaranteed their preservation, it gave virtually complete power to a single legislative body.

The test of history confirmed these predictions because freedom, which means the right to make errors and to adopt wrong policies (to commit sins), could not endure under a government based on inflexible, dogmatic principles, whether established by right reason or Divine revelation. Such maxims as that written by Jefferson, "Only lay down true principles, and adhere to them inflexibly," lead to tyranny when acted upon, regardless of whether it was the Church, the king ruling by Divine Right, a Marx, Lenin, Stalin, or Hitler who formulated them.

The conservative position, consequently, was not the opposite of the liberal, but rather was in the center between two extremes. It did not stand for authority against freedom; instead it was a guard against the universal tendency of men to confuse the relative with the absolute, and the all too human with the Divine. Hamilton and Burke were not opposed to the use of human reason (like Luther they welcomed correction by arguments based on scripture or right reason) but they remained constantly aware of the limits of reason and revelation and of the hazards that both introduced into human history.[801]

These random reflections upon the conservative and liberal traditions as exemplified by Hamilton and Jefferson have been caused by the rereading of a book by twelve Southerners, published in 1930, entitled, *I'll Take My Stand: The South and the Agrarian Tradition*,[802] in which the "Southern way of life" was contrasted with the "American or prevailing way," and the distinction was described "in the phrase Agrarianism versus Industrialism." The agrarian society, they said, "is hardly one that has no use at all for industries, for professional vocations, for scholars and artists, and for the life of cities." Rather, it was "one in which agriculture is the leading vocation. . . . The theory of agrarianism is that the culture of the soil is the best and most sensitive of vocations, and that therefore it should have the economic preference and enlist the maximum number of workers."

The resemblance of this statement to Jefferson's "Those who labor in the earth are the chosen people of God" was not accidental because it was derived from him, and the group shared his hostility to government and his belief in individualism, the small community, and what is called state rights. The very term they used to designate their program came out of the leveling and liberal traditions, since agrarianism, as a radical doctrine based upon the principle that monopoly in land was the root of economic injustice and should be remedied by an equal division among free-holders, was introduced into America by Thomas Paine.

These modern reformers repudiated what they called liberalism, priding themselves upon the "antique conservatism" of the South which, according to John Crowe Ransom, was the heritage from "a strain which came out of Europe most convinced of the virtues of establishment, contrasting with those strains which seem for the most part to have dominated the other sections, and which came out of Europe feeling rebellious toward all establishments." Allen Tate went further and claimed that the South "was a feudal society," but, he regretfully confessed, it was "without a feudal religion." Its religious impulse, consequently, "was inarticulate simply because it tried to encompass its destiny within the terms of Protestantism, in origin, a non-agrarian and trading religion."

Lyle Lanier, another contributor, thought that the peculiar virtue of an agrarian society was political democracy, the great movement for human freedom which began with the Renaissance and culminated at the close of the eighteenth century with the formation of the American and French republics. But democracy was being destroyed by the "counter-influence" of the industrial revolution and could be preserved only by restoring the agrarian economy. Frank Owsley contended that at the time of the Civil War there were "two divergent economic and social systems, two civilizations, in fact."[803] The North was commercial-industrial, and South, agrarian. "The fundamental and passionate ideal for which the South stood and fell," he wrote, "was the ideal of an agrarian society . . . the old and accepted manner of life for which Egypt, Greece, Rome, England and France had stood."

Two of these writers are poets and critics, one is a philosopher, and the other a historian, so that the confusion of thought and terminology found in these not untypical quotations is disappointing. They begin with a definition of an agrarian society as one in which agriculture was the predominant way of life, but which did not exclude industry, commerce, and the arts. Finance was not mentioned, but since they did not advocate a return to barter, it can be assumed that they had no objections to the use of the market and of money as the medium of exchange. Most of the United States conformed to this definition until late in the nineteenth century, but Mr. Owsley stated that at the time of the Civil War there were two civilizations within the nation, one commercial and industrial, and the other agrarian. He ignored the profitable and extensive agriculture of up-state New York, Pennsylvania, New Jersey and the Connecticut Valley, not to mention the Middle West; and also the tobacco industry in Virginia and North Carolina; the textile mills in upper South Carolina and at Augusta and Columbus, Georgia; the iron foundries and coal mines of Virginia, Georgia, Tennessee, and Alabama; and the social and financial importance of the merchants, lawyers, and bankers in the pre-Civil War South.

Mr. Tate described the South as feudal, ignoring the distinctions between serfdom and chattel slavery and those between investiture of land and holding it in fee simple. Mr. Lanier called the same society democratic, while Mr. Ransom found that its peculiar virtue was its sympathy to the English establishment even though it had no Church or formal aristocracy, and its religious tradition, like that of the whole United States, was predominantly Calvinist and Baptist.

The inhabitants of the southern United States did have a culture and a tradition, but not a separate one. They lived in a society which had been produced out of medieval Europe by the Renaissance, the Reformation, the Commercial, Scientific, and Industrial Revolutions, Capitalism, and Political Democracy. Their spiritual and intellectual fathers were the giants whose teachings shaped and formed the whole Western world and who were shared in common by all men in the West. The differences which distinguished the South from other areas of the

United States were, as a whole, minor and inconsequential, and, in actual fact, were less important than the differences to be found within the section itself.

The mixed agriculture of the valleys of Virginia and Tennessee and of the Lexington and Nashville basins had more in common with the agriculture of Pennsylvania, New York, New Jersey, and New England than it did with the industrialized, single-crop agriculture of the cotton, rice, and sugar plantations in other areas of the South. The southern mountaineers had a different dialect as well as different modes and customs of life from those who lived in the Piedmont and the Coastal Plain, but the greatest internal difference was that between urban and rural people which existed, with notable exceptions, in all parts of the country until the day of the automobile, the paved road, electricity, the telephone, radio, television and the consolidated school.

The South, however, had a sense of unity within itself and of separation from the rest of the United States, which was caused, according to Ulrich Phillips, by its determination that "it was and should remain a White Man's country."[804] Through a series of political and economic accidents, Negroes were concentrated in the southern United States in greater numbers than in other areas, and their enslavement continued for approximately sixty years longer. The southern states seceded from the union to defend this institution of slavery and precipitated a civil war in which they were defeated. The memory of this common effort and of the "Lost Cause" preserved this Southern feeling of distinction and difference from the rest of the nation,[805] but it seems strange that a group of intellectuals would consider it more important than the common heritage they shared with the entire West.

The Agrarians did so, however, because they were writing at the height of the speculative expansion of the American economy which preceded the depression of 1929. The tawdriness of the national culture as exemplified by its political, economic, social, and religious leaders in this drab era alienated them, and they looked back, conservatively they thought, to a gentler, richer period. They were tired of progressivism, of go-getting, of bigness, of mechanization, which they identified with northern industrialism. They rightly connected liberalism and materialism and rejected both, but by accepting the Jeffersonian principles they abandoned conservatism and became not only liberals and materialists but also Manichaean and Pelagian heretics. They made the Pelagian assumption that man was naturally virtuous and had the choice between the good or evil forces which the Manicheans said struggled for domination of the world. The good, they said, was the agricultural life; the bad, the industrial life—both ways of making a living. (Karl Marx himself did not so rigidly hold to a doctrine of economic determinism.) They were also pessimistic, like Jefferson and the liberals, since they knew that the continued development of science and industrialism, the corrupting forces, was almost inevitable, and they believed that religion, art, and the amenities of life could not survive under such conditions.

"Religion," they affirmed, "is our submission to the general intention of nature that is fairly inscrutable; it is the sense of our role as creatures within it." Their God, however, was so weak that He could not continue to work in a "nature industrialized, transformed into cities and artificial habitations, manufactured into commodities," because this was "no longer nature but a highly simplified picture of nature." Their art, man's greatest and most nearly creative activity, was similarly weak and ineffectual since it could not exist "in an industrial age except by some local and unlikely suspension of the industrial drive." It could not take the raw materials provided by life and draw from them their aesthetic form and meaning. Such an art is hardly art, as such a God is certainly not God. And as for the amenities, the manners and furnishings which distinguish the gentle from the coarse life, every gentle person and family always has them, regardless of location or circumstances.

This book would have no importance if its exaggeration of sectional differences and its confusion concerning the liberal and conservative traditions were found in it alone. Unfortunately, however, this is not the case, and almost all American historians are guilty of similar distortions. Samuel E. Morison and Henry S. Commager, whose textbook *The Growth of the American Republic* is justifiably praised, state concerning the break between Jefferson and Hamilton that it was not personal, but the "political expression of a deep lying antagonism between two great American interests—the planting-slaveholding interest, typified by Virginia; and the mercantile-shipping-financial interest, typified by Massachusetts. . . . American political history until 1865 is largely the story of these rival interests, capitalist and agrarian, Northern and Southern, contending for the control of the government."

This statement is less justifiable than any made by the Agrarians because they at least recognized that the owner of a plantation growing crops for sale was a capitalist. What is even stranger, however, is the assertion of a supposed political antagonism between the merchants, ship-owners, and financiers of international trade, and the producers of the exports which were the basic of that trade. None of these groups could have existed without the others and they were further united by their common opposition to the protective tariff and other limitations upon free trade. The real political conflict was between those whose interests were international and others whose primary concern was the expansion of the internal American economy: the industrialists, the growers of crops for the domestic market, and the nationalists.

The major controversies that divided the American people in this period are obscured by this central interpretive paragraph of Morison and Commager's book. Two great debates were being conducted simultaneously: the one between liberals and conservatives over the proper role of the federal government in relation to the states, the individual citizens, and the economy; and the other over slavery. The two debates were related in that those who thought that slavery was immoral and should be ended by action of the federal government advocated the strengthening of its powers, while those who insisted that slavery must be continued (even though most of them also believed it to be immoral) defended individual freedom (including the right to hold other men as slaves) and state rights.[806]

This forced contraction of political and moral debates into a framework of economic and sectional conflict has characterized most twentieth-century studies of the American past. Frederick J. Turner,

Walter P. Webb, and many others explained the development of American democracy and freedom by the presence of a frontier of unsettled lands and concluded with the fear that the government would become tyrannical when these no longer existed. Conflicts over land policy and other economic questions occupied most of their attention, and by dismissing intrasectional differences as of no consequence, they termed them sectional. Charles A. Beard, an economic determinist (most of the time) who used Marxian terminology, depicted the past as a conflict between the industrial, commercial, and financial bourgeoisie and the feudal landowners of the South. Vernon L. Parrington (who, without defining it, was the first to use the term agrarian in its modern sense as a synonym for agriculture), writing on American intellectual history, distinguished between the good contributors who were southern or western agrarians and socialists (and some easterners who were wise enough to share their views) and the bad who were either defenders of mercantilism and industrialism or effete easterners influenced by corrupt Europeans.[807]

Jefferson, in these varied interpretations was the good symbol of the South, the West, agriculture, the frontier, and feudalism, depending upon the writer, but in all cases he was the spokesman for freedom, equality, and democracy. Hamilton, on the other hand, was the evil symbol of aristocracy, authoritarianism, and exploitative northeastern capitalism.

The two men were in fundamental opposition, but the differences that separated them were not primarily economic or sectional. Their disagreements had a political, philosophical, and theological basis, and can best be expressed by the phrase "liberal against conservative."

When George Washington became president of the United States and Jefferson and Hamilton were the leading members of his cabinet, the nation was weak, virtually bankrupt, and dependent upon Europe and European possessions both for its tools and equipment and as a market for its agricultural produce. It owned vast areas of unsettled lands west of the Appalachians, but these were occupied by semi-hostile Indian tribes, and

American control was challenged by the British from Canada and the Spanish from Louisiana and the Floridas.

Hamilton believed that the federal government had to have strength to meet these problems and to discourage domestic adventurers, who, he thought, wanted to create anarchical conditions so that they could seize tyrannical power and destroy freedom. His aim was to supply this strength, which, with a capitalistic economy, required an abundant supply of liquid capital; a trustworthy medium of exchange; an effective mercantile and transportation system; and an industrial establishment which would not only provide the necessary manufactured goods, but whose workers would wear the wool and cotton, eat the meat and vegetables, and smoke and chew the tobacco produced by American agriculture.

He wanted to enlist the "ambition and avarice" of all men in support of the government, to tie them to it through "ligaments of interest," but, at the same time, "to make them subservient to the public good." The disparities of wealth and power created by such a system, if controlled, would, he knew, be dangerous, so he argued that "Your government must meet this state of things, or combinations will in process of time undermine your system."

Jefferson, however, thought that these same dangers could best be solved by leaving individuals free to follow their own inclinations and interest as guided and controlled by natural law. Governmental power was the great danger to be guarded against, and anarchy, if that should result, was preferable to a state which imposed any but the most simple and necessary restraints upon personal freedom. He could not defeat Hamilton's financial measures (funding the national debt and assuming the state debts, and chartering the Bank of the United States) because the "avarice" of the wealthy and powerful groups in a majority of the states was enlisted in support of them, but he had more success in stopping the remainder of the program.

Hamilton's other proposals—for a regulatory protective tariff, for subsidies for industry and agriculture, and for the sale of public lands at a price sufficiently high to pay for internal improvements and civilizing institutions in the newly opened areas—lacked the support of a powerful and established interest and also promised to limit speculative opportunities. They were defeated and the subsequent industry and commerce, internal improvements, and settlement of the western lands was individually initiated without governmental regulation, direction, or control. Industry began to develop not as the result of public need or plan, but as an incidental effect of the British and French blockades and counter-blockades during the Napoleonic Wars and of the self-imposed American non-intercourse and embargo acts.

The defeat of the recharter of the first Bank of the United States in 1811 eliminated the last of Hamilton's programs. The disastrous consequences of this triumph of liberalism and laissez faire were made apparent by American military and economic weakness during the War of 1812, and Jefferson's successors, Madison, Monroe, and John Quincy Adams, turned back to Hamilton. This second era of conservatism was ended in the 1830s by Jackson, Van Buren, and Calhoun, who, divided as they were about such matters as the presidential succession, nullification, and patronage, were united in opposition to the principle of governmental direction and control of the economy. The liberal principles of Jefferson, that the best government was the least government and that economic enterprise was governed by laws with which men interfere at their peril, were not effectively challenged again until the close of the nineteenth century.

The resulting anarchy in the realms of finance, industry, commerce, and agriculture had the effect that Hamilton anticipated. Individual freedom was destroyed in countless areas by the unrestricted power of private tyrannies established by exploitive corporations. Only the speculators profited as the economy moved through an unrestrained cycle of boom and bust to the financial ruin of farmers, merchants, bankers, manufacturers, and transportation companies. Violence became the accustomed mode of settling disputes over land, water and poker in the Far West, white supremacy in the South, the right of labor to organize, and the conflicting ambitions of rival corporations.

The correction of these evils has been a long and painful return, not yet completed, to the conservative principles of Hamilton and an abandonment of the liberal illusion that unrestrained man will be a sheep not a wolf. Freedom, as Hamilton pointed out many years ago, "is never found in despotism or the extremes of democracy, but in moderate governments,"[808] and can only be preserved by subjecting every man to public authority and protecting him from its abuse through law and tradition. The poets, philosophers, historians, and politicians who have used Hamilton and Jefferson as symbols of opposing class, economic, or sectional interests have done a disservice to history because they have obscured the differences between the liberal and conservative traditions which actually separated them, and thus contributed to the misunderstanding not only of the American past but also of contemporary political and economic conflicts.

Appendix 3

See Chapter 11

A New Birth of Freedom

Thomas Payne Govan

March 17, 1954

Dear Dr. Williams,

Μy proposed subject of study is the American attempt to establish a social order that had as its principal purpose the enlargement of human freedom; and as such, I believe, it lies within the field of interest of the Fund.

This American revolution, which had its sources in the Judaic-Christian tradition and the British development of constitutional government, began in the eighteenth century, but is still going on; and from its beginning there was a group of political theorists who insisted that it and the traditions from which it sprang were man's best hope, perhaps his only hope, of establishing a society "which unites public strength with individual security."

Since 1946 I have been engaged in the preparation of a biography of Nicholas Biddle, President of the Second Bank of the United States, which will be turned over to the publisher, E. P. Dutton and Company, in September, 1954.[809] My study of this early nineteenth-century conservative nationalist, and of the predecessors and contemporaries

452

who shared his general point of view, has led me to question the usual interpretation of American history, which categorizes them as the conscious advocates of an oligarchical government by the rich, the well-born, and the able.

Their purpose, like that of their liberal opponents, was individual freedom in an orderly society; but they, in my opinion, were wiser than the liberals in that they better understood the difficulties which stood in the way of the achievement of this end. Their point of view was expressed in the Constitutional Convention by Alexander Hamilton, who said, "Those who mean to form a solid republican government ought to proceed to the confines of another government. As long as offices are open to all men, and no constitutional rank is established, it is pure republicanism. But if we incline too much to democracy, we shall shoot into a monarchy." He declared himself "to be as zealous an advocate for liberty as any man, whatever," and he warned his fellow-members, "Give all power to the many, they will oppress the few. Give all power to the few, they will oppress the many. Both . . . ought to have power that each may defend itself against the other.[810]

The recognition of the dangers of trusting the few or the many, the individual or the organized group, was one of the main differences which distinguished these traditional conservatives from the liberals, but it has seldom been emphasized by students of the American past. The history of this United States too frequently has been written in terms of the economic conflicts between classes or sections without adequate recognition of the more fundamental ideological differences concerning the best means of achieving individual freedom.

Two debates have occupied the attention of the American people and have been the principal source of political controversy during their national history. Only one of these, slavery, took a sectional form, and it was settled by the Civil War; the other, which was concerned with the proper relation between individuals and government, was essentially national and has continued to the present day. Beginning with Alexander Hamilton and continuing through the administrations of James Monroe and John Quincy Adams, the proponents of the American System of governmental direction, support, and control of social and economic institutions and processes were in the ascendancy.

They acted upon the assumption that the United States was a single nation, and that its citizens had complementary rather than conflicting interests. Their concern was the strength of the nation as a whole, which involved the protection and the support of every individual, and the instrument they used was the national government.

The intention of these traditional conservatives and nationalists was misrepresented by their political opponents, who, motivated in part by ideology and in part by party interest, succeeded in defeating and reversing the whole program under the guise of relieving the country from tyranny and exploitation. The opposing point of view, that of classical liberalism with its deterministic laws of population and wages enunciated by Malthus and Ricardo, was most effectively represented in the United States by Thomas Jefferson (the political ideologist and the organizer of the opposition party in the 1790s) and his uncritical follower, Andrew Jackson. They believed that economic, social, and political matters were controlled by natural laws with which men interfered at their peril, and that the government was best which governed least.

Their victory, which was accomplished by Jackson and his successor, Martin Van Buren, was won in the name of the common people, but it opened the way for the excess of speculative exploitation and private tyranny by powerful individuals which characterized all phases of the latter half of the nineteenth century in the United States. At the close of the century, the United States began a slow return to the point of view of the proponents of the American System, and began to act on the assumption that a society could be free only where individual liberty was restrained and prevented from becoming despotic, while, at the same time, being protected and cherished.

This return from anarchic individualism to a moderate program of social control was resisted by those who based their opposition on the tenets of Jefferson, Jackson, and the classical liberals; and also by another group under the influence of Marxian socialism, who insisted that freedom could be obtained only through a dictatorial state with power to eliminate private property and profits and to establish a rigidly planned and controlled economic system. These collectivists, like the classical liberals, based their conclusions upon positive laws derived from the scientific study of society. The traditional conservatives were not so certain, for their authority was historical experience; but where the liberals ignored the danger from the unrestrained individual and the collectivists ignored the danger of the unrestrained state, conservatives remained aware of the hazards of trusting either the individual or the state.

This middle position has been valued and discussed less than its extreme opponents, largely because of its very lack of certainty or finality and also because it gives no promise of an ultimate utopian harmony in which the best interests of all are to be advanced automatically, or in which all conflicts and problems are to be resolved. And yet, it seems to me, this conservative view may constitute men's greatest hope for achieving a measure of security and freedom, because this anti-deterministic, non-dogmatic, essentially pragmatic rather than positivistic, attitude both values and advocates individual liberty and collective action, but remains aware of the dangers inherent in both.

These conservatives, in my opinion, relied upon an older and more valid conception [that is, the Bible] of the nature of man and society than did their opponents; and their contributions to the cause of individual freedom were of more lasting importance than the contributions to the same cause by those who based their actions upon the rationalistic philosophy of natural law.

The conservatives consciously and deliberately were not seeking to establish a perfect society in which there would be no conflicts or problems. If government were given power to rectify all that was considered wrong, individuals and groups would seize control and use the power for other ends. These usurpers, like the Committee of Public Safety in revolutionary France, the tyrants Napoleon, Hitler, Stalin, and many others in man's unfortunate search for order and freedom, would not reform society, but rather seek to eliminate those whom they feared and those who had the temerity to dissent from their rule.

The task of the conservatives was to guard against this continuing danger and to establish a principle of judgment against which to measure whatever the organized society accomplished and always to find it wanting and in need of improvement. The final truth, the perfect society, could never be possessed, so they were patient and urged that evils be suffered as long as they were sufferable. They were not weak, or opportunistic. Rather they had the wisdom to understand the powerful hold that fear, superstition, and greed had upon all individuals and the institutions and groups with which they were associated, and how difficult a task it was to establish a society "which united public strength with individual security."

I have already done much of the fundamental research upon which these tentative conclusions are based, but they need further examination and criticism before they are incorporated into articles and a book in which I will attempt to set forth this conservative conception as one of the sources of American freedom. Some of the individuals whose political theories and acts will be examined are Alexander Hamilton, John Adams, John Quincy Adams, Henry Clay (after 1824), John C. Calhoun (before 1824), Thomas Jefferson (the author of state papers and the responsible office-holder, not the ideologist), James Madison, Matthew Carey, and Nicholas Biddle.

The proposed year of research and writing will be of great advantage to me as a teacher and historian, and the year 1954-1955 is the most opportune from my personal point of view. A year ago, for various reasons, I voluntarily resigned as Professor of History and head of the department at the University of the South, Sewanee, Tennessee. This year I have had an appointment as Visiting Professor of History at Tulane University, but I have made no commitments for 1954-1955. I plan to continue teaching at the graduate as well as the undergraduate level, but if I make a new connection at this time, it will be a number of years before I can apply for a leave of absence of sufficient duration to do the work described above.

I am, as a consequence, applying to the Fund for the Republic for a grant of seven thousand dollars ($7,000) to enable me to do the proposed research and writing at Cambridge, Massachusetts and Washington, D.C. during 1954-1955.

Sincerely,
Thomas P. Govan

Appendix 4

See Chapter 13

Free to Be Merely a Man

Thomas P. Govan

The Enigma of Human Rights

The central problem of politics in the twentieth century, as in centuries past, is the creation of an orderly society in which each individual can be free, and numerous political thinkers throughout the ages have attempted to define the conditions under which such a society can be achieved. Most of these definitions can be reduced to three basic affirmations which Prime Minister Nehru of the Republic of India restated a short time ago as the guiding principles of his government, "The freedom of the individual, the equality of men, and the rule of law." These constitutional principles, important and useful as they are, are not the whole of the matter. There is another aspect, less capable of being defined than the others, which is described by the late James Weldon Johnson, an American Negro poet, in that portion of his autobiography which told of his first trip out of the United States:

> From the day I set foot in France I became aware of a
> quick readjustment to life and environment. I recaptured
> for the first time since childhood the sense of being just a

human being. I was suddenly free; free from a sense of
impending discomfort, insecurity, danger; free from the
conflict with the Man-Negro dualism and the innumerable
maneuvers in thought and behavior that it compels; free
from the problems of the many obvious or subtle
adjustments to a multitude of bans and taboos; free from
special scorn, special tolerance, special condescension,
special commiseration: free to be merely a man.

This right to be "merely a man" is one of the most important of all
human rights, and yet it is probably the one that is most difficult of all
to establish and maintain. There is a quality in the human mind
which balks at the idea that a man is simply a man. Each person is
aware that a man is somehow both more than and less than a man, and
is frightened by the knowledge. All of the great religions try, by making
this knowledge an explicit part of their teaching, to rid it of this
frightening quality, but they are never quite successful. They teach
that most devils and demons have no fundamental reality, that they
are, in large part, creations of the human mind itself, and that they
lose all power if the mind which created them ceases to believe in the
reality of its creations. Men are, however, seldom capable of accepting
this great fact. They continue to create devils and demons, and, as
soon as they are created, to believe in their independent existence,
and, finally, to fear them.

Men are not content to fear these disembodied creatures of the
mind; they have given them a dwelling place. And the one most often
selected is the bodies of men. This is the theme of Aldous Huxley's
book, The Devils of London,[811] a study of possession and demonology
in seventeenth century France. After examining the evidence he comes
to the conclusion that the priest burned as a wizard had, in fact, made no
pact with the Devil. He was destroyed by his human enemies; but lest
men in the twentieth century take too much comfort, Huxley adds:

Few people now believe in the Devil; but very many enjoy
behaving as their ancestors behaved when the Fiend was
a reality as unquestionable as his opposite number. In

order to justify their behavior, they turn their theories into dogmas, their bylaws into First Principles, their political bosses into gods, and all who disagree with them into incarnate devils. This idolatrous transformation of the relative into the absolute, and the all too human into the divine, makes it possible for them to indulge their ugliest passions with a clear conscience. And when the current beliefs come, in their turn, to look silly, a new set will be invented, so that the immemorial madness may continue to wear its customary mask of legality, idealism, and true religion.

These conclusions, it seems to me, are true. They are the facts with which all men have had to deal, but they are, nevertheless, no cause for despair or resignation. They merely indicate how difficult and complex is the task which must be continuously undertaken, that of enabling each man or woman, each group of men and women, to be only what they are; neither devils, nor demons, nor scapegoats for the sins and shortcomings of others.

Freedom, Equality and Law

The reason for this continuing and demonic difficulty is to be found in the universal tendency to transform the relative into the absolute, the all too human into the divine. Take the definition of Human Rights with which this paper began: the freedom of the individual, the equality of men, and the rule of law; and see how terrible each one becomes if allowed to rule in isolation and without the restraint of its opposite. The doctrine of the free individual found expression in nineteenth century British politics and economics in the belief that the State had no right to regulate or control the individual's use of what was called his property. It was immoral for government to intervene in regard to the hours or conditions of work or the terms of contracts between individuals, because each must be free. One result was a starvation and suffering unparalleled in a country which was fundamentally rich and secure; but lest Americans

459

think this merely a fault of the British, they should be reminded that in the nineteenth century human slavery was justified by this same doctrine of the free individual. Calhoun and other spokesmen for the slaveholding States argued that it would be an infringement of their rights as free individuals to limit their power to enslave others.

In the same way the doctrine of human equality became transformed in the French Revolution of the eighteenth century and in the Russian and German revolutions of the twentieth century into an instrument of unqualified tyranny by those holding state power. All men were equal, but the equality was that of slaves who had no right to appeal from the dictates of the organized society. And when the term, "the rule of law" is used, it must be remembered that laws can be unjust as well as just and promote tyranny as much as freedom.

The Rationalist Answer

There is no easy or simple way out of this dilemma. Herbert J. Muller in *The Uses of the Past* has examined each of the great civilizations of history and shown how each in one way or another has tried to solve the age old problem of the reconciliation of individual liberty with the control necessary for social order. Always he finds the attempts fail. Freedom is destroyed by the absolute authority of Church or State which seeks to rule "without enlisting the free consent of their subjects or permitting free criticism of the principles of their authority."

Muller believes that he has a new solution to offer. To avoid the fate of their predecessors, men must adopt "a liberal rationalistic faith, rooted in the Greek heritage." Their only hope, he says, "lies not in prayer, but in more thought and in more earnest responsible endeavor," because the plainest lesson we learn from history "is that men cannot count on miracles." To support this thesis, he quotes an aphorism of the seventeenth century mathematician and mystic, Pascal, "Thought makes the whole dignity of man, therefore endeavor to think well—that is the only morality." And then Muller adds that "thinking well" requires the thinker to recognize the limitations of human thought and the hazards which thought itself introduces into the life of man. Muller, it seems, has hit upon the heart of the matter. He has, however, erred when he has based himself so exclusively on "the Greek heritage." The Greeks did have something to do with it, but it was Greek thought as modified by the great Hebrew Prophets and restated and reinterpreted by St. Paul in the first century, by St. Augustine in the fifth; and by Martin Luther, Richard Hooker, and Pascal himself, at the beginning of the modern period. Muller, like so many contemporaries who consider themselves rationalists, fundamentally misunderstands the meaning of prayer and miracle, because to many of the greatest of religious thinkers, prayer has been the affirmation of the limitation of human thought and of the hazards it introduces into human history, not a petition to escape from those limitations or hazards. And thought itself has been the miracle, not divine intervention to prevent the tragic consequences of its shortcomings.

What Muller has done is not to provide a new solution to the age old problem, but to make a separate affirmation of his faith in that which has found expression in the political and religious tenets of the Anglican Reformation and of the British and American revolutions. I recognize that I am in grave danger in daring thus to find the proper solution for the problems which beset all men in the religious and political tradition in which I have been reared. Bigots in all ages have done the same. They have made the relative into the absolute, and the all too human into the divine. But in thus affirming these traditions, I believe I am protected, because it is the essence of both that the relative should not be confused with the absolute, and the human remain separate from the divine.

The Anglican Reply

Anglicanism, it seems to me, finds one of its best expressions in the writings of Richard Hooker, the sixteenth century Englishman in whom the liberating spirit of the Renaissance, which honored every human faculty, was checked by a genuine humility concerning the limits of knowledge. In one place, for instance, he says, "dangerous it were for the feeble brain of man to wade far into the doings of the Most High: whom although to know be life, and joy to make mention of his name, yet our soundest knowledge is to know that we know him not as indeed he is and our safest eloquence concerning him is our silence." And in another he warns us not to say too much concerning God lest we fall into error.

The same spirit finds essential expression in the Preface to the American *Book of Common Prayer*, written in Philadelphia in 1789, the year the American Constitution was put into effect. The Preface begins:

> It is a most invaluable part of that blessed 'liberty wherewith Christ hath made us free' that in his worship different forms and usages may without offense be allowed, provided the substance of the faith be kept entire; and that, in every Church, what cannot be clearly determined to belong to Doctrine must be referred to Discipline; and therefore, by common consent and authority, may be altered, abridged, enlarged, amended, or otherwise disposed of, as may seem most convenient for the edification of the people 'according to the various exigency of times and occasions.'

And then having thus clearly distinguished between the doctrine which is unalterable, and the discipline, which can be changed, the Preface and the Prayer Book which follows, do not state what belongs to the separate categories, because to do so would be to make possible the transference of the relative into the absolute or the human into the divine.

Anglicanism thus recognizes that in regard to the beliefs and issues that move men to action, there is not unity but disagreement. It does not regret this situation, rather it rejoices in it because a Church, a nation, or a group that is held together by conformity instead of love is not truly united. The Church's historic task is to hold in fruitful tension the contradictory and paradoxical aspects of truth and reality as they are given to men through revelation and reason. The united community it seeks is not one in which all differences are resolved, but rather a community in which men who differ are held together almost because of their differences through the frank and humble acknowledgment by each of the individuals involved that he too is a sinner and there is no health in him. Anglicanism has few absolutes but this one from the General Confession is central, secondary only to the two commandments, *Thou shalt love the Lord thy God with all thy heart, and with all thy soul, and with all thy mind,* and *thy neighbor as thyself.*

And Its Constitutional Concomitant

It is not of Anglicanism, however, that I wish to write, but of the political movements that were profoundly influenced by its spirit, the British and American revolutions that had their beginnings in centuries past but are still going on. These continuing revolutions, in my opinion, are man's hope, perhaps his only hope, for a society combining a relatively permanent social order with a substantial degree of individual freedom. This conviction has been strengthened by Ralph Ellison's *Invisible Man,*[812] an American Negro, who, in the epilogue to the novel of that title, remembers the deathbed declaration of his grandfather:

> Son, after I'm gone I want you to keep up the good fight. I never told you, but our life is a war and I have been a traitor all my born days, a spy in the enemy's country ever since I gave up my gun back in the Reconstruction. Live with your head in the lion's mouth. I want you to overcome 'em with yeses, undermine 'em with grins, agree 'em to death and destruction, let 'em swoller you till they vomit or bust wide open.

The Invisible Man was puzzled by this message.

> Could he have meant, he queried, hell, he must have meant the principle, that we were to affirm the principle on which the country was built, and not the men. Did he mean say 'yes' because he knew that the principle was greater than the men, greater than the numbers and the vicious power and all the methods used to corrupt its

463

name. Was it that we of all, we, most of all, had to affirm
the principle . . . not because we would always be weak,
not because we were afraid or opportunistic, but because
they had exhausted in us, some—not much, but some of
the human greed and smallness and the fear and
superstition that had kept them running.

The principle, as defined by the *Invisible Man*, is the recognition that only in division is there true health. "Let man keep his many parts," he said, "and you'll have no tyrant states. America is woven of many strands: I would recognize them and let it so remain. Our fate is to become one, and yet many."

"Let man keep his many parts and you'll have no tyrant states." This sentence by Mr. Ellison is the key to the distinction between the British and American revolutions, on the one hand, and that of the French, on the other. For these revolutionary movements are quite different in purpose, method, and philosophy, and while the British and American constitute man's hope, the French and its nineteenth and twentieth century successors lead only to the repetition of the age old error, the transformation of the relative into the absolute, the all too human into the divine.

The National Assembly of France, the revolutionary successor of the Estates General, began this process in the Declaration of the Rights of Man and Citizen which was adopted on August 27, 1789. Here they stated "that ignorance, forgetfulness, or contempt of the rights of man are the sole causes of public misfortune and the corruptions of government." They consequently defined these rights with great explicitness and perpetually guaranteed their protection. "Men are born and remain free and equal in rights;" "The aim of every political association is the preservation of the natural and inalienable rights of man; these rights are liberty, property, security, and resistance to oppression." Many other statements of high aim and purpose can be quoted from this momentous document but they are all essentially negated by the third one, which says, "The source of all sovereignty resides essentially in the nation; no group, no individual may exercise authority not emanating expressly therefrom."

The nation by this definition, was bound to be free from all corruption and misfortune, because the sources of this corruption and misfortune, ignorance, forgetfulness or contempt for the rights of man, had been eliminated. Unfortunately the definition was not correct, and the nation as sovereign swallowed up all the individuals, first in the terror and then under the tyrant Napoleon; just as in the twentieth century, another revolutionary movement which defined property and profits as the sole causes of corruption and misfortune, became a bloodthirsty Moloch and has devoured and is devouring the rights of all individuals.

The founders of the British and American revolutions, on the other hand, were not so certain that they knew the source and cause of corruption or misfortune or that they had discovered the correct principles of a permanent social order. The British monarchy, in the eighteenth century, was the product of a long historical development, not of a consciously developed theory of political organization, and the only explicit principles to be found in it were those coined by students to describe what already existed. The British had a constitution, but no one could say exactly of what it consisted. They had a king, in whose name and with whose consent all governmental acts were performed, but the power of the man who occupied this sovereign throne were checked and limited in innumerable ways. They had a House of Commons, chosen by ballot to represent the body of the people, but the actual members of this House were indebted to a very few men for their selection and large numbers of Englishmen were entirely unrepresented. And yet this strange, unwieldy, complicated, and confusing government was considered by many contemporaries to be the only existent one which united "public strength with individual security," and the Americans, who were revolting against it, consciously modeled their own political system upon it.

They, in their Declaration of Independence, said that "All men are created equal" and "are endowed by their Creator with certain unalienable rights." They added that governments are instituted among men "to secure these rights," but then they began to shift their ground. "Whenever any form of Government," they wrote, "becomes destructive of these ends, it is the Right of the People to alter or abolish it and to institute new Government, laying its foundations on such principles and organizing its powers in such form, as to them shall seem most likely to effect their Safety and Happiness." And when in 1787, they came to organize their final form of government, they acted in the same spirit. "Give all power to the many," Alexander Hamilton said in the Constitutional Convention," and they will oppress the few. Give all power to the few, they will oppress the many. Each must have power to protect itself from the other." Thus tentatively, experimentally, uncertainly, they stated their principles, always on guard against being too rigid, too explicit, too certain.

From Slavery to White Supremacy

One of the problems which confronted them was slavery and it may seem strange that this new nation, this revolutionary movement which I have been audacious enough to designate as one of man's best hopes, was founded by men who themselves held other men as slaves. They did not eliminate the institution, instead they protected it, and many both within and without the country thought that this betrayal of the principle upon which the government was founded was final. The founders of the American Revolution, however, were wiser than their critics. They did not abolish slavery because if they had done so, they would not have obtained the effective consent of the mass of the people, and they preferred to establish a society in which all men could gain freedom rather than one in which all men were said to be free.

They compromised with what they considered to be wrong not because they were "weak, afraid or opportunistic," but because they were aware of "the human greed and smallness and the fear and superstition" that kept all men running. They also believed that "the principle was greater than the men," and their confidence seemed justified when seven of the original States, by voluntary action, eliminated slavery within their borders by the close of the eighteenth century. The rest were expected to follow but they did not. Slavery, instead of dying, expanded into new territories, and, in the debates concerning the admission of Missouri, slaveholders proved conclusively that they intended to make the institution permanent.

Most of them admitted that it was immoral and in conflict with the fundamental principle upon which the country was founded. But they had been frightened by the insurrection and massacre which accompanied the ending of slavery in Santo Domingo. "The relation which now exists between the two races in the slave holding States," John C. Calhoun said, "has existed for two centuries. It has grown with our growth and strengthened with our strength. It has entered into and modified all our institutions, civil and political. No other can be substituted. We will not, cannot, permit it to be destroyed. If we were base enough to do so, we would be traitors to our section, our families, and to posterity."

He made this statement in 1836 and from it he never departed though he recognized that he was offending the moral sense of the other members of the national community by his stand. "Every portion of the North," he admitted in 1850, "entertains views and feelings more or less hostile to [slavery]. Those most opposed regard it as a sin. Those less opposed regard it as a crime. While those least opposed regard it as a blot and a stain on the character of the nation." But to the southern section, he insisted, it was an institution which could not be destroyed "without subjecting the two races to the greatest calamity, and the section to poverty, desolation, and wretchedness." The South, he said, "has no compromise to offer and no concession or surrender to make," and it was the acceptance of this stand by a majority of the people of the slaveholding States which led to the Civil War.

This conflict which separated the nation into geographical sections, each hostile to the other, was about slavery, not the relation between the two races, and in the North as well as the South, a majority of those descended from Europeans believed that the Negro was basically inferior. They did not think it right that he should be enslaved, but they would not fight other white Americans in order that he could be free. Abraham Lincoln was not unaware of this fact, and he made certain that the war, which was unavoidable, was not fought against slavery but for nationalism.

It was not until the closing months of the war that he acknowledged its connection with slavery. "One eighth of the whole population," he said in his second inaugural, "was colored slaves. These slaves constituted a peculiar and powerful interest. All knew that this interest was somehow the cause of the war." He made no apology or explanation because he, like the founders of the Republic, believed it more important to make possible the accomplishment of moral ends than to make moral affirmations, and the war, fought for the union, had made possible the ending of slavery. There was no hatred, bitterness, or self-righteousness in him. Neither was he weak or unforceful. I do not know if he ever read a statement by Thomas Jefferson concerning slavery that "I tremble for my country when I reflect that God is just, that his justice cannot sleep forever," but the major assertions of his apologia are based upon this theme.

> Neither party, the North or the South expected for the war, the magnitude, or the duration which it has already attained. Neither anticipated that the cause of the conflict might cease with or even before the conflict itself should cease. Each looked for an easier triumph and a result less fundamental and astounding. Both read the same Bible and pray to the same God, and each invokes His aid against the other. It may seem strange that any man should dare to ask a just God's assistance in wringing their bread from the sweat of other men's faces, but let us judge not that we be not judged. The prayers of both could not be answered. That of neither has been answered fully. The Almighty has His own purposes. Woe unto the world because of offenses; for it must needs be that offenses come, but woe to that man by whom the offense cometh. If we shall suppose that American slavery is one of those offenses which must needs come, but which, having continued through His appointed time, He now wills to remove, and that He gives to both the North and South this terrible war as the woe due to those by whom the offense came, shall we discern therein any departure

from those divine attributes which the believers in a living God always ascribe to him? Fondly do we hope, fervently do we pray, that this mighty scourge of war may speedily pass away. Yet, if God wills that it continue until all the wealth piled up by the bondsmen's two hundred and fifty years of unrequited toil shall be sunk, and until every drop of blood drawn by the lash shall be paid by another drawn with the sword, as was said two thousand years ago, so still it must be said, The judgments of the Lord are true and righteous altogether.

The war ended slavery but that was only the beginning. Fifty years later James Weldon Johnson had to arrive in France in order that he could experience for the first time since losing the innocence of childhood the sense of being "merely a man." And in between was all the pain and suffering of reconstruction, the slow climb of millions of men and women from the degradation of slavery and the adjustment of others who had always been free, to this new situation. These tasks, among the most difficult ever confronted by any national group, were made harder by the 1883 decision of the Supreme Court which declared the Civil Rights Act unconstitutional and deprived the federal government of the power to aid in the transition. Control of the relations between the two races was turned back to the States, dominated and controlled by white voters, and the resulting disenfranchisement, the hardening of the segregation barriers, the lynchings, and the race riots caused many to believe that America once more had permanently betrayed its fundamental principles.

The Court's decision, according to Ralph H. Gabriel, a contemporary historian, was a tacit recognition that in the United States "a caste system had crystallized, and the sanction behind it was its acceptance in the North." A few protested, but only a few, and the reason for its general acceptance "was to be found in the fact that, as early as 1883, Northern folkways were developing similar, though not identical, patterns to those of the postwar South." A new bondage called "white supremacy" had taken the place of slavery to prevent the Negro from participating freely and fully in the American society in the North, the East, and the West as well as the South. "It is founded on force," Gabriel says, and "it represents a denial of the American democratic faith." He can see no way out, because the discipline by which white supremacy is enforced constitutes, in his view, "a makeshift solution for a problem which is without solution."

The Future Right to Be Human

Such extreme pessimism is unwarranted. There is no solution, it is true, but also there is no problem except as it has been artificially created by denying to the Negro people as a group the full status of members in the American nation. The doctrines which are used to justify this denial of the American democratic faith are as false, and the fears which cause them to be believed, are as needless, as those which gave to slavery its too long endurance. But slavery was overthrown, and so will be its successor. The moral sense of mankind cannot be thwarted without peril, as Lincoln pointed out at the close of the Civil War, and it should be remembered what happened once, can happen again.

"Woe unto the world," he quoted, "because of offenses; for it must needs be that offenses come, but woe to the man by whom the offense cometh." If the people of the United States, or those in some of its parts, become stubborn and refuse to compromise, tension will mount and violence and bloodshed may follow.

The compromise and acceptance cannot all come from one side, and if any group says, as did John C. Calhoun in 1850, that it "has no compromise to offer no concession to make," then upon it must lie the responsibility for the breakdown of constitutional processes. The danger of the present situation and the hostility it has engendered do not invalidate the principle upon which the country was founded or the contention that it is this revolution which constitutes one of man's best hopes for a society in which there is both freedom and order. It was not the revolution's intention to provide a perfect society without corruption or misfortune, but rather to give to its members a continuing principle of moral judgment against which to measure

that which they have and to know always that it is imperfect and must be improved.

No revolution can do more, and it is not for men to ask why God, in His infinite wisdom, established this limit. It is sufficient that He did, and if they pretend that He did not, they will once again repeat the age old error of making the relative into the absolute, the all too human into the divine. Governments must have power and their citizens must obey, but not absolutely, because if absolute power is given to government to define what is evil and to rectify it permanently and at once, to make practice conform completely with theory, then those who are given this power will not use it for these ends. They will turn their "theories into dogmas, their bylaws into first principles, and all who disagree with them into incarnate devils."

We, who in this generation are given this great problem to solve, must always remember that the men opposed to us are merely men, not devils or demons; and we must be patient, not because of weakness, fear, or opportunism, but out of the same understanding of human greed, smallness, and superstition that distinguished the founders of the American nation. And if we have this wisdom, if those who have physical power are generous and brave and those without power courageous and self-restrained, then once again we will have a new birth of freedom and government of the people, for the people, and by the people will not perish from the earth.

Appendix 5

See Chapter 13

True Freedom I
by Thomas Payne Govan[813]

Men are free, but they do not want freedom. Each fears and resents freedom, and only occasionally, through grace, do men, nations, or other social organizations willingly accept the freedom that is theirs. In the legend of the Grand Inquisitor, Dostoyevsky writes, "So long as man is free he strives for nothing so incessantly and painfully as to find someone to worship. But man seeks to worship what is established beyond dispute, so that all men would agree at once to worship it." When man worships and follows that which is established beyond dispute, however, he loses his own freedom and seeks to destroy the freedom of all others. He can be free only so long as he says with Saint Paul that "we know in part and we prophesy in part. But when that which is perfect is come, then that which is in part shall be done away . . . For now we see through a glass darkly; but then face to face; now I know in part; but then I shall know even as I am known." (1 Corinthians 13: 9-10, 11-12)

The acceptance of mystery, uncertainty, and insecurity in perfect confidence and trust is the acceptance of human freedom, but the attempt to deny this true situation of man is a denial of freedom. Man's idolatrous desire for certainty of knowledge, perfect peace, and complete understanding, to be as the gods, is the source of man's slavery. The God who made man in His image made man free, but the gods men want and create for themselves destroy freedom. Those of us who call ourselves Christian know this to be true, but despite this knowledge we, like our pagan brothers, continue to eat of the tree of knowledge of good and evil, to build towers of Babel, and we forget the wrath and power of the jealous God we offend by thus making Christ into an idol, a destroyer of freedom, not the God who made us free.

We are unwilling to imitate Him, who though he "was in the form of God did not count equality with God a thing to be grasped, but emptied himself, taking the form of a servant, being born in the likeness of men, and being found in human form, he humbled himself and became obedient unto death, even death on a cross" (Philippians 2:6-9). We are not willing in humility to count others as better than ourselves, but rather seek to earn and deserve the salvation, already freely granted to us, by being better and wiser than others, by having the correct doctrines, or the true principles of order. We can only be free so long as we remember that we are but creatures with limited knowledge and understanding, that always before us there is to be found unexplored areas and unanswered questions, and that within what we think we have established as firm knowledge, there is always error, incompleteness, and inadequate statement.

When we forget or ignore these limitations, we forge chains to enslave ourselves and others, for whenever human knowledge and understanding is taken as a final and true statement, it ends in determinism, a denial of freedom . . . and all such determinisms must be denounced by the Christian as false whether it is the church, the state, or philosophers that seek to persuade us they are true. To question the finality of these teachings is not to deny their usefulness or their partial and limited truth, but rather is to affirm that they, no matter how soundly they may be based, are not the whole of the story: that humans have still more to learn.

Appendix 6

See Chapters 11 and 18

Agrarianism, Sectionalism, and State Sovereignty Denounced:

A Refutation of Thomas Jefferson, John Taylor of Caroline,
Andrew Jackson, John C. Calhoun and the Historians
Who Have Been Misled by Their Teaching

Thomas P. Govan
November, 1960

Twice within the last one hundred years, in 1861 and today, southern political leaders and a majority of their white constituents have permitted what John C. Calhoun described as "a low, sordid, selfish, and sectional spirit" to take possession of their minds. They have challenged the basic affirmations of the Declaration of Independence, written by another southerner, Thomas Jefferson, and have risked division and separation with all the attendant dangers. The substantive question at issue is the relation between whites and Negroes, and in both crises white southerners have sought to deny to Negroes the freedom and equality that they, like all men, are due. No one denies this fact, but, and there is always a but, the statement is made not only by white southerners but also by many

American historians that the rights of Negroes are not truly the issue at stake.

According to this explanation, the white southerners, in defending their right to differ from the rest of the nation in regard to the Negro, are not seeking to deny the moral and metaphysical affirmations of the Declaration of Independence. These phrases have little to do with the more fundamental issues of freedom which are being decided in the sectional contests for economic power between the Northeast, the South, and the West. The attack on slavery in the nineteenth century, and, by implication, that on segregation today, are said to have little or no concern with their apparent objects, they are merely smoke-screens devised by the most subtle enemies of freedom, the capitalistic business interests centered in the Northeast, for their selfish, sectional desires to dominate and exploit the agrarians of the South and West. The defense of slavery or segregation by white southerners thus becomes a necessary means for the protection not only of the general agrarian interest but also the true American freedom, the right of local self-government with the consent of the governed, and if they are finally defeated, so runs this historical argument, then American liberty will be destroyed.

National power, in this interpretation of American history, is the enemy of freedom, and the doctrines of state sovereignty and of a strict interpretation of the Constitution of the United States, developed by Jefferson and Calhoun (earlier referred to in a different context), and by John Taylor of Caroline and Andrew Jackson, are freedom's most effective protectors. None of these early national leaders was himself a sectionalist. Calhoun alone, and he only in the latter part of his political career, could be appropriately so designated, and then, in his self-appointed role as spokesman for the South, he was seeking some way to preserve the American union intact. Each also would have denied that he was an agrarian, for agrarianism in their time was a radical doctrine based on the principle that monopoly in land is the root of all economic injustice. And though all four, on particular occasions, were defenders of state rights, each also, on other occasions, was an advocate of national power. They are,

475

nevertheless, the original formulators of this view of American history, and among them, Jefferson is the leader. For this reason, his statements alone will be examined and analyzed, though, if space permitted, confirmation and endorsement of what he wrote could be found in the speeches and writings of the other three.

One other cautionary note: Jefferson was a many-sided person, whose thought covered almost the whole range of human experience. He wrote many letters and said many things, sometimes contradictory things, so that any quoted statement, unless compared and contrasted with other statements, may constitute a misrepresentation of his thought. Jefferson could also hold quite contradictory views about one subject, and nowhere is this more clearly illustrated than in his thought and expression on freedom. In the Declaration of Independence, he said and believed that freedom and equality are the moral and metaphysical foundations of all true and viable governments, but he was also certain that American freedom was an accident based on particular and temporary historical circumstance. Writing to James Madison, he said that Americans could be free "only as long as we remain virtuous; and I think we shall be so, as long as agriculture is our principle object, which will be the case, while there remain vacant lands in any part of America. When we get piled upon one another in large cities, as in Europe, we shall become corrupt as in Europe, and go to eating one another as they do there." At another time he wrote, "The mobs of great cities add just so much to the support of the government, as sores do to the strength of the human body," and he also believed that "Those who labor in the earth are the chosen people of God, if ever He had a chosen people, whose breasts He had made His peculiar deposit for substantial and genuine virtue."

Such theoretical assertions are difficult to refute, or to prove, but against them may be quoted such counter-assertions as that of Karl Marx who spoke of the "idiocy of rural life" from which the cultivators of the land would be delivered by the proletarian revolution. The answer to Jefferson and Marx, however, is not to pose theoretical statement against theoretical statement, rather it is to avoid theory altogether, and to rely on observation and experience, contemporary and historical. America has remained free, at least as free as it was in the eighteenth century, even though it has many great cities and only a small part of its population makes its livelihood through the farm. Perhaps we do eat one another, and we certainly are corrupt, but cannot the same accusation be made against those Americans, in every generation, who have cultivated the land? Farm blocs in Congress are not an example of virtuous, disinterested action, nor are the boulders that too frequently have been packed in cotton bales.

A similar appeal to history must be used to judge Jefferson's contention that in the American political system, the several states, as the sovereign parties who compacted together, are the exclusive and ultimate judges as to what the compact was intended to be. The concept of sovereignty has never been formally accepted or defined in any of the basic documents of the American nation, and in its constitutional framework there is no group, individual, or body that even in theory possesses the unlimited and unrestrained authority that sovereignty is said to be. The state governments and people are limited not only by their own self-adopted constitutions but also by the Constitution, laws, and treaties of the United States, and, in point of time, the United States, rather its predecessor, the Continental Congress, was a defacto government as soon as, if not before, the component states.

Jefferson devised this theory in justifiable protest against the Alien and Sedition Acts, which probably should have been held to be unconstitutional, and which were unwisely and unjustly, perhaps even tyrannically, enforced. In most other instances, however, the arguments he originated, and his proposed remedy, state interposition,[814] have been used not to oppose tyranny by the national government, but to prevent it from doing something useful and essentially moral that the majority thought it should do. Jefferson, nevertheless, was thinking only of freedom. He and John Taylor were the theorists of the opposition to the neo-mercantilist measures of Alexander Hamilton, and Hamilton, in their view, not only was opposed to freedom but also was seeking to advance sectional and selfish interests at the expense of the public good. They sincerely believed that farmers were more virtuous than other people, that governments and all other established institutions, at all times and in all places, were inimical to freedom, and that social action to promote, protect, or restrain individual activity, by definition, was wrong. They also believed that economic interests were essentially, almost exclusively, competitive, that aid to merchants, financiers and manufacturers was necessarily harmful to farmers, and that national strength was dangerous and destructive, not a desirable objective for a free people.

Hamilton's policies and political philosophy, viewed from this partial perspective, seemed to confirm the charges brought against them. He did not think that unrestrained men were or could become virtuous, nor did he think that virtue, as the term was generally used, was necessary for freedom. A government which based itself on virtue, he believed, would necessarily be tyrannical for the men that it governed, even though they might so desire, could not live up to its demands. Men who thought of themselves as virtuous, in his opinion, were self-deceived, for they and the institutions they created were alike governed by the passions of ambition, avarice, and interest. But Hamilton also was confident that Americans, just as they were, could establish a free, partially just, and strong nation if their passions could be made subservient to the public good. Ambitious, avaricious, and interested men (all are described by this definition, you, me, Alexander Hamilton, and, let it not be forgotten, Thomas Jefferson and John Taylor of Caroline) would find, if Hamilton's intentions were carried out, that it would be to their advantage to promote the public good. Economic interests were complementary as well as competitive, but in every complex society many opportunities existed for particular men and institutions to exploit and deprive others. Some power had to exist by which such men and institutions could be restrained, and Hamilton, therefore, argued for a government strong enough to thwart their schemes and to protect national freedom from external enemies and internal political adventurers.

Hamilton, in the beginning, had his way, and during the first forty years of American experience under the Constitution, the national government, in cooperation with the states, guided, protected, and sustained the economy regardless of whether the Federalist or the Republican party was in power. It also prohibited the further importation of slaves and kept this immoral institution from being established in most of the national territories in the vain hope that this example would lead slaveholders voluntarily to free their slaves. It did not do more because it could not overcome the resistance of white southerners, who, in the words of one of their spokesman in the Constitutional Convention, said, that "the security the Southern States want is that their Negroes not be taken from them."

In 1828, however, Hamilton's political philosophy and point of view were overthrown. Andrew Jackson was elected President, with John C. Calhoun as vice-president, and throughout the rest of the century and into the next, the principles advocated by Jefferson and Taylor were the guiding rules of the nation except for one brief interval during the Civil War and its immediate aftermath. The results of this planned policy of governmental weakness and nonintervention were not what its originators thought it would be. Agriculture did not prosper and unrestrained men and institutions, competing freely with one another, did not prove to be virtuous. The nation became mechanized and industrial, the greater part of its population lived in cities, and these results, ironically, were interpreted to mean that Hamilton, rather than Jefferson, had had his way.

The climax occurred in the late 1920s with an unrestrained speculative expansion followed by a spectacular and disastrous financial collapse, and in 1930, there appeared a book, *I'll Take My Stand: the South and the Agrarian Tradition*, written by twelve Southerners, which, perhaps more explicitly than any other, portrays the philosophical, moral, political, and theological confusion of Americans when writing of their past. These young intellectuals were alienated by the America they knew, by the tawdriness and corruption of the national culture and of its political, economic, social, intellectual, and religious leaders. They were tired of progressivism, of go-getting, of bigness, of mechanization, and looked back, conservatively they thought, to a gentler, richer period. The agrarian society they desired was not one that had "no use at all for industries, for scholars and artists, and for the life of cities;" rather it was "one in which agriculture is the leading vocation. . . . The theory of agrarianism is that the culture of the soil is the best and most sensitive of vocations, and that therefore it should have the economic preference and enlist the maximum number of workers."

479

The resemblance of this statement to Jefferson's, "Those who labor in the earth are the chosen people of God," is obvious, and the group shared his essential hostility to action by the national government and his belief in individualism, the small community, and state rights. The very term they used to designate their program came out of the leveling and liberal tradition, but these modern reformers repudiated liberalism. They prided themselves rather on the "antique conservatism" of the South, which, according to John Crowe Ransom, was the heritage from "a strain which came out of Europe most convinced of the virtues of establishment, contrasting with those strains which seem for the most part to have dominated the other sections, and which came out of Europe feeling rebellious toward all establishments." Allen Tate went further, describing the South as a "feudal society," though, he regretfully confessed, it was "without a feudal religion." Lyle Lanier, on the other hand, thought that the peculiar virtue of an agrarian society was political democracy, the great movement for human freedom that began with the Renaissance and culminated in the formation of the American and French republics. Frank Owsley repudiated this nationalist heresy. At the time of the Civil War, he wrote, there were "two divergent economic and social systems, two civilizations" in the United States. The North was commercial-industrial, the South agrarian. "The fundamental and passionate ideal for which the South stood and fell was the ideal of an agrarian society . . . the old and accepted manner of life for which Egypt, Greece, Rome, England and France had stood."

The writers of the separate essays recognized that they were not in total agreement and each accepted responsibility for what he had written, but the confusion of thought and terminology, nevertheless, is surprising. All accepted a definition of an agrarian society as one in which agriculture was the principal occupation, but not one which excluded industry, commerce, and the arts. But most of the United States conformed to this definition until well into the nineteenth century, and yet Owsley stated that at the time of the Civil War there were two separate and distinctive civilizations in the United States. Tate called the South feudal, but in doing so ignored the distinction between serfdom and chattel slavery and between investiture in land

and ownership in simple. Lanier said the South was democratic, but Ransom found it peculiarly sympathetic to the English establishment, though it had no formal aristocracy or established church, and its religious traditions, like those of the other parts of the country, were predominately Baptist, Methodist, and Calvinist.

Despite this confusion of terminology and thought, *I'll Take My Stand* has a continuing influence. Most of the contemporary intellectuals who call themselves neo-conservative have adopted its essentially liberal, individualistic, and exclusively materialistic interpretation of the American past. Like the agrarians, they hold the national government and its unifying policies responsible for all the evils of modern life, and advocate as a remedy the Jeffersonian prescription of unrestrained individualism, state rights, and laissez faire. The extremists among them exalt competition into the sole rule of life. They are ruthless Darwinians, exulting in a nature that is red in tooth and claw, and denounce social legislation as a positive wrong. Freedom and equality, instead of being the moral and metaphysical foundations of all true and viable governments, are sentimental vaporings by naive idealists, for only the strong, who have seized freedom, have any right to it.

Arrayed against these conservatives are the modern liberals, many of them historians, who, in the twentieth century, have repudiated the Jeffersonian principles. Like Hamilton in the early years of the American republic, they argue for social control of the economy and an expansion of public expenditures as means for promoting genuine freedom and the general welfare. They point to the interdependence of all economic and social groups and to the indivisible character of their freedom and prosperity. For this reason they are in the forefront of those demanding the full incorporation of the Negro into the American society with all the freedom and privilege that he had hitherto been unjustly denied, and they denounce the southern political leaders, their conservative allies, and the appeal both make to the constitutional principles of Jefferson, Taylor, Jackson, and Calhoun.

The hostility to these principles, paradoxically, does not extend to the men who uttered them, and the liberals, almost unanimously, consider themselves Jeffersonian. Like the agrarians and neo-conservatives, who repudiate liberalism when acting on liberal principles, the liberals reject Hamilton though essentially adopting his policies and point of view. The most obvious example of such a liberal is Arthur M. Schlesinger, Jr., who, in his multi-volume history of the Roosevelt administrations, attacks everything that he defends in his widely-influential *Age of Jackson* except organized labor, the Democratic party, and the American people. But he is not alone. There are many Hamiltonians in the twentieth century who write as Jeffersonians about the events of the past, and the source of their confusion is to be found in the works of four men, all liberals, who, more than any others, have influenced intellectuals in their understanding of American history. Vernon Parrington, Frederick J. Turner, Walter P. Webb, and Charles Beard are the most prominent names in twentieth century American historiography, and though they differ in emphasis, they all are essentially Jeffersonian in their hostility to what they call the "business group." They also are sectionalists, finding in sectionalism and sectional conflicts the true history of the American nation, and, with the exception of Charles Beard, they say that American freedom has been a temporary possession produced by an abundant supply of unexploited land.

The farmers in the South and West, according to these historians, have been the defenders of equality and freedom against the selfish desires and ambitions of eastern business groups, and the important conflicts in the nation's history have been those about money, tariff, internal improvements, and land. Their conclusions have not gone unchallenged. In recent years Turner's frontier thesis has been subjected to sharp critical attack, and Beard's economic interpretation of the Constitution has been sustained only by an apologist who says that Beard was right even though he stated his thesis incorrectly, asked the wrong questions, used the wrong evidence, and did not understand what his conclusions should have been. Parrington's evaluations of American writers are almost universally disregarded by literary critics and intellectual historians, and the predictions made by Turner and Webb as to the growing importance of sectional self-consciousness have turned out simply to be wrong. But no one has challenged the whole corpus of their theoretical structure, the naive economic determinism that each of them, like the agrarians and neo-conservatives, almost uncritically accepts, and their determination to ignore, as unworthy of attention, the moral, the metaphysical, the theological debates about the meaning of freedom and equality that have constituted so important a part of American history.

Even their discussion of economic matters has been marred by their Jeffersonian bias, for they, like him, believe these questions to be essentially moral. A single gold standard is virtuous, true, and right when argued for at the beginning of the nineteenth century in the name of farmers against the mercantile and financial groups, but is selfish, wicked, and wrong when defended by the spokesmen for business at the close of the same century. The protective tariff is an unjust instrument through which the rich exploit the poor, though Hamilton, when he initially proposed the measure, was arguing for small farmers and an essentially non-existent manufacturing group, and was violently opposed by the wealthiest established interests, the growers of export crops and the international merchants, bankers, and brokers. But the chief weakness of their treatment of these subjects is their belief that these economic debates were sectional in character. At particular times and on individual questions there were votes in the Congress in which the members from one of the geographical areas voted with surprising unanimity on one side or another of these questions, but the explanation most often is to be found in an analysis of political loyalties and party divisions. Intrasectional divergences of economic interest are just as characteristic of the American nation as sectional commonality, and neither is as significant a factor in shaping political opinions as is national unity, on the one side, and local and particular interests, on the other.

What Americans have debated most seriously about is not these matters of purely economic concern. The important sources of division have actually been, first, the proper role of the nation in its relation with the states and individual citizens, and second, the position of the Negro in the national society, and of these, only the second, and it but partly, has taken a sectional form. The first of these debates is predominantly political, the second predominately moral, but the majority of American historians have followed their teachers, Parrington, Turner, Webb, and Beard, by discussing the political differences as if they were moral, and dismiss the moral demand for the freedom and equality of the Negro as a disguise for selfish and sectional economic ambitions.

What is needed, most particularly at this moment, is a reexamination by American historians of their understanding of the nation's past. By accepting the agrarian, sectional, and state sovereignty arguments either originated by or derived from the writings of Jefferson, Taylor, Jackson, and Calhoun, these historians have fallen into the error which twice during the past one hundred years has led white southerners into a tragic and disastrous course. Accepting false principles as true, eleven southern states seceded from the union and attempted to build a new nation because they believed their freedom, their equal position in the nation, was in danger, and in the contemporary crisis, the segregationists, at least most of them, are likewise certain that what they are defending is the freedom and equality they are due in the American nation. At the close of the Civil War, Lincoln, himself, was bothered by this same fact, and though he was puzzled that any men would dare to pray to a just God for assistance in wringing their bread from the sweat of other men's faces, he wisely concluded that it was better to follow the scriptural injunction to judge not that ye be not judged.

If the question were one of merely historical interest, Lincoln's solution might well be adopted, but once again the nation is confronted with an essentially identical moral dilemma, and though secession and war seem unthinkable, southern governors and legislators, as well as white leaders of powerful private organizations, are making violent threats of resistance to federal court decisions and law. They hold to the teaching, partly fostered by historians, that their freedom and equality require the enslavement or enforced subordination of others, and forget that unless freedom and equality be universal, unless all men possess it by right, then none do. The principles enunciated in the

Declaration of Independence are not sentimental ideals, they are moral and metaphysical truths rooted deep in human experience, and if they are neglected or obscured, the United States will follow the path to destruction through tyranny that so many other nations have taken.

The choice confronting the American people is the choice described by John C. Calhoun in the Congress after the War of 1812, when, in the speech partly quoted at the beginning of this paper, he said, "Blessed with a form of government at once combining liberality and strength, we may reasonably raise our eyes to a most splendid future, if we only act in a manner worthy of our advantages. If, however, neglecting them, we permit a low, sordid, selfish, and sectional spirit to take possession . . . this happy scene will vanish. We will divide and in its consequences will follow misery and degradation."

Appendix 7

See Chapters 10 and 21

Hamilton, the Bank, and the National Economy

Thomas Payne Govan

Alexander Hamilton became Secretary of the Treasury on September 11, 1789, and ten days later the House of Representatives, believing, as it said, that "an adequate provision for the support of public credit" was a matter of high importance not only to the nation's honor but also its prosperity, directed him to prepare a plan for this purpose. This directive was an order, not a request, because the Secretary of the Treasury, more completely than the other department heads, was an administrative officer of the Congress as well as a member of the executive.[815] The welfare of the national economy was thus made a part of his official responsibility, and his initial report, recommending the common refunding of the national and state debts, was as much concerned with "the individual and aggregate prosperity of the citizens of the United States" as it was with the financial character and reputation of the nation.

Hamilton similarly recommended the establishment of a national bank, which he described as "a political machine of the greatest importance to the State," because it would be a nursery of national wealth through the aid it would render to trade, agriculture, and manufacturing.[816] This proposal, like his earlier one in regard to the public debt, was made without the advice or formal approval of President George Washington, probably because (though no explanation was ever made) both men believed that prior consultation between them would have constituted an improper interference by the chief executive in a matter that was the exclusive concern of the Congress and the Secretary of the Treasury.

The bill chartering the bank was thus not "an administration measure," and Washington was free to veto it, when it was presented for his signature in February 1791, without breaking any expressed or implied commitment. The other members of the executive were likewise free to approve or disapprove, and Hamilton had no reason to protest, nor did he do so, when Thomas Jefferson, The Secretary of State, and Edmund Randolph, the Attorney-General, in reply to the President's request for their opinions, recommended that the charter be vetoed on the ground that it was unconstitutional. Washington, almost certainly, had strong doubts as to the advisability of chartering the bank; doubts strengthened by these adverse opinions from men he respected and trusted, and though he permitted Hamilton to reply to Jefferson and Randolph, he requested James Madison, who had led the opposition to the bank in the Congress, to prepare a veto message.[817]

This message was not used. Washington signed the charter, but, as was his custom, gave no explanation. He did what he thought proper, his reasons were his own, and it is not possible to know whether it was Hamilton's defense of the bank's constitutionality that convinced him, or his acceptance of Jefferson's advice that "unless the President's mind on a view of everything which is urged for and against this bill, is tolerably clear that it is unauthorized by the Constitution; if the pro and con hang so even as to balance his judgment, a just respect for the wisdom of the Legislature would naturally decide the balance in favor of their opinion."

The exercise of the veto power, the Secretary of State continued, should be reserved for cases where the Congress had been "clearly misled by error, ambition, or interest,"[818] and it would be ironic, in the light of subsequent developments, if it were this argument that led Washington to sign the bill. Jefferson's original objections were entirely constitutional, but soon afterwards he was convinced that the charter had been passed through the Congress by votes of interested members who were seeking to subvert the republic. He, John Adams, and John Taylor of Caroline were to become the most noted spokesmen for a diverse group of Americans, who, though they agreed on little else, shared in common the belief that the bank was an aristocratic institution, injurious to the nation, most particularly the farmers.

Through it and the funding system, a "paper junto," led by "an aristocracy of bankers," an "oligarchy of Shylocks," and other "sycophants" of Great Britain, had converted the government into an immoral "scheme of finance" that, "instead of dispensing public welfare," dispensed "unequal wealth."[819] In brief but powerful sentences, Taylor proclaimed: "Public creditors subsist upon the national labour. Prosperity to a paper credit, is adversity to the mass of the people. Increment of wealth to the one, is diminution to the other."[820] These dogmatic assertions were the foundation on which the bank's opponents built their case, but their views of this subject were derived not so much from their own and the nation's experience as they were from the attacks made on the Whig-created Bank of England and the British funding system by Viscount Bolingbroke, Jonathan Swift, and other Tory propagandists in the reigns of Anne and George I.[821]

These partisan defenders of the interests of the landed aristocracy had charged that the mercantile and credit system was an organized plan of plunder and extortion, a fraud on the nation and the majority of its people. The only safe currency was gold and silver, the commercial classes should be subservient to the agriculture, for as Swift, in a passage highly valued by Taylor, wrote: "I ever abominated that scheme of politics . . . of setting up a monied system in opposition to the landed. For I conceived there could not be a truer maxim in government than this, that the possessors of the soil are the best judges of what is for the advantage of the nation."[822]

It was statements such as these by speculative theorists and propagandists, more than the operation of the bank, that were the source of the hostility of Taylor, Adams, and Jefferson to the institution that Hamilton had devised, and their charges of gambling, fraud, corruption, and injustice, though they believed them, were more ideological than moral. As defenders of agriculture, they seemed to believe that economic activities were exclusively competitive, a sort of internal war in which there were spoils to be gained, and if one individual or group profited, all others suffered loss. In Hamilton's view, however, the competitive and conflicting interests of men buying from and selling to each other, though always present and to be reckoned with, were not as significant as their mutual interdependence. The provision of a sound and effective currency, regardless of whether it was paper or specie (gold and silver) was a measure to which no one should object, a matter of common interest to the farmer and the merchant, the debtor and the creditor, the rich and the poor. Each would benefit, none would suffer, for, as Hamilton wrote, "in the present state of things, the health of a state, particularly a commercial one, depends on a due quantity and circulation of cash, as much as the health of an animal body depends upon the due quantity and regular circulation of the blood."[823]

He advocated a banknote currency for the United States, not from hostility to farmers or a prejudice in favor of merchants, but from the conviction, based on experience and study, that gold and silver were too scarce, as well as too valuable in other ways, to be used as the ordinary medium of exchange. If they were substituted for the paper already in circulation, to say nothing of the much greater amount that would be needed as the economy began to expand, a great part of the nation's internal transactions would have had to be "carried on by barter: a mode inconvenient, partial, confined, destructive both of commerce and industry."[824]

Few in the nation would have been willing to make such a sacrifice of convenience and profit, as had been proved by the colonial and revolutionary experiences, for Hamilton, it must be remembered, was not the initiator of the "paper system" in the United States. If the public debt had not been refunded or the national bank established, there would still have been fundholders and paper money (issued by state banks) exerting all the influences that Taylor, Adams, and Jefferson deplored. Fraud, speculation, and gambling, it seems highly probable, would likewise have continued. They were produced in the nation, as in all others, by the "avarice of individuals," their inordinate desire for exorbitant profits, and it was one of Hamilton's reasoned expectations that the provision of a stable and plentiful supply of credit and currency would lessen the incidence of these economic evils and abuses through opening opportunities for profit in more socially desirable channels of traffic.

The initial benefit of his measures, it was true, went to fundholders and city-dwellers, chiefly merchants, who could borrow from the bank and its branches, but the other groups would profit equally from the increased economic activity stimulated by this addition to the nation's capital, credit, and currency. The interdependence of all economic groups was more than a theory, it was a fact of experience, and Hamilton, seeking to convince those who disbelieved, wrote: "Nothing can be more mistaken than the collision and rivalship which almost always subsist between the landed and trading interests, for the truth is they are so inseparably interwoven, that one cannot be injured, without injury, nor benefited, without benefit to the other. Oppress trade, lands sink in value, make it flourish, their value rises, encumber husbandry, trade declines, encourage agriculture, commerce revives."[825]

He recognized, however, that men were beings "governed more by passion and prejudice than by an enlightened sense of their interests," and that they frequently lost sight of this "mutual reaction" when the "seductions of some immediate advantage" tempted them "to sacrifice the future to the present." Some men would seek immediate, short-term profit, wherever profit was found, regardless of the dictates of honor, their own long-range interests, or those of the nation, and neither moral indignation nor patriotic exhortation was of use as a weapon of prevention: a fact of human nature learned reluctantly by Hamilton during the Revolution, when Samuel Chase of Maryland, a Signer of the Declaration and a Member of the Congress, turned "the knowledge of secrets to which his office gave him access, to the purposes of private profit, by employing emissaries to engross (buy up wholesale) an article, flour, of immediate necessity to the public service."[826]

Hamilton, as righteously indignant as his own opponents were later to be, denounced Chase "as a traitor of the worst and most dangerous kind," and solemnly warned his fellow-countrymen that "when avarice takes the lead in a state, it is commonly the forerunner of its fall." But he soon came to the realization that individual corruption was only a symptom, not the source of the disease. The depreciation of the currency, though in the situation unavoidable, was "as pernicious to the morals as to the credit of the nation," and its effects were to be found in "the constant thinness of our armies, the impossibility . . . of recruiting them otherwise than by compulsion, the scarcity of hands in husbandry and other occupations, the decrease of our staple commodities, and the difficulty of every species of supply."[827]

Thousands of ordinary citizens, farmers as well as merchants, the rich and the poor, like Chase, were seeking to take advantage of the times "to raise themselves above indigence by every little art in their power," and Hamilton, though an aide de camp of Washington and ardently desirous of a combat command, was forced to the conclusion that it was only "by introducing order into our finances—by restoring public credit—not by gaining battles" that victory would be won. The nation's troubles were more economic than military, and, in an effort to find a remedy, he devoted whatever time he could spare to the study of history and political economy in the books that he had used at King's College before the Revolution, and which he had abandoned, as Washington said, to devote his "soul," his "probity," and his "sterling virtue," wholeheartedly to the American cause.[828]

It was thus as a soldier intent on military victory that Hamilton first became concerned with the problems of money and credit, and was convinced through his study that a sound and effective financial system could never be established on the basis of governmental credit alone. Some new principle was needed, for in the American situation the "moneyed men," instead of having their profits enhanced through upholding the government's credit, frequently found it to their interest "to undermine it," and Hamilton, for this reason, insisted that "the only plan that can preserve the currency is one that will make it the immediate interest of the monied men to cooperate with government in its support."[829]

He had no property or income, except his army pay, and if he had any partiality or prejudice when he made this suggestion, it was against these "monied men," who, like almost all civilians, from the viewpoint of the soldier, were promoting their selfish private interests while he and his companions were making sacrifices for the cause. But Hamilton now had become a realist, and when confronted with an actuality that could not be overcome, he no long wasted his energies on futile grumblings or denunciation. Instead he sought to use it, perhaps to outwit it, and in April, 1781, when thinking of ways to persuade merchants and other "monied men" to subscribe to governmental stock, he stated as a fact, without approval or disapproval, that "individuals will not have confidence enough in our public councils to embark any considerable part of their fortunes with us on the ordinary principles of a loan. Stronger inducements, the prospects of commercial advantages, securities different from the mere faith in the United States must be held out, to tempt them to engage with us."[830]

To "give individuals ability and inclination to lend, in any proportion to the wants of the government," he continued, "a plan must be devised, which by incorporating their means . . . with those of the public will . . . erect a mass of credit that will supply the defect of monied capitals and answer all the purposes of cash; a plan which will offer adventurers immediate advantages analogous to those they receive by employing their money in trade, and eventually greater advantages; a plan which will give them the greatest security the nature of the case will admit for what they lend, and which will not only advance their own interest and secure the independence of their country, but in its progress have the most beneficial influence upon its future commerce and be a source of national strength and wealth."[831]

The plan he envisioned was that of a national bank of issue, subject to governmental control and inspection, but directed and operated by private stockholders who had paid for their stock with national securities, and his chief purpose in making this proposal was to meet the nation's need for a trustworthy and effective currency and an expanded supply of credit. The one great advantage of such an

institution was its ability to raise "a vast fabric of paper . . . on a visionary basis," and here Hamilton fully agreed with one of his later critics, John Taylor of Caroline, who, with indignant fury, protested that banknotes "may be infinitely multiplied by a printing press, and are unlimited so long as the nation is able to pay six pounds specie, for every hundred pounds of idea, which a bank may be pleased to emit."[832]

But, instead of objecting to this feature, Hamilton thought it advantageous. Buyers and sellers would use paper, even though its value was based on a fiction, as readily as gold or silver, just so long as they had confidence in its stability. "A degree of illusion," he wrote, "mixes itself in all the affairs of society. The opinion of objects has more influence than their real nature;"[833] and one of the virtues of a bank-issued currency was its capacity for indefinite expansion without arousing doubt or distrust concerning its value. In three private unpublicized letter (the first undated and to an unknown correspondent, probably written in the winter of 1779-1780; the second to James Duane, a member of Congress from New York, on September 3, 1780; and the third to Robert Morris, newly appointed Superintendent of Finance, on April 30, 1781), he urged the importance of establishing a national bank. "In my opinion," he wrote, "we ought not to hesitate because we have no other resource . . . We have little specie; the paper we have is of small value and rapidly descending to less; we are immersed in a war for our existence as a nation, for our liberty and happiness as a people; we have no revenues or credit."[834]

The American situation resembled that of Great Britain at the time that the Bank of England was established, for there "the long and expensive wars of King William had drained (the nation) of its specie, its commerce began to droop for want of a proper medium, its taxes were unproductive and its revenues declined." But, instead of despairing and doing nothing, its "administrators wisely had recourse to the institution of a bank," which not only "relieved the national difficulties" of the moment but also provided the means "for the immense efforts (Great Britain) has been able to make in so many illustrious and successful wars" during the eighteenth century. "Tis by this alone," he added, "she now menaces our independence," and he thought that the Americans should profit from the example.[835]

The public importance of the Bank of England and the contributions it had made to governmental and military strength were Hamilton's chief interest during the Revolution, but he also pointed out that such banks, in times of peace, had "proved to be the happiest engines that ever were invented for advancing trade." Most of the great commercial nations and cities (Holland, Hamburg, Venice, Genoa, and others) had established similar institutions, and through them had enhanced their commerce, riches, and power. "The tendency of a national bank," he wrote, "is to increase public and private credit," both of which were needed in the United States, for as the former would give "power to the state for the protection of its rights and interests," so would the latter facilitate and extend "the operations of commerce among individuals. Industry would be increased, multiplied, agriculture and manufactures stimulated, and it was these measures, not the condition of the national treasury alone, that marked "the true wealth and prosperity of a state."[836]

Unfortunately for Hamilton and other proponents of public banks, these institutions seldom attracted notice when they were operating effectively and soundly. Governments collected taxes and borrowed, individuals bought and sold, the nation and its economy were strong and prosperous, and almost no one bothered to ask the reason why. The evidence was there for those curious enough to inquire, but despite its overwhelmingly favorable character, numerous "enlightened and respectable" observers were convinced that the whole principle and practice of banking was dangerous and wrong. For confirmation, they looked not to Great Britain, Italy, Germany, and Holland, where, as Hamilton said, "after an experience of centuries" there existed not a question as to the utility of public banks. Instead they remembered the disastrous collapse in 1720 of the bank organized by John Law in France as part of his speculative Mississippi scheme, and they seemingly believed that such would be the inevitable fate of all similar institutions.[837]

In words that he later could have used to answer Taylor, Jefferson, and Adams, had he ever chosen to do so, Hamilton wrote in regard to these exaggerated fears:

"All that has been said against [these banks] only tends to prove that like all good things they are subject to abuse and when abused become pernicious. The precious metals by similar arguments may be proved to be injurious; it is certain that the mines of South America have had great influence in banishing industry from Spain and sinking it in real wealth and importance. Great power, commerce and riches, or in other words great national prosperity, may in like manner be denominated evils; for they lead to insolence, an inordinate ambition, a vicious luxury, licentiousness of morals, and all those vices which corrupt government and precipitate the ruin of a nation.

"No wise statesman," he added, should "reject the good from an apprehension of the ill," for "the truth is in human affairs, there is no good, pure and unmixed; every advantage has two sides, and wisdom consists in availing ourselves of the good, and guarding as much as possible from the bad."[838]

Here Hamilton stated his political and economic credo, from which he never departed, and his proposal to the Congress in 1790, that it charter the Bank of the United States, was in accordance with it. He did not hope for perfection, nor was it attained, but the Bank more than fulfilled his most optimistic expectations. For twenty years, from 1791 to 1811, it usefully served the United States, faithfully performing its public and private functions, and the results of its operations were found, as its president accurately claimed in one of the few public statements ever made by the Bank, "in the rapid advancement of agriculture, manufactures, and commerce, the solidity of private as well as of public credit, the ease with which the moneyed operations of government, of societies, and of individuals to an immense amount are carried on, the accumulation of wealth, and the general prosperity of the nation."[839]

The Bank provided a sound, elastic currency of almost equal value in all parts of the United States, and through its large capital, its numerous branches, its possession of the government deposits, and its established credit in Europe and the Far East, facilitated inter-regional and international payments, and equalized the balance of specie capital among the different commercial cities. It also acted as "the general guardian of commercial credit," expanding and contracting its loans and its dealings in domestic and foreign exchange in accordance with the needs of the national economy, and no major depression, no wide-spread or disastrous financial panic, occurred in the United States during these years, despite the severe and fluctuating pressures engendered by a world almost continuously at war.[840]

Three of the nation's leading students of political economy, Mathew Carey, Nicholas Biddle, and Condy Raguet, believed that the Bank was almost exclusively responsible for this fortunate state of affairs, as did also the officers and directors of the Bank of New York, who testified that in all cases of "sudden pressure upon the merchants," the national bank came "to their aid in a degree which the state banks are unable to do."[841] It also aided these local banks, whenever they found themselves temporarily pressed, and the protection thus provided was of direct benefit to the manufacturers and farmers. It was bank credit in the form of notes and deposits, not individual or corporate capital and wealth, that enabled the merchants to purchase and export American products, and thus the producers would be among the worse sufferers, if through the inability of the banks to lend during a depression, the merchants were unable to buy.

The national treasury also benefited from this Bank-induced prosperity and regularity, for, according to Albert Gallatin, Secretary of the Treasury under Jefferson and Madison, it was the Bank's ability and willingness to lend to the importers at times of monetary pressure as well as during periods of ease that enabled the government "to collect with so great facility, and with so few losses, the large revenue derived from the impost (tariff)." He likewise was convinced that the Bank "was a necessary and useful institution without which the Treasury operations would be costlier, riskier, and much less convenient."[842] It provided a safe depository for the public funds, transferred them from place to place and made the government's payments without charge to the Treasury, and whenever the national revenue was inadequate for immediate needs, enabled the government to keep its payments current by loans or advances.

It was so obviously useful that Jefferson, when President, though not changing his views or abating his hostility, was forced begrudgingly to admit that his Secretary of the Treasury (Albert Gallatin) "derived immense convenience from it," because, the President added, "it gave the effect of ubiquity to his [sic] money wherever deposited." Funds placed in the branches "in New Orleans or Maine" were "transformed in an instant into money in London, Paris, Amsterdam, or Canton," and not even Jefferson's indignation at what he called "the open hostility of that institution to a government on whose treasuries they were fattening," made Gallatin willing to transfer the deposits to "Republican" banks.[843]

The Secretary of the Treasury knew nothing of this alleged hostility of Jefferson's. He received only cooperation and non-partisan fulfillment of duty, much more, he believed, than could or would be given by the state banks, regardless of the political affiliations of their officers and directors. And in words reminiscent of those Hamilton had used, he justified his rejection of Jefferson's desire on the ground that "a national bank, deriving its charter from the national legislature, will, at all times, and under every emergency, feel stronger inducements, both from interest and a sense of duty, to afford to the Union every assistance within its power."[844]

The test of history thus proved Hamilton a true prophet. The Bank, instead of being, as Taylor, Jefferson, Adams, and other opponents continued to charge, "the curse and scourge of the nation," was in truth "the main spring of its prosperity;" a fact that became obvious during the War of 1812, after the Congress, in part for political reasons unconnected with the Bank, had refused to renew its charter.[845] Without a national currency or an effective source of credit, the United States had almost as much difficulty in providing means for this war as it had earlier had in financing the Revolution, and one of Congress' first acts after peace had returned was to create a new Bank of the United States.

Former opponents of the earlier Bank took the lead in the establishment of its successor, and, with the usual enthusiasm of converts, they thought all their problems were solved. They forgot, perhaps did not believe, Hamilton's warning that "every advantage has two sides," and were almost totally surprised in 1818, when the ineffectiveness and corruption of the Bank's management was the major factor in precipitating a depression. For a time all the old cries against banks and bankers were heard once again, but soon afterwards a new and more effective management, under Nicholas Biddle, was installed.[846] Prosperity returned, all was as before, and farmers, manufacturers, and merchants relearned (though not well enough, as the administrations of Andrew Jackson were to show) the truth of Hamilton's earlier quoted statement that "in the present state of things, the health of a state, particularly a commercial one, depends on a due quantity and circulation of cash, as much as the health of an animal body depends upon the due quantity and regular circulation of the blood."

Appendix 8

See Chapter 24

American Slavery

Thomas Payne Govan

In 1639, thirty-three years after the English began to settle "in that part of America commonly called Virginia," the free men of Maryland, with the consent of their Lord Proprietor, stated that "all the inhabitants of this province, being Christians (slaves excepted), shall have and enjoy all such rights, liberties, immunities, privileges, and free customs within this province as any natural born subject of England hath or ought to have or enjoy in the realm of England." Like many others before and since, they were more concerned with their own freedom than the freedom of others, and the parenthetical words, "slaves excepted," were an assertion that blacks, as a Chief Justice of the Supreme Court was later to say, were considered as "a subordinate and inferior class of beings, who had been subjugated by the dominant race" and "had no rights which a white man need respect."

This view of blacks "as beings of an inferior order altogether unfit to associate with the white race either in political or social relations" was accepted in all of the colonies and their enslavement was legally permitted in Massachusetts, Rhode Island, Connecticut, New York, New Jersey, Pennsylvania, and Delaware, as well as in Maryland,

Virginia, the Carolinas, and Georgia. Only a few morally sensitive individuals protested against this explicit denial of the teachings of the English Constitution and the Christian churches, and even during the revolutionary struggle against Great Britain, John Laurens of South Carolina and Alexander Hamilton of New York could gather little support for a proposal to permit black slaves to gain their freedom through enlistment in the Continental Army.

The Declaration of Independence and the Constitution of the United States, with their common assertion that the purpose of government was to establish freedom, justice, and equality, did increase the number of whites opposed to slavery, and in the nation's first quarter century, seven of the states began the process of emancipation. The national Congress, by the Northwest Ordinance of 1787, permanently prohibited slavery in the territories north of the Ohio and west of the mountains, and many Americans thought that within a few years this unjustifiable institution would be abolished throughout the United States.

They optimistically believed that slave labor was more costly than free and that this economic fact would lead the owners to consent to emancipation. Unfortunately, slavery was not unprofitable. Instead, the invention of machines to spin, weave, and gin cotton created a new source of profit for the owners of slaves, and the spread of cotton culture into the newly opened areas of the southwest provided a market for the surplus produce and slaves of earlier settled areas. The owners were unwilling to give up these profits, but, even more importantly, they became afraid to risk the dangers involved in emancipation.

One of the defenders of slavery in the Constitutional Convention had said that he "was not apprehensive of insurrections," but shortly afterwards an event occurred outside the United States that basically altered the proslavery argument. The blacks and men of color on the island of Santo Domingo, influenced by French revolutionary doctrines, rose against the whites; and the ensuing wars and massacres sent a wave of fear through the slaveholding regions of the United States, a fear apparently confirmed in subsequent years by the plots of

Gabriel Prosser and Denmark Vesey and the insurrection of Nat Turner.

Slavery became more than an economic institution. It was, in the opinion of large numbers of whites, the sole means through which the two races could peaceably occupy the same territory, and fear of the blacks became even more influential than a greedy desire for profit in inducing slaveholders to defend the institution and to insist that it must be permanent. Emancipation by legislative or judicial action stopped at the Ohio and the southern boundary of Pennsylvania and when Missouri was admitted to the Union, slavery spread west of the Mississippi. The nation did not totally abandon its hopes for emancipation. Slavery, by the terms of the Missouri Compromise, continued as a morally condemned institution, permanently prohibited in the northern part of the national territory and begrudgingly permitted to the south only after an explicit expression of the popular will.

Some thirty years later the situation changed, and the Congress, with the approval of the President, placed slavery and freedom on an equal moral plane through what came to be called the Compromise of 1850. The doctrine of popular sovereignty, which said that when territories became states, they were to be "received into the Union, with or without slavery, as their constitution may prescribe at the time of their admission," was prescribed for the territories of New Mexico and Utah. And on May 30, 1854, in the Kansas-Nebraska Act, the Congress, again with the approval of the President, not only repealed that portion of the Missouri Compromise that prohibited slavery in the northern territories, but also stated that it had become national policy "not to legislate slavery into any Territory or State, nor to exclude it there-from, but to leave the people thereof perfectly free to form and regulate their domestic institutions in their own way, subject only to the Constitution of the United States."

The Kansas-Nebraska Act offended many whites, some because it equated freedom and slavery, but others because it permitted black slaves to be taken into territories that previously had been reserved for white settlement alone. Anti-black sentiment, it seems, was as potent a source of opposition as anti-slavery, and this white attitude was strengthened on March 6, 1857, when Chief Justice Roger B. Taney, in the case of *Dred Scott v. Sanford,* held that there was no distinction between "property in a slave and other property," and that under the Constitution, a citizen of the United States could not be forbidden to take his property with him when he moved from one area of the nation to another.

The constitutionality of state laws prohibiting slavery was not an issue in this case, but the broadness of the Chief Justice's language cast doubts on their validity, and in the campaign of 1860, the Republican party received support from many whose opposition to the spread of slavery was based on their fear and hatred of blacks. These opponents of the spread of slavery also believed that blacks were "beings of an inferior order . . . altogether unfit to associate with the white race in political or social relations," and the war, when it came the following year as a result of the secession of eleven slave states, was fought for the Union, not to free the blacks. "My paramount object," President Abraham Lincoln wrote, ". . . is to save the Union, and is not either to save or to destroy slavery. . . . What I do about slavery and the colored race, I do because I believe it helps save the Union; and what I forbear, I forbear because I do not believe it would help to save the Union."

He justified the Emancipation Proclamation on military grounds, and though there is reason to believe that he objected to slavery because he knew it was wrong, he concealed these views until his second inaugural. Here, in what was to be almost his last statement to the American people, he abandoned moral neutrality, denouncing slavery as an evil, offensive to God, and pledging the nation, if it should be necessary, to continue the war "until all the wealth piled by the bondsman's two hundred and fifty years of unrequited toil shall be sunk, and until every drop of blood drawn with the lash shall be paid by another drawn with the sword." These sacrifices were not required. The war ended a few weeks later, and during the period of reconstruction that followed, the Republican leaders of the nation, angered by the intransigence of the unrepentant rebels and seeking to find a way to strengthen their political party, not only eliminated slavery but also provided full civil rights for the freedmen by the thirteenth, fourteenth, and fifteenth amendments to the Constitution of the United States. The apparent purpose of these Republicans was to make sure that the affirmations of the Declaration of Independence would apply to blacks as well as to whites, but, if such have ever been their aim, it was abandoned in 1877, when Rutherford Hayes and his party, to gain the presidency, returned control of relations between the races to the individual states.

The nation turned back to the view first expressed in the early part of the seventeenth century, that blacks were excluded from the "liberties, immunities, privileges, and free customs" that whites rightfully enjoyed, and though many blacks, supported by a few whites, protested, their protests were not heard or read in any significant way. A legend arose that the blacks were content with their assigned subordinate place, and this legend found apparent confirmation in the writings of American historians, most of whom accepted the view that the United States, from its beginning, had been a white man's nation, and that the blacks, as a dependent and inferior race, were to be ignored except when their presence aroused disputes among the whites as had happened with the slavery controversy and during reconstruction.

Only a few of these historians were admitted racists. Most would have disavowed the name and, if asked for their personal opinion, would have admitted that slavery and also the later denial to the blacks of their constitutionally established social, political, and civil rights were both departures from the correct course of national conduct. But, as objective, detached, and uninvolved scholars, they also believed it would be improper for them to permit this disapproval to appear in their writing. They wanted to guard themselves and their accounts of the past from partisanship, an easy distinction between good and evil, right and wrong, and in the pursuit of this praiseworthy objective, they came to distrust and ignore sources that patently were partisan and self-interested, propaganda, not factual description. In regard to much of the past, this objectivity, this avoidance of partisanship, made possible greater knowledge and understanding, but not so with slavery in the United States. For here the sources containing the viewpoint of the slave were to be found in personal narratives, written or dictated by those who passionately hated the institution, who were sure it was unjust and dehumanizing, and most of whose stories were used as abolitionist propaganda. So prevalent was the distrust of these accounts that historians of slavery almost entirely ignored them, turning instead to more neutral sources, and after a time, with a few notable exceptions such as the autobiographical writings of Frederick Douglass and other prominent blacks, their very existence was forgotten.

The present book is an effort to repair this omission, to use the more than five thousand narratives by ex-slaves as sources not for a complete description of what slavery actually was—Stanley Feldstein is too modest a historian to make such a presumptuous claim—but rather to provide an opportunity for these previously unheeded witnesses to be heard. "It is very important for the reader to understand," Mr. Feldstein writes "that, to the fullest extent possible, this study relates only what these narratives say about slave—life and the institution—it is not a history of slavery, nor is it offered as the 'true' story of slavery. It is exactly what the subtitle implies-that is, what the slaves whose stories were written down said about slavery."

Readers, however, will have difficulty in heeding this cautionary advice. This account of slavery has the ring of truth, and nowhere more than in its numerous descriptions of the refusal of slaves to become what the institution tried to make them be, "a chattel; a thing; a piece of property." The slaves were men, and though their masters, as many of the narratives attest, used "every instrument of cruelty" for the purpose "of obliterating the mind, of crushing the intellect, and of annihilating the soul," they did not succeed.

What the author calls "the dehumanization process—the making a thing of a human being"—was a constant characterization of the institution as described by those who experienced it; but the spirit of humanity within the slaves could not be destroyed; and despite the pain, the cruelty, and torment that appears on almost every page of this book, it yet remains a magnificent, almost joyous testimonial to the determination of men to retain not only their humanity but also their humaneness under the most adverse circumstances, to continue defiantly to say, as Aaron Siddles, a fugitive, did say, "By the law of Almighty God, I was born free."

He and all his fellows were indeed born free and were entitled to freedom. The denial of this freedom on this continent for more than three hundred years was a damnable wrong, one of the most horrid examples of man's inhumanity to man, and though Stanley Feldstein may not have written "the true story of slavery," he has done a better and more useful thing, he has made it possible for his readers to feel, to know, and to understand what it was like to be a slave.

Bibliography

Anderson, John M., ed. *Calhoun: Basic Documents.* State College, PA: Bald Eagle Press, 1952.

Appleby, Joyce, Lynn Hunt, and Margaret Jacob. *Telling the Truth about History.* New York: W. W. Norton and Company, 1994.

Archer, Peter. *The Queen's Courts: An Account of the Various Courts and Tribunals Which Administer English Law.* Penguin Books, 1956.

Arendt, Hannah. *The Human Condition.* Chicago: University of Chicago Press, 1958.

Armentraut, Donald Smith. *The Quest for the Informed Priest, a History of the School of Theology.* Sewanee, TN: University of the South, 1979.

Bailyn, Bernard. *The Ideological Origins of the American Revolution.* Cambridge, MA: Belknap Press, 1967.

Bailyn, Bernard, ed. *The Debate on the Constitution: Federalist and Antifederalist Speeches, Articles, and Letters During the Struggle for Ratification, September 1787 to February 1788.* The Literary Classics of the United States, Inc., 1993.

Bancroft, George. *The History of the United States From the Discovery of the American Continent,* 10 vols. Boston: Little, Brown and Company, 1834-1882.

Barzun, Jacques. *Romanticism and the Modern Ego.* Boston: Little, Brown and Company, 1943.

_____. *God's Country and Mine, a Declaration of Love Spiced with a Few Harsh Words.* Boston: Little, Brown and Company, 1954.

_____. *From Dawn to Decadence: 500 Years of Western Cultural Life, 1500 to the Present.* New York: Harper Collins, 2000.

Beard, Charles A. *An Economic Interpretation of the Constitution.* New York: Free Press, 1941.

———. *The Rise of American Civilization.* New York: Macmillan, 1968.

Bellah, Robert N. "Civil Religion in America." *Daedalus.* Winter 1967 1-21.

Bingham, June. *Courage to Change, an Introduction to the Life and Thought of Reinhold Niebuhr.* New York: Charles Scribner's Sons, 1961.

Bird, Kai. *The Color of Truth, McGeorge Bundy and William Bundy, Brothers in Arms; A Biography.* New York: Simon and Schuster, 1998.

Blackstone, William. *Commentaries on the Laws of England.* 4 vols. Oxford: Clarendon Press, 1766-1769.

Blight, David W. *The Civil War in American Memory.* Cambridge, MA: Harvard University Press, 2001.

Book of Common Prayer, 1979. New York: Seabury Press, 1979.

Boorstin, Daniel J. *The Genius of American Politics.* Chicago: University of Chicago Press, 1953.

———. *The Americans: The Colonial Experience.* New York: Random House, 1958.

Booty, John. *The Episcopal Church in Crisis.* Cambridge, MA: Cowley Publications, 1988.

Bridenbaugh, Carl. *Mitre and Sceptre: Transatlantic Faiths, Ideas, Personalities, and Politics, 1689-1775.* New York: Oxford University Press, 1962.

Brinkley, Alan. *Liberalism and Its Discontents.* Cambridge, MA: Harvard University Press, 1998.

Brookhiser, Richard. *Alexander Hamilton, American.* New York: Free Press, 1999.

Brown, Robert E. *Charles Beard and the Constitution, a Critical Analysis of "An Economic Interpretation of the Constitution."* Princeton: Princeton University Press, 1956.

Buber, Martin. *I and Thou.* New York: Charles Scribner's Sons, 1970.

Burnham, Frederic B., ed. *Postmodern Theology, Christian Faith in a Pluralist World.* San Francisco: Harper and Row Publishers, 1989.

Buttrick, George A. *Christ and History.* New York: Abington Press, 1963.

Cam, Helen C., ed. *F. W. Maitland, Historical Essays.* Cambridge, UK: Cambridge University Press, 1957.

Clark, Henry B. *Serenity, Courage, Wisdom: The Enduring Legacy of Reinhold Niebuhr.* Cleveland: Pilgrim Press, 1994.

Commager, Henry Steele ed. Alexis de Tocqueville's *Democracy in America.* New York: Oxford University Press, 1947.

Conrad, Alfred H., and John R. Meyer. *The Economics of Slavery and Other Studies in Econometric History.* Chicago: Alsline Publishing Co., 1964.

Cooke, Jacob E., ed. *Alexander Hamilton,* a Profile. New York: Hill and Wang, 1967.

Crowe, Charles, ed. *The Age of Civil War and Reconstruction, 1830-1900.* Homewood, IL.: Dorsey Press, 1966.

Cunningham, Noble E. *In Pursuit of Reason, the Life of Thomas Jefferson.* New York: Ballantine Books, 1987.

Davies, D. R. *Reinhold Niebuhr: Prophet for America.* New York: Macmillan Company, 1948.

Davies, W. Merlin. *An Introduction to F. D. Maurice's Theology.* London: SPCK Press, 1964.

Davis, Harry R., and Robert C. Good. *Reinhold Niebuhr on Politics.* New York: Charles Scribner's Sons, 1960.

Deglar, Carl N., ed. *Pivotal Interpretations of American History, Volume I.* New York: Harper and Row Publishers, 1966.

Dobell, Bryon, ed. *A Sense of History, the Best Writings from the Pages of American Heritage.* New York: American Heritage Press, 1985.

Dumond, Dwight L. *Anti-Slavery Origins of the Civil War in the United States.* Ann Arbor: University of Michigan Press, 1939.

Eaton, Clement. *Freedom of Thought in the Old South.* Durham: Duke University Press, 1940.

Elkins, Stanley, and Eric McKitrick. *The Age of Federalism.* New York: Oxford University Press, 1994.

Ellis, Joseph J. *Founding Brothers: The Revolutionary Generation.* New York: Alfred A. Knopf, 2001.

Ellison, Ralph. *The Invisible Man.* New York: Vintage Books, 1972.

Emery, Naomie. *Alexander Hamilton, an Intimate Portrait.* New York: Putnam Press, 1992.

Feldstein, Stanley. *Once a Slave: The Slaves' View of Slavery.* New York: William Morrow and Company, 1971.

Fiske, John. *The Critical Period of American History, 1783-1784*. Boston: Houghton Mifflin, 1888.

Fleming, Thomas. *Duel: Alexander Hamilton, Aaron Burr, and the Future of America*. New York: Basic Books, 2000.

Flexner, James Thomas. *The Young Hamilton: A Biography*. New York: Fordham University Press, 1977.

Flowers, Betty Sue, ed. *Bill Moyers, a World of Ideas*. New York: Doubleday, 1989.

Fogel, Robert W. *Without Consent or Contract, the Rise and Fall of American Slavery*. New York: W.W. Norton and Company, 1989.

_____. *Time and the Cross, the Economics of American Slavery*. Boston: Little, Brown and Company, 1974.

Foner, Eric. *The New American History*. Philadelphia: Temple University Press, 1990.

Foner, Philip S., ed. *Basic Writings of Thomas Jefferson*. New York: Willey Book Company, 1944.

Fox, Richard W. *Reinhold Niebuhr, A Biography*. New York: Harper and Row, 1987.

Freeman, Joanne B., ed. *Alexander Hamilton, Writings*. New York: The Library of America, 2001.

Gabriel, Ralph Henry. *The Course of American Democratic Thought*. New York: Ronald Press Company, 1940.

_____. *The Course of American Democratic Thought, an Intellectual History Since 1815*. 3rd ed. with Robert H. Walker. New York: Greenwood Press, 1986.

Garraty, John A., and Jerome L. Sternstein, eds. *Encyclopedia of American Biography*. New York: Harper Collins, 1974 and 1997.

Genovese, Eugene D. *The Political Economy of Slavery: Studies in the Economy and Society of the Slave South*. New York: Pantheon Books, 1956.

Govan, Thomas P. *Banking and the Credit System in Georgia, 1810-1860*. New York: Arno Press, 1978.

_____. *Free to Be Merely a Man*. New York: The Episcopal Church, 1956.

_____. "History of the Second Army." In *Studies in the History of the Army Ground Forces*. Washington, DC: Headquarters, Army Ground Forces, September 1, 1945.

_____. *Nicholas Biddle, Nationalist and Public Banker.* Chicago: University of Chicago Press, 1959.

_____. "Radical America, the Continuing Revolution." A course of twenty television lectures sponsored by the American Bicentennial Commission of Oregon, aired several times over station KOAC-TV and later published in mimeographed form by the Oregon Educational and Public Broadcasting Service.

_____. *The Rejection of Denominational Idolatries.* New York: The Episcopal Church, Forward Movement Press, 1975.

_____. *Training in Mountain and Winter Warfare, Study 28.* Washington, DC: Army Ground Forces, 1946.

Grantham, Dewey W. *The South in Modern America, a Region at Odds.* New York: Harper Collins Publishers, 1994.

Grog, Gerald N., and George Athan Billias eds. *Interpretations of American History, Volume I, to 1877, Volume II, Since 1877.* 6th ed. New York: Free Press, 1992.

Hammond, Bray. *Banks and Politics in America: From the Revolution to the Civil War.* Princeton: Princeton University Press, 1957.

Handy, Robert T. *The Social Gospel in America.* New York: Oxford University Press, 1966.

Hartz, Louis. *The Liberal Tradition in America: An Interpretation of American Political Thought Since the Revolution.* New York: Harcourt Brace and World, 1955.

Heilbroner, Robert L. *The Worldly Philosophers, the Lives, Times, and Ideas of the Great Economic Thinkers.* 7 eds. New York: Touchstone, Simon and Schuster, Inc., 1953-1989.

Henry, William A. 3rd. *In Defense of Elitism.* New York: Doubleday, 1994.

Hildreth, Richard. *The History of the United States, 1788-1821*, six vols. 1848-1852. New York: Harper & Brothers, 1877.

Himmelfarb, Gertrude. *On Looking into the Abyss, Untimely Thoughts on Culture and Society.* New York: Alfred A. Knopf, 1994.

Hofstadter, Richard. *The American Political Tradition and the Men Who Made It.* New York: Vintage Books, 1948.

Horton, Myles. *The Long Haul.* New York: Doubleday, 1990.

Howarth, David. *1066, the Year of the Conquest.* New York: Viking Press, 1977.

Jennings, Frances. *The Creation of America: Through Revolution to Empire.* Cambridge UK: Cambridge University Press, 2000.

Kennedy, Roger G. *Burr, Hamilton, and Jefferson: A Study in Character.* New York: Oxford University Press, 2000.

Little, David. *Religion, Order, and Law.* New York: Harper Torchbooks, Harper and Row, 1969.

Lovin, Robin W. *Reinhold Niebuhr and Christian Realism.* Cambridge, UK: Cambridge University Press, 1995.

MacArthur, Douglas. *Reminiscences.* New York: McGraw-Hill, 1964.

MacQuarrie, John. *Twentieth Century Religious Thought: The Frontiers of Philosophy and Theology, 1900-1960.* New York: Harper and Row Publishers, 1963.

Maier, Pauline. *American Scripture, Making the Declaration of Independence.* New York: Alfred A. Knopf, 1997.

Maitland, F. W. *The Constitutional History of England.* Cambridge, UK: Cambridge University Press, 1968.

Malone, Dumas. *Jefferson and His Time.* 6 vols. Boston: Little, Brown and Company, 1948-1981.

Maurice, Frederick Denison. *Has the Church or the State the Power to Educate the Nation?* London: J. G. and F. Rivington, St. Paul's Church Yard and Darton and Clark, Holburn Hill, 1839.

———. *The Kingdom of Christ.* 2 vols. London: James Clarke and Co. Ltd. Reprinted by J. M. Dent and Co., 1959.

———. *The Prayer Book.* Republished in London: James Clark and Co. Ltd., 1966.

McClain, Frank M. *Maurice, Man and Moralist, 1805-1872.* London: S. P. C. K., 1972.

McCullough, David. *John Adams.* New York: Simon & Shuster, 2001.

McDonald, Forrest. *Alexander Hamilton.* New York: W. W. Norton and Company, 1979.

———. *The Presidency of Thomas Jefferson.* University of Kansas Press, 1976.

———. *We the People.* Chicago: University of Chicago Press, 1958.

McDonald, Forrest, Leslie E. Decker, and Thomas P. Govan. *The Last Best Hope, a History of the United States.* 2 vols. Reading, MA.: Addison-Wesley Publishing Company, 1973.

McGrane, Reginald C., ed. *The Correspondence of Nicholas Biddle Dealing with National Affairs, 1807-1844.* Boston: Houghton Mifflin Company, 1919.

Miller, John C. *Alexander Hamilton: Portrait in Paradox.* New York: Harper, 1959.

————. *The Federalist Era, 1789-1801.* New York: Harper Torchbooks, Harper and Row Publishers, 1960.

————. *Origins of the American Revolution.* Boston: Little, Brown and Company, 1943.

Miller, William Lee. *Arguing about Slavery: The Great Battle in the United States Congress.* New York: Alfred A. Knopf, 1996.

Miller, Perry. *The New England Mind: The Seventeenth Century.* Boston: Beacon Press, 1953.

Mitchell, Baudus. *Alexander Hamilton, a Concise Biography.* New York: Oxford University Press, 1976.

Modares, Larry, and James M. SoRelle. *Clashing Views on Controversial Issues in American History, Volume I, the Colonial Period to Reconstruction.* Guilford, CT: The Dishkin Publishing Group, Inc., 1995.

Morgan, Edmund S. *The Birth of the Republic 1763-1789.* Chicago: University of Chicago Press, 1956, 1992.

Morison, Samuel Eliot, and Henry Steele Commager. *The Growth of the American Republic.* 2 vols. in 10 eds. New York: Oxford University Press, 1930-1960.

Moritz, Charles. *Contemporary Biography (1969).* New York: H. W. Wilson Company, 1970.

Morone, James A. *The Democratic Wish, Popular Participation and the Limits of American Government.* New York: Basic Books, 1990.

Muller, Herbert J. *Adlai Stevenson: A Study in Values.* New York: Harper and Row, 1967.

Namier, Lewis B. *England in the Age of the American Revolution.* New York: St. Martin's Press, 1961.

Niebuhr, H. Richard. *Christ and Culture.* New York: Harper Brothers, 1951.

Niebuhr, Reinhold. *Beyond Tragedy.* New York: Charles Scribner's Sons, 1937.

_____. *The Children of Light and the Children of Darkness*. New York: Charles Scribner's Sons, 1944.

_____. *Christian Realism and Political Problems*. New York: Charles Scribner's Sons, 1953.

_____. *Christianity and Power Politics*. New York: Charles Scribner's Sons, 1940.

_____. *The Irony of American History*. New York: Charles Scribner's Sons, 1952.

_____. *Leaves from the Notebook of a Tamed Cynic*. Hamden, CT: Shoe String Press, 1956.

_____. *Moral Men and Immoral Society*. New York: Charles Scribner's Sons, 1932.

_____. *The Nature and Destiny of Man*. 2 vols. New York: Charles Scribner's Sons, 1941.

Niebuhr, Reinhold, and Alan Heimert. *A Nation So Conceived, Reflections on the History of America from Its Early Visions to Its Present Power*. New York: Charles Scribner's Sons, 1963.

O'Brien, Conor Cruise. *The Long Affair: Thomas Jefferson and the French Revolution, 1785-1800*. Chicago: University of Chicago Press, 1996.

_____. *The Great Melody: A Thematic Biography of Edmund Burke*. Chicago: University of Chicago Press, 1992.

Parrington, Vernon L. *Main Currents in American Thought*. 3 vols. New York: Harcourt Brace, 1927-1930.

Patterson, James T. *Grand Expectations: The United States, 1945-1974*. New York: Oxford University Press, 1996.

Peterson, Merrill D. *Adams and Jefferson, a Revolutionary Dialogue*. New York: Oxford University Press, 1976.

_____. *Thomas Jefferson and the New Nation, a Biography*. New York: Oxford University Press, 1970.

Phillips, Ulrich Bonnell. *American Negro Slavery*. New York: Appleton and Company, 1918.

_____. *The Course of the South to Secession, an Interpretation*. Edited by E. Merton Coulter. New York: D. Appleton-Century Company, 1939.

Polkinghorne, John. *Belief in God in an Age of Science*. New Haven, CT: Yale University Press, 1988.

Porter, David L. *African-American Sports Greats, a Biographical Dictionary.* Waterford, CT: Greenwood Press, 1995.

Porter, John F., and William J. Wolf. *Toward the Recovery of Unity.* New York: Seabury Press, 1964.

Ramsey, Arthur Michael. *The Gospel and the Catholic Church.* Reprint, Cambridge, MA: Cowley, 1990.

_____. *F. D. Maurice and the Conflicts of Modern Theology.* Cambridge, UK: Cambridge University Press, 1951.

Rauschenbusch, Walter. *Christianity and Social Crisis.* Louisville: Westminster-John Knox, 1992.

Rogow, Arnold A. *A Fatal Friendship: Alexander Hamilton and Aaron Burr.* New York: Hill and Wang, 2000.

Rossiter, Clinton. *Alexander Hamilton and the Constitution.* New York: Harcourt Brace and World, Inc., 1964.

_____. *Alexander Hamilton and the Growth of the New Nation.* New York: Harper and Row, 1964.

Schlesinger, Arthur, Jr. *The Age of Jackson.* Boston: Little, Brown and Company, 1945.

_____. "The Ages of Jackson." T*he New York Review of Books* (December 7, 1989): 48-51.

_____. *The Age of Roosevelt.* Boston: Houghton Mifflin, 1951-1960.

Sellers, Charles Grier. *The Southerner as American.* New York: E. P. Dutton and Company, 1966. 1st ed. Chapel Hill: University of North Carolina Press, 1960.

Silk, Leonard. *The Economists.* New York: Basic Books, Inc., 1978.

Smith, Ronald Gregor. *The New Men, Christianity and Men's Coming of Age.* London: S. C. M. Press Ltd., 1955.

Smith, Morton. *The Republic of Letters: The Correspondence between Thomas Jefferson and James Madison 1776-1826.* New York: Norton Press, 1995.

Stein, Susan R. *The Worlds of Thomas Jefferson at Monticello.* New York: H. N. Abrams, 1993.

Stone, Ronald H. *Reinhold Niebuhr, Prophet to Politician.* New York: Abington Press, 1972.

Sumner, David E. *The Episcopal Church's History, 1945-1987.* Wilton, CT: Morehouse Publishing, 1987.

Tillich, Paul. *Systematic Theology, Volume III* (on history). Chicago: University of Chicago Press, 1963.

Tracy, David. *Plurality and Ambiguity.* New York: Harper and Row Publishers, 1989.

Turner, Frederick Jackson. *The United States, 1830-1850: The Nation and Its Sections.* New York: Henry Holt, 1935.

Twelve Southerners. *I'll Take My Stand: The South and the Agrarian Tradition.* New York: Harper and Brothers, 1930.

Vidler, Alec R. *F. D. Maurice and Company.* London: S. C. M. Press, 1966.

_____. *Witness to the Light.* New York: Charles Scribner's Sons, 1948.

Von Holst, Hermann E. *Constitutional and Political History of the United States.* 8 vols. Chicago: Callaghan and Company, 1889-1892.

Wallace, Anthony. *Jefferson and the Indians: The Tragic Fate of the First Americans.* Cambridge, MA: Belknap Press, Harvard University Press, 1999.

Ward, John William. *Andrew Jackson, Symbol of an Age.* New York: Oxford University Press, 1955.

Warren, Robert Penn. *The Legacy of the Civil War.* New York: Random House, 1960.

Wills, Gary. *Inventing America: Jefferson's 'Declaration of Independence.'* Garden City, NY: Doubleday, 1978.

Wilson, Clyde N., ed. *Twentieth Century American Historians.* Vol. 7 of *Dictionary of Literary Biography.* Detroit, MI: A Bruccoli Clark Book, Gale Research Company, 1983.

_____. *American Historians, 1607-1865.* Vol. 30 of *Dictionary of Literary Biography.* Detroit, MI: A Bruccoli Clark Book, Gale Research Company, 1984.

_____. *American Historians, 1866-1912.* Vol. 47 of *Dictionary of Literary Biography.* Detroit, MI: A Bruccoli Clark Book, Gale Research Company, 1986.

Woititz, Janet Geringer. *Adult Children of Alcoholics.* Pompano Beach, FL: Health Communications, Inc., 1983.

World Almanac and Book of Facts. Mahwah, NJ: World Almanac Books, 1975-2000.

Wood, Gordon S. *The Creation of the American Republic, 1776-1787.* Chapel Hill: University of North Carolina Press, 1969.

————. *The Radicalism of the American Revolution.* New York: Alfred A. Knopf, 1992.

Wood, H. G. *Frederick Denison Maurice.* Cambridge, UK: Cambridge University Press, 1950.

Wreszin, Michael. *A Rebel in Defence of Tradition, The Life and Politics of Dwight Macdonald.* New York: Basic Books, 1994.

Book Reviews

The 1940s

Govan, Thomas P. "Slavery and the Civil War," *Sewanee Review* 48, No. 4 (October-December 1940).

> Gabriel, Ralph Henry. *The Cause of American Democratic Thought.* New York: Ronald Press Company, 1940.
>
> Dumond, Dwight L. *Anti-Slavery Origins of the Civil War in the United States.* Ann Arbor: University of Michigan Press, 1939.
>
> Phillips, Ulrich Bonnell. T*he Course of the South to Secession, an Interpretation.* New York: D. Appleton-Century Company, 1939.
>
> Eaton, Clement. *Freedom of Thought in the Old South.* Durham: Duke University Press, 1940.

___. "Not Profit and Loss," *Sewanee Review* 50, No. 3 (July-September 1942): 426-427.

> Perkins, Howard Cecil, ed. *Northern Editorials on Secession.* New York: Century Company, 1931.

___. *The Journal of Southern History* IX, No. 4 (December 1943): 569-570.

Madeline, Sister M. Grace. *Monetary Banking Theories of Jacksonian Democracy.* Philadelphia: Dolphin Press, 1943.

___. *The Southern Historical Review* XII, No. 1 (February 1945): 117-118.

Henry, Robert Selph. *First With the Most, Nathan Bedford Forrest, 558. Indianapolis:* The Bobbs-Merrill Company, 1944.

___. *The Journal of Southern History* XIV, No. 4 (November 1948): 566-567.

Tilley, Nannie M. *The Bright Tobacco Industry, 1860-1929.* Chapel Hill: University of North Carolina Press, 1948.

___. *The Journal of Southern History* XV, No. 2 (May 1949).

Murray, Paul. *The Whig Party in Georgia, 1825-1853.* Chapel Hill: University of North Carolina Press, 1948.

The 1950s

___. *The American Historical Review* LXVII, No. 4 (July 1952): 1004-1005.

Cline, Roy S. *Washington Command Post: the Operations Division.* Washington, DC: Department of the Army, 1951.

___. *The Mississippi Valley Historical Review* 38, No. 4 (March 1952): 701-702.

White, Leonard D. *The Jeffersonians: A Study of Administrative History, 1801-1829.* New York: Macmillan Company, 1951.

___. *The Journal of Southern History* XIX, No. 3 (August 1953): 387-389.

Anderson, John M., ed. *Calhoun: Basic Documents.* State College, PA: Bald Eagle Press, 1952.

___. *The American Historical Review* LIX, No. 1 (October 1953): 167-168.

> Smith, Robert Ross. *The Approach to the Philippines.* Washington, DC: Center of Military History, Department of the Army, 1953: 623.

___. *The Mississippi Valley Historical Review* XL, No. 4 (March 1954), 731.

> Butterfield, Lyman H. *John Witherspoon Comes to America: A Documentary Account Based Largely on New Material.* Princeton: Princeton University Library, 1953.

___. *The American Historical Review,* Vol. LX, No. 3 (April 1955): 621-622.

> White, Leonard D. *The Jacksonians: A Study in Administrative History.* New York: Macmillan Company, 1954.

___. *The Journal of Southern History* XXI, No. 3 (August 1955): 593-595.

> Heath, Milton Sydney. *Constructive Liberalism: The Role of the State in Economic Development in Georgia to 1860.* Cambridge: Harvard University Press, 1954.

___. *The Mississippi Valley Historical Review* XLII, No. 3 (December 1955): 565-566.

> Ward, John William. *Andrew Jackson, Symbol of an Age.* New York: Oxford University Press, 1955.

___. *The Pennsylvania Magazine of History and Biography* LXXXI, No. 3 (July 1957): 328-329.

> Bruchey, Stuart Weems. *Robert Oliver, Merchant of Baltimore, 1783-1819.* Baltimore: Johns Hopkins Press, 1956.

___. *The Business History Review.* (Autumn 1957): 72.

Schneider, Wilbert M. T*he American Bankers Association, Its Past and Present.* Washington: Public Affairs Press, 1956.

___. *The Journal of Southern History* XXIV, No. 1 (February 1958): 114-117.

Meyers, Marvin. *The Jacksonian Persuasion: Politics and Belief.* Stanford: Stanford University Press, 1957.

___. *The Mississippi Valley Historical Review* XLIV, No. 4 (March 1958): 721-724.

Hammond, Bray. *Banks and Politics in America from the Revolution to the Civil War.* Princeton: Princeton University Press, 1957.

___. *The American Historical Review* 64, No. 4 (July 1959): 1013-1014.

Balinsky, Alexander. *Albert Gallatin: Fiscal Theories and Policies.* New Brunswick, NJ: Rutgers University Press, 1958.

The 1960s

___. *The Mississippi Valley Historical Review* 47, No. 3 (December 1960): 499-500.

Dorfman, Joseph, and R.G. Tugwell. *Early American Policy: Six Columbia Contributors.* New York: Columbia University Press, 1960.

___. *The Pennsylvania Magazine of History and Biography* LXXXIV, No. 4 (October 1960): 494-495.

Hopkins, James P., and Mary W.M. Hargreaves, eds. *Papers of Henry Clay, Volume I: The Rising Statesman, 1794-1814.* Lexington: University of Kentucky Press, 1963.

___. *The Church Review of the Church Society for College Work of the Episcopal Church* (February 1961).

Baly, Denis. *Academic Illusion*. Greenwich, CT: Seabury Press, 1960.

___. The *Brown Daily Herald Supplement* (April 18, 1961).

Warren, Robert Penn. T*he Legacy of the Civil War*. New York: Random House, 1959.

___. *The American Historical Review* 67, No. 4 (July 1962): 1057-1058.

Abernathy, Thomas P. *The South in the New Nation, 1789-1819*. Baton Rouge: Louisiana State University Press, 1961.

___. *The American Historical Review* 68, No. 1 (October 1962): 244-245.

Rothbard, Murray N. *The Panic of 1819: Reactions and Policies*. New York: Columbia University Press, 1962.

___. *The Historical Magazine of the Protestant Episcopal Church* XXXII, No. 1 (March 1963): 49-56.

Bridenbaugh, Carl. *Mitre and Sceptre: Transatlantic Faiths, Ideas, Personalities, and Politics 1689-1775*. New York: Oxford University Press, 1962.

___. *The Pennsylvania Magazine of History and Biography* LXXXVIII, No. 4 (October 1964).

 • Hopkins, James P., and Mary W.M. Hargreaves, eds. *Papers of Henry Clay, Volume I: The Rising Statesman, 1794-1814*. Lexington: University of Kentucky Press, 1963.

- ___. *Papers of Henry Clay, Volume III: Presidential Candidate, 1821-1824.* Lexington: University of Kentucky Press, 1963.

___. *The Journal of American History* LII, No. 1 (June 1965): 163-164.

MacArthur, Douglas. *Reminiscences.* New York: McGraw-Hill, 1964.

___. *The Business History Review* (1963) (specific reference unknown).

Swift, David E. *Joseph G. Gurney: Banker, Reformer, and Quaker.* Middletown, CT: Wesleyan University Press, 1962.

___. *The Bulletin of Bexley Hall Seminary,* Rochester, NY, Vol. 8, No. 3 (October 1964): 3-4.

Porter, John F., and William J. Wolf, eds. *Toward the Recovery of Unity: the Thought of Frederick Denison Maurice.* New York: Seabury Press, 1964.

___. *The Pennsylvania Magazine of History and Biography* LXXXVIII, No. 4 (October 19645): 494-495.

Rossiter, *Clinton. Alexander Hamilton and the Constitution.* New York: Harcourt Brace and World, 1964.

___. *The Prism,* the magazine of the University Christian Foundation at New York University, No. 1 (March 1964): 3-4.

- Von Balthasar, Hans Urs. *A Theology of History.* New York: Sheed and Ward, 1963.
- Buttrick, George A. *Christ and History.* New York: Abington Press, 1963.
- Tillich, Paul. *Systematic Theology.* Vol. 3. Chicago: University of Chicago Press, 1963.

___. *The Journal of American History* LII. No. 2 (September 1965): 387-388.

Conrad, Alfred H., and John R. Meyer. *The Economics of Slavery and Other Studies of Economic History.* Chicago: Aldine Publishing Company, 1964.

___. *The Journal of Southern History* 31, No. 1 (February 1965): 119-120.

Grimes, Alan P. *Equality in America: Religion, Race, and the Urban Majority.* New York: Oxford University Press, 1964.

___. *The Journal of Southern History 32*, No. 2 (May 1966): 231-234.

Genovese, Eugene D. T*he Political Economy of Slavery: Studies in the Economy and Society of the Slave South.* New York: Pantheon Books, 1965.

___. *The Pennsylvania Magazine of History and Biography* XC, No. 4 (April 1966): 271-272.

Gilchrist, David T., and W. David Lewis, eds. *Economic Change in the Civil War Era: Proceedings of a Conference on the Civil War, Held March 12-14, 1964.* Greenville, DE: Eleutherian Mills-Hagley Foundation, 1965.

___. *The Florida History Quarterly* XLIV, No. 3 (January 1966): 242-243.

Perkins, Bradford. *Casttereagh and Adams, England and the United States, 1812-1823.* Berkeley: University of California Press, 1964.

___. *The Pennsylvania Magazine of History and Biography* XCI, No. 2 (April 1967): 235-236.

Hoyt, Edwin P., Jr. *The House of Morgan.* New York: Dodd Mead and Company, 1966.

___. *The* Review reference unknown. A typed version is among Govan's papers.

Sibley, Joel H. *The Shrine of party: Congressional Voting Behavior, 1841-1852.* Pittsburgh: University of Pittsburgh Press, 1967.

___. *The Florida Historical Quarterly* XLVIII (October 1968): 189-190. Each successive volume reviewed in the year following its publication.

Hemphill, W. Edwin. *The Papers of John C. Calhoun.* Columbia, SC: University of South Carolina Press.

Vol. III, 1818-1819 (1967)
Vol. IV, 1819-1820 (1969)
Vol. V, 1820-1821 (1970)
Vol. VI, 1821-1822 (1972)
Vol. VII, 1822-1823 (1973)
Vol. VIII, 1823-1824 (1975)
Vol. IX, 1824-1825 (1976).

___. *The Pennsylvania Magazine of History and Biography,* Vol. XC, No. 4 (April 1966): 271-272.

Gilchrist, David T., and W. David Lewis, eds., *Economic Changes in the Civil War Era: Proceedings of a Conference on American Economic Institutional Change, 1850-1873, and the Impact of Civil War, Held March 12-14, 1964.* Greenville, DE, Eleutherian Mills-Hagley Foundation, 1965.

___. *The Business History Review* XLII, No. 1 (Spring 1968).

Leiman, Melvin N. J*acob N. Cardozo: Economic Thought in the Ante-Bellum South.* (New York: Columbia University Press, 1966.

___. *The Journal of Southern History, 34,* No. 3 (August 1968).

Muller, Herbert J. *Adlai Stevenson: A Study in Values*. New York: Harper and Row Publishers, 1967.

___. *The Pennsylvania Magazine of History and Biography* CXII, No. 3 (July 1968): 397-398.

Shapiro, Seymour. *Capital and the Cotton Industry in the Industrial Revolution*. Ithaca, NY: Cornell University Press, 1967.

___. *The American Historical Review* 74, No. 1 (October 1968): 280.

Woodman, Harold D. *King Cotton and His Retainers: Financing and Marketing the Cotton Crop of the south, 1800-1925*. Lexington: University of Kentucky Press, 1968.

___. *The Journal of Southern History* LVI, No. 1 (June 1969): 136-137.

Kirwan, Albert D., ed. *The Civilization of the Old South: Writings of Clement Eaton*. Lexington: University of Kentucky Press, 1968.

The 1970s

___. *The Pennsylvania Magazine of History and Biography* XCIV, No. 4 (October 1970): 560-561.

Brown, Norman D. *Daniel Webster and the Politics of Availability*. Athens, GA: University of Georgia Press, 1969.

___. *The Pennsylvania Magazine of History and Biography* XCIV, No. 1 (January 1970): 122-123.

Cave, Alfred A. *An American Conservative in the Age of Jackson: The Political and Social Thought of Calvin Cotton*. Fort Worth: Texas Christian University Press, 1969.

___. *The Journal of Southern History* XXXVI, No. 4 (November 1970).

> Callcott, George H. *History of the United States, 1800-1860: Its Practice and Purpose.* Baltimore: Johns Hopkins Press, 1970.

___. *The* Review reference unknown. A typed version is among Govan's papers.

> Curtin, Philip D. *The Atlantic Slave Trade: A Census.* Madison: University of Wisconsin Press, 1969.

___. *The American Historical Review* 76, No. 4 (October 1970): 1597-1598.

> Lesesne, J. Mauldin. *The Bank of the State of South Carolina: A General and Political History.* Columbia: University of South Carolina for the South Carolina Tricentennial Commission, 1970.

___. *The Florida Historical Quarterly* XLIX, No. 4 (April 1971): 407-408.

> Curtis, James C. *The Fox at Bay: Van Buren.* Lexington: University of Kentucky Press, 1970.

___. *The Journal of American History* 58, No. 1 (June 1971): 174-175.

> Hammond, Bray. *Sovereignty and an Empty Purse: Banks and Politics in the Civil War.* Princeton: Princeton University Press, 1970.

___. *The Business History Review* XLV, No. 3 (Autumn 1971): 374-375.

> Sharp, James Roger. *The Jacksonians versus the Banks: Politics in the States after the Panic of 1837.* New York: Columbia University Press, 1970.

___. *The Journal of American History* LVIII, No. 1 (June 1971): 143-144.

Stourzh, Gerald. A*lexander Hamilton and the Idea of Republican Government*. Stanford: Stanford University Press, 1970.

___. *The Journal of Southern History* 38, No. 1 (February 1972): 122-123.

Robin, Donald L. *Slavery in the Structure of American Politics, 1765-1820*. New York: Harcourt Brace Jovanovich, Inc., 1971.

___. *The* Reference unknown. Review found among Govan's papers.

Heilbroner, Robert L. *The Future of History: The Historic Currents of Our Time and the Direction in which They are Taking America*. New York: Harper and Brothers, 1971.

___. *The Journal of Southern History* LX, No. 3 (December 1973): 813-814.

Durden, Robert F. *The Grey and the Black: The Confederate Debate on Emancipation*. Baton Rouge: Louisiana State University Press, 1972.

___. *The Business History Review* XLVII, No. 1 (Spring 1973): 108-109.

Erickson, Erling A. *Banking in Frontier Iowa 1836-1865*. Ames: Iowa State University Press, 1971.

___. *The Maryland Historical Magazine* (Spring 1974): 106-107.

Blessinggame, John W. *The Slave Community: Plantation Life in the Ante-Bellum South*. New York: Oxford University Press, 1972.

___. *The Journal of the New York Historical Society* (January 1974): 69-70.

McFaul, John M. *The Politics of Jacksonian Finance* Ithaca:
Cornell University Press, 1972.

___. *The Journal of Southern History* 40, No. 1 (February 1974): 475-476.

Monroe, John A. *Louis McLane: Federalist and Jacksonian.*
New Brunswick, NJ: Rutgers University Press, 1973.

___. *The Wisconsin Magazine of History* (August 1976): 65-66.

Perkins, Edwin J. *Financing Anglo-American Trade: The House
of Brown, 1800-1880.* Cambridge, MA: Harvard
University Press, 1975.

The Govan Archives

The Episcopal Church, U.S.A.

All of Govan's papers can be found in the Episcopal Church U.S.A.'s archives, whose archivist is Mark J. Duffy These papers include the text of this book and all other extant papers.

Episcopal Church, U.S.A.
Research Office
606 Rathervue Place, Box 2247
Austin, Texas 78768-2247
Phone: (512) 472-6816
Fax: (512) 480-0437
Email: research@episcopalarchives.org
Web: http://episcopalarchives.org

Records Administration Office
Episcopal Church Center
815 Second Avenue
New York, New York 10017-4594

Copies of most of this material is also in the Archives of the University of Oregon, Eugene, Oregon. The following is a list of his papers in general topical categories:

531

The Bank of the United States and the Issues Surrounding It

"Banking and the Credit System in Georgia, 1810-1860"

'The Miracle of Funded Public Debt"

"The Enemies of Banking and Bankers"

"Jefferson's Moral Crusade, 1780-1801"

"The Fundamental Issues of the Bank War"

"The Fall of the House of Biddle"

"Hamilton, the Bank and the National Economy"

Liberal versus Conservative Understanding

"Apologia Pro Vita Sua"

"The Liberal and Conservative Traditions in the United
States"

"The Principles of Freedom, the Hamilton-Seabury
Debates"

"John C. Calhoun, the Nationalist Renegade"

"John C. Calhoun, a Reappraisal"

"Jefferson and Hamilton: A Christian Evaluation"

"The Johnson-Goldwater Election, 1964"

Alexander Hamilton, Federalist and Conservative

"The Rich, the Well-Born, and Alexander Hamilton"

"Alexander Hamilton and Julius Caesar: A Note on the
Use of Historical Evidence"

The Sectional Controversy

"The Ante-Bellum Attempt to Regulate the Price and
Supply of Cotton"

"John M. Berrien and the Administration of Andrew
   Jackson"
"Agrarianism, Sectionalism, and State Sovereignty
   Denounced"
"Agrarianism, Sectionalism, and Jeffersonian Democracy:
   A Moral Inquiry"
"Agrarian and Agrarianism: A Study in the Use and Abuse
   of Words"
"Those Mysterious Southern Agrarians"
"Was the Old South Different?"
"The Importance and Dangers of Myth"

Slavery and the Civil War

"Slavery and the Civil War"
"Was Plantation Slavery Unprofitable?"
"Not Profit or Loss"

The Christian Faith and the University

"The Mission of the Church in the University"
"The Christian Faith and the University"
"The Christian Faith and the University, a Reply to the
   South African Universities"
"The American College and University, a Christian
   Critique"
"The Faith, the Church, and the University"
"The Teacher Needs Theology"
Mitre and Sceptre, a review
*The Recovery of Unity: The Thought of Frederick Denison
   Maurice,* a review
"The Task and Purpose of the University, the Educational
   Writings of F. D. Maurice"
"Faith and Doubt"

A Christian Understanding of Freedom

"Free to be Merely a Man"

"Christian Freedom"

"A New Birth of Freedom, the English Background"

"This Nation Under God: Theological Reflections on
American History," a book proposal

"Faith and Freedom"

"Freedom and Equality"

"The Rejection of Denominational Idolatries"

The Christian Faith and the Historian

"The Study and Writing of History"

"The Christian Understanding of History"

"Revelation and the Historian"

The Lecture Series

"A New Birth of Freedom," Five Lectures at Beloit

"We Hold These Truths," the Deems Lectures at NYU

"Radical America: The Continuing Revolution,"
Twenty Television Lectures in Eugene, Oregon

Books to which Govan contributed a major essay

*The Age of Civil War and Reconstructions, 1830-1900: A Book
of Interpretive Essays.* Charles Crowe, ed. Homewood,
Illinois: The Dorsey Press, 1966. Chapter 2, "Those
Mysterious Southern Agrarians," pp. 44-52.

The Southerner as American. Charles Grier Sellers, Jr., ed.
New York: E.P. Dutton and Co., Inc., 1966. Chapter 2,
"Americans Below the Potomac," pp. 19-39.

Pivotal Interpretations of American History, Volume I. Carl N.
Deglar, ed. New York: Harper and Row Publishers,

Harper Torchbooks, 1966. Chapter 7, "Was Plantation
Slavery Unprofitable?" pp. 159-183.

Once A Slave: A Slave's View of Slavery. Stanley Feldstein.
New York: William Morrow and Company, Inc., 1971.
Introduction, pp. 13-24.

Books Govan authored

Banking and the Credit System in Georgia, 1810-1860. New
York: Arno Press, 1978. 315 pp. His doctoral thesis
written in 1937.

Nicholas Biddle, Nationalist and Public Banker, 1786-1844.
Chicago: University of Chicago Press, 1959. 429 pp.
His major biography.

Endnotes

Preface Notes

1   Micah 6:8.

2   *The Gettysburg Address.*

3   Thomas Payne Govan, *Nicholas Biddle, Nationalist and Public Banker, 1786-1844* (Chicago: University of Chicago Press, 1959).

4   Decker was also at the University of Oregon and a friend of Govan's.

5   Forrest McDonald, Leslie E. Decker, and Thomas P. Govan. *The Last Best Hope, a History of the United States, Volume I to 1865; II Since 1865* (Reading, MA: Addison-Wesley Publishing Company, Inc., 1972). This reference is from Volume I, 335-336.

6   Samuel Eliot Morison and Henry Steele Commager, *The Growth of the American Republic, Volumes I and II* (Oxford University Press: New York; First Edition 1930, Fourth Edition 1950, Tenth Printing 1960).

7   Thomas P. Govan, *Radical America, the Continuing Revolution,* a television course given for credit at the University of Oregon (History 307), produced and directed by Mack W. Schwab and published in mimeograph form by the Oregon Education and Public Broadcasting Service, 1975-1976, 110. (See Chapter 28).

Introduction Notes

8   Bray Hammond was an assistant secretary of the Federal Reserve Board and the author of *Banks and Politics in America* that Govan reviewed and

Sovereignty and an Empty Purse: Banks and Politics in the Civil War. He was deeply respected by Govan.

9   See Chapter 3.

10   Ibid. Also see the Collect for Peace, 1979 *Book of Common Prayer,* 57.

11   Gerald N. Grob, George Athan Billias, eds., *Interpretations of American History, Patterns and Prospects; Volume 1 to 1877, Volume II Since 1877,* sixth ed. (New York: The Free Press, a Division of Simon and Schuster, Inc., 1967, 1972, 1978, 1982, 1987, 1992), Volume I, 454; Volume II, 472. This reference is from Volume I, 2-3.

12   Ibid., 3-4

13   George Bancroft, *History of the United States from the Discovery of the American Continent,* 10 vols. (Boston: Little, Brown and Company), 1834-1882. See Grob and Billias *Volume I,* 5, 74-76, 111-112, 160-161.

14   Richard Hildreth, *History of the United States, 1788-1821,* 6 vols, (New York: Harper and Brothers, 1848-1852). See also McDonald, Decker, and Govan, *Volume I,* 335-336.

15   McDonald, Decker, and Govan, 336.

16   John Fiske, *The Critical Period of American History, 1783-1784* (Boston: Houghton Mifflin, 1888), 53. See Grob and Billias *Volume I,* 161.

17   Grob and Billias, *Volume I,* 33, 210.

18   McDonald, Decker, and Govan, *Volume I,* 231.

19   Ibid., 336.

20   Vernon L. Parrington, *Main Currents in American Thought,* 3 vols (New York: 1927-1930).

21   Govan's essay "Slavery and the Civil War" is found in the Govan Archives.

22   Ibid.

23   Ibid.

24   Grob and Billias, 214.

25   Ibid., 117.

26   Ibid.

27   Ibid., 118.

28   Ibid., Richard Hofstadter, *The American Political Tradition and the Men Who Made It* (New York: Alfred A. Knopf, 1948, 1951), viii.

29   Ralph Henry Gabriel, *The Course of American Democratic Thought* (New York: The Ronald Press Company, 1940), 452.

[30] Govan's essay "Slavery and the Civil War" is found in the Govan Archives.

[31] Grob and Billias, *Volume I,* 262.

[32] Govan's article "Jefferson and Hamilton, a Christian Evaluation" is found in the Govan Archives.

[33] Ibid.

[34] See Appendix 1, "Apologia Pro Vita Sua."

[35] Govan refers to this history especially in his essay, "The Rejection of Denominational Idolatries." See Chapter 23.

[36] The *Book of Common Prayer,* 1979, 866.

[37] A Collect for Peace, the *Book of Common Prayer,* 57.

[38] Article XIX, the *Book of Common Prayer,* 871.

[39] Ibid., Preface, 9.

[40] Ibid., 10.

[41] Ibid., 9.

[42] See Appendices.

[43] See Chapters 11 and 22.

[44] Grob and Billias, Volume II, *Patterns and Perspectives,* 23-25.

[45] Paul Murray, *The Whig Party in Georgia, 1825-1853* (Chapel Hill: University of North Carolina Press, 1948), 219. Reviewed by Thomas P. Govan in *The Journal of Southern History,* Vol. 15, No. 1, February 1949, 111-112.

[46] Ibid., 120-122.

[47] Grob and Billias, *Volume I,* 182-195.

[48] Ibid., 194-195. The quotation is from Gordon S. Wood, *The Creation of the American Republic,* 1776-1787 (Chapel Hill: University of North Carolina Press, 1969), 513-518.

[49] Ibid.

[50] Robert Bellah, "Civil Religion in America," published in *Daedalus,* Winter, 1967, 1-21.

[51] Ibid.

[52] Thomas P. Govan, *Nicholas Biddle, Nationalist and Public Banker, 1746-1844* (Chicago: University of Chicago Press, 1959), Preface, ix.

[53] Op. cit., "Free to Be Merely a Man." See Appendices.

[54] Forrest McDonald, Leslie E. Decker, and Thomas P. Govan, *The Last Best Hope: A History of the United States* (Reading, MA: Addison-Wesley Publishers, 1973), Volume I, Preface, v.

55   Op. cit., McDonald, Decker, and Govan, v.

56   Ibid.

57   Thomas P. Govan, *Radical American, the Continuing Revolution* (Oregon Educational and Public Broadcasting Service, 1977), Preface, i.

58   Ibid.

59   Ibid.

60   Op. cit., McDonald, Decker, and Govan, *Volume I*, Preface, v.

61   Quoted from an early draft of a paper on John C. Calhoun, written by Govan while at Tulane. The paper, without this quotation, was delivered at the American Historical Association meeting in December 1955, entitled, "An Appraisal of Calhoun as a National and Sectional Leader." This paper is found in the Govan Archives.

Chapter 1 Notes

62   I knew a little about the Govan family directly from Tom and Jane, but learned more from interviews with Jane in 1990 and 1991. I came to know the rest of the Govan family through telephone conversations and a stream of letters with a few of them over the past ten years. From these conversations and letters, along with Tom's letters and papers, I have pieced together a brief family narrative. Members of the Govan family interviewed by telephone were Elizabeth (Betty) Tucker Conn, Tom Govan's niece; Richard Conn, Elizabeth's former husband, and their two children, Amy and Carol; James Bunnell, Tom's nephew-in-law, and his daughter Sarah E. Bunnell; Thomas James Tucker, a nephew.

63   An Elizabeth Conn interview, 1998.

64   Sacco and Vanzetti were two Italian immigrants living in Boston who were arrested in 1920 during the "Red Scare," so-called, after the Russian Revolution on charges of being anarchists and of an alleged hold-up and murder. Seven years later, they were finally found guilty and executed. Overwhelming evidence since attests to their innocence.

65   From a 1998 James Bunnell letter when he sent me a picture of the Tenth Street house. He was married to Govan's niece, Kate Tucker.

66   Letter from Thomas J. Tucker to Crocker, September 13, 1999.

67   From a James Bunnell interview, February 10, 1998.

68   Ibid.

69   From an interview with Thomas Tucker, 1998.

70   Ibid.

71   Op. cit., Thomas Tucker letter.

72   Ibid.

73   Ibid.

74   Ibid.

75   Ibid.

76   From an interview with Elizabeth Tucker Conn, 1999.

77   Ibid.

78   Op. cit., Elizabeth Tucker Conn interview.

79   Ibid.

80   The *Chattanooga Times*, August 7, 1966, Book Page, 15. This was an article about Gilbert's retirement from the paper and from his position as chief librarian at the University of Chattanooga.

81   Ibid.

82   Op. cit., Thomas Tucker letter.

83   Ibid.

84   Op. cit., James Bunnell interview.

Chapter 2 Notes

85   From an interview with Jane Govan, 1990.

86   Thomas P. Govan, "Apologia Pro Vita Sua." See Appendix 1. This was an address to a group of college chaplains and faculty at Whitinsville, Massachusetts in the fall of 1955.

87   Ibid., "Apologia."

88   Op. cit., Jane Govan interview.

89   Ibid., p. 4.

90   Op. cit., "Apologia," p. 2.

91   Ibid., p. 3.

92   Ibid.

93   Ibid., p. 5.

94   Ibid., p. 5.

95   Ibid., p. 6.

96   Ibid.

97   Ibid.

98 Ibid.

99 Ibid.

100 Ibid., p. 7.

101 Ibid., p. 6.

102 Ibid., p. 7.

103 Ibid.

104 Ibid.

105 See Thomas P. Govan, "Banking and the Credit System in Georgia, 1810-1860," in the Govan Archives. Published in *The Journal of Southern History*, Vol. 4, 1938, 164-182.

106 Ibid.

107 Ibid.

108 Forrest McDonald, Leslie E. Decker, Thomas P. Govan, *The Last Best Hope, a History of the United States* (Reading, MA: Addison-Wesley Publishing Company, 1973), Vol. I, Preface, v.

109 Ibid.

110 Ibid., 10.

111 Ibid.

112 Ibid.

113 Op. cit., *The Last Best Hope*, Vol. II, 645.

114 Ibid.

115 Thomas P. Govan, *Banking and the Credit System in Georgia, 1810-1860* (New York: Arno Press, 1978), 312.

Chapter 3 Notes

116 A letter from Cora Louise Belford to Crocker, October 2000.

117 From an interview with Jane Govan, spring 1990.

118 Letter from the Reverend George T. Hall to Jane Govan, March 16, 1979.

119 From a telephone interview with Harriet Price, one of Jane's closest younger friends, May 3, 1998.

120 The preceding narrative was pieced together from meetings with Jane Govan and telephone conversations with other family members.

121 See "Apologia," in Appendix 1.

122 *The Last Best Hope*, Vol. 1, v. 5

[123] The *Book of Common Prayer*, Preface, pp. 10-11.

[124] Bernard Bailyn, ed. *The Debate on the Constitution, Part I*, (New York: Literary Classics of the United States, Inc., 1993), 3-4.

[125] Ibid.

[126] From Govan's unpublished notes. See also preface for the *Book of Common Prayer*, paragraph 1, and the Collect for Peace, 57.

[127] Ibid., preface, paragraph 1.

[128] All things from which, in "The Great Litany," we pray to be delivered. The *Book of Common Prayer*, 149.

[129] From Govan's unpublished notes. See also the Preface.

[130] Op. cit., "Slavery in the Civil War."

[131] Ibid.

[132] Ralph Henry Gabriel, *The Course of American Democratic Thought* (New York: The Ronald Press Company, 1940), 452.
Dwight L. Dumond, *Anti-Slavery Origins of the Civil War in the United States* (Ann Arbor: University of Michigan Press, 1939), 143.
Ulrich Bonnell Phillips, *The Course of the South to Secession, an Interpretation*, ed. E. Merton Coulter (New York: for the American Historical Association by D. Appleton-Century Company, 1939). 170.
Clement Eaton, *Freedom of Thought in the Old South* (Durham, North Carolina: Duke University Press, 1940), 343.

[133] It was a book review by Thomas P. Govan of the Howard Cecil Perkins, ed. *Northern Editorials on Secession* (New York: The Century Company, 1931), entitled "Not Profit and Loss," *Sewanee Review*, Volume 50, no. 3, July-September 1942, 426-427. This review is in the Govan Archives.

[134] Ibid.

[135] Ibid., 1.

[136] Op. cit., "Was Plantation Slavery Unprofitable?"

[137] *The Last Best Hope*, Volume I, 535.

[138] Ibid., 536.

[139] Govan, "Was Plantation Slavery Unprofitable?" in the Govan Archives, the last sentence of the essay.

[140] Carl N. Deglar, ed., *Pivotal Interpretations of American History, Volume I* (New York: Harper and Row, 1966), 234.

[141] Harold D. Woodman, ed., *Slavery and Southern Economy* (New York:

Harcourt Brace World, 1966). Hugh G. J. Aitkin, *Did Slavery Pay?*
(Boston: Houghton Mifflin Company, 1971).

Chapter 4 Notes

142   From an interview with Jane Govan, October 1990.
143   Reinhold Niebuhr, *The Nature and Destiny of Man, Volume I*, The Gifford
       Lectures (New York: Charles Scribner's Sons, 1941), 300.
144   Robert T. Handy, *The Social Gospel in America* (New York: Oxford
       University Press, 1966), 14.
145   Walter Rauschenbusch, *Christianity and Social Crisis* (Louisville,
       Westminster-John Knox, 1992), 209.
146   As quoted by Henry B. Clark, *Serenity, Courage, Wisdom, The Enduring
       Legacy of Reinhold Niebuhr* (Cleveland: The Pilgrim Press, 1994), 94.
147   Op. cit., *The Nature and Destiny of Man, Volume II*, Preface, v.
148   By this time, Reinhold Niebuhr's major works consisted of the following:
       Leaves from the Notebook of a Tamed Cynic (1929), *Does Civilization Need
       Religion?* (1927), *Moral Man and Immoral Society* (1932), *Beyond Tragedy*
       (1937), *Christianity and Power Politics* (1940).
149   Op. cit., Henry B. Clark, 78.
150   Robin W. Lovin, *Reinhold Niebuhr and Christian Realism* (Cambridge:
       Cambridge University Press, U.K., 1995) 221.
151   Ibid., 208.
152   Reinhold Niebuhr, *Moral Man and Immoral Society* (New York: Charles
       Scribner's Sons, 1932), xi-xii.
153   Op. cit., Lovin, 6.
154   Ibid., Lovin, 10-11.
155   Ibid., 4.
156   Reinhold Niebuhr, *The Children of Light and the Children of Darkness* (New
       York: Charles Scribner's Sons, 1944), the Foreword, xiii and 1.

Chapter 5 Notes

157   From an interview with Jane Govan, 1990.
158   Ibid.
159   "History of the Second Army," in *Studies in the History of the Army Ground*

Forces, Washington DC: Headquarters, Army Ground Forces (September 1, 1945).

[160] Ibid., the frontispiece of "History of the Second Army."

[161] Ibid.

[162] This was *not* the view of General Douglas MacArthur and his headquarters staff.

[163] The President and Congress responded to this threat by ordering the National Guard into federal service on August 31, 1940, and by passing the Selective Service Act of September 16, 1940. George C. Marshall was appointed chief of staff.

[164] Op. cit., "History of the Second Army," 59.

[165] Ibid., 122

[166] Govan's review in *American Historical Review,* Vol. LVII, no. 4, July 1952, 1005. This is a quote from Govan's review of Roy S. Cline, *Washington Command Post: the Operations Division* (Washington DC: Department of the Army, 1951), 413.

[167] Ibid.

[168] Op. cit., "History of the Second Army," 55

[169] Op. cit., Govan's review of Sister M. Grace Madeline, *Monetary Banking Theories of Jacksonian Democracy* (Philadelphia, Dolphin Press, 1943) xi, 186. Reviewed by Govan in *The Journal of Southern History,* Volume IX, no. 4, December 1943, 569-570. Quotation from 569.

[170] Ibid.

[171] Ibid.

[172] Ibid., 570.

[173] Robert Selph Henry, *"First With the Most" Forrest* (Indianapolis: The Bobbs-Merrill Company, 1944), 558. Reviewed by Thomas P. Govan, *Southern Historical Review,* Volume XII, no. 1, February 1945, 117-118.

[174] *Training in Mountain and Winter Warfare,* Study No. 23, Capt. Thomas P. Govan, Historical Section, Army Ground Forces, Washington, DC, 1946.

[175] An earlier title of this paper was "The New Guinea and Bismarcks Campaign."

[176] An earlier title of this paper was "The Reorganization of Command in the Pacific and the Planning for the Invasion of Japan."

[177] In the course of preparing this book, I made several inquiries to army

sources in search of these texts to no avail. The National War College, the Office of Military History in Washington, DC, the United States Military History Institute in Carlisle Barracks, Pennsylvania, and in particular, the Army Military Research Center at the Institute in Carlisle Barracks—all of them have searched their archives for these monographs without success. It seems that Govan's historical literary efforts for MacArthur have been silenced forever. I cannot help asking what happened to them and why. I have no certain answer but can speculate on the basis of several significant hunches.

[178] Thomas P. Govan, a review of Robert Ross Smith, *The Approach to the Philippines* (Washington, D.C.: Center of Military History, Department of the Army, 1953) 623, in the *American Historical Review*, Vol. LIX, no. 1, October 1953, 167-168.

[179] Thomas P. Govan, a review of Douglas MacArthur's *Reminiscences* (New York: McGraw-Hill, 1994, viii, 438, unknown journal, June 1945), 163-164.

[180] Ibid.

[181] Ibid.

[182] From an interview with Jane Govan, October 1990.

Chapter 6 Notes

[183] Letter from Laura Roper to Crocker, June 6, 2000.

[184] Ibid.

[185] Ibid.

[186] Ibid.

[187] *Nicholas Biddle, Nationalist and Public Banker, 1786-1844,* Thomas P. Govan (Chicago: University of Chicago Press, 1959), Preface, vii.

[188] Ibid.

[189] Ibid., from his "Note on Sources," 414.

[190] Ibid.

[191] Arthur Schlesinger Jr., *The Age of Jackson* (Boston: Little, Brown and Company, 1945), 557.

[192] Op. cit., *Nicholas Biddle*, Preface, vii.

[193] Thomas P. Govan, "Fundamental Issues of the Bank War," *Pennsylvania*

Magazine of History and Biography, Volume LXXXII, no. 3, July 1958, 305-315. This essay is in the Govan Archives.

[194] Ibid.

[195] Ibid.

[196] *American Historical Review,* Vol. LII, no. 3, April 1947, 600.

[197] Op. cit., Govan, "Fundamental Issues," Govan Archives.

[198] Arthur M. Schlesinger Jr., "The Ages of Jackson," *New York Review of Books,* December 7, 1989, 48-56. Quoted in Grob and Billias *Volume I,* 270-281.

[199] Grob and Billias, 275-276.

[200] Ibid., 276-277.

[201] "Nicholas Biddle at Princeton," *Princeton University Library Chronicle,* IA (1947), 49-66. "An Unfinished Novel by Nicholas Biddle," *Princeton University Library Chronicle,* X (1949), 124-136. "The Death of Joseph Dennie: A Memoir" by Nicholas Biddle, *Pennsylvania Magazine of History and Biography,* LXXV (1951), 36-46.

[202] *Taking Sides: Clashing Views on Controversial Issues in American History, Volume I. The Colonial Period to Reconstruction* (6th edition), eds. Larry Modares and James M. SoRelle (Guilford, CT: The Dushkin Publishing Group, Inc., 1995). Issue 9, "Did the Bank War Cause the Panic of 1837?" Govan's article, "The Fundamental Issues of the Bank War," explains why and how the Bank War did cause the Panic of 1837. Professor Peter Temin takes the negative side.

[203] Op. cit., Laura Roper letter.

Chapter 7 Notes

[204] From Govan's March 17, 1954 proposal to the Ford Foundation's Fund for the Republic via Dr. Logan Williams, President of the University of Texas. See Appendices, "A New Birth of Freedom," p. 2.

[205] Ibid.

[206] Ibid.

[207] From a letter of the Right Reverend G.P. Mellick Belshaw, April 1, 2000.

[208] From a letter of Laura Roper to Crocker, September 27, 1999.

[209] From various family sources.

[210] From a telephone interview with James Bunnell, February 10, 1998.

211 "Apologia Pro Vita Sua," Appendices.

212 Nannie M. Tilley, *The Bright Tobacco Industry, 1860-1929* (Chapel Hill: University of North Carolina Press, 1948), xlv, 754. Reviewed in *The Journal of Southern History*, Volume XIV, no. 4, November 1948, 565-567.

213 *The Journal of Southern History*, Vol. XV, no. 1, February 1949, 76-77.

214 Roy S. Cline, *Washington Command Post, the Operations Division* (Office of the Chief of Military History, Washington, D.C., Department of the Army, 1953, reissued 1996), 623. Reviewed in the *American Historical Review*, volume LXIX, no. 1, October 1953, 167-168. Robert Ross Smith, *The Approach to the Philippines*, Washington, D.C., Center of Military History, Department of the Army, 1953, reissued 1996), 623. Reviewed in the *American Historical Review*, Volume LXIX, no. 1, October 1953, 167-168.

215 *The Journal of Southern History*, Vol. XVIII, no. 1, February 1952, 68.

216 Paul Murray, *The Whig Party in Georgia, 1825-1853* (Chapel Hill, University of North Carolina Press, 198), vii, 219. Reviewed by Govan in *The Journal of Southern History*, Vol. XV, no. 2, May 1949, 111-112.

217 Ibid., 112.

218 Thomas P. Govan, "The Rich, the Well-Born, and Alexander Hamilton," in Notes of Documents, *Mississippi Valley Historical Review*, Volume XXXVI, June 1949 to March 1950, 675-680.

219 See Chapter 6.

220 See "The Fundamental Issues of the Bank War," in the Govan Archives.

Chapter 8 Notes

221 Donald Smith Armentraut, *The Quest for the Informed Priest, a History of the School of Theology* (The School of Theology, the University of the South, Sewanee, Tennessee, 1979), 280.

222 There are nine provinces in the Episcopal Church. The twenty-two dioceses of the southeastern regions of the United States, who "owned" and oversaw the University of the South, was Province II.

223 Myles Horton, *The Long Haul* (New York, Doubleday, 1990), 86.

224 Letter from Laura Roper to Crocker, July 23, 2000.

225 Ibid.

226 From an interview with Jane Govan, 1989.

227 From a telephone interview with Thomas J. Tucker, November 3, 1997.

228 They were insured through a Nashville agency, Pacific National Fire Insurance Company, which paid them the $5,000 they were due.

229 Letter from Scott Bates to Crocker, February 8, 2000, quoting Ellen Webb, whose husband, John, taught American history at Sewanee after Tom left.

230 Op. cit., Armentraut, 282.

231 Ibid.

232 From an interview with Jane Govan, 1990.

233 Quoted from the 1998 Lambeth Conference report by the theological faculty in their June 9, 1951 protest to the trustees. Op. cit., Armentraut, 282. The Lambeth Conference is a conclave every ten years of all Anglican diocesan bishops worldwide, in which they discuss the issues and pass resolutions intended to influence the thinking and actions of the member churches. Racial inclusions had been emphasized at the 1948 conference.

234 David E. Sumner, *The Episcopal Church's History, 1945-1985*, (Wilton, CT: Morehouse Publishing, 1987), 35.

235 From an interview with Jane Govan, 1989.

236 Ibid., 1990.

237 Op. cit., Armentraut, 283.

238 Ibid., 284.

239 Ibid.

240 Ibid., 285.

241 Ibid., 295.

242 Ibid.

243 Ibid., 288.

244 Ibid., 287.

245 Ibid.

246 In Tom's file there is a copy of an August 8, 1944 letter from Dr. Charles Johnson, Director of the Department of Social Sciences at Fisk University, Nashville, Tennessee, to Myles Horton, a friend of Tom's and head of the Highlander Folk School in Monteagle, Tennessee. Horton had written Johnson asking about "the state law regarding White and Negro students at a private educational institution." Dr. Johnson replied:

"In 1901 a statute was enacted prohibiting the teaching of Whites and Negroes in the same school, academy or college and makes it unlawful for a teacher, instructor, professor or educator to teach Whites and Negroes in the same classroom or building. This was directed at Fisk University at the time when White instructors' children were attending the university, and made violation a misdemeanor punishable by $50.00 fine for each offense and imprisonment of 30 days to six months. The Gupton-Jones College of Mortuary Science openly violated this statute with impunity. Although Whites and Negroes are segregated within the classroom, they are taught together 'in the same classrooms and buildings.'"

Chapter 9 Notes

247 David L. Porter, ed., *African American Sports Greats, a Biographical Dictionary* (Waterford, CT: Greenwood Press, 1996), pp. 284-285.

248 The Govans' New York experience was drawn largely from telephone conversations with Cora Louise Belford, March, 2000.

249 Op. cit., Armentraut, 296.

250 Ibid.

251 Ibid.

252 Ibid.

253 Ibid., 296-297.

254 Ibid., 297-298.

255 Ibid., 302.

256 Ibid., 302-303.

257 Ibid., 305.

258 Ibid., 306.

259 Ibid., 307.

260 Ibid., 306.

261 Ibid., 307.

262 Ibid., 309.

263 From an interview with Jane Govan, 1990.

264 Reinhold Niebuhr, *The Irony of American History* (New York: Charles Scribner's Sons, 1952), 173.

265 Richard W. Fox, *Reinhold Niebuhr, A Biography,* (New York: Harper & Row, 1987, paperback, 345) 242.

266 Ibid., 245.

[267] I know this from personal knowledge. Schlesinger has mentioned it repeatedly in his writing; and Kennon told me personally about Niebuhr's influence on him.

[268] Quoted in *Contemporary Biography*, 1964, 26.

[269] Jacques Barzun, *God's Country and Mine, a Declaration of Love Spiced with a Few Harsh Words* (Boston: Little, Brown and Company, 1954), 339.

[270] Ibid., 334.

[271] Ibid., 335.

[272] Ibid., 336.

[273] Ibid., 337.

[274] Ibid., 313-331.

Chapter 10 Notes

[275] "Slavery and the Civil War," is in the Govan Archives.

[276] Op. cit., *I'll Take My Stand,* 359.

[277] Samuel Eliot Morison and Henry Steele Commager, *The Growth of the American Republic,* 2 volumes (New York: Oxford University Press, 1930-1960 in ten editions.)

[278] Ibid., *Volume I,* 383.

[279] Ibid., 537.

[280] "The Liberal and Conservative Traditions in the United States," unpublished essay. See Appendix 2.

[281] Ibid.

[282] Letter from Govan to Jacques Barzun, March 1953.

[283] Letter from Govan to Barzun, March 30, 1953.

[284] Ibid.

[285] Quoted from the *New York Times,* March 29, 1953.

[286] Op. cit., Govan letter to Barzun.

[287] Ibid.

[288] Quoted by Govan in his letter to Barzun, March 30, 1953.

[289] Ibid.

[290] Letter from Barzun to Govan, April 3, 1953.

[291] Ibid.

[292] From a telephone interview between David Underdown and Crocker, October 2000.

Chapter 11 Notes

293 From an interview with Jane Govan, 1999.

294 Letter from Laura Roper to Crocker, June 13, 2000.

295 Letter from Govan to Thomas S. K. Scott-Craig, February 1, 1955.

296 Govan's reviews from this period can be found in the Book Reviews section.

297 *The Journal of Southern History*, Vol. 20. No. 1, February 1954, 77-78.

298 Ibid.

299 Sellers, Charles Grier, Jr., ed., *The Southerner as American* (New York: E.P. Dutton and Co., Inc., 1966), pp. 19-39.

300 See the discussion of Hamilton's speech to the Constitutional Convention in Forrest McDonald, *Alexander Hamilton* (New York: W.W. Norton and Company, 1979), 95-107.

301 All quotations in this section are from Govan's proposal for *A New Birth of Freedom*. See Appendix 3.

302 Forrest McDonald, Leslie E. Decker, and Thomas P. Govan, *The Last Best Hope, a History of the United States* (Reading, MA: Addison-Wesley Publishing Company), 2 volumes, 537 and 1055, respectively.

Chapter 12 Notes

303 David E. Sumner, *The Episcopal Church's History 1945-1995* (Wilton CT: Morehouse Publishing, 1987), 77.

304 Ibid., pp. 77-82.

305 Letter from Laura Roper to Crocker, June 6, 2000.

306 Ibid., June 13, 1998.

307 Ibid., September 27, 1999.

308 Op. cit., September 14, 2000.

309 Letter from Roger Blanchard to Govan, March 10, 1955.

Chapter 13 Notes

310 At the time, women could not be ordained; therefore, women assistant chaplains were trained lay women.

311 For administrative purposes, the Episcopal Church was divided into nine provinces.

312 An unpublished paper by Glen Martin.

313 Govan's response to Martin's paper.

314 Ibid.

315 Ibid

316 Ibid.

317 Govan's address, "The Mission of the Church in the University," pp. 5-6. See the Govan Archives.

318 Thomas P. Govan, *Free to Be Merely a Man*, a *Faculty Paper*, published by the Episcopal Church, 1956.

319 Ibid.

320 The essay, "Christian Freedom," is in the Govan Archives.

321 Thomas P. Govan, "A New Birth of Freedom," his 1963 lectures at Beloit, Wisconsin.

322 F. D. Maurice, *Has the Church or the State the Power to Educate the Nation?* (London: J.G.F. Rivington, St. Paul's Churchyard, and Darton and Clark, Holborn Hill, 1839, 364.) See Lecture 1.

Chapter 14 Notes

323 From Govan's 1956 report to the Commission on College Work.

324 *Faculty Notes*, December, 1958, 3.

325 *Faculty Notes*, Spring 1957, 1.

326 Announced in *Faculty Notes*, Spring 1957. Govan wrote several papers for these meetings:

"The Mission of the Church in the University"

"The Christian Faith and the University"

"We Believe"

"The American University, a Christian Critique"

These papers are in the Govan Archives.

327 Govan's essay "The Christian Faith, the Church, and the University," is in the Govan Archives.

328 Ibid., p. 6.

[329] Ibid., p. 1.

[330] Declaration of Independence, paragraph 2.

[331] Op. cit., p. 14.

[332] Ibid.

[333] Ibid., p. 15.

[334] Ibid.

[335] Ibid., p. 16.

[336] Ibid.

[337] Ibid.

[338] Ibid

[339] Ibid., p. 17.

[340] Ibid., p. 19.

[341] Ibid., p. 20.

[342] Ibid.

[343] Ibid.

[344] Ibid., p. 21.

[345] This list of Colloquy participants is instructive because although it is a superb group of qualified scholars and theologians, they produced a surprisingly weak document.

The Rev. C. Fitzsimmons Allison, Ph.D.
Assistant Professor of Church History
School of Theology, University of the South
Sewanee, Tennessee

The Very Rev. Robert F. McGregor
Dean
Trinity Cathedral
Newark, New Jersey

The Rev. Frederick H. Arterton, D.D.
Assistant Warden
College of Preachers
Washington, DC

The Rev. Albert T. Mollegen, D.D.
Professor of New Testament Language and Literature, Apologetics, and Christian Ethics
Protestant Episcopal Theological Seminary of Virginia
Alexandria, Virginia

The Rev. William H. Baar, Ph.D.
Episcopal Chaplain and Director of Brent House
University of Chicago
Chicago, Illinois

The Rev. Arnold S. Nash, D.D.
Professor of the History and Sociology of Religion
University of North Carolina
Chapel Hill, North Carolina

A. Denis Baly
Visiting Lecturer in Political Science
Kenyon College
Gambier, Ohio

The Rev. W. Norman Pittinger, S.T.D.
Professor of Christian Apologetics
General Theological Seminary
New York, New York

The Rt. Rev. Stephen F. Bayne, Jr., S.T.D.
Chairman, Bishop of the Diocese of
Olympia, Seattle, Washington

William H. Poteat, Ph.D.
Professor of Theology
Episcopal Theological Seminary of the Southwest
Austin, Texas

A. John Coleman, Ph.D.
Professor of Mathematics
University College, University of Toronto
Toronto, Canada

The Rev. John F. Porter
Episcopal Chaplain
Michigan State University
East Lansing, Michigan

Marshall Fishwick, Ph.D.
Professor of American Studies
Washington and Lee University
Lexington, Virginia

The Rev. John W. Pyle
Canon
Cathedral of St. John the Divine
New York, New York

The Rev. Hans W. Frei
Professor of Theology
Yale University
New Haven, Connecticut

The Rev. Robert N. Rodenmeyer, S.T.D.
Professor of Pastoral Theology
Church Divinity School of the Pacific
Berkeley, California

Thomas P. Govan, Ph.D.
Executive Secretary for Faculty Work
National Council of the Protestant Episcopal Church
New York, New York

Thomas S. K. Scott-Craig, Ph.D.
Professor of Philosophy
Dartmouth College
Hanover, New Hampshire

Virginia Harrington
Professor of History
Barnard College, Columbia University
New York, New York

The Rev. Jones B. Shannon
Executive Director
Church Society for College Work
Washington, D.C.

The Rev. Louis M. Hirshson, D.D.
President
Hobart and William-Smith Colleges
Geneva, New York

The Rev. William A. Spurrier
Chaplain
Wesleyan University
Middletown, Connecticut

Richard Hocking, Ph.D.
Professor of Philosophy
Emery University
Atlanta, Georgia

The Rev. Richard B. Scott
Episcopal Chaplain
Cornell University
Ithaca, New York

The Rev. Harry H. Jones
Executive Secretary
Province of New England (Province 1)
Whitinsville, Massachusetts

William Stringfellow, L.L.B.
Attorney; Church Society for College Work Representative
Columbia and New York University Law Schools
New York, New York

Wilber G. Katz, S.J.D.
Professor of Law
University of Chicago
Chicago, Illinois

The Rev. Charles L. Winters, Jr., D.Th.
Assistant Professor of Dogmatic Theology
School of Theology, University of the South
Sewanee, Tennessee

William L. Kolb, Ph.D.
Professor of Sociology
Newcomb College, Tulane University
New Orleans, Louisiana

The Rev. Philip T. Zabriskie
Executive Secretary, Division of College Work
National Council of the Protestant Episcopal Church
New York, New York

[346] The *Book of Common Prayer*, pp. 41-42.
[347] Ibid., p. 57.
[348] From "A Collection of Prayers," drawn together by the Reverend John Crocker, Sr., 1954.

Chapter 15 Notes

349 The American Historical Association, the Southern Historical Association, and the Mississippi Valley Historical Association.

350 *The Christian Scholar,* Vol. XL, no. 1, March 1957, 6-20.

351 *The Christian Scholar,* Vol. XL, no. 2, March 1957, 126-127.

352 Ibid., 126.

353 Ibid., 127.

354 Letter from Govan to Donald R. McNeil, Interim Director of the American National Historical Research Center, March 9, 1959.

355 Letter of Roger Shugg to Govan, October 17, 1956.

356 Letter from Govan to Roger Shugg, October 22, 1956

357 *Mississippi Valley Historical Review,* Vol. XLIV, no. 4, March 1958, 721-724.

358 Ibid.

359 Ibid., 723.

360 Ibid., 723-724.

Chapter 16 Notes

361 Letter from Govan to Roger Shugg, March 11, 1957.

362 Ibid.

363 One of the readers was Ralph Hidy, Indor Strauss Professor of Business History at Harvard Business School who wrote McDonald a highly laudatory letter (March 11, 1957) about Govan's manuscript. He urged publication.

364 Letter from McDonald to Govan, January 12, 1958. Govan talked with McDonald about his own desire to return to university history teaching as soon as possible. He had served the church for three years and he felt that was long enough. For all of his disingenuousness, McDonald genuinely wanted to help. Now with an "in" at Brown, he began working on bringing Govan to Brown also. James Hedges, the leading American historian at Brown at the time, was much impressed with Govan, enough to promise to speak to Barnaby Keeney, president of Brown, and to see, as McDonald put it in his January 12 letter, "if something could be

worked out immediately re: an offer in the fall." In fact, the offer came for the following year when Hedges would be on sabbatical.

[365] This was the Faculty Board of University Publications, which authorized all publications of the Press.

[366] Letter from Govan to Donald McNeil, March 23, 1959.

[367] Clifford L. Lord was Dean of the School of General Studies at Columbia University.

[368] Letter from Govan to Donald McNeil, March 16, 1959.

[369] Letter from Govan to Roger Shugg, March 23, 1959.

[370] Letter from Lord to McNeil, March 16, 1959.

[371] Ibid.

[372] Letter from McNeil to Govan, February 26, 1959.

[373] Letter from Govan to McNeil, March 9, 1959.

[374] Letter from Shugg to Govan, March 11, 1959.

[375] Ibid.

[376] Letter from Shugg to Govan, March 19, 1959.

[377] Ibid.

[378] Letter from McNeil to Govan, March 19, 1959.

[379] Letter from Govan to McNeil, March 19, 1959.

[380] Letter from McNeil to Govan, March 17, 1959.

[381] Ibid.

[382] Ibid.

[383] Letter from Govan to Lord and McNeil, March 23, 1959.

[384] Letter from McNeil to Govan, April 1, 1959.

Chapter 17 Notes

[385] D. M. L. Farr in the *Canadian Historical Review*, Volume XXII, no. 1, March 1961, 59.

[386] The reviews of *Biddle*:

> *The Pennsylvania Magazine of History and Biography*, Vol. 84, no. 3, July 1960, 369-374, reviewed by Bray Hammond of Johns Hopkins University.

The American Historical Review, Vol. LXIX, no. 1, October 1963, 165-166; reviewed by Charles M. Wiltse, Office of the Surgeon General, Army Medical Services.

The Political Science Quarterly, Vol. LXXV, no. 4, December 1960, 635-636; reviewed by Irwin Unger, Long Beach State College.

The American Political Science Review, Vol. LIV, no. 2, June, 1960, 539-540; reviewed by Richard P. McCormick, Rutgers University.

The Mississippi Valley Historical Review, Vol. XLVII, no. 1, June 1960, 124-126; reviewed by Stuart Bruchey, Michigan State University.

The American Quarterly, Vol. XII, no. 2, Summer 1960, 216-217, reviewed by James H. Stowe, San Francisco State College.

The Journal of Economic History, Vol. XX, no. 3, September 1960, 481-482; reviewed by Paul W. Gates, Cornell University.

Pennsylvania History, Vol. XXVII, no. 4, October 1960, 425-426; reviewed by Jeanette P. Nichols, University of Pennsylvania.

The Ohio Historical Quarterly, Vol. LXIX, no. 3, July 1960, 317-319; reviewed by Reginald C. McGrane, University of Cincinnati.

Business History Review, Vol. XXXIV, no. 3, Autumn 1960, 390-391; reviewed by Lance E. Davis, Purdue University.

The Journal of Southern History, Vol. XXVI, no. 2, May 1960, 243-244; reviewed by Ray F. Nichols, University of Pennsylvania.

Indiana Magazine of History, Vol. LVI, no. 2, June 1960, 178-179; reviewed by George Rogers Taylor, Amherst College.

Wisconsin Magazine of History, Vol. XLIV, no. 2, Winter 1960-1961, 143-144; reviewed by Peter J. Coleman, Washington University.

The Canadian Historical Review, Vol. XLII, no. 1, March 1961, 59-60. Reviewed by D. M. L. Farr, Carleton University.

Bulletin of the British Association for American Studies, March 1961, 62-64.

Several newspaper reviews were also in Govan's file including *The London Times Supplement,* March 15, 1960, and *Morning Advocate,* Baton Rouge, Louisiana, June 5, 1960, E 2.

[387] Volume 84, no. 3, July 1960, 369-374.
[388] Princeton University Press, Princeton, 1957.
[389] *The Mississippi Valley Historical Review,* Vol. XLIV, no. 4, March 1951, 721-724.
[390] *Nicholas Biddle,* 413, the last sentence in Govan's book.
[391] Op. cit., *Pennsylvania Magazine of History and Biography,* 369.
[392] Ibid.
[393] Letter from Govan to Shugg, October 22, 1956.
[394] Op. cit., Hammond, 372.
[395] Preface, ix.
[396] Op. cit., Hammond, 374.
[397] See Chapter 5 in this book.
[398] For example, George Rogers Taylor of Amherst College and Roy F. Nichols of Pennsylvania University.

[399]   Op. cit., *Pennsylvania History*, 426.

[400]   Op. cit., *Wisconsin Magazine of History*.

[401]   *Biddle*: Notes on sources, 414.

[402]   *American Political Science Review*, Vol. LIV, no. 2, June 1960, 539-540.

Chapter 18 Notes

[403]   Report to the National Commission on College Work, Spring, 1959, 1.

[404]   Ibid.

[405]   Ibid.

[406]   Conversation with Govan, 1960.

[407]   Part of the letter of agreement from Barnaby C. Keeney, president of Brown University, to Govan, September 7, 1960.

[408]   This was an adjunct professor's salary for a course taught in 1960 as reported by the Brown University history department.

[409]   Govan's course followed the theme of his lecture at the University of Virginia, "The Liberal and Conservative Traditions in the U.S.A."

[410]   Report in *The Journal of Southern History*, Volume XXVII, February-November 1961, 59.

[411]   Charles Grier Sellers Jr., ed., *The Southerner as American* (Chapel Hill: University of North Carolina Press, 1960), x, 126. The book was reprinted in 1966 by E. P. Dutton and Co. in paperback.

[412]   Op. cit., *I'll Take My Stand*.

[413]   *The American Historical Review*, Vol. XLVI, no. 2, January 1961, 468-470.

[414]   Ibid.

[415]   Review of Seller's *The Southerner as American* by C. Vann Woodward in *The Journal of Southern History*, Vol. XXVII, February 1961, 92-94.

[416]   Ibid.

[417]   Govan's essay, "The Liberal and Conservative Traditions in the United States," is found as Appendix 2.

[418]   Letter from C. Van Woodward to Govan February 28, 1961.

Chapter 19 Notes

[419]   Op. cit., Armentraut, 418.

[420]   From a letter written but never sent.

421 Cora Louise Belford, wife of Lee Belford, chairman of the NYU Department of Religion, and an old friend of the Govans.

422 What matters is not only what we do, say adhering to the letter of the law, but how we do it and in what spirit. Govan found the Sewanee faculty falsely self-righteous about their own behavior and uncharitably judgmental of the ESCRU members. The disposition of their hearts was the problem. He called them back to a spirit of humility, of forgiveness, and of love. See Galatians 2:16-20.

423 Matthew 25: 40; John 13: 31.

424 Matthew 25:18, 24-30.

425 It seems that Allison had been to see a psychiatrist in Washington over the situation and had told Tom about what the psychiatrist had said.

426 From the conference announcement.

427 Written in April 1961 from Brown University.

Chapter 20 Notes

428 Letter from Govan to Professor David Underdown at the University of Virginia, May 7, 1964. Underdown had succeeded Govan in American history at Sewanee in 1954 and had recently moved to Virginia.

429 Letter from Govan to Crocker, December 19, 1965. In 1965-1966, I was in Cambridge, England on a sabbatical funded in part by the Division for College Work of the Episcopal Church, thanks to Govan's strong intervention on my behalf. What he wrote me in December was vintage Govan: full of irony and humor at his own expense. I had written an open letter to my college congregation at Brown University about the monument to the Magna Carta at Runnymede given to England by the American Bar Association. It stands out on a small plot of land given to the U.S. by Britain in gratitude for the monument that celebrates the continuity of law in Great Britain and the United States ever since Magna Carta. I had spoken gratefully of the Constitution, the Civil Rights Movement, the recently passed Civil Rights Law, and the leadership shown by President Johnson in the wake of John F. Kennedy's assassination. Law, which for so long had served the purposes of injustice and oppression during slavery, post-Civil War tenant farming, all sorts of discrimination, and the denial of voting rights, was now serving the

purposes of freedom and justice. On July 2, 1964, Congress had passed an omnibus civil rights bill banning discrimination in voting, jobs and accommodations. On August 6, 1965, another bill was passed in response to the March from Selma to Montgomery, Alabama, providing federal protection for black voting rights. The United States, were demonstrating that reform was possible and the future full of hope in spite of Kennedy's death.

At Christmas, Govan responded to my letter "occasioned" as he put it, "by your visit to Runnymede and that one acre of American soil given by the British in gratitude for the fact that we have the Irish and not they any longer." He "reluctantly" admitted that he had found my letter "convincing." In fact, however, he was tweaking my dewy-eyed views at Runnymede because the United States still had a long way to go in bringing blacks justice. He ended, "I meant this to be a message of Christmas cheer, and certainly the knowledge that you and Ellie have had this year has been a bright thought for both of us." He was being honest instead of cheerful, but even so, he knew he had been more responsible for my sabbatical than anyone else, and he felt good about that.

[430] Ibid.

[431] Charles Moritz, *Current Biography*, 1969 (New York: H.W. Wilson Company, 1970), 279.

[432] Ibid.

[433] From a McDonald letter to Govan, March 13, 1963.

[434] Dwight McDonald's letter to Govan, March 13, 1963.

[435] Arthur Schlesinger, Jr., *The Politics of Hope* (New York: Houghton Mifflin, 1962).

[436] Op. cit., McDonald's letter.

[437] Op. cit., McDonald's review of *The Politics of Hope*, 3.

[438] Arthur Schlesinger, Jr., *The Age of Jackson* (Boston: Little, Brown and Company, 1945).

[439] Ibid.

[440] Ibid.

[441] Ibid.

[442] Ibid.

[443] Op. cit., McDonald's letter to Govan.

444 From an interview with Jane Govan, 1990.

445 From a letter from Michael Allen to Crocker, January 1, 2000.

446 Ibid.

447 Ibid.

448 Ibid.

449 Letter from Michael Allen to Crocker, February 22, 2000.

450 From a telephone interview with Allen, March 4, 1997.

451 Ibid.

452 Op. cit., Allen's letter, January 1, 2000.

453 Ibid.

454 Ibid.

455 From a mimeographed text on orange paper found among Govan's papers.

456 See Chapter 30, "The Final Years".

Chapter 21 Notes

457 Carl Bridenbaugh, *Mitre and Sceptre: Transatlantic Faiths, Ideas Personalities, and Politics, 1689-1775* (New York: Oxford University Press, 1962), xvi, 354.

458 Thomas P. Govan, "The Historian as Partisan Prosecutor and Judge" *Historical Magazine of the Protestant Episcopal Church*, Volume XXXII, no. 1, March 1963, 49-56.

459 From a Govan letter to a historian friend about Bridenbaugh's book, January 1964.

460 Ibid.

461 From an interview Jane Govan, 1990.

462 Op. cit., Govan's review, 56.

463 Alan P. Grimes, *Equality in American, Religion, Race, and the Urban Ministry* (New York: Oxford University Press, 1964), 136. Reviewed by Govan, *The Journal of Southern History*, Volume XXXI, no. 1, Feb. 1965. 119-120.

464 Ibid., Govan's review.

465 Eugene D. Genovese, *The Political Economy of Slavery: Studies in the Economy and Society of the Slave South* (New York, Pantheon Books, 1965), xiv, 304. Reviewed by Govan in *The Journal of Southern History*, Vol. XXXII, No. 2, May, 1966, 231-234.

466 bid., Govan's review, page 232 of *The Journal of Southern History*.

467 Ibid., *The Journal of Southern History*, 233.

468 etter from Arthur E. Link to Govan, September 7, 1962.

469 Ibid.

470 Letter from Govan to Link, October 17, 1962.

471 Op. cit., Link, September 7, 1962.

472 Op. cit., Govan, October 17, 1962.

473 Ibid.

474 Letter from Link to Govan, October 27, 1962.

475 Letter from Govan to Link, November 3, 1962.

476 Ibid.

477 Letter from Govan to Philip F. Detweiler, March 8, 1963.

478 Govan's essay, "Agrarianism, Sectionalism and Jeffersonian Democracy, A Moral Inquiry," is in the Govan Archives.

479 Ibid.

480 Ibid.

481 Ibid.

482 Crowe's preface to Tom's article ("Those Mysterious Southern Agrarians").

483 Thomas P. Govan, "Was Plantation Slavery Unprofitable?" in *The Journal of Southern History*, Volume XIII, 1942, 513-535.

484 Carl N. Deglar, ed. *Pivotal Interpretations of American History, Volume I*, (New York Harper and Row, 1966), 163-183.

485 Ibid., Preface.

486 Ibid.

487 The last sentence of Govan's article, page 28 of the essay.

488 Op. cit., Preface.

489 See Appendices.

490 Letter from Govan to Alfred D. Chandler, April 17, 1964.

491 See Appendices.

492 Ibid., p. 5.

493 Ibid., p. 6.

494 See "The Miracle of Funded Public Debt," in the Govan Archives, and "Hamilton, the Bank and the National Economy," in the Appendices.

495 Ibid., p. 2.

496 Ibid., p. 3.
497 Ibid.
498 Ibid.
499 Ibid.
500 Ibid., 4.
501 Govan's proposal for an "Albert Gallatin Institute" at NYU, is in the Govan Archives.
502 Quoted from the proposal.
503 Ibid.
504 Ibid.

Chapter 22 Notes

505 See II Kings, Chapters 22-23, and Deuteronomy, Revised Standard Version of the Bible.
506 T. P. Govan, "The English Background," an address delivered at the University of Oregon in August 1966, and later rewritten as the first chapter of a proposed book, *A New Birth of Freedom.* This quotation is from page 13 of the first chapter.
507 William Blackstone, *Commentaries on the Laws of England,* 4 volumes (Oxford: The Clarendon Press, 1766-1769).
508 F. W. Maitland, *The Constitutional History of England* (Cambridge, U.K.: Cambridge University Press, 1968), 539. Helen C. Cam, ed., *F.W. Maitland, Historical Essays* (Cambridge: Cambridge University Press, 1957), 278.
509 Ibid., Maitland, 2.
510 Op. cit., "The English Background."
511 Ibid., The indented quotation was not referenced by Govan but it may well be from Lewis B. Namier, an English "deconstructionist" historian with whom Govan was not usually sympathetic.
512 Ibid., 7.
513 Ibid., 12.
514 David Little, *Religion, Order, and Law* (New York: Harper Torchbooks, Harper and Row, 1969), 269.
515 French, Spanish, and Roman.
516 Govan, "The English Background," 12-13.
517 Ibid., 13.

518 Ibid.

519 Ibid., 12.

520 Op. cit., Little, 131.

521 Ibid.

522 Ibid.

523 Ibid.

524 Isaiah 6:1-8.

525 Romans 7:15-25.

526 1979 *Book of Common Prayer*, 41-42, 61-62.

527 Govan, "The English Background," 10.

528 Isaiah 6:8.

529 Micah 6:8.

530 From a letter from Jack Maddex, professor of American history at the University of Oregon, to Crocker, September 27, 2002, Maddex was present at the lecture.

531 Letter probably from a graduate student named John to Govan, September 2, 1967.

532 Ibid.

533 Op. cit., Maitland, 1-6.

534 Ibid., 1.

535 Ibid., 4.

536 Ibid., 5.

537 These quotations come from a later, but more or less identical proposal for the same book dated June 20, 1971, four years later.

538 Letter from Lawrence Grove to Govan, March 6, 1967.

539 From Lincoln's Second Inaugural Address.

540 Op. cit., "The English Background," 8.

541 Ibid.

542 Ibid., p. 18.

543 Ibid.

544 See the Deems Lectures in the Govan Archives.

Chapter 23 Notes

545 Letter from Govan to Michael Allen, October 4, 1968.

546 Letter from Govan to Crocker, December 22, 1967.

547 Letter from Govan to Stanley Feldstein, January 9, 1968.

548 Letter from Govan to Allen, December 22, 1967.

549 Letter from Govan to Feldstein, January 1968.

550 Letter from Feldstein to Govan, January 16, 1968.

551 Letter from Govan to Crocker, Spring 1968.

552 Letter from Govan to Crocker, December 22, 1967.

553 Letter from Govan to Feldstein, July 28, 1968.

554 Ibid.

555 From a September 27, 2002 letter from Jack Maddex, Professor of American History at the University of Oregon.

556 Ibid.

557 Ibid.

558 Ibid.

559 Letter from Govan to Allen, August 4, 1968.

560 Op. cit.

561 Ibid.

562 Bayne to General Theological Seminary on Ninth Avenue, New York City; and Moseley to Union Theological Seminary, Morningside Heights, New York City.

563 Letter from Govan to Warren Turner, April 13, 1970.

564 Ibid.

565 Ibid.

Chapter 24 Notes

566 Letter from Govan to Crocker, October 1971.

567 Telephone interview with Cora Louise Belford, September 1997.

568 Ibid.

569 Telephone interview with Elizabeth Conn, September 30, 1997.

570 Interview with James Bunnell, February 3, 1998.

571 Ibid.

572 Ibid.

573 From a telephone interview with Sarah E. Bunnell, September 1998.

574 All the remaining quotes are from the Sarah E. Bunnell interview.

575 Ibid.

576 Ibid.

[577] Ibid.

[578] Ibid.

[579] Ibid.

[580] Ibid.

[581] Ibid.

[582] Ibid.

[583] Ibid.

[584] Ibid.

[585] Ibid.

[586] Ibid.

[587] Ibid.

[588] Ibid.

[589] Ibid.

[590] Ibid.

[591] Ibid.

[592] Ibid.

[593] Ibid.

[594] Ibid.

[595] Ibid.

Chapter 25 Notes

[596]   The nine reviews are:

1.   T.P. Govan, review of *Adlai Stevenson: A Study in Values*, by Herbert J. Muller, *The Journal of Southern History* 34 (August 1968): 483-484.

2.   __, review of *Capital and the Cotton Industry in the Industrial Revolution*, by Seyman Shapiro, *The Pennsylvania Magazine of History and Biography*, 91 (July, 1968): 397-398.

3.   __, review of *The Civilization of the Old South: Writings of Clement Eaton*, edited by Albert D. Kirwan, *The Journal of American History*, 61 (June, 1968): 136-137.

4.   __, review of *The Future of History: The Historical Currents of our Time and the Direction in which They are Taking*

America, by Robert L. Heilbroner, (1967): reference unknown.

5. ___, review of *The House of Morgan,* by Edwin P. Hoyt Jr., *The Pennsylvania Magazine of History and Biography,* 91 (April, 1967): 235-236

6. ___, review of *Joseph N. Cardozo: Economic Thought in the Ante-Bellum South,* by Melvin N. Lieman, *The Business History Review,* 42 (Spring 1968): 104-105.

7. ___, review of *King Cotton and His Retainers: Financing and Marketing the Cotton Crop of the South,* by Harold D. Woodman, *American Historical Review,* 74 (October, 1968): 280.

8. ___, review of *The Papers of John C. Calhoun,* edited by W. Edwin Hemphill, *The Florida Historical Quarterly,* 48 (October, 1968): 189-190.

9. ___, review of *The Shrine Party: Congressional Voting Behavior,* by Joel H. Sibley, (magazine unknown): 195-196.

[597] Carl N. Deglar, *Pivotal Interpretation of American History,* Harper Torchbooks (New York: Harper and Row Publishers, 1966) 163-183.

[598] Letter from Govan to Robert F. Fogel, October 1, 1967.

[599] Ibid.

[600] Ibid.

[601] Letter from Govan to Fogel, October 17, 1967.

[602] Ibid.

[603] Robert W. Fogel, *Time on the Cross, the Economics of American Slavery* (Boston: Little, Brown and Company, 1974), 286.

[604] Review by C. Vann Woodward in *The New York Times* Book Review, November 5, 1989, 16.

[605] Robert W. Fogel, *Without Consent or Contract, the Rise and Fall of American Slavery* (New York: W.W. Norton and Company, 1989), 539.

[606] Report in *The New York Times,* Wednesday, October 15, 1995, D-1-D-6 and a two-column editorial.

[607] Muller, Herbert J. *Adlai Stevenson, a Study in Values,* reviewed by Govan in *The Journal of Southern History,* 34, No. 3 (August, 1968).

[608] Eisenhower's moralistic campaign against Adlai Stevenson in 1952 in

which he declared a "crusade to clean up the men in Washington" left by Truman's administration.

609 Stanley Feldstein, *Once a Slave: the Slaves' View of Slavery* (New York: William Morrow and Company, 1969; paper in 1971), 285.

610 Letter from Govan to Feldstein, January 9, 1968.

611 Letter from Feldstein to Govan, January 16, 1968

612 Letter from Govan to Feldstein, January 18, 1968.

613 Ibid, January 25, 1968.

614 Ibid, March 19, 1968.

615 Ibid, July 28, 1968.

616 Ibid, August 6, 1968.

617 Op. cit., *Once a Slave*, 285.

618 Letter from James Landis, senior editor at William Morrow and Company, to Govan, March 3, 1970.

619 From a Govan conversation with Crocker during the 1970s.

620 See Govan's "Introduction to *Once a Slave*," op. cit., p. 22

621 Ibid.

622 Ibid.

623 Ibid, p. 23.

624 Thomas Payne Govan, "Nicholas Biddle, 1786-1844," an article in the *Encyclopedia of American Biography*, eds. John A. Garraty and Jerome L. Sternstein (New York: Harper Collins, 1974): reprinted in the Second Edition, 1997, 100-102.

625 Letter from Govan to John A. Garraty, July 10, 1970.

626 Ibid.

627 Ibid.

628 Op. cit., *Encyclopedia of American Biography*.

629 Ibid.

Chapter 26 Notes

630 Quoted from a June 20, 1972 proposal for another book, *Alexander Hamilton and His Adversaries*.

631 Ibid.

632 See Chapter 7. *Mississippi Valley Historical Review*, Vol. XXXVI, 1950, 675-680.

633   Published in *The William and Mary Quarterly*, Vol. XXXII, No. 3, July, 1975, 475-480.

634   Ibid., 480.

635   Ibid.

636   Letter from Govan to Crocker, December 22, 1970.

637   Forrest McDonald, Leslie E. Decker, and Thomas P. Govan, *The Last Best Hope, A History of the United States, Volume I to 1885; Volume II, Since 1865.* (Reading, MA: Addison-Wesley Publishing Company, 1972, 1973), Vols. I and II, 1056.

638   From an interview with Jane Govan in Sherrill House, Alexandria, VA, 1990.

639   Letter to Larry Wilson from Govan, December 16, 1969.

640   Letter from Wilson to Govan December 29, 1969.

641   Letter from Govan to Crocker, December 22, 1970.

642   From a telephone interview with Robert M. Berdahl, July 25, 1997.

643   From Govan's June 20, 1971 proposal, 3.

644   Ibid.

645   A letter from Govan to Paul L. Ward, June 13, 1971.

646   A summary of his purpose; from the June 20, 1971, proposal, 1.

Chapter 27 Notes

647   University of Oregon Student Course Guide, 1968-1969, 39.

648   From a discussion of Crocker and Feldstein in New York in February, 2003.

649   Ibid.

650   Ibid.

651   Stanley Feldstein, *Once a Slave: the Slaves' View of Slavery* (New York, William Morrow and Company, 1970). See Chapter 25.

652   Letter from Stephen A. Channing to Govan, February 14, 1968.

653   See "Slavery and the Civil War," Appendices, Chapter 3.

654   Letter from Govan to Stephen Channing, February 24, 1968.

655   Letter from J. Lewis Shapiro to Govan, April 7, 1968.

656   Letter from John F. McElligott to Govan, March 14, 1969.

657   See Gospel of St. Mark 5:1-13.

[658] Tom refers here to one of the deepest mysteries of human nature: why we human beings seek to kill the ones we love and need most. How does the dynamic of love-hate, hate-love work? The mystery was lived out in the crucifixion of Jesus. The Cross is its symbol, and in one way or another, *we all* find this to be true in our lives. So, Tom asks, "Why be bothered when you find this to be true?"

[659] Letter from Govan to John F. McElligott, June 25, 1969.

[660] Letter from John McElligott to Jane Govan, March 21, 1979.

[661] Letter from Leonard Bernstein to Govan, July 20, 1970. This person is not to be confused with the well-known conductor and composer by the same name.

[662] Letter from Diana Klebanov, February 19, 1972.

[663] Murphy's article was in the July 4, 1981 *Boston Globe* op. ed. page; his letter was undated.

[664] Samuel Smith was a republican senator from Baltimore for over twenty years. He was a Jeffersonian on most matters except the Bank of the United States, which he strongly supported. As chairman of the Senate Finance Committee in 1830, when the Bank came under serious attack from President Andrew Jackson, he presided over the publication of a committee report, which showed Jackson not only to be wrong, but ignorant, and seriously embarrassed the president. The report turned out to be word-for-word identical to a report written in the Bank's defense by Nicholas Biddle, president of the Bank.

[665] Letter from John S. Pancake to Govan, January 19, 1979.

[666] Letter from Ira Cohen to Jane Govan, February 17, 1981.

[667] See Jane's version of this story in Chapter 1.

[668] From a phone interview, September 1, 1997 with William Robert Ellis Jr.

Chapter 28 Notes

[669] See Govan's November 1972 introduction to the Educational Program of the American Revolution Bicentennial Commission of Oregon in the Govan Archives. This quote is from page 1 of the introduction.

[670] Ibid.

[671] "The Declaration of Independence."

672 Op. cit., 3.

673 Ibid., 2-3.

674 Ibid.

675 Ibid.

676 Ibid.

677 Ibid.

678 Quoted in Govan's review of Robert Penn Warren's *The Legacy of the Civil War* (New York, Random House, 1960, 109) in the Brown (University) Daily Herald Supplement, fall, 1960. The words are Warren's.

679 Op. cit., 3.

680 Micah 6:8.

681 Ibid.

682 Ibid., 6.

683 Ibid.

684 *The Hungry Eye*, the monthly bulletin of the Oregon Educational and Public Broadcasting Service, July, 1974, 1.

685 Ibid.

686 From a letter of Laura Roper to Crocker, November 9, 2000.

687 The cover of *The Hungry Eye* featured excerpts from "The Declaration of Independence."

688 Ibid.

689 Schwab became a close friend of the Govans.

690 Quoted from the introduction of "Radical America, the Continuing Revolution, 3, a short section called "Evaluation." See the Govan Archives.

Chapter 29 Notes

691 Quoted from the brochure announcing the lecture series.

692 Letter to Lee A. Belford from Govan, February 2, 1975.

693 See Lecture I, 2. All of these lectures are in the Govan Archives.

694 Ibid.

695 Ibid., 5. "We hold these truths to be self evident ... "

696 Ibid., 17.

697 Ibid.

698 Ibid.

[699] Ibid., 17-18.

[700] Lecture II, 1.

[701] Ibid.

[702] Ibid., 5.

[703] Ibid.

[704] Ibid.

[705] Ibid.

[706] Ibid., 14.

[707] Ibid., 14-15.

[708] Lecture III, 9.

[709] Ibid.

[710] From a Govan conversation with Crocker in 1976.

[711] From a 1976 letter to Crocker.

[712] Thomas P. Govan, "The Rejection of Denominational Idolatries" (Forward Movement Press, 1975), 13. This essay is in the Govan Archives

[713] Ibid., 12

[714] Ibid., 11.

[715] Ibid., 12.

[716] Ibid.

[717] Ibid., 13.

[718] Ibid., 12.

[719] Ibid., 13.

Chapter 30 Notes

[720] By university rules, one's retirement would come at the end of the semester before one's seventieth birthday. Tom's birthday was in January so he would retire the previous December, 1976.

[721] Letter from Henry Alpert to Govan, June 6, 1971.

[722] Letter from Henry Alpert to Govan, February 17, 1976.

[723] Ibid.

[724] Letter from Govan to Crocker, December 20, 1976.

[725] Ibid.

[726] Letter from Govan to Crocker, March 17, 1977.

[727] Ibid.

728 Ibid.

729 From a phone interview with Robert Berdahl July 25, 1997. Berdahl, by this time, was president of the University of California, Berkeley.

730 Letter from Govan to Crocker, April 5, 1977.

731 Mollegen was already in Goodwin House, and was bored by many of the nonintellectual people there. He yearned to have Tom and Jane's company so they could drink together and discuss things.

732 Letter from Mollegen to Govan, January 25, 1978.

733 Letter from Stephen Haycox to Govan, July 26, 1978.

734 From a memo written by Jane Govan at the request of St. Mary's Church in Eugene to explain what home care and hospice care are all about. "They hit me too early," she said. "I should have had the sense to refuse," but she did it anyway.

735 Op. cit., Berdahl telephone interview.

736 *The New York Times,* July 29, 1978.

737 Op. cit., telephone interview with Berdahl.

738 Ibid.

739 Govan had written his old friend Jones Shannon about his condition. Shannon mentioned this in his reply to Govan on January 22, 1979.

740 Op. cit., Jane Govan's memo.

741 Letter from Jane Govan to Crocker, November 11, 1978.

742 Letter from Jane Govan to Crocker, February 5, 1979.

743 Letter from James Govan, a nephew, to Govan, January 25, 1978.

744 Op. cit., Jane Govan's memo.

745 Letter from Kate Bunnell to Jane Govan, April 18, 1979.

746 Op. cit. Jane Govan's memo.

747 *Book of Common Prayer,* 483.

748 Op. cit., Jane Govan's memo.

749 Ibid.

750 Allison had been teaching at Sewanee when the Episcopal Society for Cultural and Racial Unity sit-ins at the Claramont Inn took place. They had argued heatedly about the issue.

751 The Reverend Thomas F. Pike was a curate under Michael Allen at St. Mark's-in-the-Bowery during two of Govan's early years at NYU and was a close friend.

752 Suzanne Reid had been a colleague of Govan's in the College Work Department of the Episcopal Church.

753 Cora Louise Belford was the Reverend Lee Belford's wife, a southerner and a close friend.

754 Two members of Govan's former office staff.

755 Bowen, Zabriskie, and Chitty were members of the Executive Council of the Episcopal Church staff when Tom worked there between 1955 and 1962.

756 Harriet Price had been a student leader of the Canterbury Association and a member of the National Commission for College Work during the late 1950s and was a younger intimate friend of the Govans, especially of Jane's.

757 Letter from the Reverend Christopher F. Allison to Jane Govan, March 16, 1979.

758 Old friends and members of St. Mark's-in-the-Bowery.

759 Letter from Michael Allen to Jane Govan, May 4, 1979.

760 "The News Bulletin" of the University of the South, undated.

761 From a telephone interview with Thomas J. Tucker in the fall of 1997.

762 This reference is to the story of Legion told by Jesus. Legion was filled with unclean and evil spirits. Jesus was ready to cast them out so that Legion could be returned to his right mind. But the spirits, as Mollegen always said, needed a body to be housed in and begged Jesus to send them into the herd of swine grazing nearby. Jesus did as they asked. The swine, invaded by evil spirits, panicked and plunged over a cliff into the sea. Legion was returned to his right mind. Mollegen wanted Jane to be in her right mind and come to Goodwin House.

763 Letter to Jane Govan from Mollegen, March 12, 1979.

764 Letter to Jane Govan from Daniel Corrigan, November 4, 1986. The reference to "La Casa Gonzales" is obscure. Corrigan's wife Elizabeth had no idea what it meant. It must, however, have referred to some form of "heaven on earth" where good friends meet in close fellowship.

765 From a copy of Pierson's address to the History Department of the University of Oregon. Several copies were among Jane's papers.

766 The editorial never materialized; the undated letter speaks for itself.

767 Undated letter to Joan Pierson from Robert M. Berdahl just before Tom's death. Berdahl gave a copy of this letter to Jane Govan who noted on it that "No editorial appeared."

768 She sent me, for example, all of Tom's F. D. Maurice books, a gold mine of out-of-print works.

769 Telephone interview, May 3, 1998.

770 Ibid.

771 Ibid.

772 Ibid.

773 Op. cit., telephone interview with Harriet Price, May 3, 1998.

774 Ibid.

775 Ibid.

776 As a follow-up to our May 3, 1998 telephone conversation, Harriet Price sent me a long compendium of comments about Jane, her relationship with Jane, and quotes from Jane's letters over the years, in this note and hereafter, called Harriet's Notes, May 11, 1998.

777 The quotation is from an article entitled "Venture in the Arts," which Jane wrote for the art exhibit at the National Study Conference in Colorado Springs, 1959.

778 Harriet's Notes, May 11, 1998.

779 Ibid. Quote from Jane Govan's letter of January 14, 1984.

780 Ibid., letter of March 21, 1984.

781 Ibid., letter of December 22, 1988.

782 Ibid.

783 Ibid.

784 Ibid.

785 Ibid.

786 Laura Roper remembers that Jane, after a few days, was clear-headed and never confused.

787 Op. cit., telephone interview with Harriet Price. I visited her once after her stroke and tried reading parts of this book to her. She heard me but was unable to respond.

788 Letter from Laura Roper to Crocker, June 13, 1998.

789 I was on a sailing trip off the coast of Newfoundland and did not learn of Jane's death until a month later.

[790] The *Book of Common Prayer,* 485.

[791] This description of the service is in part from an October 8, 1991 letter from Crocker to Laura Roper.

Epilogue Notes

[792] See Chapter 27, p. 401.

[793] See Chapter 29, the Deems Lectures.

Index

A

B

Marx, Karl 152, 446, 476
Maurice, Frederick Denison
(F.D.) 190, 255, 296, 517,
524, 533
McCormick, Richard P. 230
McCrady, Edward 132, 139, 142,
162, 246
McDonald, Dwight 259
McDonald, Forrest 20, 172, 211,
214, 220, 233, 234, 342, 345
McElligott, John 353, 360, 362
McNair, Robert 139
McNeil, Donald R. 217
Mollegen, Albert T. 179, 196,
202, 397, 408, 412
Monges, René 317
Moore, Bishop Paul 399
Morgan, Edward S. 30, 31
Moseley, Rt. Rev. Brooke 314
Murphy, Jeremiah V. 365

N

National Commission for
College Work 179, 186,
194, 196, 242
Nature and Destiny of Man, The
(Reinhold Niebuhr) 93,
95, 437, 514
New Birth of Freedom, A 38,
165, 170, 241, 294, 295,
328, 342, 343, 349, 350,
423, 452, 534
New Orleans, Louisiana 49, 52,
162, 163, 167, 168, 173,
180, 182, 209, 497
New York City 85, 135, 148, 173,
176, 182, 201, 209, 232,
255, 263, 282, 314, 317, 389
New York University (NYU)
145, 173, 179, 182, 241,
243, 254, 256, 257, 269,

282, 283, 285, 300, 302,
304, 317, 334, 344, 356,
357, 358, 359, 360, 363,
364, 381, 382, 394, 524, 534
Nichols, Jeanette 229
Niebuhr, Reinhold 92, 93, 95,
135, 144, 149, 191, 437,
508, 509, 510, 512, 515

O

Once a Slave, see Feldstein,
Stanley 334, 345, 357, 509
Oregon Educational and Public
Broadcast Services
(OEPBS) 178, 376, 380
Otey Parish 126, 134

P

Parrington, Vernon L. 28, 156,
273, 448
Penick, Bishop Edwin A. 147
Penick Committee 147, 148
Perkins, Howard Cecil 89
Phillips, Ulrich B. 90, 278, 279,
338
Pierson, Stanley 392, 409, 411
Pike, Very Rev. James A. 148
Pittinger, Norman 196
Price, Harriet 13, 405, 413, 414,
416
Progressive Historians 28

R

Racial discrimination 26, 65,
79, 89, 90, 134, 144, 235,
239, 244, 245, 246, 247,
249, 250, 257, 263, 304,
312, 314, 389
Radical America 21, 372, 376,
377, 380, 394, 511

Printed in the United States
39463LVS00001B/5